Baptizing Burma

RELIGION, CULTURE, AND PUBLIC LIFE

RELIGION, CULTURE, AND PUBLIC LIFE
Series editor: Matthew Engelke

The Religion, Culture, and Public Life series is devoted to the study of religion in relation to social, cultural, and political dynamics, both contemporary and historical. It features work by scholars from a variety of disciplinary and methodological perspectives, including religious studies, anthropology, history, philosophy, political science, and sociology. The series is committed to deepening our critical understandings of the empirical and conceptual dimensions of religious thought and practice, as well as such related topics as secularism, pluralism, and political theology. The Religion, Culture, and Public Life series is sponsored by Columbia University's Institute for Religion, Culture, and Public Life.

For a complete list of titles, see page 291.

BAPTIZING BURMA

Religious Change in the Last Buddhist Kingdom

ALEXANDRA KALOYANIDES

COLUMBIA UNIVERSITY PRESS   *NEW YORK*

Winner of the 2020 Claremont Prize
Institute for Religion, Culture, and Public Life at Columbia University

Publication of this book was made possible in part by funding from the
Institute for Religion, Culture, and Public Life at Columbia University.

Columbia University Press
Publishers Since 1893
New York   Chichester, West Sussex
cup.columbia.edu
Copyright © 2023 Columbia University Press
All rights reserved

Library of Congress Cataloging-in-Publication Data
Names: Kaloyanides, Alexandra, author.
Title: Baptizing Burma: Religious change in the last
Buddhist kingdom / Alexandra Kaloyanides.
Description: New York : Columbia University Press, 2023. |
Includes bibliographical references and index.
Identifiers: LCCN 2022032445 (print) | LCCN 2022032446 (ebook) |
ISBN 9780231199841 (hardback) | ISBN 9780231199858 (trade paperback) |
ISBN 9780231553315 (ebook)
Subjects: LCSH: Christianity and other religions—Buddhism. | Buddhism—
Relations—Christianity. | Christianity—Influence. | Buddhism—Influence. |
Burma—Civilization—Christian influences. | Burma—Civilization—
Buddhist influences. | Burma—Civilization—19th century.
Classification: LCC BR128.B8 K35 2023 (print) | LCC BR128.B8 (ebook) |
DDC 261.2/43—dc23/eng/20221129
LC record available at https://lccn.loc.gov/2022032445
LC ebook record available at https://lccn.loc.gov/2022032446

Cover image: © Shutterstock

For my parents

Contents

Acknowledgments ix

Introduction 1

ONE The Book: Religious Texts of Nineteenth-Century Burma 22

TWO The School: Models of Religious Imagination in Burmese Education 66

THREE The Pagoda: Icons and Iconoclasm 117

FOUR The Portrait: American Jesus in Burma 165

Conclusion 207

Notes 213

Works Cited 261

Index 275

Acknowledgments

As with the objects I study in these pages, this book has been formed by multiple communities. There are so many in Myanmar who I want to thank for their help with my research. Saw Chit U's good humor and large network opened many doors into contemporary Karen life. Myo Thandar Nwe's innovative Burmese lessons enlivened my days and began a lasting friendship. Reverend John Hla Win Felix helped me navigate Yangon's multiple religious worlds. Mya Oo at the National Library of Myanmar and U Tin Maung Lwin at the Yangon University Library offered expertise and access to manuscript collections. Myo Myint and U Tun Aung Chain generously made time to answer my still-forming questions. While the current political situation makes me hesitate to name them, many people in Myanmar shared their family's history with the American Baptist mission, gifting me with a greater sense of the meaning of Christian evangelism in the country. I am endlessly grateful to those who welcomed me into their homes, workplaces, churches, and monasteries.

The participants in the Judson200 Tour to Myanmar, which I write about in chapter 4, gave me my first real experience of how caring Baptist communities can be. Thanks especially to Deborah Van Broekhoven, Jan Ballard, and Will Womack. Other associates of the American Baptist Historical Society supported this project at many stages. The late George Tooze, who I was lucky to have met over email, compiled the seven-volume

ACKNOWLEDGMENTS

collection of Emily Chubbuck Judson's writings that first conjured the mission for me.

I would never have been able to begin this book without the riches of Yale University. The Yale Council on Southeast Asia Studies paid for my study of Burmese; the Charles Kao Fund and the MacMillan Center funded two research trips to Myanmar; the Divinity School's Day Missions Collection furnished revelatory artifacts from nineteenth-century religious life; and the Kenneth A. Gerber Fund paid for the food at the graduate student events, where I found inspiration from and commiseration with people from across the study of religion—people like Sara Ronis, Sonja Anderson, Christina Harker, Devin Singh, Tyler Smith, and Daniel Schriever.

This book would not exist without the graduate school advisors who indulged my interdisciplinary interests while gifting me with training in their particular areas of expertise. Phyllis Granoff opened Sanskrit and Prakrit worlds to me, read my work without hesitation and with a sharp eye, and delighted in helping me discover new sources. Koichi Shinohara taught me how to ask the right questions when I was asking the wrong ones, and skillfully showed me how to rethink my approach. Skip Stout first saw potential in my proposed combination of the study of American religious history and Asian religions, magnanimously supporting it along the way. Kathryn Lofton challenged this project to have more to say and to say it better by engaging with emerging scholarship and the collective of American studies students she formed. Other teachers at Yale University—especially David Brick, Osmund Bopearachchi, U Khin Maung Gyi, Andy Quintman, Jim Scott, Tisa Wenger, and the late Stanley Insler—gave helpful feedback during this book's formation.

I am lucky to have friends from graduate school who enthusiastically read my work and inspired me with their own. A writing group with the Lofton collective provided the peer pressure that first put this project on the page. I am especially grateful to Shari Rabin, David Walker, Sarah Koenig, Emily Johnson, Lucia Hulsether, Michelle Morgan, and Tina Post for suggestions on early drafts. Kati Curts continues to be a brilliant reader, coconspirator, and dear friend. A beloved cohort of graduate students in Asian religions—including Jay Ramesh, Lang Chen, Sasha Restifo, Andrew Moore, Lynna Dhanani, and Mark Holum—indulged many after-hours research ramblings. Marko Geslani encouraged me to keep asking questions about Orientalism and his camaraderie is a reason why I still study Asian religions.

ACKNOWLEDGMENTS

And Ellen Gough's true friendship carried me through this project from New Haven to the southeast, laughing much of the way.

A postdoctoral fellowship at the Ho Center for Buddhist Studies at Stanford University provided me with two precious years to rethink this project in the company of brilliant professors, students, and visiting scholars. John Kieschnick and Paul Harrison were sage mentors who saw potential in this project when I was unsure. Irene Lin and Tatiana Deogirikar created extraordinary (and delicious) occasions for intellectual exchange. Others in Stanford's Religious Studies Department offered insights into my research, especially Adeana McNicholl, Simona Lazzerini, Michaela Mross, and Audrey Truschke. I am grateful to scholars at the University of California, Berkeley, who invited me across the bay to share works in progress. In Penny Edwards's Theravada Civilizations workshop, I tried out a theory about Kammavāca manuscripts that I developed for the first chapter. Penny has since become an encouraging mentor and a model for an expansive cultural study of Southeast Asia. Robert Sharf and Alexander von Rospatt brought me to the Center of Buddhist Studies where I presented an early version of the analysis of the Paramat sect that I write about in chapter 3.

Even as a latecomer, I have been graciously welcomed into the field of Burma studies. I first met Alicia Turner and Erik Braun on the page and was beside myself to find them even more inspiring in person. A workshop at York University that Alicia invited me to present at offered encouraging and helpful comments on my first chapter. Erik invited me to present at the University of Virginia, where I was grateful to receive generative comments on my third chapter. Alexandra Green showed me exciting new ways to take the study of Burmese material culture. Michael Edwards offered close and insightful readings of drafts of my first and fourth chapters. Hitomi Fujimura gave expert feedback on my first chapter. Tom Patton carefully read my introduction and shared smart suggestions. Don Stadtner took an early interest in this project and helped me make connections in Myanmar. Exchanges with Jason Carbine and Elliott Prasse-Freeman energized this project at critical junctures.

Scholars of other Southeast Asian and Theravada communities have similarly enriched this work. Susanne Kerekes and Trent Walker shared their expertise on neighboring Buddhist cultures to help me rethink my Burmese materials. Richard Fox mentored me in the labor of programming Southeast Asia sessions for the American Academy of Religion. Cuong Mai invited me to share findings at Appalachian State University. A Theravada Civilizations

ACKNOWLEDGMENTS

Dissertation workshop—run by Juliane Schober, Steven Collins, John Holt, and Justin McDaniel—occasioned the redesign of this project at its early stages. Ṭhānissaro Bhikkhu generously answered many questions, corrected mistakes, and gently checked in about my progress.

For the last few years that I was working on this book, I had the great fortune of being a fellow in a Material and Visual Cultures of Religion (MAVCOR) project cycle run by Sally Promey and funded in part by the Henry Luce Foundation and Yale University. I am grateful to the crackerjack collective Sally assembled. Fellows like Emily Floyd, Judith Brunton, Roxanne Korpan, Laura Levitt, Tracy Fessenden, Pamela Klassen, Cécile Fromont, Kambiz GhaneaBassiri, Chip Callahan, Suus van Geuns, Judith Weisenfeld, and Hillary Kaell pressed me to think more creatively and critically about the American and Burmese materials and economies that I write about. Sonia Hazard, another fellow on that project, included me in two endeavors she edited, one for *Church History* and the other for *Material Religions,* that sharpened my thinking about Protestant power and global diversity in nineteenth-century America.

At the University of North Carolina at Charlotte, I work with supportive and inspiring colleagues, students, and administrators. Joanne Maguire gave me the precious gift of time, without which this would be a far lesser work. Will Sherman has been a curious reader and thoughtful companion in the transition to faculty life. Reading new books and our own works in progress with him and Sean McCloud galvanized my thinking about how to shape this for the shelf. Other religious studies colleagues—Kent Brintnall, Eric Hoenes, Barbara Thiede, Julia Moore, John Reeves, Celia Sinclair, Tina Katsanos, Janna Shedd, and Letha Victor—offered help at various stages. Dean Nancy Gutierrez allowed me to defer my start date so that I could take a postdoctoral fellowship to work on the manuscript. Discussions with colleagues in neighboring departments, especially Phil Kaffen, Jill Yavorsky, Ritika Prasad, Maren Ehlers, Natalie Ornat, and Heather Bastian, illuminated my understanding of how studies of religion like this one contribute to larger undertakings in the humanities and social sciences. My students have urged me to clarify what I research and why. Graduate students like David Flaherty, Dan Staton, and Matt Argonauta have posed questions about the study of religion that have strengthened the approach I take here. And I am indebted to the citizens of North Carolina, who pay the taxes that pay my salary and fund public universities with vibrant humanities programs.

ACKNOWLEDGMENTS

A longer biography of this book begins and ends at Columbia University. I first became fascinated with the study of Asian religions in Rachel McDermott's course on Indian civilizations as a first-year student at Barnard College. Because of Rachel's encouragement, I spent my junior year studying in South and Southeast Asia, including Myanmar. I was thrilled to once again have the privilege of Columbia University's support when Matthew Engelke wrote to tell me that my manuscript had won the first Claremont Prize for the Study of Religion from the university's Institute for Religion, Culture, and Public Life. Matthew patiently shepherded this book through reviews, revisions, and the dream workshop he orchestrated with Hannah Chazin and Michael Como, who carved out time from their summers to read my manuscript and offer smart suggestions. Wendy Lochner, Lowell Frye, and Emily Shelton at Columbia University Press have kindly given their expertise and time. And the two anonymous reviewers illuminated the manuscript's potential and pointed to ways for it to speak more fluently to multiple audiences.

I am deeply grateful to my family for all of the love and support they readily offered as I wrote this book. Betsy Ruderman, Nate Wade, Tara Warner, and Shannan Foley cheered me on the whole time. Kim Wiley and Jim Ransom provided an abundance of meals and childcare. Julia Ransom and James Ransom brought new life and reasons to finish. Larry Ransom-Wiley offered boundless support and joy as this work took us from Connecticut to California to North Carolina. Finally, I am forever indebted to my parents, Sheila Wade and Michael Kaloyanides, who showed me how the world can transform through curiosity, education, travel, and love. This book is dedicated to them.

Baptizing Burma

Introduction

WHEN ANN AND Adoniram Judson arrived in Rangoon in July 1813, the air above the Bay of Bengal was sweltering. The young Americans had left Boston in the bitter cold of February 1812. Now they stood in the wet monsoon heat on the deck of the *Georgiana*, the three-masted ship that had taken them to Burma from Madras, India. From the bow they could see the towering golden Shwedagon Pagoda, as well as a scattering of smaller white and gold shrines along the horizon.

The Judsons had sailed all this way to preach the gospel, and their voyage would make history for launching the United States' first-ever overseas mission. The couples' fame would multiply in the Protestant press as accounts of their Southeast Asian adventures traveled to North America along new global postal routes. After Burma's King Bagyidaw imprisoned Adoniram in 1824 on suspicion of spying for the British at the outset of the First Anglo-Burmese War, Americans in Philadelphia parlors and New York City boardinghouses read about Ann's desperate bribes of tea, cotton, and silver flatware to secure food and protection for her incarcerated husband. Magazines published reports of Adoniram's eventual release on the condition that he serve the Burmese court as its translator in the peace negotiations that ended the war in 1826. And when Ann died shortly thereafter, at the age of thirty-six, popular books featured sketches of her lonely gravesite in southern Burma, where she would be joined months later by her daughter, Maria, the Judsons' second child to die in infancy in Burma.

INTRODUCTION

New weeklies like the *Baptist Missionary Magazine* and the *Macedonian* grew their readerships by regularly running dramatic accounts of the Judsons' sacrifices and successes on a world stage. The long-awaited baptisms of the first Christian converts in Burma were covered in these Sabbath-day magazines and reprinted in major urban newspapers, as was Adoniram's eventual completion of the first Burmese translation of the Bible in 1834 and his pioneering work compiling the first Burmese-English dictionary, which was nearly finished when he died in 1850. Ann and Adoniram Judson were among the most well-known celebrities in the early republic.[1]

As celebrated as the Baptist mission was in the United States, and as appealing as Christianity turned out to be among minority communities in Burma, the Protestant mission to Burma proved terribly disappointing. The number of converts from Burma's ethnic majority, the Bamar,[2] was so small that by the 1840s—three decades into the Baptist mission—the Protestant operation had already cut the amount of missionaries dedicated to them in half. The mission was far more successful among marginalized groups, especially the Karen, who were converting at rates never approached by the Bamar. In 1836, for example, the mission recorded 729 newly baptized Karen, whereas it had only baptized 207 Bamar in all of the twenty-three years it had been running at that point.[3] If anything, it seemed as though the Bamar grew more resistant to Christian conversion efforts, that their Buddhist identity became more pronounced, as their kingdom weakened under the pressure of the encroaching British empire. By the end of the Third (and final) Anglo-Burmese War in 1885, Burma's last Buddhist kingdom had collapsed, and the entire realm was subsumed into the British Raj. Even in the absence of a patron king, the Bamar continued assert themselves in efforts to form a distinct Buddhist country.

The continued strength of Buddhism in Burma dismayed the American missionaries. In the face of lavish pagoda repair projects and widely circulating Buddhist ritual texts, the Baptist evangelists justified their persistent presence by pointing to the attraction of Christianity among minority communities and to the popularity of their schools. The American Baptist operation was the first sustained Christian mission in the country, quickly forming more numerous and active operating posts than the few Catholic one-man operations that had preceded it and managing far more foreign and local evangelists than the smaller-scale British evangelical organizations that arrived decades after the Americans.[4] In spite of its active presence, the Baptist mission never swept the country as it had dreamed.

Adoniram Judson penned that dream in his journal in 1820 when he visited the medieval Buddhist monuments at Pagan and "took a survey of the splendid pagodas and extensive ruins," proclaiming that "the churches of Jesus will soon supplant those idolatrous monuments, and the chanting of the devotees of Boodh will die away before the Christian hymn of praise."[5] This never happened. Burma's Buddhist monuments were never supplanted by churches. Sacred Pali chants were not drowned out by Christian hymns. The number of Buddhist pagodas likely increased during the nineteenth-century American Baptist mission; Christian congregations, however, also grew exponentially. Both Burmese Buddhists and Christian minority communities amplified their religious presence in this politically contentious and culturally transformative period.

The story of the American Baptist mission to Burma, then, is a story of conversion—both failed and sweeping. Throughout the nineteenth-century mission, Burmese Buddhists largely resisted Christian evangelism, whereas people from minority communities like the Karen, the Kachin, and the Chin were being baptized in astonishing numbers. And American Baptist Christianity found itself changing in the Buddhist kingdom: missionaries who had arrived admonishing the idolatry of Buddha statues found themselves creating tree shrines and their converts hanging multicolored Jesus paintings in their churches. As eccentric as these objects might seem, it is this kind of religious material that turns out to be central to this story of conversion and opposition. This book explores this religious material culture to understand how the Burmese majority positioned Buddhism to counter Christianity, how minority communities took on Baptist identities, and how Protestantism transformed into a kind of Southeast Asian religion.

Each of the chapters to follow examines a holy object to reveal the mechanics by which different communities conjured religious worlds. By telling stories of how four powerful objects—the sacred book, the school, the pagoda, and the portrait—helped shape Burmese, American, and Baptist convert communities, this book illuminates the little-known history of religious transformation during Burma's last kingdom. Its exploration of the Baptist mission also offers a human-scale example of the multicontinental history of American missionary interactions with Asian religions.[6] I will show how worshipped books, schoolhouses filled with new globes and maps, popular reliquary shrines, and paintings of revered religious figures became key objects through which communities in Burma asserted their identities and explored new modes of being. These four object studies demonstrate that religious material was a valuable resource for communal transformation and segregation in nineteenth-century Burma. My attention to material expressions of religion draws on my research in American, Burmese, and British archives where I explored sources in English, Pali, Sanskrit, and Burmese languages. I was also able to make two research trips to Myanmar in 2013 during the bicentennial celebrations of the Baptist mission to meet Baptist communities commemorating the arrival of the Americans and to record oral histories.[7] The remembered and remaining sacred objects that appeared over and over again in my research contour this book's story of religious change.

The field of Burmese religious history has attended almost exclusively to Buddhism and the Bamar majority. The field of U.S. religious history rarely broadens its borders to include missionaries in Asia, and, when it has, it tends to cluster them for consideration of larger expressions of violent Western imperialism or, occasionally, American cosmopolitanism. This book's analysis focuses on the lives of religious things in nineteenth-century Burma in order to contribute to both of these fields and tell a story of a diverse country in which communities from a range of socioeconomic positions remake themselves and others in the waning of the Burmese kingdom and the waxing of British colonialism. Attending to the religious lives of things in multiple sites allows me to trace patterned ways in which less powerful people—especially people from ethnic and religious minority groups—worked to determine political, economic, and religious systems and were determined by them. This book shows that Burma was not a simple country of unified Buddhists defending themselves against a monolithic Western enemy, but rather a place of entangled empires and reimagined religious worlds.

My analysis of religion in Burma's last Buddhist kingdom builds on the body of scholarship on Burmese religious history that developed slowly during the isolation of Myanmar's twentieth-century dictatorship and then somewhat more quickly in the twenty-first century as the country opened up. Finishing this book in the wake of the February 2021 military coup (which I address in the conclusion) makes me feel both grateful for the research that others and I were able to do in the country and concerned about the future for the people of Myanmar and those committed to studying their complicated, wonderful cultures. The extant scholarship sketches a millennium of kings working to secure and expand their realms through military campaigns and Buddhist traditions, especially the Pali scriptures (*Tipiṭaka*), jurisprudence,[8] and the monastic order known today as the Theravada sangha.[9] The Taungoo dynasty—which ruled Burma from the middle of the sixteenth century until it was toppled in 1752 by a village chief who would be called Alaungpaya when he became the first Konbaung king—was one of the largest and richest empires in Southeast Asian history.[10] At its peak, it encompassed all of modern Thailand and much of Laos, what is now the northeastern Indian state of Manipur, and Shan regions of southwest China. Like its predecessor, the Konbaung dynasty featured ambitious kings. It also gave rise to an influential monastic and lay literati whose control, creation, and circulation of texts fabricated the images of prestige that kings used to maintain the power they had won through wars.[11] Upper-class lay Bamar people became even more influential in the British colonial period, which was established in full after the Third Anglo-Burmese War dethroned the last Burmese king in 1885, but started in southern regions in the First Anglo-Burmese War of 1824–1826 and the Second Anglo-Burmese War of 1852–1853. Lay communities in colonial Burma took over Buddhist obligations previously met by kings, such as the support of monks and rituals and the commissioning of monuments, texts, and artworks.[12] During this colonial period and into the independent Union of Burma (1948–1962), the Socialist Republic (1962–1988), the Union of Myanmar (1988–2010), and the period of political reforms (2011–2015), charismatic meditation teachers,[13] modern middle-class women,[14] and extraordinary wizards and their devotees helped create the country known around the world today as a strongly Buddhist, Bamar nation.[15]

My book seeks to supplement and complicate this history of Burma by attending to religious and ethnic minorities. But, rather than isolate my focus on a particular marginalized group, I examine Christian communities alongside more familiar Buddhist populations to consider larger patterns in which empowered *and* disempowered people used religious objects to express themselves and relate to others. I work to tell a textured and inclusive story that challenges common narratives from Burmese political rhetoric and some scholarship, narratives about Burma being a unified, harmonious Buddhist kingdom before the British arrived. I hope to shed some light on larger patterns of religious conflict and human flourishing that continue in Myanmar to this day.

INTRODUCTION

When I investigate expressions of religious and ethnic identity, I want to be clear that the boundaries of these categories are not fixed but protean and permeable. Recent political discourse and academic work describes Myanmar's minority communities in terms of "ethnicity," "race," and "religion," though the most common Burmese term for categorizing people—*lumyo*, meaning "type of person"—is more general.[16] Myanmar's current use of the term *tainghyintha* to mean "indigenous races"—which incorporates ideas of ethnic, racial, and religious identity and has been infamously deployed to violently exclude Rohingya Muslims—descends from nineteenth-century British and Burmese practices of determining groups of people.[17] The American Baptist mission played a significant role as well. Between the start of the mission in 1813 and the first comprehensive British census in 1891, American missionaries were actively involved in surveying the country's population and trying to change it through conversion. The American mission was not only the first sustained force behind the Christianization of significant segments of minority communities but it was also responsible for the development and systematization of several scripts for Southeast Asian languages. These include the first Sgaw Karen script, which was devised in 1832 by the American Baptist missionary Jonathan Wade; the first Asho script, which was devised in 1865 by the Pwo Karen missionary to the Chin Myat Goung; and the initial transcription of Jingphaw, the Kachin language, undertaken in 1877 by the American Baptist missionary Josiah Nelson and a team of Karen evangelists.[18] With the widening reach of the Baptist press, school system, evangelical preaching tours, and local leaders, these linguistic innovations accompanied Christian conversions and invented boundaries around a variety of non-Bamar people.[19] Gaining a unique script coupled with a religious identity that was shared with the increasingly dominant British could certainly be empowering. At the same time, these divisions and alliances gave rise to new conflicts.[20]

To think about the many implications of Christian conversion, I draw from recent scholarship on empire and evangelism from the fields of missionary studies, colonialism, and North American religious history.[21] A surge of monographs on American Christian missionaries abroad demonstrates their political significance to be both more sweeping and more complicated than simply a unilateral extension of U.S. power. Scholars are attending to the mechanics by which particular foreign missions contributed to American imperialism as well as to forms of cosmopolitanism.[22] This book's analysis of the American Baptist mission to Burma contributes to this scholarship by showing that there was a much greater range to missionary interactions with Asian religions. Furthermore, it argues against a prominent assertion in the study of American religious history that Protestant Christianity monopolized the United States' antebellum period.[23] What the case of the American Baptist mission to Burma shows is that the world's diversity had a meaningful effect on Protestant mechanisms for organizing that diversity and consolidating Anglo-European power. I do not go as far as to contend that a kind of balanced pluralism or happy multiculturalism characterized nineteenth-century American encounters; that romantic view of religious peoples of the world coming together to cross-pollinate cultures misunderstands the pervasive and violent power of Western imperialism. Instead, my approach navigates a space between pluralism and Protestant domination. The story I tell here is one in which multiple religious expressions and the structures for administering and consolidating those expressions are at play.[24]

This complex American evangelism was not a ruggedly individual phenomenon, but part of a larger, international effort to promote Christianity in Asia and beyond.[25] The American Baptist mission to Burma was preceded by Catholic missionary attempts in the kingdom that date back to the early seventeenth century and was joined in 1859 by British evangelists when the Church of England's Society for the Propagation of the Gospel began operations in the country.[26] Moreover, the first generation of American foreign missionaries had a complicated relationship with British institutions interested in India. In 1811, Adoniram Judson traveled to England to secure connections and funds from the London Missionary Society, but a French pirate captured his ship, and he was only able to get to London by way of a French prison.[27] Because of this dangerous ordeal and the beginnings of the War of 1812 between the United States and Great Britain, the American Board of Commissioners for Foreign Missions (which Judson helped create in 1810) ultimately decided to finance their country's first mission to "the East" without British support. After Ann and Adoniram Judson and the other missionary couple that traveled with them, Harriet and Samuel Newell, arrived in Calcutta in June 1812, the British East India Company refused to allow them to stay. The Americans split up. The Judsons eventually made their way east across the Bay of Bengal to Burma, while the Newells sailed southwest to the island of Mauritius off the southeastern coast of Africa. After giving birth

INTRODUCTION

to a child, who died on that tempestuous voyage, Harriet died shortly after their arrival, at the age of nineteen, becoming the first American missionary to die abroad.[28] The newly widowed Samuel continued on to Ceylon to explore its evangelical potential.

Despite the mission's initially perilous clashes with British institutions, its dispersed American posts in South and Southeast Asia soon formed alliances with British missionaries in the field. Most significantly for this book, the British Baptist evangelist, printer, and translator William Ward baptized the Judsons when they arrived in Calcutta. The couple had set sail from Boston as Congregationalists but then studied and adopted Baptist principles on their four-month journey from the States. Their ritual in Calcutta initiated them into the Baptist Church and formalized their departure from Congregationalism. Consequently, Adoniram resigned from the American Board of Commissioners for Foreign Missions and helped establish the Baptist Triennial Convention in 1814 (which was called the American Baptist Missionary Union after 1845).[29] Thus the particular Baptist form of Protestant Christianity that the Judsons promoted in Burma, with its signal practice of only baptizing believers through full immersion (as opposed to baptizing infants with a sprinkling or pouring of water), traces back directly through the history of British evangelism in India.

To grasp the many moving parts of this history, I fashion an approach out of a third area of scholarship: the study of religious material cultures. I explore the objects that communities in Burma from a range of socioeconomic positions found sacred in this period of unprecedented societal change. Looking beyond elite monastic and royal scriptures to the paintings, pagodas, teaching aids, and books that were revered and attacked as Buddhism and Christianity collided in nineteenth-century Burma allows me to feature multiple communities with stakes in the outcomes of the collision. Furthermore, I show them acting in patterned and surprising ways. The material and visual expressions of their engagement in this fraught political period sheds new light on how Buddhism became such an important part of Burma's political identity while Christianity transformed through its adoption by particular minority communities.[30]

This book's attention to politically powerful religious objects exists in conversation with scholarship on material cultures of American Christianity and contributes to that field by showing how objects from other religious

INTRODUCTION

traditions have interacted with American Christian cultures through missionary enterprises. This scholarship has sustained an interest in previously overlooked material dimensions of religion in North America to demonstrate the centrality of material objects to American Christians' relationship to God and the supernatural.[31] This book is informed by this development and offers insights from the still-little-studied interactions between North America and Southeast Asia that have been shaped in significant ways by the religious objects at the center of this book. Indeed, it was the American Baptist mission to Burma that sent U.S. newspapers their first illustrated on-the-ground reports of living Buddhist communities, that gifted U.S. universities many of their first Buddhist manuscripts and artifacts, and that supplied some of the first Buddhist statues and mala beads displayed in U.S. exhibitions.

These valued things are not simple reflections of more important political and social dynamics. The weaponized spirits on bejeweled Buddhist ritual texts that missionaries sent to American libraries did not just symbolize Burma's conscription of Buddhist institutions in its fight against the British. These prized Burmese Buddhist books worked to actively conjure spirits and recruit them into the Anglo-Burmese wars. The towering Burmese pagodas that garnered so much attention were not only signs of the enduring power of the Buddha's teachings; these massive gilded shrines with their Buddha relics and ritual programs were also crucial sites where visitors sensed and made sense of the Buddha and his path to nirvana. Even the most critical Christians found themselves returning to pagodas over and over again, compelled by these sensational sites to consider Buddhism's popular appeal. Likewise, when the American Baptist mission imported the first printing press into Burma in 1816, crowds began forming around itinerant preachers, seeking copies of the Christian booklets so that they could hold the new religious teachings about an almighty god and his power to forgive sins. As I will show, some printed tracts inspired baptisms, while others were cut up and molded into amulets, and a select few were adopted as magical power sources by leaders of new religious movements.

This book tells the stories of these sacred materials and the people who interacted with them in order to imagine what religious change was like on the ground in nineteenth-century Burma.[32] I ask: How did the sacred book, the school, the pagoda, and religious portraits contour the course of

INTRODUCTION

Burmese history in ways that do not fit easily into the familiar story of British colonial oppression and resourceful Buddhist opposition? In answering this question, I intervene in the scholarship on Burma that has made this story familiar, that has illuminated how Western imperial institutions devastated Burmese cultural forms and how Burmese communities inventively resisted those institutions. The study of Burma would not be where it is today without this understanding. My research, however, regularly manifested material that resisted being explained away by a story of structured domination or of collective protest. Part of this resistance came from sources produced by minority groups like the Karen who ended up converting to Christianity in large numbers. Scholars have tended to point to the material benefits that minority groups who affiliated with Westerners received, such as English-language training and access to Anglo-American social networks. This focus on rational behavior is appealing because it not only highlights the financial incentives in congregating with Christians but it also works to correct ignorant colonial-era assertions about Burma's minorities being deceived by evangelists because they were gullible or superstitious. Much of the evidence examined in the following pages could be convincingly analyzed to support these kinds of rational, economic arguments. Communities who engaged with American Baptist missionaries certainly gained access to the increasingly valuable skills of learning English and Western academic disciplines like geography, and, surely, they were interested in better-paying jobs. The downside of focusing exclusively on economic concerns is, however, that it suggests that local communities were *simply* interested in improving materially, and did not have more *abstract* concerns about things like ultimate salvation and philosophies of religion. Scholarship has tended to assume that in this period it was only upper-class Western Christians and the occasional impressive Buddhist who were seriously interested in questions about the workings of the universe, the nature of the self, and the attributes of gods. Minority groups in Burma, by contrast, are consistently cast as limited to thoughts of feeding their families and protecting their villages. This book works to understand the ways that marginalized people engaged with complex, abstract concerns through tangible things. To get at the importance of the transcendent to communities who left behind far fewer written records than their upper-class neighbors, this study looks to the material forms they used to make sense of that which exceeds the physical world.³³

While this book strives to paint a more nuanced picture than one of monolithic American missionaries facilitating colonial violence, it is still sensitive to the devastating ways that Baptists helped justify British economic and military campaigns in Burma. Even the most open-minded American missionary reports that celebrated Buddhism as the best religion in the world next to Christianity and described the Christianity of the British colonists as woefully debased still positioned Burma as religiously deficient. These reports, then, promoted the West as a rightful conqueror because it spread the true word of God. This book seeks to recognize missionary complicity and to reveal the mechanisms by which the mission's work of filling out a picture of world religions promoted a particular Anglo-American Protestantism, no matter how much that work was depicted as a benevolent embrace of pluralism.³⁴ One strategy postcolonial scholars have advanced for resisting the continued dominance of Western institutions is to focus scholarship instead on non-Western and non-Christian peoples and their stories. Inspired by this, I have studied classical and vernacular languages of Burma in order to comprehend local expressions and gain distance from pervasive English systems. Additionally, I have recorded oral histories in order to listen to the force of spoken traditions instead of perpetually privileging the written, so often the domain of modern imperialism. Likewise, I have turned to objects to try to see what stories they can tell that are not told through alphabets and the elite communities who possess them. However, this book does still draw heavily from the archives of the American Baptist mission to Burma, maintaining that Western collections have more to reveal beyond records of imperial oppression. Some readers will question whether I focus on so much American archival material because I have not spent enough time in the field, learned the languages well enough, or attended innovatively enough to a range of sensory expressions. It is true that this would be a different book were I able to spend more time with the people, languages, and sensorium of Myanmar; I hope that what I have begun here will lead to more of this kind of Myanmar-based work for myself and other scholars. What this book will show, however, is that by creatively exploring excessive Christian archives and limited Buddhist collections we can still imagine what radical religious transformation felt like in nineteenth-century Burma. These pages animate a diverse array of religious objects and communities as they move through the changing landscapes of the last Burmese kingdom and pre- and post–Civil War United States. These objects of conversion and resistance conjure the worlds they changed.

* * *

Another way to write this story would be to trace its molting and calcifying theologies. I could read the same Baptist correspondence to explain the Judsons' denunciation of infant baptism that led them to leave the Congregationalist church in spite of its position as the sole established church in their home state of Massachusetts until 1833. I could read the same Buddhist chronicles alongside earlier examples of the genre to parse particular doctrinal concerns of the Burmese sangha during the Konbaung era. This kind of intellectual history could compare and contrast reforming religious ideas among leading authors of the time.

This approach, though, could not grasp the entanglements between Burma's Christians and Buddhists. The Burmese records are so silent about the Baptists that to read them on their own terms would be to conclude that Christian converts and missionaries were an inconsequential presence in the country. The Baptist writings, by contrast, depict minority communities *and* the majority as on the brink of sweeping Christian conversion. Both literatures feature protagonists advancing pure, immutable forms of their religion. But Buddhism and Christianity do not march through nineteenth-century Burma separately and unchanged; rather, they change significantly as various communities collide, converse, compete, and categorize. By the time of the collapse of the last Burmese dynasty in 1885, Buddhism had emerged as a respected world religion that must endure without a patron king and with a sophisticated engagement with modern science and colonial society. Protestant Christianity, for its part, entered the period of total British colonization having spread in Burma for over seventy years and having gone from being an ignored port city faith of a few foreigners to an increasingly popular and domesticated Burmese religion.

To understand this kinesis, I look between the lines and beyond the texts. To explore the entanglements between Buddhists and Christians—as well as people who do not fit easily into these categories—I focus on the religious objects passed and pressed between them, actual artifacts and writings about artifacts. These objects are especially telling because the two dominant doctrinal traditions in this book, Theravada Buddhism and Baptist Christianity, both pay special attention to holy objects out of a shared concern with the way worldly materials can mediate a relationship with a central figure who is absent from this world. These traditions have long, complex, and separate histories with religious media that came into embodied contact with each other for the first time through the American mission to Burma. The Baptists and the Buddhists expected to have very different beliefs and practices from each other. The Buddhists assumed that the newly settled Americans would act like other foreigners residing in the country, such as the Portuguese, and keep their god and rituals to themselves. They were surprised, then, when the Baptists took a sustained interest in translating Christian scriptures into their languages and using terms associated with the Buddha to explain Christ's teachings about salvation. Likewise, the Baptists anticipated that the Burmese would be stunned when they arrived with their demonstrations of how the Buddha was not *really* in Buddha statues. But the Burmese were long prepared for sophisticated debates about how even though the historical Buddha is long gone, special objects with special connections to him continue to have special powers.

As the Baptists soon learned, Theravada Buddhism teaches that the Buddha's life on earth culminated in his *parinirvana,* his total enlightenment. After a career of teaching following his initial nirvana, Gotama Buddha was fully liberated from this realm of stress and suffering, called "samsara." The Buddha's achievement of parinirvana meant that he no longer generated the conditions to be reborn into samsara. Until the arrival of the next buddha, Maitreya, this world is without a living buddha.

Different schools of Buddhism have debated what the Buddha's parinirvana really means. Buddhist scriptures tell of the Buddha refusing to answer questions about the existence of buddhas after death, including about whether a buddha exists after death, does not exist after death, both exists and does not exist after death, and neither exists nor does not exist after death.[35] These unanswered questions have allowed for a wide range of interpretations of the Buddha's presence and absence. Mahayana schools, for example, have developed complex theories about how and why the Buddha is an extraordinary being who still acts in this world. Mahayana, whose name translates as "greater vehicle," sees its teachings as superior because they overcome a dualistic understanding of nirvana and samsara as separate and promise as the goal of religious striving the attainment of Buddhahood. Furthermore, Mahayana claims that the Buddha lived out a human life in a kind of show to help people see that his path is one that anyone can follow. This play at humanity, according to Mahayana doctrine, is an act of compassion by a very special being who skillfully customizes his teachings for different audiences.[36] Likewise, the Buddha's parinirvana was a compassionate act for those who would be more motivated to follow his teachings in his absence. For example, in the preeminent Mahayana text the *Lotus Sutra*, the Buddha says that for some people who think he is extinct, they will worship his remains and be inspired to follow his path.[37] For those who are ready for advanced teachings, according to Mahayana, the Buddha can be understood as a continually active being who, along with a new pantheon of Bodhisattvas, can help them attain buddhahood. The Buddha and Bodhisattvas often do this as invisible presences who engage humans through special practices and objects. Indeed, the *Lotus Sutra* features teachings about how the Buddha continues to abide in this realm and gives explicit instructions for how the text itself should be engaged as a powerful actor helping beings on the path.

Theravada does not include these Mahayana doctrines about a continually active Buddha in this world. It distinguishes itself by maintaining a realist position that insists that the Buddha was a *real* (albeit extraordinary) human being who was *really* unbound from this world, which is also *real* (not a confused dualist construction). Theravada Buddhists, then, have a particular challenge of forming a relationship with the Buddha in his absence. One long-standing Theravada practice is the use of objects as tools for remembering the Buddha's teachings and example. Theravada's pragmatic side supports practitioners who employ materials such as texts, images, and shrines to help keep the Buddha's revelations about suffering in mind and follow his path to freedom. This method assumes that these objects do not have independent agency, but that humans can find motivation in them for their own actions. The most beneficial actions are those focused on virtuous behavior and the realization of what the tradition calls the "Three Marks of Existence": the truths of impermanence, suffering, and not-self.[38] The Buddha instructed his followers to see that so much of what they perceive as permanent in the world is actually caused by conditions that are subject to change. He explained that they suffer because they cling to things thinking that they will give lasting pleasure and satisfaction, only to find them in flux.

Furthermore, the Buddha taught his followers to understand all phenomena—including what they may have thought to be their soul—as not me, not mine. Nirvana comes from realizing these truths and breaking the bonds of attachment to the world. To find true happiness, one must let go.

At the same time, Theravada Buddhists have held on to objects. The most important of these objects are the bodily relics of the Buddha. Because these relics are materially composed of the Buddha's body and extend his biography into the present, they address the challenge of the Buddha's absence.[39] Relics are simultaneously the real, continued presence of the Buddha in this world and a reminder of his absence from it. The most famous relics in Burma are the Buddha's hairs, said to be enshrined in Shwedagon Pagoda in Yangon. Local traditions hold that these were the hairs that the Buddha gave to his very first lay disciples, the merchants named Tapussa and Bhallika in Pali sources. These merchants encountered the Buddha after his enlightenment and offered him sweets and rice, his very first meal after his glorious realization of nirvana. In return, the Buddha offered them some of his wisdom, which inspired the merchants to take refuge in him and his teachings. As they were leaving, the Buddha stroked his head and gave them eight hairs. In the accounts from Burma, these merchants were traveling from lower Burma, so when they returned home and enshrined the hairs, they created the earth's first reliquary monument.[40] Shwedagon is therefore celebrated for possessing the first relics of the Buddha after his enlightenment, which are enshrined in the first reliquary on earth by the first lay disciples.

Importantly, these relics are not just inanimate remains of a dead master used to remember his instructions for letting go of attachments to the material world. Like other relics in Buddhism, these relics, being an extension of the Buddha himself, have special powers. In a spectacular episode of Shwedagon's pagoda story, after some of the hairs were stolen on their journey back to Burma, they astounded the merchants by materializing in the reliquary casket. These relics appear to have moved through walls or bilocated, two of the superpowers attained by the Buddha and advanced practitioners, according to Theravada and other Buddhist traditions. Like the Buddha when he was alive, his relics have the ability to perform extraordinary acts for the benefit of his followers.

Bodily relics are not the only objects in Theravada Buddhism with these kinds of special abilities. Theravada Buddhism has long held that there are four types of objects that contain some of the Buddha's power (called *ānubhāva* in Pali): monuments with bodily relics, monuments that contain items that the Buddha used (such as his begging bowl), monuments built over sacred texts or simply the texts themselves, and monuments with consecrated objects like Buddha images. These monuments are known as *cetiya* in Pali and *zedi* in Burmese.[41] While the Buddha himself is absent in these monuments, they are still understood to contain his power because of the extraordinary objects they contain and the ritual processes like consecration that endow them with the Buddha's presence.[42]

As I detail in this book, Baptist missionaries visiting Shwedagon Pagoda and other zedis in nineteenth-century Burma would interrogate devotees who were praying and making offerings. The missionaries would ask why they were acting as though they were in the presence of a man who died over two thousand years ago. Some devotees would explain that they were honoring the absent Buddha's teachings while others would say that the Buddha was present in that monument. This paradox of absence and presence was not entirely foreign to the American Protestants; they, too, had a complicated history with this kind of conundrum.

A core paradox of Christianity is God's simultaneous presence and absence. The tradition holds that God created heaven and earth, but that he was not created; therefore, he is fundamentally different from the material of his creation. In Christ, God became materially present in this world, but, in Christ's death, God is again absent. The Holy Spirit, the third person of the Trinity, continues to act in this world, but humans do not interact with the Holy Spirit in a corporeal way as they did with Christ. Until Christ's second coming, humans have a mediated relationship with God through certain words, practices, and objects.[43] For Christians like the American evangelists in Burma, sacraments like baptism and special objects like the bread and wine of the Lord's Supper made present an intangible god.

American Baptists based their criticism of Buddhist material culture on biblical commandments to not have other gods or make idols, by which they meant manufactured objects that were worshipped as divine. When Adoniram Judson described the pagodas at Pagan as "idolatrous monuments," he meant that all of their Buddha statues and paintings were worshipped images of a false god. Protestantism's historic concern with images extends from non-Christian objects to objects that attempt to represent Jesus, God, and other occupants of heaven. Iconoclastic Protestant reformers argued that churches with artwork such as paintings and sculptures of Jesus and the saints broke God's commandment against manufacturing idols. The American evangelists who left for Burma in the early nineteenth century were raised in a Calvinist form of Protestant Christianity that maintained a strict condemnation of religious artwork. John Calvin (1509–1564), the highly influential French Christian reformer, was a fierce opponent of religious imagery. He argued that humans who try to picture God ended up with a mental fiction, and that these imagined pictures are therefore idolatrous.[44] The Puritans who established the congregations that the Judsons belonged to in Massachusetts in the late eighteenth and early nineteenth century held a Calvinist theology and its requisite condemnation of religious imagery. The missionaries' churches did not allow murals, stained-glass windows, or statues. The first missionaries to Burma had likely never once viewed a painting or an etching of Jesus.

In spite of the starkness of their churches, these Americans came from a culture alive with supernatural power. In the period between the American Revolution (1765–1791) and the Civil War (1861–1865), there was a popular belief in magic and the occult, as well in God's mysterious ability to work miracles.[45] And it was not just God who had the power to intervene in the material world; there was a pervasive sense of active invisible beings, especially the dead. Antebellum Americans used particular religious objects—including gravestones, portraits, embroidery, and hair jewelry—to communicate with loved ones after their death.[46] Early in my research for this book, I chanced on two packets of hair in an otherwise typical archival folder containing the correspondence of Adoniram Judson's third wife, Emily Chubbuck Judson. The locks of straight brown hair were labeled as Emily's and dated from 1853, the year before her death, when she was back in the States from Burma and gravely ill. Beyond its collection and preservation, there is no evidence of how Emily's hair was used. Still, it raises the question of how the Baptists who established the Burmese mission imagined special objects, perhaps including their own community's hair relics, as capable of heavenly connections.

Like antebellum America, the Konbaung kingdom was animated by the dead and other invisible beings. Burmese culture is populated with beings called "nats," which include gods like the divine characters in Buddhist literature as well as spirits with specific ties to Burmese landscapes and communities. Some nats are said to have once been humans who suffered especially violent deaths that prevented them from cycling through normal reincarnation processes; instead, they haunt the earth. These beings tend to dwell invisibly in trees, waterways, and hills and to intervene in human affairs when provoked. Humans build homes for them and other shrines, where they make propitiatory offerings such as food and flowers. As I examine in chapter 1, a distinguished set of these spirits bears a historical connection with the lineages of Burmese kings and monks who appease the spirits by ritually crafting and installing sculptures of them in monasteries and consecrating them as royal nats. Scholarship on Burmese religions has tended to separate Theravada Buddhism from what it used to call "animism."[47] The pervasive materiality of nat practices, however, demonstrates the inseparability of nats from Burmese Buddhism.[48]

The abundance of nat shrines and Buddha images initially overwhelmed and offended the American Baptists, who had been habituated to refuse religious imagery. "One's first impressions," wrote the American Baptist Howard Malcom of Shwedagon Pagoda in 1837, "are, what *terrible* grandeur—what *sickening* magnificence—what absurd imagery."[49] Over the course of the century, however, as the mission grew, the Baptists found themselves incorporating religious imagery. Meanwhile, as their kingdom collapsed, Burmese Buddhists engaged in their own debates about whether shrines and images were polluting a pure path to nirvana. This book explores the particular religious objects that helped make new relationships with God and the Buddha meaningful in light of concerns about their presence and absence. I showcase striking similarities in attitudes toward holy materials to consider how various communities engaged each other and the world around them in this period of dramatic change.

*   *   *

The religious history this book tells is organized into four chapters, each of which focuses on one type of these holy materials. The chapters proceed somewhat chronologically, with the first exploring the religious books that shaped the earliest nineteenth-century encounters between American and Burmese communities, and the last scrutinizing the mission's legacy as revealed in twenty-first-century Burmese religious portraits. The topics and sequence of the chapters also track the movements of Baptists toward engaging God through material things and of Buddhist experiments with shifting away from objects and even the Buddha himself. While the first

INTRODUCTION

chapter begins with immaterial, imagined books understood as righteous signs of God, the last chapter shows how colorful paintings of Jesus and the Judsons become powerful presences. The Burmese Buddhist books showcased in the first chapter are not confined to the imagination but are, rather, the most materially luxurious books that the kingdom produced en masse. The Buddhist sect I investigate in the penultimate chapter rejects these kinds of lavish productions, arguing that they are signs of corruption at a time when the people of Burma must purely focus on the ultimate truth realized by the Buddha. In between two-hundred-year-old books and contemporary paintings, I tell the story of the transformations of Baptist Christianity and Burmese Buddhism through attention to the schools and pagodas that hosted key parts of these tangled processes. I treat the school as an object instead of, say, a curriculum, because I argue that it was schools' special supplies—such as globes and maps—that made Baptist education so popular, even among non-Christians. Likewise, I take up the pagoda as a fundamental object in this history because the Buddha relics and imagery it contains made it the most attractive site both for devotees seeking the presence of the Buddha and for evangelists preaching his absence. The four types of objects that form this book are intentionally heterogenous. By spotlighting seemingly disparate things, I reveal common ways that religious material culture was a powerful medium for social transformation.

The first chapter, "The Book: Religious Texts of Nineteenth-Century Burma," investigates the fascination with tangible books and sacred histories that set the religious encounters of nineteenth-century Burma into motion. This chapter moves through three major concurrent religious developments: the Karen lost book legend that explained this influential minority community's sudden and sweeping enthusiasm for Christianity by recounting a local legend about a lost sacred book and the white man prophesied to return it; the Baptist tracts that promoted Asian evangelism by asserting that Christ's life story was buried in ancient Sanskrit manuscripts; and the militarization of Burma's most beautiful book, the *Kammavāca*. These developments demonstrate that powerful religious books and their communities shaped this early period of conversion and resistance. For both Buddhists and Baptists, books acted as inanimate guides for understanding immaterial powers as well as animate forces in the material world.

INTRODUCTION

Chapter 2, "The School: Models of Religious Imagination," focuses on popular educational materials and schoolhouses in Christian and Buddhist communities in nineteenth-century Burma and features rare American and Burmese writing by and about women to consider why schools and education were so important to this period. American schools dominated British schools in number and influence and, even more curiously, were attractive among Burmese Buddhist communities, who seemed to want little to do with Christian missionaries otherwise. This chapter suggests that it was a fascination with the revelatory power of Baptist telescopes, globes, maps, and other new views of the world and its place in the universe that was crucial to making Christian education so popular in Burma. This examination of educational materials shows that Buddhists instilled pride in a newly asserted Burmese Theravada history, whereas Christians invited the adoption and expansion of increasingly powerful new cosmological visions and religious imaginations.[50]

The third chapter, "The Pagoda: Icons and Iconoclasm," studies the pagoda—Burma's most popular religious building—alongside the Paramat movement, a Buddhist sect that was critical of what it saw as excessive materiality in contemporary Burmese Buddhism. The Paramats fascinated Baptist missionaries with their iconoclastic rhetoric, which the Baptists took as evidence that the Buddhist country was giving way to Christianity. As this chapter demonstrates, Buddhist reformers engaged Americans in discussions of the Buddha's total absence to elicit sympathy for their protests against royally sponsored monastic institutions and related material practices. This chapter pairs a study of the Baptist mission's fixation on pagodas with the Paramats' criticisms of Burmese religious material culture in order to illuminate a tension felt by both Baptists and Buddhists—a tension between the sense of extraordinary power in religious objects and the conviction that true salvation is not found in the material world. I show how this mysterious Paramat movement is an example of minority communities using religious objects to assert independent identities in this period of advancing British occupation.

I continue to explore political dimensions of religious materials in the fourth and final chapter, "The Portrait: American Jesus in Burma." My analysis of religious portraits of the Judsons and of the larger context of the Buddhist visual culture in which they are displayed considers the development of Christian portraiture and its culmination in the 2013 bicentennial celebrations of the establishment of the American Baptist mission in Burma. This chapter draws on the fieldwork I conducted in Myanmar during these celebrations to study the legacy of the nineteenth-century mission and the ongoing ways in which Baptist minority communities understand the power of religious objects in their negotiation of the country's politics. It attends to the specific material qualities of Christian images at memorial sites to consider how paintings of Jesus and the Judsons create distinct and globally networked Christian communities; and it argues that the Anglo-American style of Jesus and Judson imagery reveals a Baptist practice of marking themselves as distinct from Burmese Buddhists and their religious material culture. This act of distinction is informed by an understanding that, even in the vastly Buddhist country, Christianity is the most popular minority religion.[51]

The story I tell of nineteenth-century Burma cascades through these chapters to show a fluidity to religious identity, to Christianity and Buddhism. The Myanmar of contemporary travel advertising makes it tempting to look back and think that Burmese Buddhism withstood the onslaught of Christian evangelism and British colonialism like some massive weathered but unfallen Buddhist statue. And today's politics prime us to see a contemporary, intractable American evangelical Christianity as the same fervent religion that the Judsons brought with them to Burma, just in period clothing. But this retrojection misunderstands. As the object studies in this book reveal, the power of these forceful religious traditions does not come from constancy. It comes from change. To begin to get a sense of what this change felt like, I will now turn to a surprising early Baptist encounter with a mysterious book in southern Burma.

ONE

The Book

Religious Texts of Nineteenth-Century Burma

ON SEPTEMBER 7, 1828, a group of Karen people, a large minority group in Myanmar and the Thai borderlands, went to the home of the American Baptist missionary George Boardman, who had recently moved into their town, Tavoy. An elderly, highly respected local teacher who was carrying a special book led the group. He approached Boardman and said, "My lord, your humble servants have come from the wilderness to lay at your lordship's feet a certain book, and to inquire of your lordship whether it is good or bad, true or false." Boardman, who had spent that Sunday in worship and religious discussion, continued listening.[1]

"We, Karens, your humble servants, are an ignorant race of people, we have no books, no written language, we know nothing of God or his law," the local leader announced. "When this book was given us, we were charged to worship it, which we have done for twelve years."[2]

As the American Baptist mission in Tavoy had only been established five months earlier, Boardman must have been curious to know what book these people had been worshipping for over a decade. It was likely Buddhist, as Buddhism was the country's dominant religion; however, it would have been odd for a Buddhist text to be in the possession of this minority Karen lay community rather than in a Burmese monastery.

"We know nothing of its contents," the local leader continued, "not so much as in what language it is written. We have heard of the gospel of Jesus

Christ, and are persuaded that your lordship can easily settle the question, and teach us the true way of becoming happy."[3]

The teacher then opened a large basket and proceeded to unwrap layer after layer of coverings until he finally unveiled what Boardman instantly recognized as an "old tattered duodecimo volume ... [of] the 'Book of Common Prayer, with the Psalms,' published at Oxford."[4]

Boardman told the Karen community that "it is a good book ... but it is not good to worship it. [They] must worship the God it reveals."[5] Boardman was trying to explain the Protestant insistence that their god is not present in the book, but that its mundane words can be a guide to this transcendent god. The American then proceeded to spend the rest of the evening teaching the basics of the gospel.

At the end of the night, the old teacher, who, Boardman wrote, had the air of "a kind of sorcerer, seemed disappointed at the thought that he had obtained no claim to heaven by worshipping the book so many years."[6] This Karen elder, according to this Baptist account, understood the practice of venerating the book to be extraordinarily powerful in and of itself, independent of the particular teachings the book recorded.

This disorienting and reorienting encounter with a special book speaks to a larger history of religious practice in nineteenth-century Burma. As Protestant missionaries began evangelizing in Burma, not only did Christian texts manifest in unexpected places but the production and dissemination of Buddhist scripture also became more creative. For example, in 1868, the Burmese king commissioned the world's largest "book," in the form of their entire Buddhist canon inscribed on 729 marble slabs, with each slab standing five feet tall, three feet wide, and five inches thick, crowned with a precious gem and installed in its own shrine.[7] In a response to the lavish production of Buddhist books, American missionaries, as part of their pleas for permission to proselytize, gifted Burmese kings multivolume bibles that they had gilded and wrapped in luxurious cloth. Furthermore, the Baptists' introduction of the printing press into the Southeast Asian country led to mass-produced evangelical tracts as well as newly designed scripts for Burma's previously illiterate minority groups. After blanketing the countryside with printed arguments for Christian conversion, missionaries would return to find that some recipients had read and debated the arguments, whereas others had refashioned the paper tracts into amulets worn as earrings or wrapped them in special fabrics and attached to bells to be worshipped as magical devices. The Karen, the country's first minority group to be taken with Christianity, explained their enthusiasm for the Americans' religion by recounting a local legend about a lost sacred book and the white man who would return it.[8]

This chapter argues that powerful books are at the center of this period of religious confrontation, confusion, and comparison. Today all of these groups name the nineteenth century as especially important for reforming their religious identities. Baptists take special pride in their history of establishing the United States' first overseas mission station and assert that this bold evangelism gave them a strong voice in the States and abroad.[9] Burmese Buddhists look past their twentieth-century trials with a military dictatorship, past the era of British colonial rule, back to the last line of Burmese kings in the nineteenth century to illustrate an idealized way of Burmese leadership and Buddhism coming together to rule the diverse country.[10] And the Karen point to this period as the time when their community realized its special identity and grew strong by adopting a writing system and carrying out religious reform.[11]

To understand why the nineteenth century became so crucial for these three groups, this chapter will explore each of them in turn, attending specifically to the most privileged object of the time: the sacred book. By "book," my sources and I mean bound pages with handwritten or printed words (B. *sa-ouq*).[12] I argue that an alluring fantasy of a holy past made palpable by circulating books drove the first period of religious encounter, exchange, and exclusion in nineteenth-century Burma. In other words, the sometimes corresponding and often contesting presentations of eternal revelations recorded in written texts launched the nineteenth-century American Baptist mission, empowered the simultaneous Burmese Buddhist reformation, and gave rise to an independent Karen Christian minority. The Protestant mission would claim success in its translation works and introduction of writing systems along with the gospel to Burma's marginalized peoples. At the same time, this evangelical organization would bemoan its failed attempts to convert Burmese Buddhists, whose celebration of their carefully recorded, royally purified, and luxuriously disseminated ancient religious teachings grew as the American mission expanded.

Of course, the combination of powerful books and sacred pasts is at the center of many stories in the study of religions.[13] But much of what is distinct about the version at the heart of this nineteenth-century American-Burmese encounter is the role played by new technologies—philological, nautical, and print. Together these advances powered dreams of precisely knowing sacred pasts, of ancient wisdom recovered for the here and now. New linguistic methods promised to give voice to lost prophecy; improvements in the science of sailing and the invention of the steam engine propelled religious artifacts and proselytizing people around the world at revolutionary speeds; and the evolution of printing techniques and the introduction of newly designed scripts, and then fonts, put millions of strangers into conversation for the first time.[14]

To illuminate how these developments would impact the religious cultures of nineteenth-century Burma, I will first turn to Karen communities, who worshipped books in ways that initially shocked the missionaries, but whose seemingly eccentric practices point to central religious concerns not only for this minority group but also for Burmese Buddhists and the American Baptist missionaries living among them.

Lost and Found Books of the Karen

In the nineteenth century, Karen communities circulated a story of a glorious, nearly forgotten time when they possessed a revered written language, long before they became the marginalized illiterate communities that the American Baptist missionaries found them to be. This legend told not only of these people's dignified, lettered history but also of a prophesied sacred future when the disenfranchised group would rise again with the help of a white brother who would return their lost text. This story is still told among Baptist Karen communities in Burma who account for their people's precipitous conversion to Christianity with this story of the sacred Karen book that was bequeathed long ago from an ancestral father but then tragically lost by his son, leading to generations of poverty and illiteracy for the community. The Karen prevailed in this dark period through the hopeful prophecy that the book would be returned one day by a white man coming from a distant land. When the American Baptist missionaries arrived in the mid-nineteenth century with bibles and then invented a written system for a Karen language, the Karen saw that the long-anticipated white man had come.

While this Karen book legend is told rather consistently in present-day communities, the earliest recorded versions of this legend found in nineteenth-century American missionary writings, early Karen Christian tales, and the colonial British press contain a range of details that speak to an evolving story, rather than a fixed standard account.[15] This section argues that this Karen legend is not a pre-Christian oral tradition, as it is presented today, but rather a product of the American Baptist mission and concurrent Burmese Buddhist book practices. By studying the earliest records of the lost book story, I will demonstrate that it evolved over the course of the nineteenth century from a variety of prophecies about foreigners and books to a streamlined account of the way Karen elders preserved an ancient knowledge that someday white foreigners would come to return their long-lost book of God. Further, I will suggest that this legend is not simply a quirky tale from a minor convert community, but evidence of the large role magic books played throughout nineteenth-century Burma.[16]

To read accounts of this book legend as a product of the encounter between Karen people and American Baptists is not to completely preclude the possibility that the book legend has roots in an older oral tradition that predates the nineteenth century, when the Karen had never yet met a European or an American but had stories of a future time when foreigners would come, and the Karen would become a mighty people with books of their own. The Karen, like many other unlettered people groups, preserved rich folklore and history through oral traditions.[17] The available records of these Karen book legends, however, all date to the American missionary era or later and bear marks of the encounters between the Karen and American evangelists and British colonialists.[18] The earliest recorded version of the legend pre-dates the introduction of British evangelism in Burma in 1859 and highlights the significant influence of the U.S. Baptist mission on the formation of ethnolinguistic group identities that would evolve through religious histories into later expressions of Karen ethnonationalism. As Hitomi Fujimura has shown, Karen Baptist intellectuals—despite being religious minorities in the larger Karen community, which is mostly Buddhist—were key figures in the foundation of the Karen National Association in 1881. These Karen Baptists drew on experiences with the American Baptist mission to work with the British colonial system to claim a distinct national identity. One powerful example cited by Fujimura is the Karen Baptist intellectual involvement in the British census that was based on experience with enumeration practices established by the American missions, such as the annual counting of church membership.[19] Relatedly, Ananda Rajah has shown how the Karen National Association built on Baptist practices of narrating religious histories about Karennic-speaking peoples who preceded the arrival of Burmese-speaking people to the land and have long suffered the dispossession of their lands and livelihood "caused by a *generalized* Burman Other."[20] Rajah traces this practice of separatist Karen ethnonationalism into Karen refugee camps along the Thai-Burmese border, where hundreds of thousands have fled since 1989, when Burmese armed forces began a sustained offensive against this second-largest distinct ethnic minority group identified by the state. Rajah examines instances of American missionaries working to establish concordances between Karen origin narratives and biblical stories, though he does not explore the lost book legend. In what follows, I will venture an analysis of how the presentation of this particular legend as ancient served contemporary political agendas for both the Karen and the "white foreigners."[21]

The earliest recorded examples do not mention a legendary Karen book, but they do tell of a prophecy that foreigners will be recognized as brethren who bring happiness. The first recorded account featuring emancipating foreigners appeared in 1843, thirty years into the Baptist mission in Burma, when a missionary in Tavoy published an address by Saw Quala, a Karen convert to Christianity. This first account embedded scenes of foreigners and books within a larger story of the brutality of Bamar incursions into indigenous Karen communities.

Saw Quala told of how, when Burmese control extended to Karen settlements, the Burmese took away all their rice and paddies and made the Karen their vassals. Karen men were forced to present endless tribute to their rulers (yams, ginger, elephant tusks, rhinoceros horns, wild vegetables), demanding that they leave home for days on end. The women, especially the beautiful ones, did everything they could to not be noticed by outsiders, Saw Quala's address explained; they had to hide inside and blacken their faces to put off Burmese officers.[22]

Saw Quala said that the Karen endured all of this misery, knowing that relief would eventually come. Their elders prophesized that foreigners, coming by water, would bring joy to the Karen. As their saying went, "If the thing come by land, weep; if by water, laugh." Saw Quala explained that, when the Americans arrived in Burma, his people were sure that things would finally get better. They had to; the white men had come by boat.[23]

In Saw Quala's redemptive narrative we find the earliest recorded Karen prophecy anticipating foreign aid. Note that this version does not mention anything about a long-lost book. Rather, Saw Quala's story described the Karen as illiterate before the Baptists arrived and narrated that they would go to the Buddhist monasteries when they wanted access to the power books possessed. But, according to Saw Quala, the Burmese who ran the monasteries relegated the Karen to carrying bricks, pulling weeds, and begging for food. Saw Quala recounted that it was only after the American missionary Jonathan Wade invented a script for a Karennic language in the early 1830s that the Karen began to remember another saying attributed to the Elders: "Children and grandchildren, the Karen books will yet arrive. When their books arrive, they will obtain a little happiness."[24]

Although Saw Quala's story does not have the legendary book, it does have the anticipation of being freed by foreigners, having texts of their own one day, and a final element that would become important for the later version of the Karen lost book legend: the reunion of brothers. Saw Quala told of how the Karen elders predicted that "the Karens and the white foreigners will recognize each other as brethren; and one will say, O my younger brother! And they will become real brethren, and there will be peace and happiness."[25] For Saw Quala and his 1843 audience, this must have sounded like a prophesy of the partnership that the Karen were then developing with the American missionaries, as well as with the British colonists who were pursuing alliances with the Karen in their efforts to extend the power they had gained in the First Anglo-Burmese War. Saw Quala's account can be read as an idealization of this encounter between the Karen and the Westerners that reaches back in time to recast this political present as part of the continuation of a sacred past.

It is not until 1862, nearly two decades after Saw Quala's Karen history and a decade after the Second Anglo-Burmese War, that we find our first example of a Karen book story in which the ancient Karen had a holy book that would be returned by their long-lost white brother. In her memoir of working with the Karen, *Civilizing Mountain Men*, American missionary Ellen Mason tells her readers that she heard a local Karen man relaying the story of his people's legendary book, "with such poetic fire and inspiration, it moved [her] to pencil it down that very night, almost word for word."[26] As with Saw Quala's account, Mason's foregrounds the prophecy of the coming white savior by explaining that the Karen had been "enslaved by the

Burmese" who used "their superior knowledge of books, to bind them in servitude."[27] Even though the Karen were subjugated by the dominating, book-wielding Burmese, they did preserve a memory of a single book they once possessed. Mason explained that this book "contained the words of Jehovah. Their wise men say there were seven brothers, and they, the younger, had God's word on skins. They were careless, laid it at the foot of a plantain-tree, and the White Brother carried it off, and by it became the favorite son of God.... They fully believe the White Brother is to bring it back to them from north-western lands."[28]

In the version that Mason gave, the younger brother with the book of God is the Karen ancestor, and his sibling is the white brother who leaves with the book. This American account claims that because the white brother has God's word, he is God's favorite son and offers the suspiciously convenient geographical detail that this white brother returns from a land west and north of the Karen region—a land in the direction of the United States.

Six years after Mason published her account of the Karen lost book, the evangelical Religious Tract Society in London published an elaborated version titled *The White Foreigners from Over the Water*. Like the previous two accounts, it begins by explaining that the Karen were oppressed by their Burmese rulers, who heavily taxed them. When the Karen would come into Burmese cities for trade, the Karen would sing a traditional song narrating how they used to have the words of God, but because of their trespasses, God cursed them, leaving them without books. As one verse goes:

> The Karen was the elder brother,
> And obtained all the words of God.
> God formerly loved the Karen nation above all others,
> But because of their transgression, he cursed them,
> And now they have no books.[29]

In this account, unlike Saw Quala's, the Karen had not always been illiterate. They once possessed the words of God and basked in his love, but then they were condemned to live without books. Even in these dark ages, the Karen ancestors promised that their long-lost brothers would return, and that these white foreigners would bring God and joy back to the Karen. *The White Foreigners*' rendering of Karen folklore proceeded to explain that

our ancestors said that when our younger brothers came back,
The white foreigners,
Who were able to keep company with God,
The Karens will be happy.

Our ancestors charged us thus:
Children and grandchildren,
If the king come by land, weep;
If by water, laugh.
It will not come in our days,
But it will in yours.
Hence the Karens longed for those
Who were to come by water.[30]

This version of a Karen traditional folk song included the same prediction given in Saw Quala's and Ellen Mason's accounts: white foreigners will bring happiness to the dejected, illiterate Karen. In this telling, the Karen are not simply passive people whose world is dramatically changed when American Baptists stumble into their jungles. Instead, this encounter becomes a chapter in a larger Karen story, in which the Karen are presented as waiting and ready for the white men and their sacred book. *The White Foreigners* then claimed that their oral traditions proved clairvoyant, because when the white American missionaries came by boat to Burma and encountered the Karen people, they brought them the anticipated book of God:

"Have you brought us God's book?" asked the Karens.

"Yes, we have brought you God's book; but what do you know about God's book? Have you any books?"

"No, we have no books now; but our fathers say that long ago we had God's book written on leather, and in it we were told never to worship idols. The prophet who had charge of the book was one day reading it under a tree. He fell asleep with the book on his knees, and while he slept a dog came and tore it up. Then God was angry because his book had not been taken care of. Now we have no books; but white foreigners will come and bring us God's book once again. This our prophets say."

"See, the white foreigners have come!" they cried. "You have brought God's book."

"Yes, here is God's book!" and the missionaries showed to the eager people an English Bible.[31]

The White Foreigners thus incorporated pieces of Karen legend circulating earlier, such as the auspiciousness of strangers who arrive by water, to present a single story in which the Karen lost book is returned by the white foreigners.[32]

While there are discrepancies regarding which brother is the white brother, the Karen legend in both *The White Foreigners from Over the Water* and *Civilizing Mountain Men* is based on the prophecy that a fair-skinned brother would come from a strange land to return the lost Karen book, a holy text that contains the teachings of the Christian god. By the end of the nineteenth century, this baseline was common in retellings. For example, in 1887, Donald Mackenzie Smeaton of the Bengal Civil Service published *The Loyal Karens of Burma,* an influential book-length study of the Karen people and their alliances with the British Raj that asserted that the Karen, since ancient times, knew of "the coming back of the White Book . . . and the roll of parchment or skin to be brought to them by white foreigners."[33] This cultural knowledge, Smeaton argued, was carefully preserved in the Karen's "rich bard literature, which has been transmitted from generation to generation by men whose special business it is to commit to memory the traditions, legends, songs, and homely-folk-lore." Smeaton contended that "supreme importance is attached to the correct transmission . . . of the story of God's dealings with the nation. They believed that God, who had cursed the Karen for losing the written Word, would certainly call upon them some day . . . to say how much they remembered of it."[34] While Smeaton's characterization of the transmission procedure of Karen oral traditions is persuasive, his assertion that they had long been entirely conservative and uninfluenced by Westerners is less convincing when we consider that the record of the Karen legend before the late 1860s makes no mention of the Karen once having had a written language.

Smeaton published his Karen history just after the Third, and final, Anglo-Burmese War, and he told his readers on the very first page that the Karens were the "staunchest and bravest defenders of the British rule," without whom "the rebel Burmese and Shans would, in all probability, have overrun Lower Burma."[35] Keeping in mind the key political position the Karen played in facilitating—or, as Smeaton argued, crucially enabling—total British colonization of Burma, we should read Smeaton's study of the Karen folk tradition as part of a highly politicized story. When Smeaton's Karen insist that they had carefully preserved the history of their lost sacred book, which was returned when the American Baptist missionaries brought them the Bible, they are employing history, prophecy, literacy, and the entire missionary encounter to establish themselves as an essentially Christian people, a people who lay claim to God's Word, and whose present reunion with the powerful Christian Bible righteously situated them side by side with the Western colonizers.

While this colonial context is crucial for understanding the Karen book legend, I want to be careful about dismissing it as exclusively an act of political strategy. As Matthew Engelke's study of the Friday Masowe apostolics of Zimbabwe who claim to be "the Christians who don't read the Bible" explains, books have been powerful tools of colonial subjugation, but politics is not the whole story.[36] Too often studies of religious practices among groups like the Karen only tell of utilitarian functions, depicting indigenous peoples using myth and ritual to exert agency in times of subjugation. This emphasis implies that nonpragmatic religious concerns, such as complex theologies and transcendent beliefs and experiences, belong exclusively to the world's great religious traditions. My efforts to shake this historiographic habit is inspired by scholarship on Christian missions in other parts of the globe that rethinks Christian conversion in colonial contexts and shows the limitations of seeing adoption of foreign forms strictly as symptoms of Euro-American colonialism or strategies of desperate people. For example, Nicholas May's work on the oral histories of Nisga'a Church Armies shows that this late nineteenth-century Christian movement in Canada was driven by a priority to secure the continuity of exuberant forms of worship crucial to their collective cultural survival. This resonates with Baptist Karen stories of the lost book that ensure a continuity between their past and their Christian present. May's work demonstrates that paying attention to this kind of indigenous historical practice gives us a "deeper grasp of a phenomenon such as the adoption and appropriation of what was initially a foreign religious form."[37] Similarly, Linford Fisher's *The Indian Great Awakening*—which examines the history of Native American communities and their responses to colonial Christianity in southeastern New England between 1700 and 1820—models a method of resisting characterizations of indigenous religious formations as basically utilitarian, or, conversely, entirely mystical. Fisher's project keeps the everyday, material concerns of Native lifeworlds (such as land and subsistence) in tension with the considerations of immaterial religious considerations involved in conversion.[38] Sylvester Johnson's *African American Religions, 1500-2000* addresses the related academic debate over how fully Africans converted to Christianity by showing that is more productive to attend to African participation in Christianity as a "complex of institutions, practices, statuses, and legal privileges."[39] Johnson cautions against veering toward a naturalization of this kind of participation, clarifying that "the fact that some Africans chose to affiliate with Christianity cannot be naturalized at the teleological manifestation of some inherent Black attraction to the religion, its messiah-god or its putative meekness."[40] In this book, I resist reproducing the ways that the American and Karen Baptist accounts naturalize Karen attraction to Christianity without dismissing Karen Christianity as entirely a strategic way of surviving in British Burma.

Furthermore, concluding that Karen communities simply created the lost book legend to elevate their people within a colonial hierarchy would further a stereotype of an isolated, history-less Karen, alienated from larger historical practices such as the prominent tradition of civilizations creating and circulating powerful religious books.[41] In order to understand why a book emerges as the main character in this particular Karen legend over the course of the nineteenth century, we must consider connected book practices and stories circulating in Burma in this particular period. I will therefore now turn to two additional nineteenth-century accounts of the Karen people and their religious relationships with related texts.[42]

A few years after the Karen community presented their magical *Book of Common Prayer* to George Boardman (recounted at the outset of this chapter), Francis Mason recorded a similar episode in his journal. Mason's 1835 story, like Boardman's 1828 account, features a sorcerer-like figure from Tavoy who wielded a book he and his followers believed to be divine. Mason wrote that he encountered a "prophet and necromancer ... reclining in a raised apartment between two rows of peacock's feathers."[43] The proof the local people gave that this man was sent by God was that he had a special book from heaven. The people asked if Mason would read the book for them and then convinced the prophet to produce it for the American. Mason explains that, with some reluctance, [the Karen prophet] produced a small piece of wood about two inches long, and one and a half broad, with a short handle, and wrapped in several layers of tinsel, that made jingling whenever it was handled. On removing the tinsel, in a hollow cut in the wood were several folds of cloth, under which appeared the book spread out at full length, which, to the great amusement of the people, [Mason] read as follows:—

Wheelwright,
Monk-house,
Winter &
Brooker,
London.[44]

This worshipped book turned out to be a business card from a London firm. Like Boardman, Mason expressed amusement that unlettered people had been worshipping rather mundane productions of the English press. Both of their jester-like sorcerer characters slowly remove the worshipped objects from layers of gaudy material, building suspense, only to arrive at the same punch line: these primitive people were idolizing ordinary texts.[45]

Behind these jokes, there might be an uneasiness about missionary methods. As American Baptists traveled from town to town, meeting groups of people who were asking for copy after copy of their Christian tracts, missionaries would occasionally express concern that the recipients would not treat the religious teachings with the appropriate sobriety. For example, a couple of years after Mason jotted down his peacock-feathered prophet story, American Baptist missionary Thomas Simons wrote of a group of young Muslims in Burma who were asking him for some books and who had made "ornaments in their ears made from tracts"; Simons concluded that their request must be due to a desire for a "fresh supply for the same purpose," so he refused.[46] Simons' encounter with this minority community was not the only time he had found Christian tracts being used in Burma for earrings. "At another time," Simons wrote, "I saw two men cutting up our books for ear ornaments. One pair of cylinders had already been made and were worn, and another pair were under the operation of the knife. When I spoke to them, they appeared ashamed, and hurried off into their huts, saying they were not our books."[47]

These examples of minority groups in Burma wearing sacred texts and worshipping books they cannot read to earn favorable rebirths or to promote themselves as divine prophets call to mind similar religious book practices in Asia.[48] The fact that these practices were centered on Christian texts invites a reading of them as Buddhist rituals with biblical twists, but I want to consider how Protestant text worship and book cults were at play here beyond providing the base materials.[49] As I will show see in the following section, two key books—or, rather, ideas about books—drove American evangelical work in Burma.

American Dreams of Sanskrit Bibles

American Baptist missionaries point to a single book to explain the history of their foreign missions, a history that began in Burma but spread all over the world. The book they say launched their thousand ships was, of course, the Bible—specifically, the command in the Gospels to "go ye into all the world, and preach the gospel to every creature."[50] This Christian injunction to proselytize in foreign lands gave textual authority to American Protestant campaigns establishing mission stations abroad. But an examination of the earliest American Baptist missionary records reveals that the Bible was not the only book that sent evangelists east; there was another book, and it, too, told of the life and teachings of Christ, but these sacred messages were said to have been buried under centuries of heathen darkness and superstition. This other book was an imagined ancient Indian manuscript.

The fantastical idea of an ancient Christian Indian scripture was first circulated to America in 1809, when the sermon "The Star in the East" by Claudius Buchanan became popular reading in Protestant circles. Buchanan, a minister to two hundred thousand Christians in British India, asserted that ancient Indian writings recorded specific details from the history of Christ; that Hinduism contained relics of the first faith of the earth; and that buried among all the idols and dark superstitions of Asia, was the divine light of God.[51] Several young American Protestants were so taken with Buchanan's contention that a recently discovered collection of Sanskrit scriptures celebrated a prince from two millennia ago, whose miraculous birth, life of mysterious and wonderful works, death, and resurrection are consistent with those of Christ, that they became this country's first intercontinental missionaries. Foremost among those transformed by Buchanan's sermon was the twenty-one-year old Adoniram Judson.

The romanticized history that lured Adoniram to India bears a striking resemblance to fantasies of past times nurtured not only among the Karen communities examined in the previous section but also among the Burmese Buddhists under consideration in the next section. For the Americans, a glorious past was vigorously imagined in which the grammars, texts, and religions of India married those of the Greco-Roman world. New philological discoveries of shared roots among the venerated Indian language Sanskrit and ancient Greek and Latin ignited dreams of a brilliant past when wizened South Asian philosophers debated Roman politicians and Athenian poets. At the same time as they imagined long-ago meetings of noble minds, these nineteenth-century Protestants were fascinated by stories of a sacred present in which textual discoveries of the golden age would propel the light of God into all nations before their very eyes.

The "Star in the East" sermon by Claudius Buchanan ignited these fantasies of an Indo-European golden age preserved in ancient manuscripts. Buchanan's sermon has been celebrated in the institutional histories of the American Baptist church as the singular reading that inspired Adoniram Judson to become America's first intercontinental missionary, and missionary archives preserve correspondences from American supporters who were similarly moved to make donations after reading the sermon. The biography of Adoniram by his son Edward, for example, tells of how Buchanan's description of the "progress of the Gospel in India . . . fell into Judson's soul like a spark into tinder," but a study of the sermon reveals the emphasis to be not on the advancement of Christianity in contemporary India, as Edward Judson suggested, but rather on early Indian writings and practices that, Buchanan claims, prove that the divine power of Christianity had pervaded the East since ancient times.[52]

It is this specific fantasy that we find fueling Buchanan's sermon—this vision of Indian insights in conversation with Western wisdom that made his address so exciting. A simple statistical account of the rising numbers of newly converted Christians in the East could not likely have convinced Adoniram to set sail for India. What sent the Judsons on their journey were not straightforward progress reports, but sensational stories of prophets speaking Indian tongues who discovered keys to the kingdom of God.

Later in life, Judson would often recall the momentous occasion of reading Buchanan's "The Star in the East," remembering how ludicrous, even irrational, his response was to the text. Judson saw his sudden and complete conversion to the missionary cause as necessary for overcoming the natural hesitancies that might have kept him at home, though he recognized afterward the flaws in the "vivid conception" of missionary duty he had taken from Buchanan. Judson's third wife, Emily Chubbuck Judson, wrote that, despite her husband's later repudiation of the zealous views and behaviors rooted in "The Star in the East," her husband's "missionary views were always of the most comprehensive and engrossing character; and his remarks . . . especially at the close of a day's work in private, were characterized by a high-wrought enthusiasm seldom found in persons of his maturity and years and judgments."[53] Emily explained that Buchanan's sermon led Adoniram to devour "with great greediness every scrap of information concerning Eastern countries," and that the "glowing and overwrought pictures" he found in reports of British embassies to Burma "were peculiarly congenial to his romantic spirit."[54] Ever since these early readings, Emily explained, Adoniram's "heart . . . was turned entirely to the East, and he was impatient of anything short of a life devotement."[55] Judson, in this account, was so consumed by longing for the East that only a lifetime's commitment could fulfill his desire.

Judson was not the only Protestant in America to be captivated by Buchanan's tales of the Christian truths shining through Sanskrit manuscripts. The year after Judson's death, his contemporary William Crane wrote to Emily to say that he had followed her husband's life closely and identified deeply with Judson's missionary zeal, having himself been inspired by the very same sermon that sent Adoniram east. After Crane's pastor lent him a copy of Buchanan's sermon, he "read it and revered it, with some of the same feelings, in which (perhaps during the very same month) . . . [Adoniram] imbibed . . . it, that missionary fire and zeal, which nothing but Death could extinguish."[56] In Crane's account, too, Buchanan's sermon is incendiary, inspiring unquenchable passion and admiration for foreign evangelism.

Marilla Baker Ingalls, the missionary and author of the 1857 travelogue *Ocean Sketches of Life in Burmah*, also emphasized the unique excitement of "The Star in the East" among her fellow Baptists. Ingalls began her story of American missions by explaining that "the stirring appeal of Buchanan's 'Star in the East' had crossed the waters. Judson and a few others responded to the call, and laid themselves upon the altar of missions."[57] For Ingalls, "The Star in the East" inspired martyrdom.[58] In order to understand how a single sermon could inspire such a passionate and total commitment to a life of missionary work in the East, we must examine Buchanan's arguments regarding the Christian roots of Indian texts and the responses they engendered.

Buchanan's "The Star in the East" sermon centered on the contention that newly unearthed Sanskrit scriptures celebrate a prince from two millennia ago whose miraculous birth, life of mysterious and wonderful works, death, and resurrection are consistent with those of Christ. According to Buchanan, the Sanskrit manuscripts containing these testimonies record the journey of holy men who followed a star west to gaze upon the divine incarnation.[59] The corpus of Indian religious texts that British officials, merchants, and missionaries sent back to Europe at the time of Buchanan's writing in 1809 was so vast, and often so crudely translated, it is not hard to imagine how Buchanan could have patched together pieces from here and there in order to quilt the story that Sanskrit writings bear witness to the coming of Christ. Sanskrit literature, for example, tells of countless powerful princes; thus, even with limited access to Indian writings, Buchanan could easily have found enough vague, decontextualized comparisons between Christianity and Indian religions to excite an audience accustomed to hearing how vastly different the two worlds were.[60]

Trying to track down the specific texts and translations to which Buchanan refers is a bit more difficult. Buchanan himself likely had little to no knowledge of Sanskrit and must have relied on the writings of the first generation of Englishmen living in India and their pundit partners, who translated ancient manuscripts into European languages. Buchanan wrote that the "important records" he cited "have been translated by a learned Orientalist [who] has deposited the originals among the archives of the Asiatic Society."[61] Buchanan named that Orientalist in a footnote as Mr. Wilford, who must be Francis Wilford, an early member of the Asiatic Society of Bengal, founded by William Jones. Wilford's visions of Hinduism's Christian mythology were published in a series of articles for the society's journal, *Asiatic Researches*, in which Wilford highlighted certain names, places, and ideas from Sanskrit literature to argue for their Christian and European equivalencies.[62] The specific arguments he makes regarding references to Christ in Hindu literature focus on an Indian ruler named Śālivāhana, who, Wilford contended, is mentioned in many Sanskrit texts.[63] Wilford's Śālivāhana was born to a carpenter and a virgin mother, and his birth upset the realm's king, who knew that Śālivāhana would threaten his reign. Wilford suggested that the Indians twisted more than a few parts of the story of Christ; the virgin mother was one such corruption, according to Wilford, because, in the Indian retellings, she was just a one-and-a-half-year-old baby in a cradle when she was impregnated by a serpent slithering over her sleeping body.[64] This discrepancy did not dissuade Wilford, who proceeded to comb through various accounts of this particular prince in order to argue that they echoed the life of Jesus and demonstrated that "a Saviour was expected with a regeneration of the universe, all over the more civilized parts of world, in consequence of certain old prophecies."[65] This depiction of an enlightened past when the entire civilized world possessed knowledge of the Christian god is remarkable in that it includes India. Ancient civilization was no longer confined to the Mediterranean world; now Wilford expanded it beyond the Arabian Sea to include South Asia. Wilford's philological labors promoted Indian culture to an elite status just as the country was becoming more aggressively occupied, politically and economically, by England. Wilford's associations were far from benign: his argument that Christianity once graced India implied that its confused caretakers had distorted the divine truths it once knew. Now it was up to the British to set the record straight.[66]

To understand how Wilford made his arguments for the similarities between the lives of Christ and Śālivāhana, I will parse one section in which Wilford constructed dates for Śālivāhana's lifetime that match, almost to the very year, those attributed to Christ. This dating analysis included the only directly quoted Sanskrit text in the entire 135-page essay: Wilford wrote that the Kumārika Khaṇḍa section of the Skanda Purāṇa contains a verse that translates as "When three thousand and one hundred years of the Kali Yuga are elapsed, then Saca will appear and remove wretchedness and misery from the world."[67] Cross-referencing this date with the Hindu dating era known as the Kali Yuga and with dates for the reigns of kings noted in other Sanskrit texts, Wilford argued, shows that Śālivāhana died in 79 AD after living for eighty-four years, making him just five years older than Jesus Christ.

The Sanskrit *śloka*, or verse, that Wilford translated is rendered in an older, somewhat crude, transliteration system (he gives the verse as *Tatah trishu sahasréshu śaté chápyadhicéshu cha; 'SACA námá bhavishyas'cha yotidáridra háraca*),[68] but it could be reconstructed to read:

Tataḥ (tatas) triṣu sahasreṣu śateṣu apy adhikeṣu ca |
śakanāmā bhaviṣya[ṁ]ś ca yo 'tidāridryahārakaḥ ||

The reconstructed verse above is still awkward, but this revised text could translate as "Then, in three thousand [years] and hundreds more, there will be a man named Śaka, who will be a great destroyer of poverty." Wilford's translation gave the singular for hundred (śate), whereas the more grammatically logical form would be the plural (śateṣu). By choosing the singular form over the plural, Wilford made the prophesied poverty-destroyer appear in the specific year 3,100 instead of earlier. This small translation choice allowed Wilford to use Hindu dating systems to bring Śālivāhana much closer to Western dating for Jesus's lifetime.[69]

This examination of Wilford's translation work shows how he and the pundit with whom he translated Sanskrit texts (but whom he always kept anonymous) employed translation practices that were flawed, although acceptable in this early period of translating Sanskrit into European languages, to conjure Jesus from Sanskrit literature.[70] As we will see below, Wilford was not alone in his dreams in which texts in dead Indian languages are made to speak of a time when South Asians conversed with Mediterranean civilizations, sharing not only vocabulary but also sacred revelations. While Wilford was most interested in fashioning a scholastic argument to prove that the knowledge of Christ pervaded the entire ancient world, especially India, Buchanan mobilized Wilford's arguments to make the case that the time had come for Christian teachings and peoples to return to India. The new discoveries that biblical truths are buried in ancient Indian texts, Buchanan argued, are like the Star in the East pointing the way to worship God: "Now, my brethren, as the East was honored in the first age, in thus pointing out the Messiah to the world; so now again, after a long interval of darkness, it is bearing witness to the truth of his religion; not indeed by the shining of a Star, but by affording luminous evidence of the divine origin of the Christian Faith."[71] Thus, to find God, instead of following a heavenly light, Buchanan's audience was told to look to the brilliant wisdom of God that shines through even the most confused ancient Indian holy book. Turning one's gaze textward, Buchanan promised, will reveal "that the Time is come for diffusing His religion throughout the world."[72] Whereas Wilford focused on a romanticized distant past, Buchanan said that the glories of that long-gone time were manifesting once again. The romanticism of

Buchanan and the missionaries he inspired did not only look back to an age before darkness and declension but also longingly imagined a divine present. The discovery of the holy within heathen antiquity demanded that the two now be brought together again, by flesh-and-blood missionaries, who would arrive holding the Bible. Christians must go to India and translate the gospel into the languages of their brothers shrouded in darkness who once knew its truth, but have lost it—for we were heathens once, too, Buchanan reminded his readers.

Wilford's fascination with Sanskrit literature—the enthusiasm that led Buchanan to insist on the kinship between Western Protestants and non-Christian Indians—was part of a larger interest in ancient Sanskrit texts within his circle of British officers in India, most famously William Jones, who declared in 1786 that he had discovered the linguistic kinship between Sanskrit, Greek, and Latin:

> The Sanscrit language, whatever be its antiquity, is of a wonderful structure; more perfect than the Greek, more copious than the Latin, and more exquisitely refined than either; yet, bearing to both of them a stronger affinity, both in the roots of verbs, and in the forms of grammar, than could possibly have been produced by accident; so strong, indeed, that no philologer could examine all three, without believing them to have sprung from the same common source, which, perhaps, no longer exists.[73]

By the time of Jones's declaration, a few Europeans had known of the existence of Sanskrit for decades, and echoes of Western words had been heard in Indian and Persian languages since the first sustained economic relationships were established between Europe and India at the end of the sixteenth century. But it was not until Jones's celebration of Sanskrit caught on among the European literati in the early nineteenth century that the official study of what were increasingly being called "Indo-European" languages began.[74]

This excitement around the newly coined Indo-European language family was not limited to philology. The entire range of human sciences, from history to mythology, felt the impact. In 1863, Max Müller explained that "thanks to the discovery of the ancient language of India, Sanskrit as it is called... and thanks to the discovery of the close kinship between this language and the idioms of the principal races of Europe... a complete revolution has taken place in the method of studying the world's primitive history."[75] With the history of languages being confidently mapped—featuring the noble ancestors of Sanskrit, Greek, and Latin at the center—scholars in the nineteenth century felt equipped to describe mankind's earliest civilizations. By studying the roots of Indo-European languages, academics argued that they had also unearthed the ideas and accomplishments of prehistoric society. Some went so far as to contend that humanity's first and most perfect philosophies were formed on the banks of the Ganges, while others used the connection among Sanskrit, Greek, and Latin to present Christians as descendants of an enterprising, creative, and powerful people who dominated the entire ancient world. For these scholars, "linguistic paleontology" was, as historian Maurice Olender writes, "the science of their dreams."[76]

Among these scholars dreaming in Sanskrit, Friedrich Schlegel is perhaps the most famous for using philological work as form of religious evangelicalism. Although there had been plenty of romanticization of ancient India throughout Europe, and in Schlegel's Germany especially, Schlegel's writing was particularly influential in the area of religion. We can see an example of how Schlegel saw philological discoveries as spiritual in the preface to his book *On the Language and Wisdom of the Indians,* in which Schlegel argued that

> the study of Indian literature requires to be embraced by such students and patrons as in the fifteenth and sixteenth centuries suddenly kindled in Italy and Germany an ardent appreciation of the beauty of classical learning, and in so short a time invested it with such prevailing importance, that the form of all wisdom and science, and almost of the world itself, was changed and renovated by the influence of that re-awakened knowledge. I venture to predict that the Indian study, if embraced with equal energy, will prove no less grand and universal in its operation, and have no less influence on the sphere of European intelligence. And wherefore should it be otherwise?[77]

Not all Orientalists subscribed to Schlegel's romanticized view that ancient Sanskrit texts would reawaken European knowledge, but Europe's fascination with Indian connections was strong enough to prompt the Orientalist James Darmesteter to complain in 1890 that "European scientific orthodoxy believed that through the Vedas it was in contact with the first appearance of religious thought in the Indo-European race. The Vedas became the sacred book of the religious origins of the race, the Aryan Bible."[78] Thus, philology's celebrated discoveries about the nature of Sanskrit language—its millennia-old verb roots, its elaborately inflected nouns, and its kinship with the dead European languages of Latin and Greek—inspired many in the field to find a belief system written in that language that was the primordial religion and philosophy of Europe's holy ancestors.

For Protestant foreign missionaries like Buchanan and his recruits, the holy religion hidden in Sanskrit manuscripts was the only true religion: Christianity. The nineteenth-century American Baptist missionaries to Burma were so inspired by philological fantasies of God's truths embedded in eastern books that they left the comforts of home and family to move halfway around the world. When restrictions against missionaries prohibited them from entering India and getting their hands on the celebrated Sanskrit texts, they shifted their attention to the texts and languages of Burma.

As I will show in the next section, the Burmese idealized past, like the past conjured up by scholars of ancient languages in the West, had roots in India, but the Burmese focused on the sage at the center of their Theravada Buddhist tradition, Gotama Buddha, and how his teachings were preserved in their purest form by living Burmese kings and the religious institutions they supported and regularly reformed. In these Buddhist histories, golden eras of dynastic religious purification are recalled in order to make present-day Burmese rulers shine.[79]

Burmese Glory Days and Golden Books

When his grandfather, King Bodawpaya, died in 1819, Bagyidaw assumed the throne without much opposition, but with plenty of challenges. The empire that the thirty-five-year-old ruler inherited was the second largest in Burmese history, but it was suffering internally from his grandfather's extreme religious reformation campaigns, and externally from a contested region in the northwest that bordered British Bengal.[80] The first year of King Bagyidaw's rule was filled with visits from people throughout the land who came to pledge their allegiance and to ask for royal favors. Among the visitors that first year was an American: Adoniram Judson.

It was January 26, 1820, the midst of the most pleasant and dry of the country's three seasons. King Bagyidaw had heard that Christians had arrived in Ava by boat and arranged for them to meet with his minister Moung Zah the next day. Judson and fellow American missionary James Colman met Moung Zah in the minister's palace-yard apartment and explained, for the first time in the royal court, that they were in the country as missionaries who desired to present the king with their sacred book and a petition to proselytize.

All who visited the king came bearing gifts, and Judson and his missionary community in Rangoon were overwhelmed by the question of what they should offer up to King Bagyidaw. Judson recorded in his journal that he wanted there "to be a congruity between the present and [their] character," so they decided to give "the BIBLE, in six volumes, covered with gold leaf, in Burman style, and each volume enclosed in a rich wrapper."[81] As Judson and Colman sat with Moung Zah, clasping their voluminous bible, adorned in the luxurious style of the country's most prized books, word came that the king was on his way into the palace yard. Moung Zah, dressed in his official robes, immediately rose to his feet and informed the missionaries that it was time to meet the king. Before ushering them through outdoor parades, up a flight of stairs, and into an extraordinarily majestic hall, Moung Zah asked, "How can you propagate religion in this empire?"[82] This discouraging question distracted Judson and Colman as they made their way through the enormous pillared, domed, and glittering hall. When King Bagyidaw entered in royal dress clasping a gold-sheathed sword, the entire audience prostrated themselves fully, leaving Judson and Colman as the only ones with their heads off the ground. As they remained there awkwardly kneeling, the king approached.

"Who are these . . . ?" [the king asked].

"The teachers, great King," Judson replied [in Burmese].

"What, you speak Burman—the priests that I heard of last night? When did you arrive? Are you teachers of religion? Are you like the Portuguese priest? Are you married? Why do you dress so?"[83]

After Judson answered his questions, the king took a seat, and Moung Zah read the petition, which requested royal permission to preach Christianity in Burma and protection for "those who are pleased with [the] preaching, and wish to listen to and be guided by it, whether foreigners or Burmans."[84] The king said nothing. Moung Zah then presented one of the volumes of the gilded bible, unwrapping it for him, but the king remained quiet. Breaking the heavy silence, Moung Zah spoke for the court: "Why do you ask for such permission? Have not the Portuguese, the English, the Mussulmans, and people of all other religions, full liberty to practice and worship according to their own customs? In regard to the objects of your petition, his majesty gives no order. In regard to your sacred books, his majesty has no use for them: take them away."[85]

Judson left Ava having failed to obtain permission to evangelize. Like other foreigners and minority groups in the country, the Americans could practice their own religion, but they did not have approval to try and convert members of the Buddhist majority.[86] Furthermore, King Bagyidaw wanted nothing to do with their Christian bible, no matter how familiar and impressive its ornamentation. The Burmese had holy books of their own.

King Bagyidaw was the seventh king of the Konbaung dynasty, the third and last imperial establishment in Burma's history. The first, the empire of Pagan, reigned from the middle of the eleventh century to the fourteenth, and is credited with formally installing Theravada Buddhism in Burma by bringing that religious school's canon, the Pali Tipiṭaka, from Lanka and establishing it as the country's supreme collection of holy texts.[87] The dynasties that succeeded Pagan continued this practice of mobilizing Buddhist scriptures to make claims to righteous rule; the Konbaung dynasty was no exception. Its kings activated apparatuses of empire that allowed it to control multiple regions and people groups, and they particularly exploited the prestige accorded sacred books and hallowed histories.[88] As their imperial predecessors had done, the Konbaung dynasty secured its rule by promoting itself as the protector of the true Buddhism, which it advertised by publishing extravagant editions of the Tipiṭaka and commissioning dynastic and religious chronicles.[89] This final Burmese kingdom continued the practice of earlier Theravada Buddhist rulers of commissioning Buddhist chronicles (P. vaṃsa), but they elaborated on this tradition by producing the first texts that claimed to be histories of Buddhism for the Burmese domain envisioned as a united whole.[90] The collection of Konbaung Buddhist chronicles (B. *thathanawin*) comprises four texts produced from 1799 to 1861 that celebrate the series of golden ages leading up to the present that were glorious on account of righteous kings who promoted the Buddha's teachings. These chronicles were crucial for the ruling narrative of the Burmese court and their principal political partners, the Buddhist literati and clergy.[91]

An example of this narrative technique of recalling romanticized pasts is to extol present rulers in the final part of the first Konbaung Buddhist chronicle, the *Treatise on the Lineage of Elders* (P. *Vaṃsadīpanī*), written just over a decade before the Judsons arrived in Rangoon and explicitly designed as an instrument of the Buddhist reformation—known as the Sudhammā Reformation—executed by King Bagyidaw's predecessor, Bodawpaya. As Patrick Pranke's study of monastic accounts of the Sudhammā Reformation shows, what was at stake in this conflict between King Bodawpaya's and the Burmese sangha were perceptions of legitimacy, the role of the sangha to bring salvation to the world, and the prerogatives of the relationship between the sangha and the state. These monastic accounts characterize Bodawpaya's religious polices as first being orthodox and then heterodox (see chapter 3).[92] In contrast to the more complex monastic descriptions, the king and his royally appointed monastic author Mehti Sayadaw advanced a simplified history of the Reformation as entirely just. For example, Mehti Sayadaw concludes the treatise by celebrating the Sudhammā Reformation and insisting that,

> in the same way, during the lifetime of the Blessed One, disciples, and monks, having been admonished and instructed, practiced according to the rules of avoidance and the rules of observance so that [they might] escape the cycle of suffering. And after the Parinibbāna, so that [the Order] would remain true to the Blessed One's teachings, ... [there were four Synods first in India and then in Ceyon]; and in the [Burmese] city of Amarapūra, the great Elder Ñāṇābhivaṃsa Dammasenapati convened what was akin to a Fifth Synod. And so that the rules of the Blessed One passed down through this unbroken Theravada lineage might likewise be sustained in the province of Jeyyavaḍḍhana, [the venerable Paramasīrivaṃsābhidhaja] became leader of the monastic community [dwelling there]. And through his admonishments and instructions, he reunited [the monks of Jeyyavaḍḍhana] into a single Theravada [fraternity], and in doing so, caused the noble Sāsana of the Blessed One to shine forth like the sun and moon.[93]

In this final summary of the lineage's premier Buddhist chronicle, Mehti Sayadaw insisted that the royally appointed monk to head the Sudhammā Reformation reunified the clergy, making it as brilliant as it was under the Buddha. This unification, according to the treatise, followed the pattern established in the previous five Theravada Buddhist Councils, where reform and preservation of the Buddhist clergy were executed through systematic reprimands and enforced injunctions. Whereas the Western idealized past featured the confluence of ancient civilizations, and the Karen imagined a golden era when they, too, possessed God's book, the high points of Burmese royal history were marked by institutional purification through castigation and the enforcement of rigorous legality.[94]

Analogous to the first Konbaung chronicle's lineage of great monastic reform movements, the final chronicle of this textual tradition, *The History of the Buddha's Religion* (P. *Sāsanavaṃsa*), which was completed in 1861 by Paññasāmi, the tutor to King Mindon,[95] highlights these same Buddhist councils and other important religious developments and textual productions of the past to show that "under the patronage of the virtuous king, in the realm of Burma, the religion of the Perfectly Enlightened One is caused to shine brilliantly, and it reaches development, maturation, and prosperity."[96] After this argument that Buddhism fully flourished during glorious past times when virtuous kings reigned, Paññasāmi instructed that "this [history] should be appreciated by the good people who listen to it as, 'at a certain time, in a certain realm, when a certain king named so and so had elevated Buddhism, it reached development, maturation, and full bloom, just as a tree, supported by earth and water, reaches development, maturation, and full bloom.'"[97] In other words, the Konbaung chronicle directs its audience to understand the text as a description of a lineage of rulers whose sponsorship caused Buddhism to blossom.

While these court-sponsored religious-political histories played an important role in securing Burmese centers of power, it was another text that circulated out from these centers and would influence far-flung regions of the empire. This text, which coursed through Burma more robustly than any other in this period, was prized above all others for its material, ritual, and political value. This is the Burmese Kammavāca.

The Burmese Kammavāca (B. *Kammawa*) is the only Buddhist book in Burma that is adorned with precious substances and painted with powerful symbols, and that circulated widely during the Konbaung dynasty.[98] The words it contains script monastic formulas excerpted from the Tipiṭaka. Yet, in dramatic contrast to the consistency of its canonical language, the opulent visual and material features of the Burmese Kammavāca vary greatly over the course of the dynasty. In the most luxurious manuscripts, folios are sculpted from ivory, crafted from silver, and inlaid with mother-of-pearl characters. There is also a dynamic range of images, including geometric and floral patterns, auspicious or mighty animals such as birds and lions, and scenes from the Buddha's last and previous lives. The variegated substances and illustrations in Konbaung Kammavāca reflect the kingdom's multifront expansion through its takeover of Mon, Thai, and other communities and their artistic and religious traditions. They also speak to the fluctuating interests of the lay patrons and artisans who commissioned and crafted these prized Buddhist objects. By the end of the dynasty, when the Buddhist realm was shrinking from the losses of the Second Anglo-Burmese War of 1852–1853 and the Third Anglo-Burmese War of 1885, Burmese Kammavācas tended to be made of matching pages of lacquered palm leaf that were painted in gold with standardized spirit figures who often carry swords. After examining the contents and contexts of the Kammavāca, I will hypothesize that these militarized beings were understood to animate the books and that their incorporation expresses a larger anxiety about protecting Buddhism and the Burmese realm in the kingdom's final decades.

Nonilluminated manuscripts known as Kammavācas and containing the same extracts (P. *khandakā*) from the monastic code (P. *vinaya*) section of the Pali Tipiṭaka are common to monastic ceremonies in all Theravada-dominant countries, especially Sri Lanka and Thailand, but it is only in Burma that these otherwise plain, palm-leaf texts are rendered in gold, ivory, silver, or pearl, illustrated with auspicious designs, Buddhas, and spirits, and produced in significantly large numbers.[99] Both the nonilluminated and illuminated manuscripts are used as a script for the ceremonies required for the most important monastic rituals. Kammavācas carefully excerpt the most important Pali-language ritual passages from the vast Tipiṭaka, making these ritual manuals both conveniently abridged and assuredly orthodox. All Kammavāca manuscripts reproduce extracts from the Tipiṭaka's set of ritual formulas for the following monastic ceremonies: 1) higher ordination (P. *upasampadā*); 2) the annual presentation of monastic robes (P. *kaṭhina*); 3) the ceremony following the marking of the territory (P. *sīma*) for the purpose of releasing the monks within the territory from having to be with their basic set of three robes at dawn (P. *ticivarena-avippavasa*); 4) the marking the area where *uposatha* rituals take place (P. *uposathāgāra*); 5) the election of a senior monk (P. *thera-sammuti*); 6) the assignment of a monk's name (P. *nama-sammuti*); 7) the dedication of a place in the monastery where food can be stored (P. *kappiya-bhūmi-sammuti*); 8) the acquisition of monastery land

(P. *kuṭī-vatthu-olokana-sammuti*); and 9) the release of a monk from the need to stay with his teacher (P. *nissayamutti-sammuti*).[100] These crucial ritual formulas and their careful ceremonial pronunciation link the communities conducting the ritual to a Theravada lineage that claims to be the oldest, purest Buddhist order in the world. The Theravada community's claim to authority depends on its treatment of the Pali Tipiṭaka as the most faithful record of the Buddha's teachings. That the Pali text in Burmese Kammavācas is unchanging and matches Kammavāca texts throughout the Theravada Buddhist world is used to support a Burmese assertion that their country preserves and protects a pure form of Buddhism.[101]

In addition to being an authoritative ritual text for Theravada communities, the Kammavāca is also the book that brought Europe one of its first—if not its very first—Pali texts. In 1776, a Barnabite missionary to Burma, Father John Mary Percoto, translated portions of the Kammavāca into Italian. In the early 1830s, a British Wesleyan missionary in Ceylon, Benjamin Clough, published an English translation with such an abundance of footnotes that it is clear that Clough's audience of philologists, antiquarians, and Westerners specializing in Asia still had very little general knowledge of Buddhist literature.[102] In 1875, J. F. Dickson published his own English translation of the Kammavāca's higher monastic ordination text because, he explained, neither the Pali language text nor a complete translation was easily available to his fellow scholars. Dickson first gave the Pali text in Roman characters and then his English translation, indicating that study of Pali had grown enough in Europe and North America at that point that some of Dickson's readers would want to read the Kammavāca in that Asian language.[103]

Since this initial European interest in the Kammavāca, however, very little academic attention has been paid to these texts. Charles Hallisey bemoans the loss of interest in the Kammavāca in his well-known article "Roads Taken and Not Taken in the Study of Theravada Buddhism," in which he connects the loss of interest in the Kammavāca to the loss of interest in Theravada ritual in the academy at large. The fact that Kammavācas were "the first texts which Europeans were given in their encounter with the Buddhist world" indicates, according to Hallisey, "that whoever gave those texts thought that ritual was key for understanding the Buddha's message." But, soon after this initial interest in the monastic rituals described in the Kammavāca, Hallisey explains, Orientalists such as Rhys Davids worked to exclude ritual from the history of early Buddhism in their attempt to "uncover" a rationalist—and therefore ritual-free—core of Buddhism. Hallisey calls on contemporary scholars not only to recognize how Davids's neglect of ritual has distorted the field of Buddhist studies but also to revisit ceremonies such as those described in the Kammavāca in order to understand the important place ritual action has had in Buddhist communities.[104]

While scholars have responded in various ways to the manifold critiques in "Roads Taken and Not Taken in the Study of Theravada Buddhism," few have answered Hallisey's call to revisit the Kammavāca.[105] This section steps into that silent space. But, rather than studying the text in order to understand the ancient ritual it plots, the section scrutinizes the ritual object itself: the illustrated manuscript.[106] I examine the artwork filling the margins and covers of Kammavāca manuscripts to investigate the political and religious concerns inscribed onto this key Burmese Buddhist book and therefore produced and reproduced during the American missionary era, an era this chapter argues was shaped by sacred books. As Richard Fox explains in his study of textuality and writing in Bali, "Scholars have tended to devalue such nonliterary uses of writing as secondary to a more conventional model of 'the text' understood as a medium for the transmission of religious ideas and ideals." Fox invites us to invert this to try approaching "ostensibly literary objects as if they were amulets, or even living beings." I accept Fox's invitation here as it resonates with book practices throughout both insular and mainland Southeast Asia in which humans engage with books as enlivened and able to act for and against them. Approached in this way, the Kammavāca was a kind of living defender of Burmese sovereignty in nineteenth-century Burma. Just as Fox shows that Balinese letters are also weapons with a "dangerously ambivalent power of their own," a potency that "is inseparable from the ways in which writing may be controlled and deployed to localize and materialize relations of power and patronage," I will show that Kammavāca were empowered to enact royal and religious relations throughout the country.[107]

I consider over four dozen Burmese Kammavāca manuscripts, published and unpublished, from Burmese and international collections, dating from the earliest extant fragments, which may date to the eighteenth century, through the nineteenth-century production boom.[108] These manuscripts come from the most prominent Burmese manuscript collections such as those held in the National Library of Myanmar and the British Library, as well as those held in smaller collections, such as the Mon State National

Museum and Library and university collections in the United States. I examined many of the manuscripts considered here in person between 2012 and 2018, and I have also included manuscripts that I have not examined myself but that have been published in museum catalogs.[109]

I will argue that the visual and material features of Burmese Kammavāca exhibit the way the Burmese court and powerful monastic institutions employed precious books to dominate a diverse country with threatened borders.[110] These special books were not just tools of empire, however. Over the course of the nineteenth century, they became animated by weapon-wielding spirit lords conscripted to protect a kingdom at war with the British. Furthermore, studying the reverberations of Kammavāca practice and politics illuminates the ways in which Christian book practices were received and transformed in nineteenth-century Burma.[111]

Burmese Kammavāca manuscripts, especially those likely to be among our oldest extant examples, feature an array of precious substances, such as ivory and pearl, as well as a range of illustration types, scripts, and

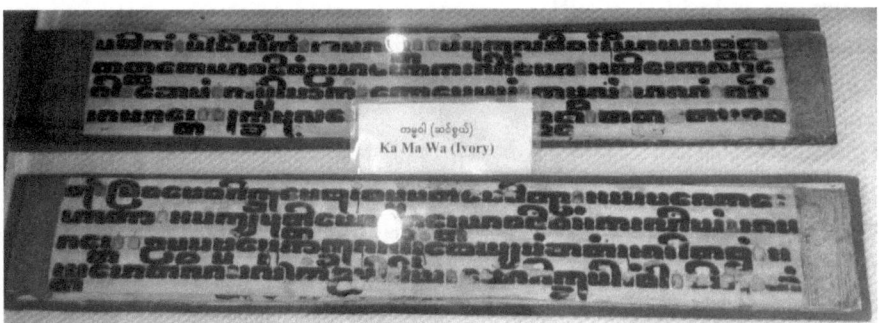

FIGURE 1.1 Ivory Kammavāca folio, Yangon University Library. Photo by author.

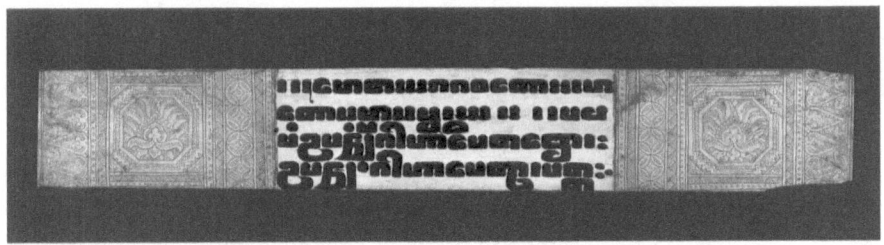

FIGURE 1.2 Ivory Kammavāca folio. Photo courtesy of the British Library.

formatting. With their varied influences from the different regions that the Konbaung conquered, the manuscripts reflect the diversity of the Konbaung empire and its history of capturing artisans during its military campaigns.[112] A particularly striking Kammavāca is held in Yangon University Library (see figure 1.1).[113] Thin ivory plates have been pasted to pages of lacquered palm leaf, each painted with four lines of a special script known as tamarind-seed script (B. *magyi-zi*), a squarish and thick writing system that is rarely used in the Konbaung period and later, except in Kammavāca manuscripts. This ivory manuscript is flanked with small margins featuring a lacquered gold and red cinnabar design resembling monastic ceremonial fans. There is no date inscribed on the folios, but the library's curator has estimated that they were created sometime between the seventeenth and eighteenth centuries.[114] A similar manuscript Kammavāca in the British Library features gleaming, translucent ivory folios with four lines of tamarind-seed script (see figure 1.2).[115] While these rare ivory Kammavācas are among the most precious, pride of place belongs to another Kammavāca manuscript, made of mother-of-pearl (see figure 1.3). Folios of this manuscript are held in the British Library, the Royal Asiatic Society, and the Chester Beatty Library in Dublin; each institution holds one folio and dates it to the eighteenth century.[116] The finely carved, iridescent pearl forms not only the four lines of tamarind-seed script occupying the center third of the folio but also the designs in the large margins. Intricate flame-like shapes blaze out into the margins of the British Library folio and, in the Chester Beatty Library piece, form four stupas, a sprinkling of flowers, and two fan-like designs. The mother-of-pearl designs are placed against a dark purple-black cloth that forms a dramatic background for the shimmering pearl and may have come from a garment worn by royalty or a monk. The artist or artists who crafted this manuscript first lacquered the cloth, and while the lacquer was setting they inlaid the carved pearl characters and design elements. Noel Singer writes that the flame motif suggests that this rare manuscript is the result of Thai artists who visited the Burmese kingdom.[117] This suggestion is persuasive, although the hypothesized Thai craftsman were just as likely to be captives of, rather than visitors to, the Konbaung realm, taken during one of the Burmese-Siamese military conflicts, such as the Burmese siege of Ayutthaya during the Burmese-Siamese War of 1765–1767. The Thai imprint on what became a dominantly Burmese tradition of sponsoring highly ornamented Kammavācas presses me to

FIGURE 1.3 Mother-of-pearl Kammavāca folio, held in the Chester Beatty Library (CBL Bu 1248.5). © The Trustees of the Chester Beatty Library, Dublin.

FIGURE 1.4 Detail of the 1792 Kammavāca held in the Royal Asiatic Society of Great Britain and Ireland (RAS Burmese 86). Photo by the author.

think about the relationships between artistic practices, Buddhist rituals, and military operations. Whether collaborative and consensual or fraught and violent, these relationships emphasize the importance of considering political contexts when we study religious expression.

Early Kammavāca also feature scenes of the Buddha. One example held in the Royal Asiatic Society bears an exact eighteenth-century date: the Burmese year 1152 (1792 AD) (see figure 1.4).[118] This Kammavāca from the reign of King Bodawpaya features the Buddha in the *bhūmisparś-mudrā*, his most common gesture in Burma. The Buddha is flanked by his disciples Sāriputta and Moggallāna, who kneel and hold up their hands together in an *añjali-mudrā*. These disciples sit on lotus thrones that complement the Buddha's, and all of the space encompassing this noble triad is sumptuously illustrated with vibrant leaves.[119]

Another manuscript showcasing the Buddha is a striking golden and black Kammavāca crafted before 1826 that features the rounded Burmese script instead of the square tamarind-seed script.[120] The Buddha is alone here, as he is said to have been on the night of his enlightenment. His right hand reaches down, calling on the earth to witness his extraordinary realization. Large leaf-like illustrations fill the top corners, perhaps suggesting the Bodhi tree that hosted this amazing event. Prominent halos and golden flames encircle him, celebrating the brilliance of the newly awakened one. The extant folios of this Kammavāca must have been crafted before 1826 because they were acquired by Captain Frederic Marryat during his participation in First Anglo-Burmese War, which was waged between 1824 and 1826.[121]

I will now examine a sampling of Kammavāca that are likely from the late Konbaung era and suggest the emergence of a standard royal look. In contrast to Kammavācas rendered in lustrous pearl or gleaming ivory or featuring the Buddha calling the earth to witness his enlightenment, there is a Kammavāca that was seemingly mass produced, with each manuscript featuring folios of lacquered, gilded palm leaf or cloth with red paint, six lines of tamarind-seed script per page, and distinctive guardian figures fortifying folios and covers. Likely because of seeming mass produced, these later Kammavācas are less common in museum exhibitions. While there are dozens of other very similar manuscripts held in other collections, I focus on the following previously unpublished examples from the American Baptist Historical Society, Yale University, British Library, and the National Library of Myanmar manuscripts because those are the examples I have been able to examine most carefully in person and the manuscripts about which I have been able to attain the most acquisition information.

I will use these examples to suggest that this standardized Kammavāca is a later development of the Konbaung manuscript tradition, and I will hypothesize that its spirit lords and weapon imagery came to dominate this prized manuscript tradition in the period between the Second Anglo-Burmese War of 1852–1853 and the collapse of the last Buddhist kingdom in 1885. I will venture further to suggest that this standardized manuscript tradition comes specifically from Mandalay, the royal city built by King Mindon in 1857, and I will argue that the newly militarized visual program reveals a larger anxiety about protecting Buddhism and the Burmese realm at the end of its last kingdom.

The three decades before the Third Anglo-Burmese War of 1885 were saturated in royal support for Buddhist institutions as well as a heightened sense of political danger. This danger was felt in three concentric ways: 1) within the Mandalay royal court itself, there was concern over who would succeed King Mindon, since he had over seventy legitimate heirs and no set plan for passing on the crown; 2) within the independent kingdom, there were various minority groups who were at odds with the Bamar majority and who were seeking autonomy through strategic forms of alliance with the British; and 3) on the borders, the British were moving into position to take over the last remaining independent domain of the Konbaung kingdom. In each of these nested realms, the Burmese authorities were concerned about losing their power and positions. The most visible response to this anxiety was King Mindon's lavish material support of Buddhism. As Myo Mint demonstrates in *Confronting Colonialism: King Mindon's Strategy for Defending Independence (1853-1878)*, a key part of King Mindon's campaign to fend off the British was to stage an expensively visible Buddhist revival. This revival included the restoration of pagodas throughout the country (including parts of the country controlled by the British, such as Rangoon), substantial donations to the sangha, and the construction of new shrines and institutions. The Burmese landscape was dramatically transformed through glittering new golden pagoda spires, bamboo-scaffolded monasteries, and massive Buddha statues donning fresh paint and new robes. This renovated Buddhist horizon proclaimed to all who gazed upon it that the Burmese were the righteous defenders of a vibrant Buddhist realm.[122]

King Mindon's Buddhist revival inlaid political concerns with religious ones and cultivated both a confidence in Burmese power at the same time as it revealed an anxiety about its surrender. As Alicia Turner and Erik Braun have shown, in the second half of the nineteenth century, there was a common sense among the Buddhist peoples of Burma that when the kingdom fell, the *sāsana* (the Buddha's teachings and institutions), too, would fall.[123] The Burmese worried that, without a devout king to sponsor the monastic order, textual traditions, ritual practices, and objects of veneration crucial for the continuation of the Buddhist tradition, the end of Buddhism would soon be upon them. In the Burmese reading of canonical texts and commentaries, the Buddha foretold that the sāsana was impermanent (like all things) and would last five thousand years in this world at most, but could become extinct far sooner. Throughout Burmese Buddhist history there have been periods of concern about the acceleration of these end times, but, in the second half of the nineteenth century, when Burma was falling, piece by piece, into the hands of the British, the Buddhist apocalypse seemed even more immanent.

One well-preserved Kammavāca that displays the tradition's turn to weapons in these anxious times was taken from the chest of the last Burmese king, Thibaw (r. 1878–1885), by the American Baptist missionary Marilla Baker Ingalls, whose career in Burma I study in detail in the next chapter. This manuscript is now housed in the archives of the American Baptist Historical Society together with a note that explains that Ingalls took the manuscript "by permission of the Court Minister," which seems somewhat suspicious at first, given how much looting there was of Thibaw's palace after the British victory.[124] Still, archival records of Ingalls's long and extraordinary career working as a solitary missionary in a Burmese community in Thonze describe cordial visits she made to various royalty in Mandalay, so it is possible that she was on good enough terms to allow her to obtain this manuscript with official Burmese royal permission before Thibaw was deposed. If this were the case, Thibaw and his ministers may have seen some advantage in circulating an impressive Buddhist object out into Western communities as something that could concretely communicate the power of Burmese Buddhist

FIGURE 1.5 American Baptist Historical Society Kammavāca detail. Photo by the author.

THE BOOK

FIGURE 1.6 American Baptist Historical Society Kammavāca detail. Photo by the author.

FIGURE 1.7 Yale Kammavāca detail. Photo courtesy of the Yale Art Gallery.

traditions. On the American Baptist Historical Society manuscript this power appears in the form of two types of guardian figures: one who wears a tapered head piece, large shoulder accents, and billowing pants (see figure 1.5), and another winged creature with similar clothing, but whose head piece is turban-like (see figure 1.6). Both figures carry swords.[125]

THE BOOK

A similar turbaned, sword-wielding figure appears on the cover boards of one of the two Kammavācas housed in the storage facility for the Yale University Art Gallery (see figure 1.7).[126] The cover boards also feature painted birds—like those in the British Library's ivory Kammavāca with the octagonal designs—as well as winged, weapon-less spirit lords. The second Yale Kammavāca also employs red and gold paint and has six-lined pages. It is ornamented with similarly costumed figures—visual features further illustrating how these later manuscripts tend toward a standardized aesthetic program (see figure 1.8).[127]

One final example of this standardized manuscript from a Western collection comes from the British Library and features a standing guardian figure in royal clothing, with two celestial wings, and holding a large sword whose pointed tip breaks through the painting's border to nearly touch the shiny, lacquered text (see figure 1.9).[128] This manuscript was donated in 1895. Comparing this manuscript to those manuscripts held at Yale University and the American Baptist Historical Society, it is clear that all of these late nineteenth-century ritual objects are following a standardized material and visual program that includes lacquered and gilt palm-leaf folios, each with six lines of tamarind-seed script per page.

This standardized late Konbaung-style Kammavāca can also be found in Myanmar's national libraries and museums. The Mon State National Museum and Library, for example, features an encased collection of folios from at least four Kammavāca manuscripts (see figure 1.10), and the Kayin State Cultural Museum displays a very similar collection. The majority of folios in both of these state collections contain royally costumed guardian figures. The most informative Kammavāca collection I examined in Myanmar was that held in the National Library of Myanmar. I was granted access to only two Kammavāca

FIGURE 1.8 Yale Kammavāca folio. Photo courtesy of the Yale Art Gallery.

FIGURE 1.9 British Library Kammavāca detail. Photo by the author.

THE BOOK

of this style, although the library's director, Daw Mya Oo, said there were three others like it. The guardian figures on the National Library of Myanmar manuscripts resemble the elaborately costumed figures above, and one type holds a sword (see figure 1.11).[129] These Kammavāca do not have dedicatory text recording their provenance, but Daw Mya Oo said they came from Mandalay Palace. It appears that this standardized style may have been established after King Mindon moved the Kobanung court to Mandalay in 1857.

Than Htun, a specialist in Burmese lacquer, explains that King Mindon's Mandalay "provided quarters for diverse craftsmen including the lacquer artists of Yundan, 79th Street," which ran along the moat of King Mindon's palace. According to Than Htun, these craftsmen produced great quantities of lacquered Kammavāca folios and boxes, though they did not seem to produce much in the way of other fine lacquer works. Than Htun suggests that Mandalay lacquer craftsmen did not want to compete with the fine lacquerware that came out of Pagan, the top lacquer producer of the time. Than Htun adds that King Mindon sponsored Mandalay's lacquer industry and its primary product, Kammavācas, "by donating many of them to thousands of monasteries across Myanmar."[130] It is quite possible that the late Konbaung-era manuscripts considered here were among the mass quantity of Mandalay lacquered Kammavāca that King Mindon distributed throughout the

FIGURE 1.10 Mon State National Museum and Library Kammavācas. Photo by author.

FIGURE 1.11 National Library of Myanmar Kammavāca. Photo by author.

country. The question this raises, then, is: Why would King Mindon feature weaponized spirit lords instead of floral arrangements or Buddha scenes on the Kammavāca he sent from the center of his realm's power to its peripheries? Who are these particular figures, and how should we understand their rise to prominence on the kingdom's most beautiful mass-produced book?

The guardian figures that take over late Konbaung Kammavaca may be generic *dewas* (devas, deities), or the more specific sprits known in Burma as *nats*, invisible beings closely connected to the protection of Burma and the history of monarchies in the country. As Bénédictine Brac de la Perrière has shown, the foundation myth of Burma's pantheon of thirty-seven nats asserts that the cult of these nats began with the first Burmese king to reign over the Irrawaddy River valley, King Anawratha (r. 1044–1077). The local population refused to do away with their local religious practices and adopt an orthodox form of Buddhism, so King Anawratha installed thirty-six statues representing local religious devotions as well as a statue of the king of the gods, Thi'dja (the Burmese version of the Indian god Indra), around his newly constructed royal pagoda. Since then, Burmese kings have been thought of as actively harnessing the power of these local spirits and subordinating them under Burmese Buddhist institutions. Burmese legends about the nats feature stories of their human lives, when they were threats or rivals to kings and, as a result, suffered a horrible death. The violence of their demise keeps them from the standard reincarnation process and binds them to the earth. Kings would appease these spirits by elevating their status to that of a nat, which was achieved through rituals involving sculpting a statue of the spirit and installing it in a new temple. This was akin to a royal coronation, in which the spirit would receive a royal title, a palace temple, and a dominion. Burmese kings would then revise the official list of the nats they kept to accommodate newly crowned spirits, but they seem to have kept the total number of nats in the pantheon at thirty-seven.[131]

Brac de la Perrière writes that the strength of Burmese royal power "lay in the concentrated ritual activity—as much centered on Buddhism as on the cult of the nats—in regions subservient to the king. The nats thus seem not only to be tied to but are an actual expression of the process of Burmese unification."[132] Thus the nats were seen as powerful both because of the material ways they influenced local communities, and because of the ways they consolidated and extended Burmese political power.[133]

This work of using religious material to consolidate and extend Burmese political power was particularly important during the Konbaung dynasty, when competing people groups tried to assert their independence from Burmese rule. The Burmese responded to these internal and peripheral threats by mobilizing local spirits along with Burmese Buddhist ritual practices. This was part of a well-established tradition in the region in which kings modeled themselves after classical South Asian and Southeast Asian emperors who used royal patronage of Buddhist institutions, rituals, and objects to amalgamate the territorial power of the court. The dominance of Burmese authority was regularly renewed by court-ordered reforms of the monastic hierarchy. The Konbaung lineage elaborated on this tradition, actively defining Theravada orthodoxy as Bamar and promoting Burmese communities over neighboring groups. In her study of modern Buddhism in Myanmar, Juliane Schober writes that "ethnic vassals were mobilized through the ritual theater of the court and through the construction of religious monuments and works of royal merit."[134] The commissioning of Kammavāca texts could likely have been one such merit-making, minority-absorbing activity, with the Burmese court extending its influence by inserting itself into powerful Buddhist ritual objects put to work throughout the realm.

Furthermore, the Konbaung kings did not limit their political-religious arsenal to orthodox Buddhist tools; by the end of the dynasty, these manuscripts show that they grew increasingly dependent on the power of local spirits.[135]

The armed spirits' rise to prominence on Burma's prized Kammavāca tells of a larger effort of this lineage of kings to use the power of books to subsume religious ritual activity under Burmese royal aegis. As a weakening country at war with the British, the Burmese must have found it strategic to tighten the bonds between their political institutions and religious materials and beings. Of course, this kind of political-religious partnership has a long and storied history in the larger Buddhist world. Examining this specific Konbaung manuscript tradition details one example of that alliance in its particular Burmese, ritual, and material forms.

While court practices carried a lot of weight, monks with a range of relationships to royalty also advocated for the commissioning and circulation of Kammavāca. In one piece of evidence of monastic attitudes toward these special manuscripts' material and visual features, Ledi Sayadaw, the famous Burmese founder of the modern insight meditation movement, advised the ritual specialists who recited Kammavāca texts to use highly adorned versions. As Erik Braun writes in his study of Ledi Sayadaw and the insight movement, this prominent Burmese Buddhist figure understood that "the sight of such aesthetically impressive dhamma texts would scare away many troubling spirits before one had even begun to read."[136] For Ledi Sayadaw, the richly ornamented and illustrated Kammavācas were important for purifying the ritual spaces in which the texts were recited. Perhaps for King Mindon and other Konbaung court figures, the spirit lords on impressively adorned Kammavāca were meant to scare away troubling beings both invisible and visible.

* * *

When American Baptist missionaries came into contact for the first time with Burmese Buddhists and Karen minority peoples, there were plenty of misunderstandings. Adoniram Judson recognized that even after two-and-a-half years of dedicated study of Burmese he was only just beginning "to see his way forward in this language, and hope[d] that two or three years more will make it somewhat familiar."[137] Slowly, but desperately, the first wave of American missionaries learned Burmese and began to study the languages of minority groups—first of the Karen, but soon of the Kachin and Shan. In the midst of this struggle for communication, a valued object and the romantic past it conjured emerged to determine how these groups would define the grounds for comparison, conversion, and contestation. Some in the West, based on readings of Sanskrit texts and new understandings of the shared heritage of Indo-European languages, imagined a golden age when India knew Christ. It was this vision that inspired the first American missionaries to set sail for the East, and, when they could not enter the country that held divinely inspired Sanskrit texts, they turned to Burma. When Karen people first met these Anglo-American foreigners who wanted to tell them about God and his gospel, they said they heard echoes of familiar legends in the arrival of these strangers. Within a couple of decades of the America Baptist mission, Karen people were worshipping printed evangelical texts wrapped in luxurious cloth, and soon thereafter a growing number were claiming the Christian god as their own, his Bible as their long-lost book, and the missionaries as the younger brother who left them in a nearly forgotten holy time. Burmese authorities had long dismissed the Karen as an uncivilized people, without letters, without history, without power. Many Karen shared this majority's Buddhist beliefs and practices, as well as their spirit worship, and even if the Karen could not read the glorified Buddhist books, they still regarded them as mighty and sacred. But Burmese histories ignored the Karen, concerned as they were with the specific Burmese lineage that traced itself back through great Burmese kings, through Sinhalese rulers and Indian potentates, and finally to the Buddha. These religious-dynastic chronicles made concerted efforts to link earlier periods when Buddhism fully prospered under the aegis of virtuous kings to the present Burmese emperor.

Eight years after Judson traveled up the Irrawaddy River in 1820 to present a gilded Bible carefully wrapped in silks to the newly crowned King Bagyidaw, Boardman first reported Karen people elaborately venerating English texts they could not read. In 1834, Judson knelt down before God to offer him the last leaf of his long-labored translation of the Bible into Burmese. And, during this entire time, the Burmese crafted exquisite Kammavāca volumes to carry powerful messages and armed spirits throughout the country.

This chapter has argued that sacred books were an integral part of the earliest interactions between Christian missionaries and both Burmese Buddhists and Karen communities.[138] As the Baptists made Burma their new home, and the Karen made the Baptists their brothers, the Bible made God's presence known in the Buddhist kingdom. This was still the realm of the Kammavāca and its royal spirits, who only became more active as the century went on, preserving Buddhism as the religion of the land. While this status kept the Burmese from attending churches, they did start to explore one Baptist place. As I show in the next chapter, the second phase of the Baptist mission to Burma concentrated on building schools filled with maps, globes, and other world-conjuring devices to attract large numbers of Burmese students.

TWO

The School

Models of Religious Imagination in Burmese Education

AMERICAN BAPTIST MISSIONARIES were among the first, if not the first, to introduce telescopes and globes to Burma. In 1826, Jonathan Price wrote that, in just thirteen years since the American Baptist mission had been established, Burma had "progressed at least a century in knowledge and civilization," predicting that "in a very short period [it would] be induced to throw away its superstitious forms . . . its false astronomy, and more fatal, false system of geography, and thus be laid open for the glad work of apostolic men to enter the breach to force the ramparts and save the souls of the enslaved, benighted waiting multitude."[1] Price's dramatic vision was never realized. However, his notion that Burma would soon reconsider its astronomical and geographical systems through contact with the American evangelists, was, for the most part, right on.

This chapter focuses on educational devices and school houses in order to try and understand what it was about telescope-trotting evangelists and American Baptist education that made them so popular in Burma. This chapter also explores what emerging female-centric pedagogies suggest about changing approaches to promoting religion in the Baptist mission and in the Konbaung court. In the first two-thirds of the nineteenth century, American schools dominated British schools in number and influence and, even more curiously, were attractive among Burmese Buddhist communities who seemed to want little to do with Christian missionaries otherwise. Even if they did not have much interest in studying the Bible, Burmese families seemed fascinated by the revelatory power of the telescopes, globes, maps, and other new views of the world on offer in Baptist classrooms. Of course, American Baptist schools were influential places where local people went to gain the technical skills necessary to advance economically and socially under British occupation—that is to say, the schools were particularly effective technologies of Western imperialism. But they were also places for local communities to explore, adopt, or reject powerful new cosmological visions and religious imaginations. This analysis is part of this book's larger effort to complicate simple utilitarian, economic explanations for why minority groups converted to Christianity.

This chapter begins with early nineteenth-century Burmese encounters with Christian teaching aids and the mid-nineteenth-century Baptist debates over the use of material resources for English-language education (as opposed to instruction in Burmese and other vernaculars) for boarding schools for Eurasian students, and for schools for girls and women. It then showcases the extraordinary objects—including a metal dog and a shrine tree—that distinguished the missionary site credited with baptizing the most Burmese Buddhists. It concludes with a close reading of an odd section of the prominent 1861 Pali-language royal Buddhist chronicle the *Sāsanavaṃsa*, which celebrates highly educated Burmese women as a way of promoting the power of the Burmese realm.

This chapter's assorted examples of educational objects and practices in the nineteenth century charts new religious worlds that Baptists and Buddhists were working to materialize. Baptists strove to solve what they saw as the problem of pervasive idolatry with richly supplied schools. Buddhists experimented with Western astronomical and geographic instruments to remake their claims to an independent Burmese kingdom and a continuously committed sangha. Woven through both of these efforts were stories about women. Baptist and Burmese patriarchies paid particular attention to the role women educators and educated women played in their campaigns to secure power in Southeast Asia.

I will show that when Baptist missionaries in the field petitioned for more money, labor, and things, they were arguing for an evangelical approach that focused on children and women. This approach emphasized daily, repetitive, multisubject, device-rich education in local languages as the key to undoing the education those pupils received in their local communities through female-directed homeschooling, shrine practices, monastic teachings about

Buddhist systems of salvation, and classical Indian understandings of earth sciences. In other words, after a few decades of work in Burma, Baptist evangelists began to see idolatry not as a static state of being, but rather as a systematic, multimedia form of education authorized by women. These missionaries insisted that this idolatry training could only be countered with a systematic form of well-furnished Christian education.

In the United States, Baptist leadership—mostly male—continued to argue for an evangelical approach that prioritized itinerant male preaching to adults. Promoters of this older model insisted that a simple, apparatus-free technique of a man talking to local people was closest to the biblical commission to "go, preach the gospel to every creature." Even as Burmese communities seemed to grow more assertive in their expressions of a Buddhist identity over the course of the nineteenth century, these U.S.-based leaders held on to a fantasy that the right male preachers with the right command of local languages would eventually turn hearts toward God. These leaders acknowledged that Christian schools and teaching aides could help prepare students for God's saving grace, but they hesitated to employ teachers, many of whom were women, or devote resources to expensive networks of day schools and female institutes.

This chapter features three prominent female American Baptist missionaries and educators in nineteenth-century Burma: Lydia Lillybridge, Ellen Bullard Mason, and Marilla Baker Ingalls. Lillybridge's conflict with male leadership inspired her to establish an independent network of day schools; Mason was ultimately expelled from the American mission because of her vigorous opposition to male Baptist authorities; and Ingalls made an extraordinary career for herself as a solitary missionary who earned praise among leading male American missionaries and British colonial officials for popularizing Christianity in a strongly Burmese Buddhist area. By poring over letters that Lillybridge and Mason wrote to other women, I demonstrate how the gender dynamics of these documents differ from those of the largely male-dominated materials explored elsewhere in this book. Ingalls's writings show that she worked independently, rather than under a male authority, to draw on Southeast Asian object practices to root Christianity in the local religious landscape. I want to be careful, though, not to suggest that these American women should be celebrated as pioneering feminists prevailing over powerful men to bring an emancipating modern education to underserved girls of Burma. In their own ways, Lillybridge, Mason, and

Ingalls contributed to imperial violence, and accounts of their careers should recognize both their efforts to challenge oppressive systems and to desecrate non-Christian religions.

The chapter's final section on the smart women of the *Sāsanavaṃsa* shows an overlapping concern with female education in the seemingly distant domains of the central Konbaung elite and the peripheral Baptist posts. Both of these operations focused on women as an important resource, as a kind of possession that signaled their virtuous power. I will show that the *Sāsanavaṃsa*'s collection of stories of women who surprise the men around them with their mastery of the classical Buddhist language of Pali works to promote Burma as the world's most superior Buddhist realm. Scholars in the past have paid little attention to this portion of the text, in part because few historians on Burma study the original text and instead use a flawed English-language translation from 1952. I will parse the Pali to show that, when read closely, it offers glimpses into a Buddhist imagination that conjures women as key figures in a campaign to dominate the region.

Telescopes, Globes, and Maps

The story of the impact of American Baptist teaching aids and schools in nineteenth-century Burma begins with early Burmese encounters with itinerant Baptist preachers and the world-conjuring devices they carried. Throughout the records of these encounters, we see a fascination with the revelatory, and perhaps even magical, power of the telescopes, globes, maps, and other devices (such as magic lanterns and "chrainotropes") that American Baptist missionaries circulated along with their printed and oral messages of the Christian god and his unique powers of salvation. For example, between 1826 and 1827 Jonathan Price was invited on multiple occasions to the Burmese royal court at Ava, in central Burma, to show his dazzling views of land and sky. There, he treated a high-ranking prince to his first vision of "Saturn with his ring and 3 satellites."[2] The head Buddhist monastic tutor of the queen entertained Price's views on religion when he promised she would be able to see the moon and the planets. Price fulfilled this promise in a return visit, when he brought a large telescope. The Buddhist monk, according to Price, seemed "beyond measure astonished and delighted with the new scene which he found before him."[3] Because of his telescope, the

Baptist missionary became quite popular in the court of King Bagyidaw, the Burmese monarch whose reign (1819–1837) included the First Anglo-Burmese War of 1824–1826.

While some missionaries, like Price, saw Burmese enthusiasm for Western astronomical and geographical devices as helping to clear the path for Christian evangelism, more expressed frustration that all the local people really wanted were these devices, and that they simply rejected the accompanying Baptist teachings. The American missionary Eugenio Kincaid, for example, wrote in his journal on July 14, 1833, that the people he was meeting in the royal city of Ava "professed great anxiety to know more of Geography and Astronomy, but had no wish to investigate the subject of religion." Still, Kincaid continued the practice followed by his fellow missionaries of integrating religious messages with geographic materials in his evangelical work in spite of the Enlightenment-style way the Baptists sometimes divided these subjects into the fields of "science" and "religion" in their published reports. Kincaid was also savvy about using Burmese curiosity about Western representations of the world to secure elite support for his evangelical work. On October 28 of that same year, Kincaid wrote in his journal about a prince who had asked Kincaid for globes, so Kincaid sent him "a map well shaded and colored"; according to Kincaid, the prince "was very much pleased with it, and sent word he would be happy to render [him] any favor in his power." Like Price, Kincaid courted royal favor with new Western devices for picturing the world and its place in the universe.[4]

Thomas Simons likewise gained royal favor and attention to Christian messages through two- and three-dimensional depictions of the world. In 1836, when this American Baptist missionary (who would go on to marry Lydia Lillybridge, the educator I explore later in this chapter) was evangelizing in the royal city of Ava, he wrote in his journal about the great interest people of all stations—including royalty, monks, and lower-class working people—showed in the maps he displayed of the solar system and the earth. He even carried around a large metallic, heliocentric mechanical model of the solar system called an "orrery" and found that large crowds gathered to see it. Simons noted a particular day when he was giving away books, and a crowd formed that was so big it filled the verandah and the yard. He "showed them the map of the world and a large orrery, and explained them to them. They remained silent and attentive, some occasionally asking questions."[5] In addition to relaying this stunning scene, the published version of Simons's journal entry adds a telling editorial postscript assuring American readers that missionaries in Burma were "not unaware of the improper uses to which [religious tracts] are sometimes applied, nor unguarded against the impositions to which benevolent effort is ever exposed from the giddy and profane, both in Christian and heathen lands."[6] The unnamed editor of the *Baptist Missionary Magazine* who wrote this note strains to insert a division between the sacred and profane into Simon's Burmese scene and adds that even people in Christian lands like the United States find themselves dizzy in the company of new print productions and models of the universe. This postscript tells of large, overlapping explorations of a range of things, from the geographic situation of enemy countries to the awesome movements of mysterious world systems and the various beings and soteriological possibilities they might host.

Burmese Maps of the Universe

The Burmese, we know, did not simply accept the Western worldviews that the missionaries peddled as facts; they also modified them or used them to modify their own spatial renderings. For example, in 1873, the penultimate Burmese king, Mindon Min (r. 1853–1878), upon examining a missionary's map, explained that the map was drawn incorrectly because Burma was depicted too small. A few days later, a royal geographer brought a new map, which partially copied the missionary map, but represented Burma as twice as large.[7]

Furthermore, the Burmese had their own visual and material models of the universe, which were often based on Buddhist traditions. The Buddha famously taught his disciples to avoid speculation about the origin and nature of the universe because, he said, that would not free them from their suffering but rather confuse them further. Still, the Burmese, like other Buddhist communities, imagined and reimagined the universe based on scriptural accounts of heavenly and hellish realms. Traditionally, Burmese Buddhists saw the universe as centered around Mount Meru. A Burmese *parabaik* (accordion-style manuscript) from the mid- to late nineteenth century depicts Mount Meru as a great bejeweled pillar coming out of the ocean and surrounded by the cosmic fish Ananda (see figure 2.1). The yellow circle in the upper left with the rabbit is the moon, and the red circle in the upper

FIGURE 2.1 Mount Meru, nineteenth-century Burmese Parabaik. © The Trustees of the British Museum.

THE SCHOOL

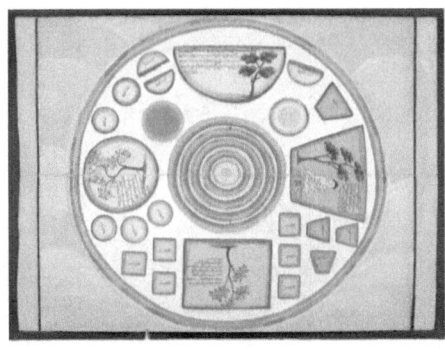

FIGURE 2.2 The Four Great Islands, nineteenth-century Burmese Buddhist cosmology manuscript. Courtesy of the British Library.

right a green peacock is the sun; the circles around the sun are planets. Another Burmese *parabaik* gives us a rather different vantage point to consider the Burmese cosmos with its rare top-down view of Mount Meru ringed by seven mountain ranges (see figure 2.2). The white background represents a vast ocean in which there are four major continents, including the southern one, Jambudipa, the land where buddhas appear. This manuscript is undated, but is likely from the late nineteenth century, after American Baptist missionaries and British colonial officials had been in the country for decades. The top-down view and the perfectly circular enclosure of this universe is rather distinct for Burmese parabaik and may be influenced by Western maps and globes.

In a monastic complex in Pakokku built in 1813, the same year that the Judsons arrived in Burma, a wall mural features another rendering of Mount Meru. In it the Buddha is shown dwelling in Tavatimsa Heaven at this central mountain's summit. As Alexandra Green explains, "Mount Meru's general position above entrances enhances the notion of karmic cause and effect once within the temple because it is in relationship to the mountain that spiritual hierarchies were posited."[8] Here Green is referring to the traditional Buddhist teaching that one's position in the universe, whether here in the land where the Buddha taught, in a heaven or in a hell, is the result of one's past actions. The more wholesome the actions one performs, the more one could advance into heavenly realms, while unwholesome actions land one in hell realms. Following the Buddha's path to completion, to nirvana, gets one out of the system all together.

Burmese Buddhists often tried to teach this system to American Baptist missionaries, explaining that Christian teachings of salvation through God did not make sense, given the rules of karma. Sure, they would say, the idea of a mighty god intervening to stop one from having to endure the consequences of one's past unwholesome actions was appealing, but this could not really work, because the responsibility for liberation fell on oneself. The Burmese recognized that their world was filled with all sorts of divine beings and spirits, so they were not necessarily opposed to being introduced to another god. And as the Burmese engaged more and more with Western geography and astronomy, they became inclined to revise earlier Indian models of the universe, including Buddhist ones. What most people in Burma refused to do, however, was to give up practices of accruing merit, such as paying respect to Buddha images and monks, making offerings, and upholding vows to behave ethically. Mainstream Burmese Buddhism held that it was through these practices that one could advance into divine abodes, avoid hell realms, and be ultimately emancipated from the suffering inherent in the system. It seems that, even as they were willing to reimagine the layout and mechanics of these world systems, nineteenth-century Burmese communities were committed to a soteriology in which the sāsana was the only way to escape from the stress and pain of these systems.

Most of the Burmese people who tried to explain merit and other Buddhist truths to American missionaries had learned these teachings from their families, community ritual practices, and the country's monastic schools. Burma's Buddhist education system earned international acclaim in the nineteenth century because of the many British and American reports about the country's extraordinary high literacy rate. As Alicia Turner has shown, the British perception of Burma as the most literate country in "the East" contributed to British notions of Burma as being exceptionally civilized and advanced. Turner explains that even when the first British census in Burma was taken in 1872 and calculated that 24.37 percent of men and 1.37 percent of women could read and write—percentages that were higher than what was found in the rest of British India but still far lower than colonial estimates—"the census takers themselves disputed their accuracy, citing personal experience over their scientific enumeration methods."[9] While the Burmese education system did not reach as much of the population as the British imagined, it was still a relatively sophisticated organization that drew upon the sizeable resources the country invested in Buddhist monasteries. Village, town, and city monasteries regularly took in local boys starting at age six or seven and taught them to read, recite, and write in Burmese and Pali. This language training prepared the boys for temporary monastic ordination, the coming-of-age ritual that Burmese families performed as an act of merit and a display of social status.[10] Many communities also had homeschools run by laypeople for boys and girls. Children in both types of schools memorized classical Buddhist texts and were taught that being able to read, recite, and write the Buddha's teachings was essential for preserving the sāsana. As discussed in the previous chapter, British colonial encroachment, the waning of Bamar political control, and the introduction of Western technologies, disciplines, and Christianity gave rise to new anxiety that the Buddha's teachings would quickly vanish from the earth. In this anxious state of anticipating an advancing Buddhist apocalypse, Burmese communities renewed their commitment to educating the next generations about the Buddha's teachings.

In addition to the study of Buddhist subjects, Burmese education also included some training in skills and sciences that would serve lay careers. Monastic education was in charge of teaching elite children advanced subjects such as Burmese history, law and jurisprudence (P. *dhammasattha*), astrology, and military skills.[11] The royally sponsored monastic reforms discussed in the previous chapter (and explored further in the next) included criticism of monks who were teaching practical forms of knowledge in order to help their lay communities earn better livings and have more material resources that they could use to support the sāsana (and therefore the monks who were teaching them those subjects). We also know that Burmese debates over monastic education often took up the Buddhist term for worldly (P. *lokāyata*) knowledge in order to criticize efforts to teach disciplines geared toward societal success rather than advancement toward nirvana. As I will detail regarding Lydia Lillybridge's debate with the Baptist mission's male authority figures, the Christian communities struggled with a similar concern about their schools being too focused on preparing students for financial and social success in the increasingly colonized country.

However much Buddhist monastic schools and Baptist missionary schools resisted preparing students to prosper under British control, they were pressured again and again to begin teaching Western subjects, especially geography, arithmetic, and land-measuring. In the 1860s, the chief commissioner of British Burma, Arthur Phayre, designed a program in which monks received free Burmese-language textbooks in these kinds of subjects. Phayre was well aware of the country's esteemed book culture (discussed in chapter 1) and knew that the physical object of the book would be a welcome donation. The problem for the British was that monks, even after accepting the books, tended to refuse to introduce these Western subjects into their curriculum.[12]

Particularly relevant for this chapter's questions about the Burmese interest in nineteenth-century Baptist schools are accounts of monastic critics of Western education who focused their condemnation on the dangers of teaching mapmaking. Juliane Schober writes about how when the new head monastic authority in Burma in 1909 finally agreed to soften the official stance on incorporating colonial education, he still "objected firmly to instruction in drawing . . . especially the drawing of maps."[13] The work of producing new visions of the world was a threat to classical forms of Buddhist education and contemporary monastic authority. Part of the hazard of learning colonial ways of drawing the country was that the British used these maps and the labor of these mapmakers to strengthen their hold on Burma. Colonial education was conspicuously interested in producing skilled land surveyors and administrators with English-language training.[14] These Burmese professionals were crucial for maintaining British authority.

While scholarship on the mechanics of colonialism in Burma and in other contexts makes it easy to see how these forms of education and labor empowered imperialism, what is harder to see is the distinctiveness of the Burmese combination of resistance to and fascination with the maps, globes, telescopes, and other world-conjuring devices presented by Baptist missionaries, first during their itinerant preaching tours and then in their popular network of schools. Why was mapmaking so threatening to Burmese monastic and royal authorities in ways that English-language instruction was not? It was surely obvious in nineteenth-century Burma that British authorities needed English-speaking administrators to control and further colonize the country. But English-language instruction did not come under the same degree of criticism in Burmese communities that mapmaking did. Likewise, it did not have the same awesome appeal of maps, globes, and telescopes, objects which appear to have had a distinct power to inspire new religious imaginations. Without paying attention to this spellbinding dimension of Burmese engagement with Baptist teaching aids, we are left with an account of Burmese people acting out of purely pragmatic motivations; we already know that they entertained traveling Baptist preachers and sent their children to Baptist schools for socioeconomic reasons. What I want to also consider is the ways that these interactions provided material resources for imagining and experiencing new immaterial power. By looking through missionary telescopes, by tracing Baptist maps, and watching the three-dimensional animation of Christian orreries, Burmese people could reimagine Jambudipa, the earth, and the cosmos, charting pathways to other worlds and new forms of salvation.[15]

Growth of Baptist Schools

The first fascinating cartographical and astronomical devices circulated in Burma through itinerant American missionaries in the first third of the nineteenth century. Starting in the late 1830s, with the establishment of the first network of Baptist schools, these materials were instead accessed inside Baptist schoolhouses. These American-run schools became the most prominent non-Buddhist schools in Burma in the period leading up to the collapse of the kingdom in 1885. This section of the chapter will sketch the establishment of American Baptist education in Burma before turning to the particular cases of the revealing educational methods of Lydia Lillybridge, Ellen Mason, and Marilla Ingalls.

In the early 1830s, American missionaries and local leaders of newly converted Christian communities began opening day schools in southern Burma. Many of these school builders were women, such as Ma Doke and Ma Min from Moulmein, Karen women who worked with Sarah Boardman, an American Baptist who became the Burmese mission's first independent woman evangelist when her husband died in 1831 (three years later she married Adoniram Judson and became known as Sarah Judson). The period between 1835 and 1853 saw the most significant growth of American Baptist schools. This was a during stretch of relative calm between the Burmese resistance movements of the late 1820s and 1830s and the Second Anglo-Burmese War of 1852–1853. As the British established their rule over lower Burma, they turned to the American school system to help maintain their control. For example, the American Baptist missionary printer Cephas Bennett became the founder of the first British government school in Burma. Under colonial rule, the Americans were instructed to not use class time for explicit religious instruction and to not pressure pupils to convert. When a Chinese student asked for baptism, it caused such a scandal that Bennett was forced to resign. The American Baptist missionary George Hough took over and was deemed so successful that by 1845 he was inspector of schools for the entire province.[16]

Like the early itinerant Baptist preachers, Baptist schools in Burma attracted Burmese attention in part through the maps and globes they possessed. The American Baptist archives are filled with requests from Burma-based missionaries for more maps and globes for their schools and with reports about the positive effects of these donated items. In 1840, for example, when Deborah Wade wrote to the American Baptist Missionary Board with an update on the state of Karen schools in Tavoy, she explained that ever since the school received "books, maps, globes, &c . . . [it had] *very much* improved, and the proficiency of the pupils during the past season has given us *great pleasure.*" Wade's use of italics here gives some sense of the joy and pride the students and teachers must have felt when their school finally included exploration of these two- and three-dimensional representations of the world. Her letter goes on to add that "the interest excited by the maps prepared in their language, has been highly gratifying."[17] Surely having these Baptist visions of vast landscapes labeled in the students' newly scripted Karen language would have been both informative and thrilling. Wade's map invited her students into a strange, yet also familiar, world where study of the earth promised passage to heavens.

Because of the success of Baptist schools like Wade's, the British were quite pleased with the work of the American schools in Burma. As the *Calcutta Review* put it in 1847:

> Too much praise cannot be bestowed on the labors of the American Baptist Mission in the education department. . . . The progress made has been wonderful; their pupils have gone forth into the villages, and have imparted to their brethren the seeds of knowledge. . . . It will be said, and truly said, "Our English rulers were, indeed, conquerors of the Burmans, and wrung from them these fair and beautiful provinces, but our American teachers were conquerors of ignorance, and dispelled the darkness from which the English never strove to rescue us."[18]

In this fantasy of Anglo-American domination, the British conquered the Burmese and extracted from them their lovely land, but it was the Americans who conquered their ignorance. It is easy to see how these two approaches worked together in a "sword in one hand, Bible in the other" kind of way. American Christian efforts, when partnered with British military operations, worked to justify—to ennoble—the colonization of Burma. In retrospect, the sword seems to have succeeded whereas the Bible largely failed. Christian missions may have been good publicity in Britain and the United States for British imperialism, but they never achieved their goal of sweeping Burmese conversion, even when the British destroyed their Buddhist monarchy and colonized the entire country. To gain some insight into how the American Baptist mission failed among the Burmese, and what the Baptists even meant by "conversion" and "idolatry," I will now consider the case of Lydia Lillybridge and her battle for Baptist educational reform and Burmese Christian conversion.

Eating in English and Educating in Idolatry: The Case of Lydia Lillybridge

Lydia Lillybridge was an American Baptist missionary to Burma active in debates about mission schools in the mid-nineteenth century, the period in which early ad hoc forms of missionary education were becoming systematized into a network of day and boarding schools. While Lillybridge was celebrated for her outstanding work as a teacher, she was also condemned for being overly assertive in her protests against boarding schools. Her distinct position as both a model for and a critic of early Baptist education in Burma makes her writings revealing windows onto the anxieties about American missionary schools and the larger project of Christian evangelism in nineteenth-century Burma. This section examines letters Lillybridge wrote between 1847 and 1853 to argue that resource debates about schools and teachers reveal changing approaches to conversion and idolatry in the mission. Earlier romantic visions of itinerant preachers blazing trails of adult Christian converts through the Burmese countryside were being replaced with institutional designs for multistage processes in which potential converts were first prepared through well-supplied, systematized, routinized, general education. In this transition, idolatry transformed in the Baptist imagination from a hypermaterialist external condition that could be totally abandoned upon hearing the truths of the gospel into a complex education system with external object-oriented practices and internal states that could only be dismantled through a continuously funded, expertly staffed, Christian, multidisciplinary education system. In other words, idolatry became redefined not only as the worship of false gods but also as the internalization of Buddhist and animist ideas about systems of salvation. In response to this new intricate understanding of idolatry (and Buddhism), the missionary system demanded more schoolhouses, teaching aids, and, perhaps most expensive of all, skilled educators. Lillybridge was one of these skilled educators, and the controversy she caused about education policy and practice shows how central schools and teachers were to the larger work of the mission.

Lillybridge's twenty-eight-year career in Burma was primarily based in the southern port town of Moulmein, a prominent center of the American Baptist mission and the British administration of colonial Burma. When Lillybridge first sailed to Burma in 1846, she was one of the mission's few single female missionaries and was remarkably successful in her efforts to resist pressure to marry one of the mission's several ministers whose wives had died in Burma.[19] In 1851, she finally agreed to marry Thomas Simons, but only after she threatened to call off the wedding (going as far as to return gifts) because she learned that the mission intended to appoint Simons to run the Moulmein Baptist boarding school and therefore use their marriage as a way to force Lillybridge to work there. Even after marriage, Lillybridge was successful in protesting Baptist educational policy, principally by establishing her own network of day schools.

From the few details about the end of Lillybridge's life that have been preserved in missionary archives, we know that she earned an international reputation for her work at Burma's Morton Lane Girls' School (a Baptist missionary school in Moulmein) and eventually had to return to the United States for health reasons in 1874. Her husband stayed in Burma and died there of cholera in 1876. Simons and Lillybridge had one daughter, who died when she was fifteen months old. After returning to the States, Lillybridge lived in Brooklyn with her sister Martha until her death on November 29, 1898. Her obituary in the *Baptist Missionary Magazine* celebrated her for "always manifest[ing] a lively interest in the missionary work of Burma" and described her as "the last one of the members of that noble missionary circle which labored in Moulmein in the year 1846," referring to contemporaries like Adoniram and Emily Chubbuck Judson.[20] Despite Lillybridge's once prominent status in the Burma mission, Baptist histories and hagiographies have not included her in their accounts of the mission and have instead focused on Adoniram Judson and his three wives (Ann Hasseltine, Sarah Hall Boardman, and Emily Chubbuck); the limited amount of non-Baptist scholarship that has explored the Baptist mission to Burma has followed suit.[21] By studying Lillybridge and then turning to the cases of Ellen Mason and Marilla Ingalls, I will offer a different perspective on the distinct role these female missionaries and their networks of students, coworkers, congregants, and neighbors played in American understandings of foreign evangelism and Buddhism. Furthermore, these women's writings shed light on the new approaches to conversion, religious identity formation, and education that were transforming Burma in the middle of the nineteenth century.

The evidence we have of Lillybridge's career is due in large part to the work she put into actively maintaining relationships with female colleagues and friends in Burma and back in the United States, most notably her close friendship with the famous author and missionary Emily Chubbuck Judson. Lillybridge and Chubbuck had worked together as teachers at the Utica Female Academy in New York in their twenties. When Chubbuck married Adoniram Judson after meeting him on the first tour he took of the States after thirty years in Burma, Lillybridge decided to join Chubbuck and sail to Burma with her as a missionary in 1846.[22] After Adoniram died in 1850, and Chubbuck returned to the States in 1851, Lillybridge and Chubbuck continued to write each other until Chubbuck's death in 1854. Because of Chubbuck's prominent status in the legacy of the mission, over a dozen of her letters from Lillybridge have been preserved in family and national archives. The following analysis draws on those letters as well as on four other letters from that same period that Lillybridge wrote to Solomon Peck, the corresponding secretary of the Foreign Department of the American Baptist Missionary Union.

Lillybridge's letters to Chubbuck and Peck focus on a criticism of English-language education and of boarding schools for Eurasian students. Lillybridge was not entirely against teaching students in Burma some English; she felt that learning this language can lead to "a fountain of knowledge [being] opened to them" and wrote that she had seen them "[sip] deliciously from that knowledge." Lillybridge described how she had seen her students' "whole character elevated" and therefore did not want to take it upon herself "to shut that fountain against others."[23] But she was still persistent in her criticism of an overemphasis on English, because it meant the she must spend her "energies in teaching [her] class to eat, and drink, and act and think in English, to the neglect of these Burmese multitudes of children that are taught nothing by idolatry and superstition."[24] This quotation, from a letter Lillybridge wrote to Chubbuck, shows her arguing that the energy that missionaries spend teaching English language and manners to select students would be better spent on educating more people from mainstream Burmese society in way that could directly counter the "idolatry and superstition" that she says their families teach them. It is noteworthy that Lillybridge used this common derogatory trope of the ignorant idol-worshipper in a private letter to Chubbuck, who also had years of experience living and working in Burma. This is not a sensationalized account of hell-bound Oriental heathens for untraveled Americans; rather Lillybridge is trying to get her friend and colleague to join her protests against English-language education. And her strongest criticism of that kind of education is that it is allowing for Buddhism and other religious traditions in Burma to maintain their authority over the country's children.[25]

Within Lillybridge's rhetoric are glimpses into how missionaries in the field saw the relationship between conversion and education. Conversion did not only mean introducing adults to Jesus and guiding them in the reception of God's grace and faith in his unique powers of salvation; it also meant changing the ideas and practices that led these adults to revere Buddha statues and spirit shrines. To convert the people of Burma to Christianity, Baptist missionaries argued, they would have to first dispel other forms of belief and ritual. Then they could plant the seeds for total faith in God. As Lillybridge writes, idolatry and superstition are not just unfortunate conditions, but forms of education. Children are not born Buddhists or animists or idolaters, according to Lillybridge; they become those things through educational processes in Burmese families, shrines, and monasteries. Furthermore, teaching in both cases—"idolatry" and Christian schools—happens through repetition. To advocates like Lillybridge, this is why education is so important: it has the power to transform a new generation in a way that isolated encounters between ministers and adult audiences never could.

Lillybridge expounded on this understanding of education, idolatry, and conversion in a letter she wrote in 1850 to Solomon Peck, corresponding secretary of the Foreign Department of the American Baptist Missionary Union, to whom she was related through her family back in the States. In this letter, which articulates her philosophy of missionary education,

Lillybridge wrote that she had never felt "the importance of schools in the work of missions" as she did then. She argued that, "if the rising generation are to be instructed in the truths of religion, it appears reasonable that they should be with us day after day, that when a good impression is made, it may be repeated again and again." Lillybridge contrasted this approach of effective daily, repetitive instruction with an image of ineffective meandering preaching: "Suppose we go from house to house, and from street to street, speaking to the ignorant children the most simple truths of God's word. They may listen attentively for the time, but without repetition, our words are like water spilt on the ground—like seed sown by the wayside. Without 'line upon line, and precept upon precept,' we cannot hope to effect much improvement in the minds or morals of thoughtless degraded children of idolaters." Lillybridge quoted Isaiah 28:10–13 to give biblical authority to her educational approach. Before concluding that she would "leave it to [her] superiors to decide upon the wiser course"—a gesture of humility to soften her bold assertions—she added that, if the mission were to "neglect schools, our efforts must be confined almost entirely to adults, or to a comparatively small number of children." Clearly Lillybridge saw that it was crucial for the mission to teach large groups of children if they were to ever counter Buddhism.[26]

Notably, Lillybridge wrote this letter to Peck the year after he published "Due Gradation of Missionary Labor" on behalf of the Board of Foreign Missions. It is likely that, shortly after receiving a copy of this report, Lillybridge wrote her letter in reply to Peck's characterization of the relative importance of schools. In his report, Peck described the work of foreign missions as being organized into three areas, with education being the third. The first, and most important, was preaching the gospel to those who had not heard it before. As the board put it, "The terms missionary and preacher are, with us, all but synonymous." The second service a missionary was to provide was translating the word of God, which included the work of printing and circulation.[27]

Peck's report shows how the board's priorities for labor in the missionary field went from the most direct form of communication to the most complex, from preaching to education. Speaking face-to-face was seen as God's commission and all other forms of communication followed from it. Here Peck imagines preaching as device-less and education as device-dependent, even though we know that itinerant preachers often brought with them tracts and—as in the cases of the touring missionaries discussed earlier in this chapter—objects like telescopes and globes. There were some very low-maintenance preachers with exceptionally good vernacular language skills who did simply go around preaching to small crowds, but even they relied on the support of local labor to carry and arrange their food, shelter, and clothing. Peck's goal was not to accurately detail the work of foreign preaching, but to rhetorically place it at the top of a patriarchal hierarchy of the mission. Only men worked as preachers. In the second department of labor, the work of translation, printing, and circulation, the men dominated the most esteemed positions: the work of translating and printing.[28] It is the third department of labor that relied most on women's work. Female missionaries—American, Burmese, and Karen—ran schools. This was an encompassing job, and one that American Baptist women did with the support of housekeepers, nannies, cooks, and other (mostly female) domestic servants.[29]

The order of operations Peck described was dictated by male American administrators and leaders based in American cities and towns who only occasionally, if ever, visited foreign missions. Naturally, foreign missionaries in distant stations would have varying understandings of the best ways to carry out their work. In Burma, where the most prominent people group resisted conversion almost entirely, missionaries began to realize that the ideal work of preaching directly to the people could not happen as quickly as they had initially imagined. We have evidence that, as early as 1817, the plan of austere public preaching was being rewritten. That year Adoniram Judson wrote that "I am extremely anxious to begin to preach in public—but have found that I could not do it to any advantage, until I have something to put into the hands of the Burmans at the same time."[30] Here we have the founder of the American Baptist mission to Burma writing four years into the mission that the strategy of direct oral preaching would not work unless it was coupled with a tangible expression of the new religion the Baptist were trying to introduce. Judson was thinking of printed translations and expository tracts, but the mission would soon elaborate on these objects to include things like the luxuriously decorated bound books like the red leather bible discussed in chapter 1; the globes, maps, and other world-conjuring devices considered in this chapter; and the Baptist shrines explored in the next section. Since the beginning of the American mission, the Burmese cultural context demanded a material means for exploring

Baptist Christianity. Remarkably, Judson's 1817 letter is preserved in the British Library because it is believed to be the earliest surviving letter from Burma via post. At the initial moment of Burma's connection to other parts of the world through this new communications technology, the first American Baptist missionary in the country acknowledges that the mission's own communication technology needed to become more complex—that it needed to add a tangible component.[31]

American Baptist missionary plans for evangelizing in Burma gave shape to changing ideas about how conversion works. The original visions of wandering missionaries preaching to people who, upon hearing, have the kind of dramatic change of heart and a new unshakeable faith that was the focus of the evangelical revivals popular in the U.S. northeast in this period were quickly abandoned in Burma.[32] The missionaries almost immediately realized how hard it was to, first, learn the languages, and, second, to convince people through conversation alone that salvation through exclusive faith in God was more desirable than Buddhist nirvana and relationships with gods and spirits.

Lillybridge's years in Burma convinced her that the Burmese would not convert to Christianity without a systematic dismantling of Buddhist education. Lillybridge's arguments about conversion were happening within a larger shift in the American understanding of conversion in the nineteenth century. As Lincoln Mullen claims in his history of conversion in the United States, over the course of the nineteenth century religion changed from being an identity that people inherited to something individuals were obliged to choose. This move toward what Mullen calls the "burden to choose" was a result of changing ideas about how religious identity was formed as well as a significant part of debates about child conversions and whether conversions happened instantaneously or gradually. Mullen shows that it was not until after the Protestant awakenings of the eighteenth century that Americans saw the conversion of children as a real possibility. The development of Sunday schools in the nineteenth century significantly contributed to a more popularly held view that students were not only capable of acquiring information but were also candidates for a full heart conversion.[33]

While Lillybridge took the position that conversion was a gradual process, and that education could prepare students for conversion, she did not write much about this kind of evangelical heart conversion happening in her classrooms. Like other missionaries working among the Bamar majority, Lillybridge acknowledged that it was very rare to for the Bamar to express an absolute faith in the Christian god's grace and sovereignty. But she did see the mission as at least successful in introducing the country to a new approach to identity formation: the notion that an individual could reject the religious system of one's family and ancestors and take on a Christian identity. In Lillybridge's Burmese context, a small but growing number of people began to accept the idea that a person in Burma could become a Christian by repudiating the Buddha's teachings and their community's obligations to local spirits. The majority still claimed that it was impossible to renounce multilifetime karmic connections to generations of Buddhists and the stores of accumulated merit or demerit. This majority argued that whether or not you *believed* in the Buddha's teachings, you were still subject to the laws of karma and rebirth. But the American Baptist mission and the British colonial incursion forced communities in Burma to accommodate, even if only at the fringes of Burmese society, an alternative worldview in which religion was an individual option. The evangelicals worked especially hard to take this new purchase on a portion of the Burmese religious imagination and invest it with the notion that Protestant conversion was an integral part of a cosmopolitan, modern identity.

In mid-nineteenth-century Burma, the mission found that Karen people seemed most interested in their alternative religious worldview. I will now to turn to one of the most illustrious Baptist missionaries among the Karen, Ellen Mason. Like Lillybridge, Mason was a prominent educator and superintendent, and, like Lillybridge, she fought with the male establishment over educational policy and resources. But, unlike Lillybridge, Mason was ultimately forced out of the mission because of the threat she posed to male and American authority. Even after leaving the American Baptists, Mason continued to be a prominent leader in the Karen Christian community, which grew widely during the course of Mason's long career in Burma.

"Woman Is the Teacher of Burma": The Campaign of Ellen Mason

Of all the American Baptist missionaries of the nineteenth-century mission to Burma, Ellen Mason may be the most outstanding, for defying male leadership, and the most derided, for her theories about religion. Mason was a strong proponent of female education and local female leadership in Burma, especially among the Karen. In 1861, she cofounded the interdenominational Woman's Union Missionary Society of America for Heathen Lands, which focused on female donors in its foreign evangelization projects, a previously undervalued source of support for foreign missions. The Woman's Union also employed single women as missionaries at a time when denominational organizations like the American Baptist Missionary Union would only support women evangelists who were married to male missionaries or planning to marry widowed missionaries once they arrived in Burma. Mason's leadership and fundraising efforts among female networks allowed her to establish the celebrated Karen Female Institute as well as several other schools for women. It also led to her eventual expulsion from the Baptist mission.

After nineteen years in Burma as a Karen specialist, teacher, and administrator, Ellen Mason was accused by the American Baptist Missionary Union's male leadership of undermining the mission. They claimed that Mason's work educating girls and women threatened American Baptist institutional authority, local British colonial authority, and even the authority of her husband, Francis Mason, a famous missionary, translator, and scholar of Karen languages and culture. When the Missionary Union's claims of subversion proved insufficient to officially strip Mason of her professional position, social status, and property, the American Baptist leaders caused a scandal around a theory she had developed known as the "God language." Inspired by patterns she saw in Karen textiles, Egyptian hieroglyphics, and an American rug, Mason made graphic and linguistic connections among ancient Middle Eastern, Burmese, and Karen cultures, hypothesizing that the patterns she saw in these disparate objects symbolized the universal and timeless language of God. Mason's material-culture-inspired theology had a limited circulation before the American Baptist leadership used it to accuse Mason of having "a direct tendency to subvert the Holy Scriptures, and encourage superstition and idolatry." While I certainly do not side with the Baptist leadership in Mason's case (there is a stronger case that they were chiefly interested in dispossessing this influential woman of her property and status), I am taken with the public way they named Baptist activity in Burma "idolatry." Perhaps, as the mission came to wield more and more powerful religious objects in Southeast Asia, the American-based leaders felt they needed to make a kind of Calvinist display of excising an idolator. Whatever their motivations, there was surely a concern that certain objects and certain women had grown too powerful abroad. In the end, the Baptist council ruled that Mason had "hallucinations amounting to monomania," and she lost her official appointment with the Missionary Union. After the death of her husband, Mason transferred to the Anglican missionary organization that was getting its footing in Burma at this time, the Society for the Propagation of the Gospel, bringing her Karen Christian community and women-centric work with her. Mason continued to work as a missionary and a promoter of female education in Burma until her death in Rangoon in 1894 at the age of seventy-seven.[34]

This section draws on a collection of letters from 1857–1859 between Mason and Viscountess Charlotte Canning, an esteemed artist and the wife of Charles Canning, the governor-general of India from 1855 through 1862 who is most remembered for his handling in 1857 of what was then then called the "Indian Mutiny" and is now referred to as the "Indian Rebellion" and the "First War of Independence."[35] These letters were in Canning's tent when it caught fire in December 1859. The Cannings encamped in Rajasthan during a kind of goodwill tour they were taking through India in the wake of the 1857 uprising against the British East India Company when a stove that had been warming Charlotte Canning as she slept set the tent on fire. In the chaos, Canning left her clothes and jewelry but saved her letters, diaries, personal papers, and paintings.[36] This archive suffered burns, but the British Library Conservation Centre began working on the damaged materials and making them available to researchers in 2017.

I examine these now legible archival materials in order to show how Mason successfully recruited this highly influential woman as a sponsor of her education programs by depicting an image of Burmese women as both exceptionally sophisticated citizens and dangerous orchestrators of idolatry. Mason's fundraising techniques combined this vision of powerful, perilous, and imperiled women with a detailed account of the construction materials and teaching aids needed to build schools. I argue that Mason, like other female evangelist fundraisers, highlighted the tangible needs and material power of Christian schools to get support from an increasingly powerful network of American and British women. While the male work of itinerant preaching was imagined to be minimalist and low maintenance, the female work of education demanded physical materials, popular teaching aids, and local and imported labor. Female fundraising networks were largely invisible in the mission's public operations (and are absent in scholarship on

Christianity in nineteenth-century Burma), yet their success relied upon effectively communicating the power of visible and tangible things in the work of evangelizing Burma.

The tent fire collection features four long letters that Mason wrote to Canning about female education in Burma between 1857 and 1859, the end of the same decade in which Lillybridge and Chubbuck corresponded about the best way to use Baptist schools to encourage Christian conversion and thwart the powerful processes of "idolatry."[37] In contrast to the low, double-digit numbers of converts reported in Lillybridge's Burmese community, Mason's Karen mission was celebrating nearly three thousand converts. In her letter from February 5, 1857, Mason explained that these converts had built approximately one hundred chapels and established approximately fifty schools. These schools, Mason wrote, "have been greatly blessed by heaven." As an example of this divine blessing, Mason told Canning that, during her four years of teaching at one of the Karen Christian schools in Moulmein, thirty-eight students were converted. But, despite all of this success and growth, Mason reported that there had been no other support for educating Karen women and girls of the region. Even though there were some three million girls and women in Burma, she noted, with seven hundred or eight hundred of them at that time under British rule, the British government did not have a single school for females, other than two Catholic schools and a newly established school in Rangoon.[38]

Mason added to these stark statistics an argument that women were, in fact, the most powerful people in the country in terms of religion and the work of British colonialism. According to Mason, a woman in Burma was "not the languishing, facile, unknowing thing of the zenana—but is strong to will and to do—and as free as the dames of ancient Rome." To this racist collage combining an Orientalist scene of secluded, weak Muslim women with a romantic rendering of independent Roman women, Mason included a sketch of a newly emerging motif: the brazen Burmese woman. Mason wrote that Karen women are "not usually bold and stubborn like the Burmese," but in their communities as in all communities in the country, "woman is the teacher of Burma." Without Christian catechism, according to Mason, women used this influential position to support "idolatry." And all the men, even those who have received Christian education, "marry ignorant heathen wives," undoing any work Americans or the British have done to educate them. What the colonial government and its American allies needed to do, according to Mason, was educate these controlling women. She insisted that "it is the women who will not believe this world is rolling in the sky; and it is the women who perpetuate ghosts, witches, and all manner of popular errors." As in Lillybridge's writing, idolatry here is depicted as a kind of false education system. It has an alternative astronomy in which the earth is flat and not "rolling in the sky" as it is in the Christian scheme; it is also a belief in beings like ghosts and witches, their power to affect change in human lives, and their receptivity to propitiation.[39]

The Karen communities that Mason worked with were not educated in Buddhist monasteries like the Bamar communities Lillybridge taught in and therefore did not get the same kind of institutional, reading-and-reciting education common to the Burmese majority, especially the male population. Because the Karen had tended to be excluded from Burma's monastic school system, their education happened largely at home, from elders and from oral traditions and during worship practices like making offerings at nat shrines or Buddhist pagodas. Baptist missionaries working with the Karen often observed this key educational discrepancy between the Bamar and the Karen. For example, when Deborah Wade, another prominent mid-nineteenth-century female missionary, wrote to her brother Lester in 1853 with a scathing criticism of the mission's renewed commitment to direct preaching at the expense of schools, she described how successful Baptist schools had been among the Karen. According to Wade, schools for this minority were "deemed highly important, because they, unlike the Burman and most of the heathen nations, had no books or literature of their own, and cannot of course read the Bible and religious books unless taught by the missionaries."[40] These missionaries to the Karen saw two key aspects of the Bamar practice of not offering monastic education to this minority: forced illiteracy and exclusion from the religious teachings contained in books. This meant that Baptist instruction to the Karen did not require prolonged, systematic undoing of complex, text-based Buddhist education, like it did in Burmese schools. This also meant that Baptist schools, with their globes and colored maps and Karen-language bibles, could harness a desire to connect with extraordinary visions of salvation, a desire not satisfied by the politically powerful Bamar.

Baptist female missionaries like Wade and Mason often focused their evangelical attentions on female Karen leaders and their influence over their community's educational processes and religious practices. Mason wrote to

Canning that women were both the figures in society who have the power to perpetuate idolatry and with the potential to promote Christianity. She also claimed that women have the ability to maintain Burma's independence or make it a British colony. Other U.S. missionaries were careful to stay out of British political developments in Burma. Some were openly critical of British colonialism and saw in Burmese resistance a reflection of the American Revolutionary War (1775–1783), in which some of their fathers and grandfathers had fought. Mason, however, positioned herself as a strong ally of the British empire, at least in her letters to this powerful English woman. She referred to the recent Anglo-Burmese war to argue that it was the women of Burma's "agents [who] wrought a war between England in Burmah." She went on to argue that "if the women of Burmah could be educated, it would not cost the Gov't one half as much as it would dues to guard these districts and keep them in order." Mason's logic here is that if women are educated, they will also be Christianized, and then they will Christianize their husbands and their children. As she explicitly wrote, "Should there ever occur another war between England and Burmah, it would be of incalculable advantage to have Christianized races among these mountain boundaries." In hindsight, Mason's letter offers a disturbing prediction of the Third Anglo-Burmese War of 1885, which colonized the entire country in part through alliances with some of the minority communities who had significant numbers of Christian converts, such as the Karen.[41] Mason's belligerent, calculating letter makes an argument to this high-ranking woman in British India that investment in female education is a savvy economic and political investment in British imperialism.[42]

Mason combines this big-picture, cost-benefit approach with a highly detailed account of the particular resources that go into constructing a successful school in Burma. In Mason's October 1857 letter, she reported to the Viscountess that local villagers had provided a vast amount of base material. Mason wrote that the very people who had originally opposed opening up a school for girls had become so supportive of the project that they donated 25,000 pieces of rattan, 2,076 pieces of thatch, 225 pounds of bark-robe, 130 mats, between 400 and 600 eggs, as well as rice, pigs, goats, 45 handmade gowns, robes, jackets, and turbans, and 10,000 days of manual labor. The British government had contributed enough teak lumber to build two large two-story buildings with a combined area of 57 by 108 feet and two tall towers. The spacious grounds, which, Mason writes, were given by

God, had since grown to three times their original size. 50 girls and women, all over twelve years old, had been taught by Mason for three seasons and part of a fourth. Mason, again invoking a romantic Greco-Roman image, proclaimed that "now this Karen Female Institute will be cherished as the Delphi of their tribes, to which they even now continually resort, and from which they cannot return without ... some shimmering from the light of science."[43] This triumphal fundraising language plays with a magical image of science literally enlightening the bodies of the female students: science is the shiny object attracting students to the school, infusing them with new glowing visions of the universe and new enlightening glimpses into religious worldviews.

Mason cultivated this sense of the supernatural power of science with the extraordinary world-conjuring devices she displayed in her schools, including maps, large globes, a magic lantern, a stereoscope, and a "chrainotrope." Mason told Canning that Providence had provided these key teaching devices along with a piano, mathematical instruments, and drawing and painting supplies for a new school she was establishing for Burmese and Shan students on the west bank of the Sittang River. Mason wanted to show the potential donor that her Toungoo school model had to be replicated in other parts of the country. Yet, even though the school was already so well furnished and even had a new teacher arriving soon from Boston, Mason reported to Canning that she only has "inexperienced Karens to help [her] while keeping exact accounts of receipts and expenditures." This accounting included

> superintending the sawing and measuring of every cubit; building the Institute and store house; with temporary dormitories, chapels, and school-rooms; clearing the land; making roads; planting gardens; gathering the wild mountaineers as protectors of the school; procuring them paddy fields adjacent, so as to make them permanent setters; aiding them in forming their society to take charge; attending to all their native and foreign correspondence; administering to all their sick.[44]

Mason's rather exhausting vision of her leading this Karen community to dramatically transform the landscape to support this school is meant to show Canning that Mason is both carefully actuarial and in genuine need of money.

What is particularly striking about Mason's writing techniques in this example and in other correspondences is the rhetorical strategies that she uses to show a righteous requirement for assistance for schools and to perform a kind of exacting management over resources to instill confidence in her as a worthy adminstrator. Mason excels at evoking specific images of villagers and land and wood and food and textiles all culminating in a grand institution of learning in a noble Western lineage that connects a celebrated ancient Greco-Roman world with the modern British empire. By detailing how much the local people have put into the process, Mason invites philanthropists and government officials to do their part by sending rupees. She also paints a picture of simple people donating things like eggs while the world around them is built up with new steam engines, postal routes, telegraphs—technologies that allow British and American support to join these people to promote Western Christian imperialism.

Mason was clearly a successful fundraiser. She received multiple donations from Canning and an 1857 British government aid grant. Between 1860 and 1861 Mason encouraged the British government to donate a powerful telescope to the Karen Young Men's Normal School, which the Accounts and Papers of the House of Commons noted "has been turned to good account."[45] And, by the 1870s, Ellen Mason's schools were widely praised in Burma and abroad. For example, Colonel Lawrie, in writing for London's *Journal of the Society of the Arts*, exclaimed that

> the energy of the American ladies ... as regards Karen women, have been remarkable, and throughout Burmah they have been the true friends of woman's elevation from the days of Mrs. Judson, after the first Burmese war, in 1826, down to those of Mrs. Mason, at the conclusion of the second war and conquest of Pegu, in 1852. I was inspector of government and aid schools in the new province in 1865–66, but among the various Burmese and Karen schools inspected there was nothing to equal as a bold success Mrs. Mason's Karen Female Institute, at [Toungoo].... Mrs. Mason [is] one of the most gifted American ladies who ever came to Burmah, and whose laborers are fully mentioned in the annals of our Indian administration. As in India, so in Burmah, the greatest hindrance to the conversion of the men is the women.... However, through American ladies like Mrs. Mason devoting themselves to the good work with untiring zeal and ability, the opposition of the natives themselves to female education—particularly of the Karens—has been subdued, and various schools have at length been

constructed, and are supported by voluntary offerings. The people are even beginning to show an interest in our arts, manufactures, and commerce; . . . Mrs. Mason's success among the Karens would appear to be an earnest call to the ladies of England to go and do likewise.[46]

Lawrie's aggrandizing celebration echoes claims Mason made in her fundraising campaigns, which surely targeted Lawrie and other British administrators in Burma. The same arguments surface here that Mason made about women in Burma deserving foreign attention because they are both powerfully influential and pitiably suppressed. Lawrie also suggests the same process of zealous Baptist education subduing local communities and preparing them for cultural and political conquest.

By the time of Mason's death in 1894, the British had fully colonized Burma. The Baptist schools begun by American missionaries like her and Lillybridge continued to be prominent centers for education in Burma. Meanwhile, the British began to establish their own schools and to pressure Buddhist monastic schools and Burmese lay-run schools to teach Western subjects. Mason's work among the Karen and her founding of the Karen National Institute for Girls and the Karen Female Education Society advanced the Karen as a distinct minority group with a particular affinity for Christianity and potential for cooperation with British colonialism. As well known as it was in some circles of the British Raj's elite, Mason's mission to the Karen was still seen as marginal to Bamar society. Indeed, even by the end of the nineteenth century it was rare for Christian missionaries to make significant inroads into Bamar Buddhist communities. This is why the final Baptist woman and educator I will now consider was so extraordinary.

Marilla Baker Ingalls's Unconventional Schools

The schools we have considered so far in this chapter are not so different from those that children in Myanmar and the United States attend today.[47] They are buildings with classrooms of children and a teacher who uses books and globes and posters to instruct children in subjects such as geography, language, and mathematics. The teaching materials I will consider in this section, however, look very different. They are a life-sized cast-iron dog, a banyan tree decorated with bible illustrations, and a train car reading room. These are the unconventional objects that the American Baptist missionary Marilla Baker Ingalls animated for her lessons on comparative religions, the materials that earned this solo evangelist's reputation of being the most successful among Burmese Buddhists.

Ingalls, or *Sayama* ("female teacher"), as she was known to her students and acquaintances, lived and worked in the southern town of Thonze from 1859 until her death in 1902. When she first arrived as a solitary missionary a couple of years after her missionary husband died, Thonze was a remote village. In 1877, the British laid the country's first rail line—the Irrawaddy Valley State Railway—through the village and quickly transformed it into a bustling station town only a few hours from Rangoon. Sir Dietrich Brandis, the renowned German tropical forester who worked with the British Imperial Forestry Service in Burma and elsewhere in colonial India, recalled how Ingalls responded to the arrival of the railway by creating "two circulating libraries, with their reading rooms well supplied with the latest literature."[48] Brandis remembered that she had "arranged for lectures to them, delivered by missionaries and others" and wrote that her circulating libraries "remain as monuments of her loving interest" in the "English and Eurasian station masters, guards, and other employees of the railway."[49] Brandis concluded that Ingalls was "greatly missed and mourned by the railway servants of Lower Burma."[50] Ingalls seems to have taken the new British railway and transformed it into a missionary machine with the same evangelical drive and creative approach that reshaped her Thonze mission into a popular center of powerful religious objects. That mission, however, did not focus on the growing locomotive colonial class. It focused instead on the local Buddhist community.

The most surprising of Ingalls's teaching materials was her enshrined dog statue, which, on festival days, would have hundreds of visitors (see figure 2.3). Even on regular days, the dog was bound to attract at least a few passersby who had come to see the strange creature at the edge of the American religious woman's land. The way Ingalls told it, the life-size dog statue would gather people around it because it seemed, at first glance, to be real. The missionary would stand by as new visitors recoiled in fear or approached the dog to offer food. When they got close enough to see that it was made of cast iron, they would ask Ingalls why she kept the dog. This was when the Baptist missionary would launch into a lesson on the irrationality of idol

FIGURE 2.3 Ingalls's dog statue in 1896. Photograph from the *Baptist Missionary Magazine*.

worship. Just as her dog statue could not chase away thieves, Ingalls argued, lifeless Buddha statues could not help devotees who came to the statues with prayers and offerings.⁵¹

She called the dog her "dumb teacher," because, she said, it wordlessly instructed countless Burmese visitors on the uselessness of venerating images. Dogs in Burma, especially compared to their U.S. counterparts, tend to have a low status. The Burmese term for "dog," *hkway*, often has a derogatory connotation. Ingalls—well known for her excellent Burmese-language skills and her extensive understanding of local cultures—was well aware of this. As she put it, "The name of 'dog' is a little offensive to the Burmans," so she was careful to "qualify and explain the comparisons" she made between her dog and the Buddha.⁵²

Ingalls's writings about her dog statue can read like other chauvinist evangelical treaties that venerate Christian missions and ridicule other religious practices. Several of the missionary accounts of Burmese pagodas I will examine in the next chapter feature a similar plot of a bold and clever Christian exposing object worship as ignorant idolatry. However, in the context of Ingalls's unique Burmese mission, a more complex story emerges. Her teaching aides tell of the power of multiple kinds of religious objects to attract attention and excite activity in nineteenth-century Burma. While Ingalls presented the dog statue as a device to demonstrate the powerlessness of idols, her writing also reveals how local image practices became a part of her missionary work, transforming it from aniconic, text-based evangelism to religious activity centered on venerated objects. While Ingalls may have intended for her dog to teach people to stop worshipping false gods, the dog seems to have joined a Burmese pantheon.

Ingalls's most detailed account of her famous dog is "My Dumb Teacher," an essay she published in the May 1896 issue of the *Baptist Missionary Magazine*. This was a decade after the British won the Third Anglo-Burmese War and colonized the entire country. While Ingalls still worked as a solitary missionary for the American Baptist Missionary Union, she also made connections to important British officials (like Brandis) who likely facilitated her work and saw it as supporting their colonial occupation. In "My Dumb Teacher," Ingalls writes about a day when she was at her home in Thonze and heard a half-dozen people approaching her dog outside. She recognized one of the men, so she invited the group onto her land. As they got closer to the dog, they exclaimed, "He haw!" The woman "seemed timid," so Ingalls told her, "Though he is chained up to that post, give him something to eat and he will not harm you." Then, the woman, who was carrying a tray of dried meat and vegetables, "walked up and put down the tray at the feet of the dog, but then she crouched back and looked up into the face of the dog and saw that it was a dumb image and picked up her tray." The Burmese visitors asked why the dog was there, and it was at this point that Ingalls "put questions to them" about the power of statues. Here is her catechism:

> "Is he not here to guard me from thieves and dacoits, and help me in various ways?"
>
> "But he cannot do anything," they replied.
>
> "Don't deride my American dog," I continued. "See, he has ears and eyes and feet," and then we got up and peered into those ears and eyes. It all came back to me. They smote upon their breasts a little and put up their hands to me in a respectful attitude.
>
> "We do not like to dispute the great teacheress but it is impossible for this dumb image to hear you or see you, or do anything for you." . . .
>
> "I am only following out your customs if I trust in a dumb image, and you are right. It cannot hear me when I ask for protection and it cannot guard me while I sleep."
>
> "Ah! That is good," said the man, "your words are now true and wise and good."

I continued "It cannot do anything for you or any other person," and then I told them that I had brought it here to show up their false customs of making an idol, calling it a god, and trusting in it for help. They said their god was consecrated, but I told them it was not changed in power after it came from the maker's hand, and that my old dog passed through a fire-consecration when he was made, but he had no life or power."[53]

This episode likely amused many readers of the *Baptist Missionary Magazine*. The anecdote depicts unnamed Asian individuals being tricked into thinking a cast-iron dog is real. Readers also might have delighted in the image of Ingalls craftily suggesting the protective power of the dog, thereby putting her visitors in the position of explaining that a statue cannot hear commands or chase away thieves. From this point of view, Ingalls cleverly got the Buddhists to make the very argument that Christian missionaries were making against treating Buddha statues as though they were living beings able to respond to prayers.

Another point of view, however, is glimpsed by the story's inclusion of the visitors' explanation of the difference between her dog statue and their enshrined Buddhas. The visitors told Ingalls that their statues were consecrated, by which they meant that a Buddhist monk or group of monks had empowered their Buddha statues through a special ritual. Kate Crosby argues that a consecrated statue "is empowered not through the Buddha himself being immanent in the statue, but through a process of empowerment, in which the Buddha's powers are transmitted into the statue."[54] Crosby's argument allows for an adherence to the doctrines about the Buddha's absence from this world that I outlined in the introduction to this book while allowing for Buddha statues to possess the powers of the Buddha. Surely not all disciples have made this fine distinction between the presence of the Buddha and the presence of his powers. As Donald Swearer explores in his book-length study of image consecration, *Becoming the Buddha*, there is a long-standing practice in Theravada Buddhism in which Buddha images are able to make the Buddha himself present. Swearer argues that consecrated images of the Buddha "mediate the universal and the particular to the lives of individuals for whom the Buddha is not just a distant ideal but a present refuge, protector, and grantor of boons."[55] The Burmese Buddhists whom Ingalls invites to her property try to explain to her the particular power consecration has to transform mundane, man-made sculptures into extraordinary representations of the Buddha with the ability to act in the world on their behalf. Ingalls tries to repudiate this by describing the welding process that made her dog statue as a "fire consecration" and then asserting that this "consecration" still did not grant the statue power or life. Her Burmese visitors, though, do not accept her equation between her dog statue and their consecrated Buddha statues.

This account suggests that there is more going on in their way of approaching the dog than a simple mistake. Specifically, it raises the question of why the woman might have gone to place dried meat and vegetables in front of the dog in the first place and then decided against it. Ingalls suggested that the Burmese woman really believed her statue was a living, breathing, dangerous dog that she could pacify with something to eat. But then, when she got close enough to see it was made out of cast iron instead of flesh and bones, she knew it would be pointless to feed it. But what if the woman knew that the dog was metal the whole time? What if she was not so easily fooled into thinking that a dog statue was a real dog? In that case, what would be the point of offering real food to a dog statue? Ingalls's typical American reader may not have understood this as anything besides superstition, but those with knowledge of Burmese culture would have immediately recognized this action as a common ritual.

Throughout Southeast Asia, Buddhist statues and shrines to local spirits attract edible offerings. In Burma, it is an especially common tradition to present food to the local spirits known as *nats* because they are understood to cause mayhem when upset. Nats are said to do things like flood a village's crops if its villagers fail to show signs of respect as they pass the nats' abode.[56] Regular offerings of food and signs of respect are meant to pacify nats and coax them into helping their devotees by doing things like bringing about good fortune or curing an illness. Even putting to the side questions of how much these Burmese people really believed in spirits, it is still clear that their community had a tradition of presenting food to images and objects recognized as special.[57]

Returning now to the Burmese woman's behavior in front of the dog statue, I want to consider a scenario in which she goes to present food because she thinks it is a kind of nat shrine. In this mindset, the woman sees a statue at the edge of the land belonging to a religious leader and determines that she should make an offering there as she would at other sacred shrines. But, once she gets close enough to see that the statue does not have other food offerings in front of it, she realizes that it is not sacred and therefore not fit for an act of sacrifice.

Unlike Anglo-American readers who had not traveled to Asia, Ingalls would have been quite familiar with this scenario of a person offering food to a statue. Ingalls surely wanted those readers to picture her revealing that Buddha statues are just as powerless as a metal dog and convincing Burmese people to stop worshipping them and become followers of Jesus Christ. What else might she have been conveying to her visitors? Was Ingalls not also positioning her dog as a material connection to immaterial, sacred power? By resembling Burmese shrines and being said to have gone through a fire consecration, was the Baptist's dog proving idols powerless, or was it taking on the power of an idol?

What was the result of this religious mimicry? Ingalls wanted to say that it ultimately led to Burmese people abandoning idol worship and converting to Christianity. She wrote that "God, the living God, is able to use various means to bring light to his creatures." Here she suggested that she was serving this God by means of the dog statue. In this kind of ends-sanctify-the-means argument, Ingalls presented her unconventional evangelical work as eventually resulting in Christian conversion. Indeed, her essay features a follow-up scene in which the man from the group returns to Ingalls's property to "show up the dog and convince his other friends of the folly of idol-god worship." Ingalls reported that the man told her "that he and the other couple had never gone to the idol-god since that day." Ingalls was clearly suggesting that the Christian teachings she gave with the aid of her dog statue eventually led people to abandon idol worship. But then she adds that the man described as trying to persuade his friends of the foolishness of image veneration accepted a few theological leaflets from Ingalls and then made a telling exclamation: "That has done more for me than these kinds of books!" Ingalls replied to the man's praise for the dog statue by inviting him back to "get lessons from the dumb teacher." The man said he would accept her invitation and stated that "at the great festival last year I heard the dog had over three hundred visitors, men, women, and children." Ingalls told her readers: "This was true; on great occasions, many of the district people come in to look at him, and there is not a day but what he has some visitors."[58]

In the end, the man seemed most impressed with the hundreds of people who came out to visit the dog. It was the dog's power to attract visitors that helped win him over. This dumb teacher was not Ingalls's only attraction: an adorned tree on her property also taught Christian lessons and demonstrated the material ways Baptist Christianity transformed when it took root in Burmese soil (see figure 2.4). Ingalls called it her "great sign tree." It was a massive banyan on the missionary's property in Thonze. Tacked all around its wide, ropey trunk were biblical illustrations, one featuring a tall, bearded Jesus standing next to his disciples in bright white robes. Alongside these Christian visual aids, Ingalls hung other images, including advertisements for American medicines and portraits of Queen Victoria. Passersby, noticing the adorned tree, would approach it to find a black-and-white photograph of that empress whose realm was eclipsing Burma's. The Christian queen was portrayed in profile, wearing a voluminous gown, medals of honor, a white lace veil, and a miniature diamond crown. Next to her was a Burmese translation of John 3:16: "For God so loved the world, that he gave his only begotten Son, that whosoever believeth in him should not perish, but have everlasting life." This pairing of monarchy and religion would not have surprised Thonze villagers who lived in or remembered a time when a Konbaung king ruled their land under the banner of Buddhism. Before Ingalls's sign tree showcased biblical quotations about everlasting life and Christian imagery, it was revered for the great spirits who were said to live in its branches.

Locals coming to pay homage to it explained to the Baptist that "this tree was more than a hundred years old; that the great nats (spirits) had their headquarters up in the tree, and if they did not revere them and present offerings, they would send great calamity upon them." This banyan tree, like so many trees, rivers, and rocks throughout the country, was treated as an abode of spirits and a special place to propitiate them. According to Ingalls's 1897 essay entitled "Our Great Sign Tree" and featuring a photograph of the banyan, the Burmese people who approached the tree had always "taken off their sandals, closed their umbrellas, and had their heads bowed down in the attitude of Buddhist worshipers." It was not only their bared feet and respectful postures that signaled to Ingalls that they treated the tree as a sacred object; they also "emptied their trays of rice under the tree," making the kinds of offerings Ingalls had seen in front of spirit shrines.[59] By examining the origin story she tells in "Our Great Sign Tree" and then investigating particular signs she featured on the tree's trunk, I will consider how the shrine might have attracted Burmese people to the Baptist mission because it was adorned as a conduit to the divine powers of a foreign god. In addition,

FIGURE 2.4 Ingall's sign tree in 1897. Photograph from the *Baptist Missionary Magazine*.

I will reflect on how much of Ingalls's appeal as a religious teacher may have come from her possession of special objects.

Ingalls's encounters with the tree and its worshippers started with her using it to wager theological arguments for Christianity. Ingalls wrote how she "began to tell them about the holy and good God who created the tree, when [she] heard 'Ahem!' and 'Ahem!'" She was interrupted by the Buddhist monk who ran the adjacent monastery. He was old and blind, but aware enough to notice Ingalls at the base of the banyan tree, talking to local people about Jesus Christ. The very name of this foreign god was "an offence to his ear," she explained, and caused a "scorn on his face." But "Our Great Sign Tree" depicts how the bold evangelist Ingalls followed the disapproving monk back into his monastery. Ingalls wanted to assure him that she was a friend, so she reached in her bag for a gift. All she had were her smelling salts. She gave them to the monk, which he sniffed until tears came to his eyes, and he asked if the salts might be able to cure his blindness. Ingalls explained that she "cannot do what Jesus Christ did while he was here on earth."[60] The monk was not interested in hearing about Christ, so she told him instead about her grandfather who had gone blind in old age.

Ingalls vividly described how her grandfather would find pleasure through his working senses by petting his dog and cat, playing with his grandchildren, eating sweet apples, walking among singing birds. Into this scene of sensory pleasure, Ingalls incorporated Christian teachings. She added that she read to her grandfather "out of a good book which had a gold edge and beautiful pictures," which seems like an intentional invocation of the Kammavāca manuscripts analyzed in the previous chapter.[61] The monk asked about the words in the adorned book, so Ingalls made a deal with him: if he would stop handling his Buddhist prayer beads, she would tell him. The monk agreed, and Ingalls proceeded to recite Romans 5:7–8: "For scarcely for a righteous man will one die, yet peradventure for a good man some would even dare to die. But God commendeth his love toward us in that while we were yet sinners Christ died for us." First she spoke the verse about her foreign god dying for poor wrongdoers in Pali and then in Burmese. Ingalls wrote that the monk "was too proud to say he liked to hear the text," but as she continued to visit him over the course of the year he would ask her "to 'repeat [her] Pali,' and would then add, and 'now the Burmese.'"[62]

Although this monk enjoyed hearing her recite Christian scripture both in Burma's sacred Buddhist language and in the common vernacular, he never became one of Ingalls's converts. Ingalls wrote that she "had no evidence that he felt that he was a sinner. He was a Buddhist priest, and rested on that." Ingalls may not have gotten him to think of himself as a man in need of Christian salvation, but she did earn his affection. Her visits to the monk and his spirit tree continued until the elderly monk's remaining senses finally gave way and he prepared to die. She wrote that "as he knew the Christians needed a better ground for [her] house, he called up witnesses and made his monastery and place over to [her] . . . the head man of [their] village came and planted the flags at the four corners, and this was how [she] came into possession of this tree and the land for [their] chapel and mission house."[63] Like her dog article, Ingalls's tree essay offers glimpses of the strange religious transformations happening in Thonze. Two of these glimpses are particularly illuminating: Ingalls's gift to the monk, and the medicinal advertisements her tree showcased.

I want to reconsider the exchange about the smelling salts. Ingalls may have wanted to caricature the Buddhist monk as naive by including his question about curing blindness with a pungent substance used for far simpler conditions like faintness. But why else might this monk think that Ingalls would have a powerful medicine in her bag? Did Ingalls have a reputation as a purveyor of curative substances? Ingalls took care to add that she told the monk that she could not do what Jesus had done; she surely did not want her readers to think she was going around Burma claiming the ability to cure blindness. Yet her writings do depict her telling Christian miracles stories and charming people with her foreign ways and adventurous spirit.

There is evidence that Ingalls used other medicines in this way: to bring people physical relief and to attract them to Christian evangelism. She even hung advertisements for the specific medicines that missionaries would hand out alongside Christian texts. She wrote how the trunk of her banyan tree featured "the bright, flashing notice of the Perry Davis Pain Killer, and . . . the more modern one of Dr. Jaynes' medicines. They are a blessing to Burma, and go packed off with our Bible and tracts."[64] Both Perry Davis's Pain Killer and the medicines of Dr. Jayne would have been familiar to Ingalls's readers, as they were popular remedies in North America. Dr. Jayne brand medicines were common treatments for a range of conditions from tapeworm and goiters to coughs and bruises. Even more popular, especially in Ingalls's mission, was Perry Davis's cure-all drug boldly called "Pain Killer."

Pain Killer was an analgesic made with opiates and ethyl alcohol. The medicine was common in North American pharmacies and homes as well as with American foreign mission movements in the mid and late nineteenth century. Pain Killer had multiple print ads, including text-only ones that ran in the *Baptist Missionary Magazine* declaring it "The Most Popular Medicine Extant."[65] Among the most popular of the medicine's illustrated advertisements at the time of Ingalls's sign tree—and the one that seems to match Ingalls' description of it as "bright" and "flashing"—was an advertisement that showed a fleet of six fair-skinned cherubs carrying a brown glass medicine bottle over the globe. The largest ad copy reads "Joy to the World" above smaller type branding it "Perry Davis' Vegetable Pain Killer." The message is obvious: this medicine from Providence, Rhode Island (the only place marked on the map), delivers heavenly relief the world over. We also find a similar visual in a common advertisement for Dr. Jayne's medicines in which a porcelain-skinned boy angel carrying a white lily leans through a window into an advertisement for "The Best Blood Purifier for Scrofula, Cancer, Epilepsy, Dropsy, Skin and Liver Diseases." Plump baby angels were a visual trope in nineteenth-century medicinal advertisements in the United States, but what could these images have signaled to a Burmese audience?

I would like to suggest that the figures on the medicine advertisements appeared to Burmese visitors as a kind of foreign nat or deva. Celestial spirits with wings are common in Burmese religious imagery, and Ingalls was certainly familiar them. It is possible, then, that she intentionally made the visual connection between the cherubs and the nats that the Burmese told her had resided in the venerable banyan tree. Ingalls's shrine tree, her professed connection to a foreign god, and her possession of powerful medicine may have positioned her as a kind of holy woman with extraordinary powers. This is just conjecture, as I have not found any evidence of local people describing her posters in terms of spirits or gods or of them explicitly saying that Ingalls wielded magical objects. There is, however, one interesting comment attributed to a Burmese woman that connects Pain Killer to the images on Ingalls's tree. In an 1877 essay, "A Morning at Thongzai," Ingalls strung together a series of vignettes showing various people discussing religion with the missionary. In one vignette, a woman approaches Ingalls to ask, "Have you any Pain Killer? My boy has cut his foot; your medicine once cured my brother in two days so that he went about his work. I came for this, but I want to see those big pictures. The women who came the other day say they understand your doctrines much better since they saw Jesus and the man out of the grave, and those blind and deaf people."[66] The Burmese woman's point here about visuals being more effective than doctrine echoes the argument made in Ingalls's dog shrine article by the man who said that the dog had done more for him than all of the texts he had received from the missionaries. By publishing two stories in which Burmese characters state that images are more persuasive than doctrine, Ingalls showed her readers how valuable her religious objects were. To be sure, her cast-iron dog and her decorated banyan tree might have seemed like strange—perhaps even irreverent—gateways into the Baptist mission, but Ingalls signaled that she had ingeniously used these objects to bring the Burmese to God. Harder to determine, though, is what all of this objects-based evangelism meant for the Burmese who visited the mission and for those who joined its Christian community.

What is clear is that Ingalls's sign tree, just like her dog statue, developed a reputation in the local community, attracting people to gather at the mission station. These material and visual religious objects animated her

Christian community, making it known as a site of more converted Burmese Buddhist monks than any other Baptist mission station in the country. Certainly, Ingalls's ebullient personality and extraordinary commitment to her Burmese community were partially responsible for the expansion of Thonze's Christian population; her writings beg alternative readings for her success, however. They suggest that her famous dog and decorated tree were even more powerful than her particular gifts of personality.

Ingalls, Mason, and Lillybridge were extraordinary women with distinct talents and biographies. Considered together, however, they tell of how American missionaries were most successful when they embraced the power of religious objects in Burma. Ingalls teamed up with her dog and her nat tree. Mason discovered God's language woven into Karen textiles. And Lillybridge filled her Burmese-language schools with new globes and maps of rapidly changing lands.

Women at Pagan

Attention to the role of women in education in Burma was, of course, not limited to Christian institutions. Bamar Buddhist women in the nineteenth century garnered international attention for their reading and writing skills. As Burma specialists have shown, in the British colonial period and later Burmese and British authorities exaggerated Burmese women's status as part of their efforts to promote political agendas such as the characterization of Burma as superior to its neighboring Asian countries.[67] What scholarship has revealed less about is how Konbaung patriarchies presented women's education as a part of their performance of the power and virtue of their realm. In the remainder of this chapter, I will explore a section of *Sāsanavaṃsa*, the 1861 royal Buddhist chronicle commissioned by King Mindon. In this section, the author, the royal monastic tutor Paññasāmi, narrates a series of amusing stories of smart women in the medieval Burmese kingdom of Pagan besting those around them—even monks—with their sophisticated mastery of elaborate Pali grammar.[68] I will propose that this unusual piece of Paññasāmi's chronicle offers a glimpse into a reimagined Buddhist world in which kings and monks promote Buddhist education to such a dramatic extent that even low-ranking and young women are masters of the linguistic complexities of the sāsana's canonical language. While these highly educated women are figments of the text's imagination rather than historical figures, they are still akin to the women described in the letters and publications examined earlier in this chapter. All of these nineteenth-century texts from Burma feature female educators and pupils in the stories they tell about religious power. For the female innovators Lydia Lillybridge, Ellen Mason, and Marilla Ingalls, education was the key to the Baptist conversion of Buddhist Burma. For the *Sāsanavaṃsa*, highly educated Burmese women are an amusing depiction of the Buddhist authority and success of the Konbaung kingdom.

While there is a relatively long tradition in Buddhist studies of scholars looking to the *Sāsanavaṃsa* for insights into Burmese Buddhist doctrine, practice, and history—starting with Mabel Haynes Bode (1864–1922), who published a critical edition of the *Sāsanavaṃsa* in 1897 that is still used by scholars today—there has not been an academic study of this hallmark text's atypical section on women.[69] As Michael Charney has written, the English translation that non-Pali-reading scholars working in Anglophone institutions use, Bimla Churn Law's 1952 work, "is frequently poor," as it is peppered with "grammatical errors, contradictions, and the like."[70] This may be part of the reason that even after Victor Lieberman published "A New Look at the *Sasanvamsa*" in 1976 and noted that this section on women was one of the very few elements that Paññasāmi added to what was largely a Pali translation of the 1831 Burmese-language text *Tha-thana-wun-tha sa-dan thathana-lin-ga-ya kyan*, scholars have not revisited this section to explore its enigmatic inclusion. To grasp its meaning, one must have a precise understanding of the Pali syntax that the female characters command, and Law's translation of its Pali-language lessons contains confusing mistakes. I will therefore work from the original Pali to parse how the text manifests female characters as part of the larger story it tells about the glorious history of Buddhism in Burma.

The lack of attention to this new section on women is particularly surprising when we consider just how anomalous it is: Lieberman revealed that of the *Sāsanavaṃsa*'s thirty-five sections, only four of them present new material: the preface, the introductory overview of the Buddha's career, the section that gives the history of the sāsana since the Burmese 1831 text, and this odd section on women.[71] As for the other thirty-one sections, twenty-seven are edited translations of the 1831 Burmese-language text, and four are based on the *Samantapāsādikā* (a collection of fifth-century commentaries on the Vinaya Piṭaka of the Pali Canon compiled in Lanka by

Buddhaghosa, the famous Buddhist scholar who wrote definitive interpretations of the scriptures); the *Mahāvaṃsa* (the chronicle of Lanka that gives a history of the sāsana and the dynasties that supported it); and Thai or Sinhalese sources.[72] It is obvious why Paññasāmi would add new introductory material to his translation of the Burmese text as well as a section on what has happened between the 1831 publication of that Burmese text and his completion of the translation in 1860. It also makes sense that he would add a few sections on monastic institutions and the geographic spread of the sāsana based on authoritative Pali commentarial and chronicle texts, given that Paññasāmi composed this text explicitly for an international monastic audience (as I will elaborate below, he wrote for a Sinhalese delegation). This leaves only the section on women without an easily discernible rationale for its addition. With this section's curious scenes—of a mother correcting her twelve-year-old daughter's Pali declension paradigms, a maid accidentally seeing her boss's penis, and a young girl shaming a monk for incorrectly using a first-person pronoun with the third-person verb termination—I cannot help but ask: Why? Why add these uncommon female characters when the text is otherwise not interested in incorporating new material?

I cannot know Paññasāmi's mind and do not have the evidence to know for sure whether this text is entirely original. It seems more likely that this well-educated monastic author derived it from some now lost text or oral tradition of monastic teachers using these kinds of funny stories about women to help teach their Pali pupils tricky grammatical rules. I can, however, look to the section itself and to the political and cultural contexts surrounding its publication to understand the implications of inserting the smart women it showcases into the larger religious imagination of the *Sāsanavaṃsa* and mid-nineteenth-century Burma more broadly. This way, I can show how these smart women, by virtue of being expected to be less educated than the monks and lay men around them, portray the Burmese realm as having reached unprecedented heights of Buddhist excellence.

You will notice that I am switching genres here. The other women I have considered in this chapter were actual, historical women who mobilized powerful objects as part of their educational and religious work. I studied their personal letters and published writings to ask questions of both history—about what really happened where they taught—and about the roles they cast for women in imagined Protestant religious worlds. In the following analysis of Paññasāmi's Buddhist chronicle, I will not ground the women he sketches in some factual time and place in the kingdom of Pagan; there is simply no evidence that these stories are based on real women from a millennium ago. What I can do, though, is read them as characters that Paññasāmi animates to tell a bigger story about how the Buddha's teachings have come to flourish most superbly in Burma. I will ask how, then, gender and education in this scene relate to Paññasāmi's efforts to celebrate the Konbaung kingdom: What else can the literary features of this section reveal about how Paññasāmi and his community of readers imagined the relationships between women, the Buddhist tradition, and the Burmese empire?

As I noted in the previous chapter, this royally sponsored text is clearly committed to celebrating Burma and its king as housing a kind of peak Buddhism. Paññasāmi directs his audience to understand the chronicle as relating a lineage of rulers whose sponsorship made Buddhism blossom. Furthermore, they are to recognize that the contemporary Burmese king, Mindon Min, is the living embodiment of this royal tradition. Thus, what began in India with Ashoka, the archetypal Buddhist king, and then continued in Lanka's great royal patrons, now continues in Burma. With Lanka then kingless—the British deposed the island's last king and royal patron of Buddhism, Sri Vikram Rajasinha, when they took over Ceylon in 1815—the Burmese court sought to promote itself as the one true Buddhist kingdom. They make no mention of King Mongkut reigning in the neighboring Buddhist kingdom of Siam, a silence that seems to promote Burma as *the* kingdom upholding the sāsana. This political agenda helps explain why Paññasāmi would add a section on Burmese women who have mastered Pali: by showing that even women excel at this Buddhist subject, Paññasāmi implies that the kingdom has the most excellent understanding of the Buddha's teachings.

Indeed, there is clear religious imperialism alongside evocative writing in Paññasāmi's project. The very reason he composed it was to create a text in the international Buddhist language of Pali to impress a visiting delegation of high-ranking Sinhalese monks with the state of Buddhism in Burma. This delegation arrived in King Mindon's royal city of Mandalay on February 24, 1861, and was headed by the monk Ambagahavatte Saranamkara, who would go on a few years later to establish the Rāmañña Nikāya, one of the three major Buddhist monastic orders in Sri Lanka in the late nineteenth century and throughout the twentieth century before it unified with the

Amarapura Nikaya in 2019 to form the largest monastic order in Sri Lanka, the Amarapura-Rāmañña Nikāya. Ambagahavatte had heard about the impressive state of Burmese Buddhism and decided to travel there with other monks from the Amarapura fraternity. Their year-long itinerary in the company of Burmese preceptors included a ritual renewal of the senior monks' higher ordination and a higher ordination for the novice monks who accompanied them. These ordinations happened at the famous Kalyani sima in Rāmañña and granted the Sinhalese monks authoritative ties to the Rāmañña order.[73]

In his introduction, Paññasāmi explains that this delegation's visit is his reason for composing the *Sāsanavaṃsa*: "At the request of the monks who have come to a foreign land from the island of Sihala, I will compose the *Sāsanavaṃsappadipika*."[74] It was surely not simply that the Sinhalese monks were interested in Burmese Buddhism. Paññasāmi and other monastic elites—as well as their royal sponsors—had their own interests in Sinhalese developments as well as in Sinhalese opinions about the Konbaung realm; the two Buddhist lands have an extensive history of religious interaction and competition. Furthermore, as Anne Blackburn explains, "the nineteenth century was a period of intense communication among Buddhist monks in Lanka, Burma, and Siam, as they sought to address intellectual, political, and institutional challenges to Buddhism linked to French and British colonial projects in the region." Blackburn illustrates how nineteenth-century monks in these three countries often celebrated unbroken Buddhist connections in the Indian Ocean region in a manner that emphasized continuities with the era of the third-century BCE King Asoka." Blackburn adds that "scholars of Buddhism and historians of the region have lately begun to forge a more detailed and temporally sensitive account of Buddhist mobility and religiocultural exchange and influence across South and Southeast Asian lands."[75] In Pali vamsa literature at large, Lanka had been held up as the second most important place in the history of Buddhism after the region of the Buddha's birth and career because the island is credited with fostering, purifying, and promoting the sāsana in the crucial period after it first began to decline in India. Burma had long looked to Lanka with both veneration and a kind of jealousy. Hema Goonatilake writes that rulers of Southeast Asia were long attracted to Lanka "as being not only the foremost center of Buddhism, but also the country that possessed two of the most famous relics of the Buddha, the sacred Tooth Relic and the Alms Bowl.... The highest ambition of the Pagan kings was to possess the sacred Tooth relic of the Buddha."[76] The *Sāsanavaṃsa*, therefore, works to assert that it is now Burma, not Lanka, that houses the most pure and glorious form of the Buddha's teachings.

In this context, the new section on women in Pagan who show off their advanced Pali education illustrates the Burmese kingdom as working to promote itself to a Sinhalese audience as so devoted to the *sāsana* that even second-class citizens are masters of the complex, ancient Buddhist language. "Second-class citizens" may sound like anachronistic or overly reductionist, but it is fitting here given that the Buddhist scriptures firmly established a Buddhist society as made up of four sections, with male monastics at the top and female monastics below them, followed by laymen and then laywomen. The earliest texts feature the Buddha initially refusing to admit women into the monastic order, and they explain that he finally agreed as long as they followed extra codes of conduct, including a requirement to get permission from a father or husband to be ordained (male monastics did not need any such patriarchal approval) and an agreement to always be ranked below male monastics, no matter how junior the male monastic and how senior the female monastic. Moreover, the earliest teachings established that buddhas are always male; a woman must first be reborn into a male body before they can attain the supreme state of a buddha. Despite this structural sexism, the Buddhist tradition is filled with stories celebrating the accomplishments of monastic and laywomen on the Buddhist path, and the *Sāsanavaṃsa*'s section on women builds on that more general understanding that women can accomplish celebrated feats such as study of the Buddha's complex teachings, extraordinary acts of generosity, and enlightenment.

In addition to being a part of a larger Buddhist literary tradition of narrating the accomplishments of women in order to honor the Buddha's teachings more generally, this section of the *Sāsanavaṃsa* is related to a family of Indian-language texts finding humor in women shaming men with their superior knowledge of grammar. For example, in the famous eleventh-century Sanskrit story collection the *Kathāsaritsāgara* (*Ocean of the Streams of Story*), when a queen tells her king to not splash her with water, he orders sweets to the lake where they are frolicking and throws those sweets at the servants. The queen breaks out in laughter over his mistake: he incorrectly parsed the phrase "*modakais sincaya*" to mean "throw sweets (*modaka*) when she was actually saying "do not (*mā*) throw water (*udaka*)." The joke is on the king who did not know the fundamental sound change (*sandhi*) rule for compound words by which the long "a" at the end of the term for "do not" combines with the "u" at the start of the word for water to make an "o" sound. A key part of this humor is that it is a woman with superior knowledge of Sanskrit grammar who humiliates the king.[77] As I will now show, the stories of women in the *Sāsanavaṃsa* use the same general formula as this story from the *Kathāsaritsāgara*: a man who does not get a specific grammar rule for a classical Indian language is humiliated by a woman who has mastered that rule to humorous effect.

I will now look closely at the *Sāsanavaṃsa*'s conspicuous section on women. The section narrates three amusing vignettes featuring women demonstrating their impressive Pali study, memorization, and recitation practices. In all three stories, laywomen surprise men with their technical mastery of the syntax of the complex Middle Indo-Aryan language. I will detail the language rules they illustrate in order to convey the pedagogical lesson at the center of each vignette; I will also try to point out the characterization and wordplay that make them comical. (As is always the case when trying to explaining a joke, this is sure to make it less funny.) With an examination of its content and tone, I will show that this section uses female figures to amuse readers with inside-Pali puns and make a kind of claim that classical Buddhist education reached unseen before heights in the Burmese kingdom of Pagan.

The section begins with the assertion that there was a past time in Pagan (named "Arimaddana" in the text) when even women trained in classical and liturgical Pali literature (P. *mātugāmāpi gantham ugganhiṃsu*). There were so many Pali-educated women that they would regularly run into each other and start to brag about what texts they were studying and reciting from memory. The introduction to this section gives the example of women who would compete with each other by asking: "How much of the text do you study? How much of the text do you recite?" One woman replies to these questions by explaining that "nowadays because my young sons are such an obstacle, I have become distracted, and I can't recite too many texts, so of the entire *Paṭṭhāna*, I only recite the [section known as the] 'Kusalattika.'" This passage not only features the universally familiar image of the distracted mother of young children but also surprises us to show how even a busy laywoman is able to recite from memory the "Kusalattika," "The Triad

THE SCHOOL

of the Wholesome," a text that comes from the Abhidhamma, the most scholastic part of the Pali Canon.[78]

The first story begins with a twelve-year-old girl who asks a monk on alms rounds why he has chosen for his name something with a feminine ending. Pali nouns are gendered, and the monk's name is Khemā, which has a long *ā* at the end—a normally feminine ending. The girl finds it odd that any man would have a feminine noun as his name. Her mother is quick to point out that the girl is mistaken; some masculine nouns also have a long *ā* at the end. The monk has taken such a name; the long *ā* is not a feminine ending here. The mother reminds her that there is a whole class of masculine nouns that have a long *ā*; these nouns decline like the word for "king," *rājā* (*rājagaṇa*) which ends in a long *ā* but is nonetheless a masculine noun. The daughter, not to be defeated, retorts that the word *khemā* does not belong to this group. The mother replies that sometimes it does. Paññasāmi explains what lies behind their thinking. The daughter is thinking that words like *rājā* never appear with a short *a* except when they are in a compound, like the compound *devarāja*, "king of the gods." But when *khema* is alone and not in a compound it functions like an adjective and takes on the gender of the noun to which it refers. Sometimes it is masculine, *khema*, sometimes it is feminine, *khemā*, and it can even be neuter, *khemam*. Therefore, she thinks, the word *khema* does not behave like the word *rājā*. For her part, the mother reasons that the daughter is right in that the word *khema* can appear in all three genders—masculine, feminine, and neuter—corresponding to the gender of the noun that it modifies. But, when it is used as a name, by itself and not in compound, it is masculine and has a long *ā* at the end. And so at times it also behaves as if it belongs to the group of nouns like *rājā*. Since the mother is given the last word, I assume that she has won this erudite argument.

The second vignette takes the section to a more ribald level. It begins with a landlord bathing on the top floor of his home, having a kind of heatstroke, and then sitting down. A maid doing chores below stands up and sees the landlord's "hidden place" (P. *guyhaṭṭhāna*). When the landlord realizes that this has happened, he composes the Pali phrase *sākhaṃ olokesi* as a kind of riddle for his children to interpret. First, he asks his son what it means and the son ventures that "*sākhaṃ* means 'the tree branch,' *olokesi* means 'looks up at.'" After the son's incorrect "saw the tree branch" guess, the landlord then gives the riddle to one of his daughters who says that "*sā* means 'dog,' *khaṃ* means 'the sky,' and *olokesi* means 'looked up at.'" Since "dog looked up at the sky" is also wrong, he then tries his other daughter, who correctly parses the phrase as "*sā* means 'woman,' *khaṃ* means 'the distinguishing member' (P. *aṅgajāta*), and *olokesi* means "having turned the face upwards, looked at." She gets the Pali joke: "The woman looked at the penis." In this vignette, the son's wrong answer is funny because he mistakes his father's penis for a tree branch; the first daughter's guess is funny because she mistakes their maid for a dog (part of the humor likely comes from a sexist and classist dehumanizing of the domestic servant). When the second daughter correctly solves the riddle, she not only provides a satisfying answer to the phrase puzzle but she also delights the reader by being the unlikely star Pali student.[79]

In the third and final story in the section, a novice monk makes a trip to Pagan to investigate its reputation for having women who possess great wisdom in the science of grammar (P. *saddanaya*). He meets a young woman who is watching over a cotton field and asks her for directions; he tells her that he has come from Ratnapura and that he is going to Pagan. The young girl then takes him to task for neglecting consideration of proper sentence composition, for using the first-person pronoun and the third-person aorist (past) verb termination. The novice thinks, "Even the impoverished young women guarding the fields and farms are masters of grammar, how much more so the rich older women?" (P. *khettavatthūni rakkhantī duggatā daharitthīpi tāva saddanayakovidā hoti, kimaṅgaṃ pana bhogasampannā mahallakitthiyoti*). Ashamed, he goes home. This last scene is less colorful than the first two, but it works to sum up the section's main point: like the men in the section humiliated before laywomen with impeccable Pali, Burma's beholders should acknowledge it as an impeccable model of an ideal Buddhist kingdom.[80]

Having looked closely at these stories, we can now see that they are comedic illustrations of Pali grammar lessons that do not try to make any serious, historical, or overtly political claims. They are more about the intricacies of Pali grammar than anything else. Unlike the material about Baptist educators that we examined earlier in this chapter, the women in this final text are unnamed sketches, characters. This thin characterization is part of the style of the *Sāsanavaṃsa*, and vamsa literature more generally. Yes, some characters in the *Sāsanavaṃsa* such as important kings and monks are named, but the nature of the text is to use short narratives to trace the Buddha's ecclesiastical lineage to Burma's current kingdom, pointing out instrumental kings, monasteries, and places along the way.

Considered in this context, Paññasāmi's smart female characters seem tailor made to impress the Pali-reading Sinhalese delegation with the state and history of Buddhism in this mainland Southeast Asian kingdom. When this particular monastic group was looking to reform their own lineages, Paññasāmi wanted to assure them that they had come to the right place: a model Buddhist realm.

* * *

This chapter has examined the roles that schools and women played in religious campaigns of nineteenth-century Burma. Over the course of the American Baptist mission, the country became increasingly interested in importing Western technologies such as steam power and the telegraph and learning the scientific disciplines behind those technologies. As the British occupied larger parts of the country, and the Burmese economy became more enmeshed with increasingly rich and powerful Western empires, the Burmese had ample materialist motivation to learn Western subjects. They also had more abstract, philosophical, and religious reasons to look through Western telescopes and consider Western theologies of salvation. Furthermore, Western education promoted both modern science in Burma as well as an idea of religious identity as an individual choice, a process any one person could go through in which they investigate for themselves different truths, gods, and systems of salvation. The Burmese, rather than being passive recipients of Western scientific knowledge and ideas about individual religious choice, actively engaged and challenged them.

The following chapter will consider how notions of conversion and idolatry analyzed in this chapter influenced changing attitudes toward icons and iconoclasm in Burma. I will show how the sensational object of the Burmese pagoda—the most prominent type of shrine—attracted Baptists to explore Buddhist liberation, and how it pressed them to articulate why, exactly, these popular sites were scenes of dangerous idolatry. These evangelical Christians found an unlikely ally in their campaign against pagodas: a Buddhist movement known as the Paramats. This mysterious movement engaged American Baptists in their criticism of Burmese Buddhism. Like the increasingly conspicuous Christians in their country, the Paramats took issue with the culture's focus on Buddha imagery. They argued that objects representing the Buddha were obstructing the way to the intangible goal of total freedom from this material world. For both religious minorities, holy objects were central to expressions of identity and transformation.

THREE

The Pagoda

Icons and Iconoclasm

READERS OF THE 1857 missionary travelogue *Ocean Sketches of Life in Burmah* by Marilla B. Ingalls (the "Teacheress" from the previous chapter) would first open the book to find two paired illustrations: "BURMAH AS IT WAS" and "BURMAH AS IT IS" (see figures 3.1 and 3.2). The "before" image of this before-and-after frontispiece shows a tall, narrow pagoda being worshipped by seven bowing people who are dwarfed by the large lion statues flanking the pagoda. In the background is a standard issue palm tree signaling to American and European audiences the exotic setting. "BURMAH AS IT IS"—the "after" image—shows an elevated public rest house (B. *zayat*) with an Anglo-American figure standing in one window, a group of darker figures sitting inside, and three men at the bottom of the stairs. Unlike the nondescript crouching Buddhist devotees in "BURMAH AS IT WAS," the standing figures in the foreground of "BURMAH AS IT IS" wear distinct clothing, which marks them as belonging to particular parts of Burmese society. This visual pair suggests a dramatic transformation in which popular Burmese Buddhist monuments and their devotees are cleared to make space for Christian evangelization. A bent idolatry gives way to an upright Christianity.

These prioritized prints, made from engravings by Van Incen-Snyder, show a missionary imagination of how Buddhism would give way to Christianity, a fantastic vision of Burma's religious landscape being made over by the American Baptist mission. They train a critical Western gaze onto a scene of object worship and then follow it with a cathartic image of Burma rid of

FIGURE 3.1 "BURMAH AS IT WAS," from *Ocean Sketches of Burmah*, 1857.

THE PAGODA

FIGURE 3.2 "BURMAH AS IT IS," from *Ocean Sketches of Burmah*, 1857.

idolatry. A specter of object worship was regularly conjured to illustrate the country's desperate need for Christian evangelism. As powerful as this visual trope was for raising funds for the Baptist mission, the work of actually destroying the power of pagodas and Buddha statues never took place. "BURMAH AS IT WAS" and "BURMAH AS IT IS" prove to be wishful thinking.

By the mid-nineteenth century, the American Baptist mission, watching pagodas being built and restored throughout the country, began to acknowledge its limited success among the Burmese Buddhist majority. In the late 1840s, only about half of the missionaries going to Burma were assigned to Burmese work, with the other half devoted to evangelism among ethnic minorities. This trend of reallocating resources away from the Bamar population continued into the twentieth century, with 30 percent of missionaries assigned to the Bamar in 1920 and only 10 percent in 1963.[1] While

American missionaries acknowledged their very limited success among the Bamar majority, they continued to hope that the dramatic political and societal change taking place in colonizing Burma would eventually create favorable conditions for spreading Christianity throughout the Southeast Asian country. In particular, Americans looked to the philosophical developments among the Buddhist group known as the Paramats for signs that Burmese Buddhism was cracking under the pressure of Christian teachings. The Paramat proponents that captured American missionary attention were reformist Buddhists who criticized pagoda worship and expressed a dedication to knowing the ultimate truth as taught in the *Abhidhamma*, the collection of teachings in the Pali Canon that provides a theoretical framework for the Buddhist path described in the other two collections: the collection of the Buddha's discourses (Sutta Piṭaka), and the collection of texts about the monastic community (Vinaya Piṭaka). The refusal of Paramats to worship at pagodas greatly impressed the Baptists, who, throughout the Burma mission, pointed to idol worship as Buddhism's most abhorrent practice. Furthermore, over the course of the nineteenth century, these missionaries began to see the Paramats' philosophy as a faith in God. This combination of seemingly Protestant practices and beliefs inspired American Baptist missionaries to argue that Christianity was finally making its way into Burmese hearts and minds.

This chapter pairs an investigation of the missionary fixation on Burmese pagodas with an exploration of the Paramat movement. I consider how both religious minority communities—the persecuted Buddhist reformers and the Baptists—invoked the country's popular Buddhist shrines in order to argue for the superiority of their iconoclastic doctrine. We see that pagodas and the Buddha statues they housed were central not only to the religious lives of mainstream Burmese communities but also to expressions of religious difference. As with the books and the teaching aides examined in the previous chapters, pagodas prove to be powerful objects that transformed the religious landscape of nineteenth-century Burma. Moreover, this chapter's study of the Paramats offers an illuminating analysis of previously unexplored archival evidence for this nonconformist development that has posed a something of mystery to the study of Burmese Buddhism. I will proceed by first analyzing the Baptist fixation on Burmese pagodas and what it tells us about how these shrines pressed visitors to sense and make sense of the Burmese Buddha. Then I will turn to the Paramats, to show how their positions on pagodas and Baptist statues was not an indication of their eventual Protestant conversion, as the missionaries hoped; it was the work of a Buddhist movement trying to religiously reform their country.

Pagodas as Powerful Idols in the Baptist Imagination

Long before American missionaries and British colonists arrived, Burma was famous for its countless towering pagodas.[2] For over a millennium, Burmese kings, monks, and lay people have built these monuments to honor the Buddha, dharma, and sangha. This architectural tradition traces back to the Buddha, who is said to have instructed his followers to cremate his body and to inter his relics in burial mounds that would celebrate his life and preserve his teachings, an instruction likely modeled on burial practices for ancient Indian kings. As I discussed in the introduction, the Theravada tradition describes four main types of pagodas (called *ceitya* in Pali and *zedi* in Burmese) that contain some of the Buddha's power (called *ānubhāva* in Pali): those that possess relics of the Buddha, those that possess items he used, those that possess scriptures (or are scriptures themselves), and those that possess consecrated objects like images of the Buddha. The rulers of Pagan were famously avid pagoda builders. This first kingdom founded by Bamar-speaking people built over two thousand Buddhist monuments in the thirteenth century alone, including pagodas and temples. Interred within these monuments were countless Buddha relics, images, and scriptures. For example, one extant epigraph in Pagan records that Lanka sent thirty corporal Buddha relics to Pagan in the late twelfth century.[3]

Accounts of Burma's pagoda-filled landscape had reached American shores in the late eighteenth century. George Boardman, a Baptist missionary to Burma, wrote in his journal in 1829 that, "before leaving America, [he] used to pray that pagodas might be converted into Christian churches."[4] For Boardman and other Americans, pagodas testified to the strength of Burma's idolatry and challenged evangelists to replace them with Christian monuments. Indeed, these public monuments became the principal embodied and hermeneutic site for the American Baptist mission's engagement with Buddhism.

The magnetism of the pagoda pulled missionaries toward powerful Buddhist objects, practices, and doctrines. These popular shrines and the

THE PAGODA

collective rituals that swirled around them forced missionaries into contact with the promise of ultimate freedom that Buddhism gave the Burmese. Baptists' particular physical reactions to pagodas and their accompanying interpretations of Buddhist practices and teachings provide a window into how these first Americans living in Asian lands imagined their vocation playing out. By attending to their expressions of what being at a pagoda felt like and meant, we glimpse some of the work that local material culture, communities, and doctrinal traditions did to shape the way missionaries presented Buddhism to international audiences who were just starting to become familiar with the Asian religion. Charles Hallisey has called on scholars to look at forms of what he calls "intercultural mimesis," or examples of "occasions when aspects of a culture of a subjectified people influenced the investigator to represent that culture in a certain manner."[5] Pagodas are a prime example of Burmese culture influencing Baptist investigators' representations of Buddhism and a reminder that it was not only Buddhist doctrines that shaped Western presentations of Buddhism but also objects and their communities.[6]

Missionary writings about Burma seem especially fixated on the pagoda and set on reducing its power to religious symbolism. Burmese texts from this period, by contrast, dedicate few incised palm pages to translating the popularity of their pagodas into abstract representations of the dharma. For example, in the *Sāsanavaṃsa,* the prominent Burmese Buddhist history from this period that I examined at the end of the previous chapter, references to pagodas are cursory and unadorned.[7] An earlier chronicle from the same Konbaung textual tradition, the *Vaṃsadīpanī*, likely composed in 1799, tends to simply note pagodas in lists of a meritorious royal deeds. Kings are described as building or repairing pagodas. For example, the text explains that, in the reign of King Kanitthatissa (in the ancient Lankan kingdom of Anaradhapura), "whatever monasteries, reservoirs, and pagodas were ruined and dilapidated were repaired."[8] In a rare exception to these passing references, the *Vaṃsadīpanī* provides a more detailed account of how another king at Anaradhapura, Duṭṭhgāmaṇi, laid the foundation for the Mahazedi pagoda:

> On the fourteenth waxing-moon day of Waso, he called the order of monks together and said "Tomorrow, on the full-moon Uposatha day, when the constellation Uttarasala is ascendant, we shall the lay the foundation bricks of the

Mahazedi. Let the Order of monks assemble for this occasion!" Thereupon, the king's ministers publicized [the decree] throughout the city with [the beating of] drums. And being thus informed [of the celebration], people took up observance of the Precepts, and carrying flowers in their hands, they came to the site where the Mahazedi was to be built. King Duṭṭhgāmaṇi, likewise, took up observance of the Precepts along with forty thousand ministers, and in the company of a vast retinue of people, he arrived at the site of the Mahazedi.[9]

While there are some interesting similarities between this pagoda scene and those found in Baptist accounts—such as its sonic dimensions and the flowering offering—this Burmese account does not have an author explaining pagodas to readers. The intended Burmese and Sinhalese audience for both the *Vaṃsadīpanī* and the *Sāsanavaṃsa* were already intimately familiar with their lineage's prolific pagoda building tradition. Instead of telling of the ways the shrines make the Buddha present and inspire visitors to follow his path, Burmese authors and oral traditions narrate how particular powerful things associated with the Buddha came to be enshrined in the country's famous pagodas, and how this supports the kingdom's mission to propagate the *sāsana*. Patrick Pranke explains that in Burma "the Buddha is encountered and known through his physical representations," but, Pranke argues, "more important than these objects of veneration are the many stories from the Buddha's life, which imbue the objects with meaning and render them sacred in the Myanmar imagination."[10] It is certainly true that stories of the Buddha are highly important in Burmese Buddhist communities, and that they endow pagodas and Buddha statues with meaning, but we should consider how the reverse is also true: these impressive objects imbue stories of the Buddha with meaning. The sensational form of the pagoda with its Buddha objects and collective rituals are a prime place for Burmese people to sense and make sense of the Buddha. Rather than privilege literary culture over sensory culture, we can instead consider how the two come together in sacred spaces.

Consider Burma's most famous pagoda story: that of Shwedagon Pagoda in Yangon that I recounted in the introduction. This story tells of the Buddha's first converts receiving the first Buddha relics (the eight hairs) and building the first reliquary monument dedicated to the Buddha.[11] As Donald Stadtner writes, "Such 'firsts' invest the monument with special significance."[12] I want to add to Stadtner's analysis that it is not just that

Shwedagon Pagoda *signifies* the power of the Buddha, but that it actually *possesses* it. The community's claim that it has hairs from the very head of the Buddha means that the shrine has actual physical, material pieces of the Buddha's body. Furthermore, Shwedagon is said to have objects belonging to three buddhas of the past: Kakusandha Buddha's water strainer, Konagamana Buddha's bathing robe, and Kassapa Buddha's staff. The tradition holds that these special objects actually hold some of these buddhas' power (ānubhāva). Thus, visiting the pagoda can mean coming into the real presence of a buddha, not just the presence of symbols or stories of a buddha. Following Robert Orsi's call on scholars to avoid reducing religion to social constructions and to instead approach "history and culture with the gods fully present," we should consider that, in the case of devout visitors to Shwedagon, buddhas can actually be present in the pagoda.[13]

Central questions, then, for the Baptist archival material explored in this chapter are: What did buddhas' presence in pagodas do to Baptist visitors? And what did Baptist visitors do to buddhas? The following examples will show a pattern in which American missionaries share some of the affecting multisensory interactions they have had with these structures and then move to reduce pagodas to symbols of something else, which tends to be ancient Buddhist doctrine and dangerous idolatry. In other words, these missionary writings about pagodas both reveal the missionaries being physically affected by the Buddhist buildings and show them doing the intellectual work of explaining away that powerful affect by arguing that it is a mere reflection of a fatally flawed religion.

This pattern in pagoda writings shows three important things about the American Baptist mission to Burma: 1) Burmese pagodas and other sensational forms pressed the Baptists who physically experienced them to sense the Buddha and his path to total liberation; 2) Baptist missionaries engaged Burmese monks and lay people to learn about Buddhist material culture, practices, and complex doctrines; and 3) Baptist missionaries regularly reduced the multisensory experience of pagodas and their collective rituals to symbols of abstract teachings of a long-dead man.

By seeing these three features of the American Baptist mission to Burma, we realize that missionaries were not simply dismissive or critical of Asian religions in their violent efforts to eradicate local religions and replace them with Christianity. Rather, missionaries were more like later scholars who studied and systematized Buddhist traditions by focusing on their textual traditions and abridging the complexity of lived Buddhism to a set of claims that could be compared to Christian theology. Yet, unlike the first generations of Buddhist studies scholars, Baptist missionaries in the early and mid-nineteenth century actually spent extended periods of time living among Buddhist communities having embodied experiences with their material culture and collective rituals. This does not mean that they were more virtuous because they did field work and learned vernacular languages; instead it means that they had a sensory knowledge of Buddhist culture that that informed their work in a way that scholars based in the West did not. Furthermore, it means that local objects and communities directly shaped that knowledge and participated to some extent in the way that these missionaries presented Buddhism to Western audiences. We must remember, however, that all of this happened within asymmetrical power structures, and that the authorizing practices of pagodas and Buddhist interlocutors clashed violently with the delegitimization efforts of Baptist missionaries, as will become painfully clear in the example I will recount of a missionary physically and publicly desecrating a Buddha statue.

Tracing Patterns in Missionary Pagoda Writings

In *Ocean Sketches of Life in Burmah,* the book that showcased the images analyzed at the beginning of this chapter, Ingalls wrote about the initial fascination engendered by Buddhist pagodas and then translated her embodied experience into a didactic message of despair. In one of her spellbinding pagoda portraits, Ingalls recounted her travels through a Burmese plantain grove to a "cluster of bamboo cottages," in which she happens upon

> a small gilded Pagoda and a nicely-carved monastery. The sun was just sending forth its first bright rays, which fell upon the gilded Pagoda and mingled with its golden hue, then scattered, and cast over the brown cottages and green trees, rays of extraordinary and unusual beauty. The village looked so quiet, and was so beautifully situated, that I could not resist the temptation of going there ... As we approached the village, the brown cottages were turned into poor rickety hovels, the enchanting spell which had bound my heart with so much enthusiasm was broken, and my heart set forth a deep sigh as I entered this heathen hamlet.[14]

In Ingalls's account, the sparkling gold of the rural pagoda and the scattered sunrise initially enchants this American missionary, seducing her into approaching the village. Like the monastic royal tutor in the previous chapter who gazed through Jonathan Price's large telescope and was astonished by the view of the moon and planets, Ingalls looks from a distance at a dazzling new scene. But then she quickly zooms in to shatter this captivating vision of Burmese Buddhism, transforming the alluring mirage into an unattractive portrait of poverty. Ingalls herself transforms from the fascinated traveler, absorbed by sensational foreign forms, into the disappointed visitor in a dismal village.

By the time Ingalls wrote *Ocean Sketches* in 1857, the American Baptist mission to Burma was in its fourth decade, and its evangelists had visited thousands of pagodas and written countless narratives like Ingalls's, telling of their experiences at these popular Buddhist sites. The Baptists proved especially interested in publishing accounts of pagodas. The few Catholic missionaries in the country, by contrast, focused on translating Buddhist scriptures and serving small local Catholic communities (such as the *bayingyi*, descendants from Portuguese and other traders in the port town of Syriam who were relocated to upper Burma and pressed into work as artillerymen when Burma sacked the town in 1613). The greatest impact of the Church of England's Society for the Propagation of the Gospel's small-scale mission to the country was through a Mandalay Christian school run by Reverend John Marks from 1869 to 1874 and supported by King Mindon, who sent several of his sons there to study.[15] The American Baptists, then, saw themselves as the first Protestant evangelist witnesses to Burmese religion, obliged to share detailed reports on the current state of Burmese Buddhism with the Christian world.

A common theme in the Baptist narratives is the way that the enormity, popularity, and profusion of pagodas inspires strong physical and emotional responses among the missionaries. One member of the first generation, George Boardman, wrote in his journal in 1828 that his spirit was stirred and his heart sunken by visiting pagodas in the southern city of Tavoy. Boardman explained that the number of pagodas in Tavoy was incalculable, but estimated that there were at least a thousand in the city. He surveyed the "vast numbers in all the surrounding regions" and concluded that "almost every mountain, and hill, and rising ground is tipt with a pagoda." While pagodas were "the most prominent and expensive of all the sacred buildings," a similar phenomenon of "idolatry" could be observed by looking at the country's many Buddha statues. In one temple alone, Boardman calculated thirty-five Buddha statues and estimated that one-third of them were made of alabaster. "This beautiful stone is found in large quantities in the vicinity of Ava," Boardman wrote, explaining that the white rock was "wrung by the hands of the artificer into objects of worship, and sold into various parts of the empire." Boardman was especially taken with the humanity of the Buddha figures that were carved out of it. "It ought in justice to be said of the image of Gaudama," Boardman admitted, "that they are not obscene and disgusting, as many of the Hindoo images are, but though differing in a few respects from a perfect human figure, they are neither grossly disproportion[ate], ugly, or monstrous." Many of Boardman's readers in 1829 would have some familiarity with missionary and colonial accounts from India that included condemnatory descriptions of the appearance of Hindu deities, and Boardman seems to feel an obligation to share that the Burmese, by contrast, create appealing human sculptures of their revered religious figure.[16]

We see Boardman's journal entry combining an expression of his emotional, admiring experience of Burmese pagodas and Buddha statues with imperial methods of counting and surveying them. As Barnard Cohn Barnard Cohn has shown, systematic surveying of India dates back to 1765, when James Rennell began surveying the British's Bengal territories. This developed into a vast documentation project that transformed colonial knowledge into practices of fixing and controlling India.[17] Baptist missionaries, themselves regular readers of British colonial writings, also sought to demonstrate control over the foreign land by enumerating and measuring natural and social landscapes and reporting these figures back to missionary boards and publications in the United States. Boardman calculates the dimensions of Tavoy's largest pagoda to be 50 feet in diameter and 150 feet high and tells of a "row of small bells" that are attached to the gilded iron crowing umbrella (B. *hti*), which, even when there is a "slight breeze, keep a continual chiming." Boardman declares these sensational sites to be "strongholds of sin and idolatry" and concludes that, because of the "Scriptures" and "divine promises," he "can rejoice in the full conviction that ere long the phrases of our God will be sung over all these idolatrous plains, and on these mountains and hills, and the echo shall resound from hill to fall, nor die away till every vestige of idolatry shall be swept away to be seen no more forever." Boardman's journal, which he sent to be published in the *American Baptist Magazine,* is a written version of the "BURMAH AS IT WAS" and "BURMAH AS IT IS" illustrations from Ingall's *Ocean Sketches of Burmah.* Boardman records what he heard and saw at Burma's abundant pagodas and then reduces it to a map for a total Christian destruction of Buddhism.[18] He uses emotional language echoing the evangelical expressions of strong individual experiences of God's saving grace cultivated in the United States at that time at Protestant revivals and camp meetings. The strong, embodied enthusiasm Boardman describes, though, was not due to a personal relationship with Christ, but to the encounter with Buddhist pagodas. Perhaps aware that his readers would see a dangerous resonance between the religious fervor of U.S. evangelism and Burma's enrapturing Buddhist landscape, Boardman dramatically turns his attention to the violent, total eradication of "idolatry."

Most missionaries, like Boardman, kept the violence of Christian evangelism in their rhetoric. A few, though, perpetrated actual physical violence against Burmese pagodas and Buddha statues. For example, in 1845, Edwin Bullard, a missionary among the Pwo Karen, attacked a pagoda and its Buddha statue when these sacred objects were in the process of being constructed. Bullard had noticed a "continuous line going and coming, carrying sand and lime and ornaments for the pagoda, and offerings for their priests," so he stopped some of the devotees and asked if they worshiped the sand or the lime. They, of course, said no. They tried to explain to Bullard that "after the brick is made, [they] build up a great pagoda of it, and worship that." Bullard made of show of "thr[owing] together a pile of bricks" and commanding them to "bow down, and worship" it. The devotees tried to explain further that they still would have to "make the pagoda very large, smooth the outside, and whitewash it." It is interesting that Bullard's report does not include devotees telling him that they worship the Buddha that the pagoda represents. Instead, their comments in Bullard's report suggest that they understand the collective process of making the pagoda large and complete to be the crucial work that transforms mundane materials into a sacred object.[19]

In the report, Bullard describes how he carried on with his show of explaining that even when the pagoda is large and whitewashed, it is still of these same constituent materials. He tried to convince the Pwo community that the Christian god made all of the sand and lime, and that they are

THE PAGODA

worshipping the Devil instead of this almighty god. He pleaded with them to "trust in God, and cast off the Devil and his customs." Notably, Bullard called what the Burmese experience as the presence of the Buddha the presence of the Devil; unlike other missionaries who made arguments about the absence of the long-dead human Buddha, Bullard seemed to recognize a superhuman presence, but named it "the Devil." His Pwo Karen interlocutors simply responded that they would not stop their pagoda practices, at which point Bullard became violent. He turned to address a Buddha image that monks were raising and exclaimed that their "god is unable to climb up yonder without [their] help." The monks, according to Bullard, told the missionary that the Buddha image could raise itself up if it wanted to.[20]

Bullard writes that he insisted the monks let him cut the rope if they were so confident that the Buddha statue can levitate. The gathered crowd "looked astounded and enraged," and "even the native Christians stood at a distance trembling." The Buddha image then dramatically fell to Bullard's feet. Since he did not actually cut the rope, Bullard did not know how it happened. He suspected that because the monks were all in a state of "fear and amazement" they let the rope go. Bullard took this shock as a cue to introduce himself as a Christian preacher who was there to tell them of the "living Almighty God." He then, shockingly, put "the end of [his] cane on the eye of the image," insisting that "it has an eye, but it sees not." He performed a similarly brutal act to the Buddha's nose and mouth, declaring that it cannot smell or eat offerings. Bullard reports that the audience was enraged and surprised, that all work stopped, and that everyone stared at him with mouths open. He then "preached with a loud voice till [he] was too hoarse to speak plainly any longer." Bullard concludes his report that the "countenance of some brightened up with evident joy at the sound of the gospel and the light that was springing up in their hitherto dark minds." His account turns again to the Buddha image, to which Bullard says one person even turned his back.[21]

While Bullard's violence is extraordinary, his "Why worship a brick?" logic is common in Baptist accounts of the mission to Burma. Francis Mason—the prominent early missionary to the Karen and husband of Ellen Mason, whose career I examined in the previous chapter—recorded an example of it in a letter he wrote at the end of 1830. December 28 of that year was a full moon day, when many Buddhists were gathered at pagodas for *uposotha,* a

Buddhist day of observance, so Francis Mason went with a group of Christians to visit the prominent Maulmain pagoda. Mason watched as a father showed his two-year-old child how to bring his hands together and then bow his head to the ground in reverence. An unnamed fellow evangelist asked the father, "Why do you bow down to these bricks and stones?" The father replied, "The god is inside." Mason explained that "the pagodas are reverenced on account of the images and relics of Gaudama, which are buried up within them." Mason's account goes on to tell of another encounter his group had that day at the pagoda, this time between an evangelist and a monk. The evangelist asserted that the monk "must be very stupid . . . to pray so long to that pile of stones." The monk, according to Mason, replied, "It is necessary to pray a great while, the sound has to go through so great a body of bricks and stones to reach the ears of our God." Mason elaborates on the importance of sounds at the Buddhist site by explaining that every time someone makes an offering of flowers or rice there—which was apparently quite often, given all of the floral and edible donations he observed—they ring a bell with a deer's horn. Mason's multisensory experience of the pagoda and its rituals continued to "haunt[] [his] imagination" even as he wrote the letter. He concludes that this scene was evidence that children can and should be taught religion, and he references the contemporaneous debate in the United States over Sunday schools and whether religious education and evangelism should be focused solely on adults to suggest that his disturbing tale of a Buddhist father instructing his two-year-old child to bow down at a pagoda showed just how crucial it was to teach children Christianity. Mason uses the vivid account of his lived experiences at a pagoda to make the polemical point that Buddhism, like Christianity, is something that is taught.[22] This resonates with the arguments made by the female leaders of Baptist education in Burma that I examined in the previous chapter, that the mission must give further material support and autonomy to schools if they wanted to see successful, sustained conversion in the Southeast Asian country.

Many missionary accounts of pagodas focus on smaller, less-well-known shrines, the kinds of fixtures of the religious landscape that otherwise go unnoticed in contemporary Burmese and British texts. The American Baptists were so dedicated to spreading the gospel in what they saw as far corners of the earth that they regularly made what they called "jungle tours" to distant villages, requiring many days of walking and several attendants (often Christian converts, but not always) to help carry food, shelter, tracts, and other supplies. As the mission learned that minority communities in the highlands and other remote regions were more likely to express interest in their Christian messages and materials than the lowland Bamar, they grew dependent on these tours. Still, there were always missionaries in big central cities, homes to the country's most famous pagodas, such as Shwedagon. The following two Baptist reports on Shwedagon show how the magnitude of this monument and its constant stream of pilgrims challenged its Baptist visitors it to explain its extraordinary power.

Ingalls wrote a moving account of Shwedagon Pagoda in the wake of the Second Anglo-Burmese War that casts the Rangoon pagoda as a key adversary in the colonial enterprise:

> The Burmans have filled the land with idol gods, Pagodas, and temples, served by their yellow-robed priests. Boodhism . . . which they received from India, had for ages exhibited all its fascinating forms, and interwoven itself with political and civil life. Being exclusive, it long resisted the entrance of the Gospel. But it has been smitten and shattered with a rod of iron. The recent war of 1852 seems to have struck its most heavy blows against this great edifice of evil. Pagodas were opened for concealed treasure, temples desecrated, and idols broken; some of the streets of Rangoon are now covered with the brick and stone of the former Pagodas; and golden Sway-da-gong, one of the proudest monuments of superstition in Burmah, is now surmounted by a British fort, and our morning gun is heard from its lofty terrace. To assail such a system with mere arguments, would have been like attempting to overthrow that solid Pagoda itself. The pride of the heart also has quailed before the Cross; and many have put on Christ.
>
> This work is not yet done. The Gospel must still be preached; trials endured; and fervent prayers offered before that land shall become Immanuel's land. God has been with us in mercy since the last war; and we have reason to unite together in a song of thanksgiving for the blessing which has rested upon the missions.[23]

For Ingalls, the infamous Shwedagon Pagoda tells a tale of Buddhism's past endurance, fascinating power, and present destruction. No longer a proud monument to ancient Asian religious beliefs, Rangoon's central Buddhist structure is now in ruins, having been desecrated, pillaged, demolished, and surmounted by a British fort. Where there was once a celebrated shrine, there is now a bellicose symbol of both colonial dominance and missionary achievement. Furthermore, Ingalls claims that God has been part of the British war effort because of the way colonial occupation facilitates Christian missionary efforts. While her account portrays Burma's most prominent shrine as a "monument of superstition," it recognizes that the overwhelming materiality of the pagoda itself means that evangelists cannot rely on "mere arguments." The massive and popular Shwedagon Pagoda shows Ingalls and her readers Buddhism's great power in Burma and that this power comes from both abstract doctrine and tangible religious objects.

Two decades later, Reverend Edward Stevens offered American readers his own detailed report on Shwedagon Pagoda, which appeared to have withstood colonial conquest better than Ingalls imagined. Steven's 1876 article details the monument's exact height (320 feet) and base (800 square feet), the numerous smaller buildings encircling it, the sheet iron, gold, silver, gems, and mirrors used in its construction. This article features a large illustration of the monument (see figure 3.3). Like others, Stevens was taken with the way the gold-leafed spire majestically reflects the sun's rays, and he comments on the pleasant chime of the tower's bells. Then he turns from its glistening glory to its alarming danger. Ignorant devotees, Stevens explains, see this bright luminosity as proof of the presence of the Buddha. Furthermore, pilgrims traveling from all over the country to pay homage at the shrine maintain the hazardous faith that depositing offerings and presenting prayers will secure the pilgrim great rewards in a subsequent life. Understanding these local beliefs and the specificity of these idolatrous practices, Stevens argues, is crucial for Christians: "In looking on this pagoda, an object of worship to so many millions of our fellow-men, it is the greatest importance to us, as Christians, to reflect on" why they worship it so devoutly. Here Stevens is making the point that missionaries should not dismiss the theological reasons behind living Buddhist rituals and objects; instead, they must study them. In this way, the pagoda demands that it be taken seriously, that both the philosophies and practices of its community be understood.[24]

According to Stevens, the two important tenets of Buddhism that propel pagoda practices are: 1) the concept that worship of statues and reliquaries will earn the worshipper a favorable rebirth (here Stevens is referring to a Buddhist understanding of merit [P. *puñña*]); and 2) the notion of cause and effect, the belief that one is doomed to suffer the consequences of one's sins (this is Stevens's gloss on the Buddhist teaching of karma, whereby one's unwholesome actions have unwholesome consequences). Acknowledging the

FIGURE 3.3 "The Great Pagoda of Shway Dagong at Rangoon," from *Baptist Missionary Magazine*, 1876.

strong Burmese belief in karma, Stevens responds by offering what he sees as karma's most tragic consequence: Buddhists do not recognize that "forgiveness is possible." Without God, without Jesus, they have no potential for salvation. Stevens wrenchingly imagines that, without faith in God's power of forgiveness, these people will be damned to hell. He concludes his essay by quoting Mark 16:15: "Go ye into all the world, and preach the gospel (the glad tidings of salvation in my name), to every creature; he that believeth and is baptized shall be saved, and he that believeth not shall be damned." Here we see Stevens, like other Baptist missionaries writing in this period, being both inspired to evangelize and compelled to engage Buddhism in a religious debate. In the face of the lofty, golden, and worshipped Buddhist monument, Stevens makes a theological argument for the gospel's superiority to Buddhist scripture.[25]

Like scholars of religion would do a century later, Stevens takes a popular, multisensory religious site and reduces it to a system of symbols of Buddhist belief that can be compared to Protestant faith. As Talal Asad has argued, twentieth-century scholars used the concept of the symbol to focus on belief and then define religion as a transhistorical and transcultural phenomenon. Asad shows how influential anthropologists like Clifford Geertz defined religion as "essentially a matter of symbolic meanings linked to ideas of general order" and traces this approach back through European foreign missionaries to early modern Europe when, in that post-Enlightenment society, the only legitimate space for Christianity was in individual belief.[26] We see in Steven's writings an example of this kind of approach, which explains particular Burmese religious objects and practices in terms of general beliefs in merit and karma. Stevens is not wrong that these two doctrines are important parts of pagoda practices, but his subordination of the materiality of pagodas and their rituals to abstract concepts is more of a reflection of his Protestant attitudes toward faith than Burmese ones. Following Asad's call to move away from transhistorical definitions of religions and instead toward the authorizing practices by which these kinds of definitions come about, I want to pay close attention to the ways Baptist missionaries focused on Buddhist beliefs to make Buddhism both legible and inferior.

This section has shown how Burmese Buddhist pagodas inspired missionaries to imagine and reimagine Buddhism, and how Americans expressed their attraction to and fear of Asian religions through this religious monument. In their writings back to the States, they offered readers a guided tour of Burma's dazzling monuments—with their precious metals and gems, their sonorous bells, their circumambulating pilgrims—and a lesson in Buddhist teachings on karma, merit, and rebirth. Pagoda stories concluded with a condemnation of the materiality and teachings of Burmese Buddhism and a plea for support for the missionary enterprise. The following section turns to another group of people in Burma with unusual attitudes toward the country's venerated pagodas. Taken together, these two religious minorities speak to this monument's extraordinary power to determine both mainstream Buddhist practice and the terms of religious dissent in nineteenth-century Burma.

Introducing the Paramats

The Christians were not alone in their criticism of Burmese pagodas. They found an unlikely ally in a Buddhist reform movement known as the Paramats.

The movement seems to have started near where the Chindwin River joins the Irrawaddy River, during the reign of King Bodawpaya (1782–1819).[27] King Bodawpaya ordered a brutal and sustained operation to purify the Buddhist monastic order while simultaneously promoting himself as a *cakravartin* (world ruler) who was also a living Buddha—specifically, Maitreya, the Buddha prophesied to succeed Gotama as the next buddha. Powerful monastic institutions and individual monks rejected Bodawpaya's grand claims. A lay group of reformers known as Paramats, however, signaled their willingness to support them and therefore garnered royal attention.[28] The more general public took notice, too. The oral histories of the Paramats relayed to British officials and Baptist missionaries that I explore later in this chapter recall King Bodawpaya's surprising attention to this new religious movement.

The source of the name "Paramat" is uncertain. It could be a transliteration of *Payama,* the Burmese pronunciation of the Pali term *paramattha,* which comes from the Sanskrit term *paramārtha* and means "the ultimate," or "the most sublime truth." In his consideration of the Paramats, E. Michael Mendelson provides a footnote after his first mention of the reformist sectarian movement in which he translates "Paramat" into the Pali term *paramattha,* which he defines as "the highest good, ideal: truth in the ultimate sense, philosophical truth; more generally speaking, those Buddhists at the end of the Theravada religious continuum who insist that in reality nothing really exists. The term has, in Burma, connotations of taking religious matters to extremes and is somewhat derogatory."[29] Mendelson is offering a classical Pali Buddhist definition of *paramattha* as well as an insight (likely from his original research) that this term has a negative connotation of going too far with doctrines about the true nature of things and ultimate reality.

Mendelson's etymology is compelling. As Erik Braun shows in *The Birth of Insight,* this notion of *paramattha* is key for the Abhidhamma system of thought that has been so influential in Burmese Buddhism. As Braun writes, "The Buddha is understood to have preached in ultimate (P. *paramattha*) terms in the Abhidhamma. To speak in ultimate terms means to describe reality only with regard to its genuinely existing constituent parts"—which are called *dhammas.* There are eighty-two of these genuinely existing parts, and they are classed under four categories: consciousness (P. *citta*), mental factors (P. *cetasikas*), materiality (P. *rupa*), and awakening (P. *nibbana*). These dhammas are so important, according to the Abhidhamma tradition, because investigating them and the conditions that give rise to them gives one insight into impermanence, not-self, and suffering—the "Three Marks of Existence" that I discussed in the introduction. The investigation into these Three Marks is what eventually leads to the one unconditioned dhamma: *nibbana*. It seems likely that the Paramats identified their major Buddhist commitment as one of realizing *nibbana* through an Abhidhamma approach to understanding the dhammas.[30]

Another suggestion for the etymology of the reform movement's name comes from Michael Charney, who writes that Paramat "was probably a corruption of paramitas, the ten perfections that lead to Buddha-hood."[31] This is possible, and it would connect the source of the name with the group's focus on the Buddha's path to awakening instead of on practices such as worshipping at pagodas. The sources I have found, however, do not mention the ten perfections, instead reporting on Paramat claims about ultimate truth. Regardless of where, exactly, the Paramats got their name, it seems that they were most concerned with returning to the teachings of the Pali scriptures and rejecting contemporary practices that they saw as deviating from the true path to awakening.

As this discussion of etymology suggests, the Paramats have puzzled scholars of Burmese history and Buddhism. Part of the reason is that the Konbaung chronicles and other extant official texts do not mention them. The dearth of available evidence in Burmese- and Pali-language sources about the Paramats has led some scholars to wonder if they even existed as a distinct sect, and whether the term might have just been used by mainstream Buddhists to refer derisively to all sorts of fringe figures and groups. There are a few scholars, though, who have named the Paramats as a distinct reform movement. I will sketch their work to show that one of the few things the Paramats are known to have done is criticize object worship—namely, Buddhist rituals focused on pagodas, statues, and monks. It seems that Paramats, like other communities in Burma undergoing religious transformations in the Anglo-Burmese-War period (including those converting to Christianity), pagodas became a key site for the expression of religious difference. I will also address an intriguing, but ultimately unsupported, academic claim that the Paramats were a kind of Mahayana sect. After reviewing this limited collection of scholarship, I will then turn previously unstudied evidence from the American Baptist archives to show how it fleshes out a portrait of the Paramats as a reform movement critical of both religious materiality and dominant Buddhist institutions.

Among the few scholars who have considered the Paramats as a distinct reform movement is John Ferguson. He addresses the Paramats when trying to understand King Bodawpaya's attraction to them. Ferguson writes: "Basically this group of argumentative lay Buddhists stressed the semi-Mahayanist position that all forms through which we comprehend life are, in the ultimate sense, nothing at all. To worship monks or Buddha statues is, therefore, to be misled by empty forms. Higher insight demands less attention to conventional 'folk' Buddhism and more emphasis upon speculative philosophy (Abhidhamma) and private insight (meditation)."[32] Ferguson here explains that the Paramats were lay people who argued against worshiping statues and monks. Curiously, he interprets their views as related to the Mahayana tradition, which extends the Buddhist teaching of not-self (*anattā*) to all phenomenon, including dhammas. Mahayana has a long and complex history of extending this philosophical line of thought, which is often described with the word *śūnyatā*, a Sanskrit term commonly translated as "emptiness." Ferguson sees the Paramat rejection of statue and monk worship as a claim that these things, like the individual self, are ultimately empty of an essential nature. Ferguson likely got this idea from research conducted by Mendelson, which Mendelson made available to Ferguson during Ferguson's graduate work. Ferguson also edited and completed Mendelson's 1975 *Sangha in the State in Burma*, which came out shortly after Ferguson's doctoral thesis. *Sangha and the State in Burma* characterizes the Paramats as "a group of unorthodox believers" who emphasized "*intent*, not ritual, and their tendency was to de-emphasize the importance of monks in their community roles. On a philosophical level, the term suggests Mahayanist concepts of emptiness."[33] Mendelson's intriguing connection to Mahayana teachings on emptiness points to questions about the history of Mahayana Buddhism in the region, a history that has been overshadowed by the centuries-old tradition of Burmese kings presenting themselves as orthodox upholders of the purest form of Buddhism found in the Pali scriptures (the tradition now called Theravada). While it is possible that Paramats were influenced by Mahayana traditions, I will show that the evidence Mendelson offers does not sufficiently support a claim that

Paramats held an emptiness doctrine related to Mahayana theories of *śūnyatā*.

Mendelson's account of the Paramats builds on three nineteenth-century European sources. While these sources do not provide strong evidence for the Mahayana theory, they do offer some insights into the Paramats—specifically, their criticism of Buddhist objects, and their history with King Bodawpaya. Mendelson's first source is a text by the Italian Catholic priest Father Vincenzo Sangermano (1758–1819), who was assigned to Burma from 1783 to 1806. Sangermano's text does not use the term "Paramat," but rather describes a group called the Zodi, which Mendelson understands to be identified with the Paramats. Sangermano writes that the Zodi

> began by making a great stir throughout the whole kingdom, and thereby excited the zeal of the Emperor against them. It is believed that great numbers of them still exist in divers parts of the empire, but they are obliged to keep themselves concealed. They are of Burmese origin, but their religion is totally different from that of Godama. They reject metempsychosis, and believe that each one will receive the reward or punishment of his actions immediately after death, and that this state of punishment and reward will last for eternity. Instead of attributing everything to fate, as the Burmese do, they acknowledge an omnipotent and omniscient Nat, the creator of the world; they despise the Pagodas, the Baos, or convents of Talapoins, and the statues of Godama. The present Emperor, a most zealous defender of his religion, resolved with one blow to annihilate this sect, and accordingly gave orders for their being searched for in every place, and compelled to adore Godama. Fourteen of them were put to a cruel death; but many submitted, or feigned to submit, to the orders of the Emperor, till at length he was persuaded that they had all obeyed. From that time they have remained concealed, for which reason I have never been able to meet with any one of them, to inquire if any form of worship had been adopted by them. All that I could learn was that the sect was still in existence, and that its members still held communications with each other. They are for the most part merchants by profession. This little which I have gleaned concerning them has rather induced me to believe that they may be Jews, for the doctrines attributed to them agree perfectly with those people, who, we well know, have penetrated into almost every corner of the known world, even to the remotest parts of Asia.[34]

In addition to including a strong criticism of Pagodas and Buddha statues that is common to many of the Paramat accounts from the Baptist archive, Sangermano's account of the Zodi sect tells of its ties to Bodawpaya's religious campaigns. The part of that story told by Sangermano is about Bodawpaya persecuting them harshly, not being attracted to them. Given that Bodawpaya was famously fickle with his royal favor, this could still mean that they were the Paramats that Ferguson describes. It is certainly possible that Bodawpaya pursued an alliance with the Paramats because they supported his claims to Buddhahood, but then denounced them as a display of his renewed favor to the prominent monastic order. Finally, there is the clearly more misbegotten feature of Sangermano's account: his theory that the reform sect were likely Jews. There is no evidence for this. Sangermano's speculation speaks to how fascinating religious reform movements were for Christian visitors to the Konbaung empire, and how visitors' active religious imaginations could easily map biblical worlds onto Burmese ones. The Baptists, too, I will soon show, mapped their own Christian imaginations onto the Paramats.

Mendelson follows Sangermano's writings with a large quotation from Henry Yule's 1858 *A Narrative of the Mission Sent by the Governor-General of India to the Court of Ava in 1866, with Notices of the Country, Government, and People*, which describes a "latitudinarian or heretical doctrine [that] had considerable diffusion in Burma . . . [which is] probably the same with that of the Zodi . . . [described by] Padre Sangermano." Yule says that he has heard that this "sect is still numerous, but [he has] not been able to obtain any information regarding them." Despite his limited secondhand knowledge of this sect, Yule offers the suggestion that their doctrine about true wisdom (which, he explains, is the claim that this wisdom is "not concentrated in any existing spirit or embodied form, but diffused throughout the universe, and partaken in different degrees by various intelligences, and in a very high degree by the Buddhas, is the true and only God") "seems very nearly Mr. Hodgson's Prajnika doctrine."[35] This is a reference to a contemporary of Yule, Brian Hodgson, who made a large impact on the burgeoning study of Buddhism in Europe by disseminating manuscripts on Himalayan Buddhism from the Royal Library in Nepal.[36] This shows how at the time of Yule's writings European colonial expeditions were circulating knowledge about a range of Buddhist traditions, including the Mahayana tradition of

Prajñāpāramitā, or "Perfection of Wisdom," which develops the theory that an awakened being (a bodhisattva) is one who realizes the ultimate truth of śūnyatā. It seems, then, that Yule was the first to publish a theory of a Mahayana-Paramat connection. Clearly it was not the Burmese reformers who were making this connection, but Yule.

The final source Mendelson includes is the 1882 book *The Burman*, written by the Scottish journalist and British colonial administrator James George Scott under the pseudonym "Shwe Yoe." *The Burman* includes a rich extended passage that names the sect "the Paramats" and describes them as rejecting image worship, refusing to offer alms to monks, and praying to a "godlike wisdom."[37] While Mendelson does not support his claim that the Paramats were concerned with *intent* over ritual, or that their name has to do with Mahayana concepts of emptiness, Mendelson does offer a helpful concluding reflection. He writes: "Considering the variety of usage for the word *paramat*, we might best accept it as a relative, category term attached to a variety of extremist sects by outsiders knowing little and caring less about historical details."[38] The people described as the Paramats in the Baptist writings could very well have come from multiple loosely connected groups. Indeed, nineteenth-century Burma was not a place of a homogenous, centralized, royally run, monolithic Buddhism, but rather the site of changing power dynamics among monks, lineages, royal patrons, literati, and lay supporters. Looking closely at the Paramats helps to underscore that diversity.

Before putting the Mahayana theory to rest, I will quickly note one last proponent: Maung Htin Aung's 1967 *A History of Burma*. Maung Htin Aung does not use the term "Paramat," but he does provide a rich narrative of Bodawpaya's attraction to "a new conception of the Buddha, which," Maung Htin Aung writes, "probably was a result of contact with Christianity and Mahayana Buddhism." According to Maung Htin Aung, Bodawpaya was attracted to this new way of thinking about the Buddha, but, after conflicts with prominent monks and a swell of public criticism, "Bodawpaya announced that he must have been mad to accept then new doctrine ... [and] executed the scholar responsible for its origin."[39] *A History of Burma* cites no specific sources for its description of the new doctrine and Bodawpaya's mercurial relationship to it, and, notably, Maung Htin Aung does not associate the new doctrine with criticisms of pagodas or Buddha statues. Perhaps Maung Htin Aung's work raises more questions than it answers, but I do want to highlight how it is the only academic work to suggest that this new religious movement was influenced by Christianity. As we will soon see, this was a strong conviction among the Baptists who sought out the Paramats for signs that Burmese Buddhism could give way to Protestant Christianity. While I will argue that this conviction comes from a Baptist religious imagination, Maung Htin Aung's analysis reminds us that as knowledge of Christianity permeated Burmese communities it must have exerted some influence on understandings and practices of religion.

The last, and most recent, academic consideration of the Paramats for us to examine before turning to those Baptist sources is Michael Charney's outstanding 2006 study of the Buddhist literati in the Konbaung dynasty, *Powerful Learning*. This intellectual history draws on a rich range of Burmese and Western sources and scholarship to reveal how an elite group of monks and laymen from the Lower Chindwin Valley worked with Burmese kings to fabricate images of a legitimate and prestigious dynasty. Charney addresses the Paramats in his analysis of the highly influential monk Shin Neyya, who served as chief of religious affairs in a period of increasing anticlerical sentiment calls for religious reform. Charney explains that early in King Mindon's reign (1853–1878) the Paramats began challenging the monastic order. Charney references earlier scholarship that associates the Paramats with Bodawpaya's Buddhist reform of 1812, but his review of the evidence leads him to conclude that this is "an attractive, but thus far unsubstantiated explanation."[40] As Mendelson did before him, Charney carefully concludes that there is simply not enough evidence to confidently narrate the history of the Paramats.

This is where the American Baptist archives come in. Christian evangelists in the Konbaung kingdom obtained and produced a collection of documents that helps fill in the story of the Paramats sketched by the earliest European accounts and more recent scholarship on the Konbaung dynasty. The Paramats turn out to have been a group of special interest for the Baptist mission to Burma. The American evangelists wrote about them extensively in their field notes, conducted long-form interviews with their leaders, and published several articles about religious and political conflicts between them and monastic and royal authorities. The Baptists' sustained concern with the Paramats appears to have entailed real engagement between the Buddhist movement and the Christian missionaries, and it also seems to have been a uniquely attractive way for the missionaries to hold on to a dream that Burmese Buddhism might finally crack open under the influence of alternative religious teachings. Furthermore, these Paramat interactions show how material expressions of religion, especially in the form of Buddha statues, were powerful and dangerous for both Burmese Buddhists and Christian missionaries.

Christians did not introduce Burma to anxiety about religious objects. Debates about the propriety of monastic possessions, for example, go as far back in time as our records do. A stone inscription from 1249 CE that contains the first known reference to the genre of Buddhist law known as *dhammasattha* describes a dispute about whether a Pagan monastery justly owned certain slaves and fields, or whether these people and property should be returned to the family of the lay donor.[41] The famously vicious eighteenth-century "one-shoulder vs. two-shoulder controversy" (P. *ekaṃsika-pārupana*) centered on the question of how novice monks should wear their robes and expanded into debates over other monastic possessions such as fans and hats.[42] In the particular context of the Anglo-Burmese War period, however, the criticism of Burmese Buddhist objects took on new political and religious significance. As the Burmese worried about British occupation accelerating the decline of the *sāsana*, and as the Baptist missionaries targeted the newly colonized country for conversion, Burma's famous pagodas and Buddha statues expressed both a desperate demand for continued independence and concerns about what new forms of religion would emerge under Western imperialism.

The American Baptists had struggled from the beginning of their mission to convert the Burmese Buddhist majority, but the Paramats appeared markedly different from the mainstream Buddhists that the Baptists had spent decades in Burma getting to know. First, the Paramats talked a great deal about refusing to pay homage to Buddha statues. This was exciting for the Christian proselytizers, who, as I have shown, had been consistently pointing to Burma's popular image-centric rituals as evidence of the danger of Buddhism. Second, the missionaries began to pay particular attention to Paramat philosophical expressions of dedication to the true dhamma alone. When Paramats argued that commitment to realizing the ultimate truth was far more important than the figure of the Buddha or the monks who were said to uphold the Buddha's teachings, Baptists heard this as strikingly similar to a Protestant faith in God and a Protestant rejection of mortal and material intermediaries. This combination of seemingly Protestant practices

THE PAGODA

and beliefs encouraged missionaries to insist that Christianity was finally making inroads in Burma.

I will not be arguing that the missionaries were somehow right; I do not believe that the Paramats were some kind of Christianizing community in Buddhist Burma. However, I do think it likely that there is what Chris Wingfield describes as "a degree of ethnographic accuracy" to the Baptist accounts.[43] In his study of the global collections of the London Missionary Society museum (1814–1910), Wingfield shows that early collecting practices there reveal a period of open-minded curiosity about other peoples and cultures rather than a focus on propagandistically promoting the success of foreign missions and the righteousness of the European empires that supported them. In Baptist writings about Paramats, we find both impulses. To separate the more open-minded inquiries out from the propaganda, I will read their accounts of the Paramats closely, situate them alongside extant Burmese records, and put both sets of sources in context.

The remainder of this chapter will detail this story of Protestant and Paramat interactions by focusing on about a dozen accounts of Paramats dating from the 1830s through the early 1880s. Two central questions will drive my examination of these accounts: what were the Paramats actually up to, and what can the themes of iconoclasm and religious reformation in these accounts reveal about a broader religious imagination in nineteenth-century Burma, both among the missionaries and among the Paramats? This second question is perhaps the more illuminating; its approach of attending to fabrication is inspired by scholars of religious imagination such as Shahzad Bashir, whose excellent study of cannibalism in Safavid Iran is only marginally concerned with whether loyal soldiers really ate their enemies.[44] Instead, his work is much more interested in what these kinds of accounts tell us about the sociohistorical context in which they were produced. In Bashir's case, descriptions of devouring enemy flesh show how displays of devotion to royal power were expressed in highly corporeal ways in sixteenth-century Iran. Bashir builds this argument upon the assertion that cannibalism is *always* an act of symbolic meaning, which is why accounts of cannibalism are well positioned to illuminate what that symbolic act expresses about a matrix of religious meanings.[45] Likewise, I assert that the rejection of image worship in the context of colonizing Burma is a highly symbolic act, and that reports of it can be examined for matrices of shared concerns among new religious movements in the final decades of the

Konbaung dynasty. In other words, because of the long history of image-centric religious practices in Burma, and because of the new context of Christian condemnation of Buddha statues and spirit shrines, iconoclasm must have meant something beyond an instance of refusing to revere a particular thing.

I will use this framework of religious imagination to show how, throughout these missionary accounts of Paramats, there is a pronounced interest in the ways this Burmese sect seemed to espouse a kind of Christian theology. But I will suggest that a more pressing concern for the Paramats seems to have been Buddhist reformation and political action, rather than a radically alternative belief system. The Paramats were more invested in protesting the corruption of royally sponsored monastic institutions and upholding a Buddhist tradition of commitment to knowing the ultimate truth as taught in the Abhidhhamma; they proved far less interested in propounding a new philosophy that drastically deviated from normative Buddhist thought. In other words, I will argue that the Paramats did not represent a turn within Burmese communities toward Christianity as the missionaries wanted their supporters to believe. Rather, they were a development in the weakening Burmese kingdom that reimagined Buddhist communities in relation to new religious, colonial, and paracolonial formations. Paramats strategically made connections to Christianity to promote their positions among Baptist communities—both American and convert—in order to gain sympathy for themselves as a persecuted group. They also saw those connections as a way to secure independence from royally empowered Buddhist institutions. Thus, the Paramats' engagement with the Baptists is best seen as a way for the movement to further articulate their concerns with the degradation of the *sāsana* and their commitment to keeping the Buddha's message of ultimate liberation alive in this changing political and religious landscape.

While there is a relative abundance of material about Paramat sectarianism in the Baptist collections, I must note that this data set is also limited, given that it is English-language writing in the service of the Christian mission. Even the extraordinary transcripts of interviews with Paramat leaders only exist in their English translations. I did find one Burmese-language source on the Paramats, but this does little to provide balance. Because of the country's climate and fraught political history, official

Burmese texts and the Burmese archives to which scholars have access have not preserved much on nineteenth-century sectarian issues or ethnic conflicts, which is why the American archives prove useful in trying to piece together marginalized histories. This imbalance in my source material demands that my analysis be sensitive to American bias and manipulation. It also means that there is still more work to be done scouring Burmese collections, which I hope will bring to light new material to enrich our knowledge of the Paramats and other forms of marginalized religious activity.

In what follows, I will explore the crucifixion of U Po, the only Paramat situation that is mentioned in my one Burmese source. I will then analyze reports on Paramats chronologically, beginning with the material recorded prior to the Second Anglo-Burmese War, and then proceeding to the period between the Second and Third Anglo-Burmese Wars, the time when it seems the Paramats were the most active. This chronological method helps track changes in descriptions over time and keeps this study contextualized within the successive power struggles of the Anglo-Burmese War period.

The Crucifixion of U Po

On November 28, 1869, the Burmese Christian preacher Moung Pyo and the senior missionary Edward Stevens left Rangoon to proselytize in Mandalay, which King Mindon had established as Burma's royal capital in 1857. With two boxes of books and tracts, the group first traveled three hundred kilometers north on foot for eight days to Prome. There, they picked up Moung Lan, the deacon of the Prome Baptist Church and Stevens's son, Edward Oliver Stevens. This missionary band boarded a flat towed by the steamer *Nagpore* up the Irrawaddy River to Mandalay. Stevens wrote in his journal about the changing religious-political climate as they made their way up river. Local people "constantly reminded [them] that [they] were under a different rule, and that a more guarded manner of speaking of Gaudama and his religion would be desirable" in Upper Burma. A man who met Stevens at a funeral along the way explained this custom further: "When we are in English territory, we are accustomed to speak well of the English religion; so you too, in coming into Burman territory, would do well to say more about your own religion, and less against ours, lest the spirit of opposition be engendered." Stevens reported feeling "grateful" for the reminder of the conflicts around and co-constitution of religion and politics in partially colonized Burma, where Christianity was expected to be praised by both Buddhists and Christians in British territory, and Buddhism was expected to be respected in Burmese territory. This sensitivity to religious tensions would prove useful for Stevens as he learned to navigate the capital city and began to investigate a crucifixion.[46]

The missionaries stayed in Mandalay for three weeks. In the mornings, they would travel to different parts of the city to preach and distribute tracts. During the midday heat, they went back home, and then, after dinner, they went out again to distribute more tracts. One morning they decided to break their routine to walk to the city's cemetery. They had gotten word of the grizzly fate of U Po, a man who had been crucified on orders of King Mindon because of his heretical religious claims.[47] They decided to seek out the sight of his crucifixion for themselves and found the remains of the executed body nailed to a bamboo frame that formed an X shape. They wrote that "nothing of the body remained below the chest, having no doubt been torn away by dogs and birds of prey. The upper part of the body still hung as it had been fastened, nothing remaining but the skeleton covered in parts with ... dried skin."[48]

This vision of a crucified body and the report of a man put to death for religious views made a powerful impression on the American missionary. "We could not but be moved by the sight," Stevens wrote, "as it brought so vividly before us the reality of that terrible death by which our redemption had been purchased." This corporeal reminder of Jesus dying on the cross inspired him to investigate. He discovered that U Po had not died as a result of the crucifixion; instead, he had been beaten to death in prison after he "boldly acknowledged ... heretical opinions." When King Mindon learned that U Po's body had been buried, he ordered it exhumed and hung on a cross. Clearly, the king wanted to make a public statement. But what statement, exactly? Did Mindon—the Burmese ruler famous for being an extraordinarily devoted and lavish patron of Buddhism as well for being tolerant of a circumscribed Christian presence—mean to make reference to Christianity?[49]

The Baptists were not the only ones who thought of Christ when they thought of U Po. When Stevens and his crew of missionaries tried to learn about the beliefs held by U Po, they found that many people in town appeared too frightened to talk about it. "One man told [Stevens] that Oo Po was a Christian, with whom he was personally acquainted, and to whom he . . . had given books." But others explained that U Po "was not a Christian, but rather of the Paramat sect of Buddhists," which Stevens notes is a sect that has "no confidence in the worship of idols and pagodas, and in making offering to the" monks. Stevens and his fellow missionaries concluded that this Paramat theory is "the more probable view of the case, and evidently it is the view . . . put forth by the king." Stevens knew that Mindon showed tolerance toward Christianity and would not have made such a horrifying public example of an executed Christian. While the king allowed for Christian expression and even sponsored the large Anglican church and Christian school discussed earlier in the chapter, he did not, according to Stevens, "sanction freedom of opinion on religious subjects among the Buddhists of his realm." The case of the crucifixion, then, was an extreme example of what Stevens had learned on the steamer to Upper Burma: Christians are tolerated, but speaking against mainstream Buddhism is not, especially by the Burmese. U Po's crime, therefore, was not that he was preaching Western religious ideas, but that his statements were deemed Buddhist heresy.[50]

In James Scott's mention of U Po in his 1906 *Burma: A Handbook of Practical Information*, the colonial administrator writes that U Po founded an "anticlerical" group called the "Mans."[51] Scott reports that U Po was one of King Mindon's doctors, and that the king executed him after declaring him a heretic for insisting that in true Buddhism lay people were not obliged to provide material support to the sangha, and that the true Buddhist path was one of an individual creating the conditions for his personal liberation. Scott adds that "the name of the sect is taken from Mara, which is written and pronounced 'Man' in Burmese."[52] It would be striking to have a sect named after the notorious antihero who tried to thwart Prince Siddhartha's enlightenment, but perhaps the name was an intentionally defamatory one used by critics of the movement; this would be in line with Mendelson's suggestion that "Paramat" was a derogatory term. Charney accepts Scott's account of the Mans being founded by U Po and as one of several anticlerical sects active during King Mindon's reign.[53] I have not found accounts of the Mans in Baptist sources, but those sources do support Charney's more important point about King Mindon and Shin Neyya confronting serious challenges from several lay reform movements.

The case of U Po is mentioned a quarter-century later in a Burmese tome by U Tin, *The Royal Administration of Burma*—the one Burmese-language reference I have been able to access on the Paramats. This text describes U Po's claim that the contemporary monastic establishment was not the true sangha and records King Mindon's subsequent decision to execute him. This Burmese author makes no mention whatsoever of Christianity, nor of Mahayana Buddhism. U Tin had been a bureaucrat in King Mindon's court and ended up working for the British colonial administration, and it was in that capacity that he published this work in 1931.[54] So, while U Tin's text was published over a half-century after U Po's execution, it draws on court documents from the time of the execution to which U Tin had special access, as well as from his personal experience working for that king.

U Tin describes "a physician named U Po, who was learned in the Pitakas and the Vedas [B. *dat-saya-gyi*], [who] was going about saying that he could not accept the authenticity of the present Order of monks." When King Mindon heard that U Po was arguing against the purity of the Burmese monastic institution, "he met and held discussion[s] with his scholars, and U Po was brought in to the meeting and questioned." After these discussions, U Po was "impaled and crucified." U Tin explains that this crucifixion was carried out "so that those who saw, or might hear of it, would be put in fear." U Tin also adds his opinion of the case: "It must be said that it was an evil execution." It is remarkable to find here a Burmese author providing a harsh judgment of an action of the country's celebrated Buddhist king Mindon Min. U Tin concludes his short account by noting that "U Po's sons, grandsons, and pupils were pursued and arrested; some escaped to Lower Burma and there is a leader of the Paramats, named Hsaya Hka, who is among those who escaped at that time. Even at the present there are a number of the successors of those pupils who escaped still living in Mon-ywa District."[55] U Tin, then, only identifies Hsaya Hka as a Paramat. He does not explicitly say that U Po was a Paramat; rather, he says that among the followers was this one Paramat.

This text offers a rare glimpse of Paramats in the Konbaung dynasty from a Burmese perspective. It is noteworthy, then, that there is no reference to Christianity and its influence on Buddhist sectarian disputes. Instead, U Po's religious positions are said to be based on scholarly knowledge of Buddhist canonical texts and classical scientific compendiums. There is also no mention of U Po refusing to bow down before Buddha statues. All U Tin relays is that U Po was speaking out about the impurity of monks and arguing that the current age was too degenerate for an authentic Buddhist monastic order to exist—a pair of concerns we find expressed at various times in the history of the Konbaung dynasty and in Theravada history more generally. As Alicia Turner and Erik Braun have shown, during the late nineteenth century these concerns about the decline of the *sāsana* were significantly heightened as the country lost a Buddhist throne and was subsumed into a Christian empire.[56] U Po's criticism of degenerating Buddhist institutions, then, is part of a larger cultural concern with the preservation of the Buddha's teachings during the violence of the British occupation.

Read together, the accounts by U Tin and Stevens agree that U Po was crucified for his criticism of the Buddhist order, and both assert that the Paramats were a kind of heretical sect, that U Po was one its leaders, and that a network of Paramats continued to be active, although marginalized, in Burma. In contrast to U Tin's report, Stevens's describes local people connecting U Po's attitude toward Buddhism with Christian texts and communities. Surely some of Stevens's concern with Christianity was fueled by the American's fixation on the future of Baptist evangelism in Burma. I do not, however, think that I should dismiss his interest in Christian connections as merely an expression of the missionary's personal concerns and then only accept U Tin's Burmese account as an accurate sketch of the story. Instead, I am arguing that Paramat accounts like Stevens's can help illuminate the Baptist vision of a Christianizing Burma as well as historical developments and the religious imagination of the Paramats. I will develop this by turning to the earliest records we have of the Paramats.

Accounts of Paramat Activity Before the Second Anglo-Burmese War

American missionaries had been recording encounters with the Paramats since at least as early as the 1830s. This period between the First and Second Anglo-Burmese Wars was a time of political anxiety throughout the country. The Burmese were forced to cede western and southern regions to the British to end the first war, pay a large fee, and agree to a commercial treaty favorable to the British. For the Americans in Burma and the newly established Christian convert communities, this was a period of ambitious missionary campaigns launched from urban centers in southern Burma into peripheral rural areas. As I discussed in the previous chapter, this was also a period of vigorous Baptist school building. Perhaps most significantly, this was a time of increased missionary printing work. A second mission press was set up in Tavoy and run by Cephas Bennet to supplement the Rangoon press. At its peak, the Tavoy press printed an annual total of 21,002,000 pages in three different languages.[57] A key production of the quickly growing Baptist press was the pamphlet, which, as Isabel Hofmeyr has shown in her study of Gandhi's printing experiments during South African years, "were a major medium for making ideas more portable and durable."[58] This mobile Baptist print product spread Christian messages from urban centers into more remote regions. This period of missionary work was additionally characterized by its focus on the Burmese majority, which gave way in the subsequent period to a strong emphasis on minority communities.

This section will show how the early Baptist reports of Paramats from this period are distinguished by a hesitation on the part of the American missionaries to suggest that Paramat beliefs put them on the path to Christianity. American missionaries writing about local Christians say that Paramat beliefs open up the members of that sect to Christian teachings, but the Americans were still skeptical. While this position would change in the period before the Third Anglo-Burmese War, when American missionaries would start to assert that Paramats were influenced by Christianity and were much closer to Protestant conversion than mainstream Buddhists, this early set of writings about Paramats does include the characterization of them as iconoclasts, which would become standard.

The earliest account that I have been able to find comes from Thomas Simons, a missionary in King Bagyidaw's royal city of Ava who recorded encounters with Paramats on two separate occasions in his 1836 journals. This is twenty-three years into the American mission and twelve years after the First Anglo-Burmese War. In writing about being introduced to a Paramat man and his nephew by local Christian converts, Simons explains that "the old man is a doctor by profession, and is also a leader of a sect called Paramats, (a kind of deist)." The Paramat doctor also, according to Simons, "appeared well acquainted with [the Baptists'] books, and one or two of the [Christian] assistants have a faint hope that he feels the force of truth on his heart." Simons here compares Paramats to deists, a term applied in

Anglo-American communities to people who argue that individuals can access religious knowledge by the use of reason instead of through church teachings or divine revelation. While Simons's effort to explicitly define the sect indicates that they were previously unknown to the American mission, his report states that the Paramat leader was very familiar with Christian texts.[59]

Later that year, Simons would report meeting "a young man of respectable appearance" who came to the verandah of the mission house in front of a crowd of a dozen people and read aloud a copy of the *Golden Balance* by Adoniram Judson, a widely distributed Burmese-language tract, which argued for Christ's superiority over the Buddha because of his powers to save others. The young man said that he had not seen the text before, but upon reading it pronounced that its "law was good." Simons suspected that this man was "afraid to say much, on account of the people who were around him," so Simons invited him inside where the man talked for a while with his colleague Eugenio Kincaid.[60] Simons reports that Kincaid "ascertained that he was of the sect of the Paramats, gave him suitable books to read, and invited him to call again." This account suggests that Kincaid had previous knowledge of the Paramats, and it also speaks to the social and political risks that people from the Burmese majority took when they talked to Christians about religion.[61] This, I think, is important to keep in mind as we consider the longer history of Paramat-Christian interactions. The Burmese authorities forbid Christian missionaries from courting Burmese Buddhists, instead limiting approved evangelism in the Konbaung kingdom to groups they identified as outside of mainstream Burmese society.

The last early report I will attend to comes from Howard Malcom's 1838 *Travels in South-eastern Asia*, a popular two-volume book by a Baptist authority that surveys the cultural landscape and missionary work in Burma and other Southeast Asian settings. According to Malcom, the Paramats were concentrated in Ava and in towns along the Irrawaddy River. Malcom writes that they practice "a semi-atheism, or the worship of WISDOM"; that their leaders come from the laity; and that they have some support from the nobility. Malcom explains that "they discard the worship of images, and have neither priests nor sacred books," and that this has led them to be "greatly persecuted." Malcom also writes that the Paramats were founded by a reformer named Kolan "who lived about fifty years" and who based his doctrine on a revised reading of portions of the Tipitaka. Malcom reports that

"Kolan took the Be-da-ma, (the first part of the Bedagat,) and, after revising it, adopted it as a good creed; but it is not much copied among his followers. Until lately, the Kolans have been greatly persecuted; but at present little notice is taken of them." Here Malcom is referring to the Abhidhamma and explaining that this Paramat reader revised the text and adopted it as doctrine. Interestingly, he says this is the first part of the Pali Canon, though the Abhidamma is traditionally considered the third, and last, collection of teachings.[62] I have been able to find two other missionary accounts, including one that I will discuss in the following section, that describe Paramats as being founded by a late eighteenth-century leader in Ava, but I would need more evidence—ideally evidence from Burmese or Pali manuscripts or inscriptions—to confidently depict the origins of this sect.

Notably, Malcom's entry on the Paramats does not make any connection between the sect and Christianity. He does not suggest that the Protestant tracts missionaries were circulating in the country influenced the Paramats' unorthodox religious views, nor does he mention direct contact between Paramats and Baptists. I might read this absence of Christian connection in Malcom's writings about Paramats as an informed recognition that this sect is an internal, Burmese religious development that is unrelated to Christian activity in the country. Alternatively, I could suspect that Malcom's limited time in Burma—he only went there for one extended trip to survey missionary operations, whereas missionaries like Simons and Stevens spent decades in the country—did not allow him to appreciate the dynamism and productivity of Buddhist-Christian encounters. Even without favoring either reading, I can take Malcom's report as support for a claim that there was Paramat activity in the Ava and Irrawaddy River regions in the 1830s as well as evidence that a story was then circulating regarding a Paramat leader from the late eighteenth century.

A little over a decade after Malcom's descriptions of the Paramats, another prolific missionary, Francis Mason, sent news from the central missionary post in Maulmain that referred to the sect. Mason wrote in 1850 about meeting an old man who insisted that "there was no reason for his examining Christianity whatever." This man explained that his reasoning for not wanting to hear what Mason had to say about Jesus and salvation had to do with his knowledge of the history of all religions. Mason reports that this man "was so confident that Budhism was the parent of Christianity as well as of all other religions." The old man further explained that descendants of the ur-religion of Buddhism not only include Christianity, but also the Paramats: "There are the paramats . . . we know that they, though they differ from Budhists, derive their law from Budhism: and it is precisely the same with Christ's religion."[63] Mason did not pause to add more about the Paramats, but his brief account at least gives us a glimpse into an understanding of Buddhist history in this period that cast Buddhism as the original religion and all other religions as its descendants, or, perhaps, aberrations. For this elder Buddhist, and likely for others, new religious developments in the country, such as the growth of Baptist communities and the activities of the Paramat sect, could be understood as coming from Buddhism. This genealogy would have served, in part, to explain similarities between different religions while still privileging Buddhism.[64] Like the writing of contemporary European scholars, this Burmese Buddhist's comparative religions approach served to both explain the increasingly visible variety of religions in the world and to secure his religion as superior.[65]

Five months after Mason's encounter with the old man and his family tree of religions, Stevens wrote a letter home to the United States from Maulmain that described an "unusually large number of the Paramat sect." This 1850 letter is Steven's first known writing on the Paramats, and one of two pieces that were published before his 1870 piece on the crucifixion of U Po examined above. In his 1850 letter, Stevens explains that in the town of Myede on the eastern bank of the Irrawaddy "there is an unusually large number of the Paramat sect." He tells his readers that the Paramats "reject the divinity of Gaudama, and also images and pagodas." Stevens also explains that the governor in that region was favorable to them. This 1850 report echoes Malcom's 1838 description of the Paramats in that it describes a rejection of image worship and an interest that upper-class Burmese people have in the sect. But, whereas Malcom makes no connections whatsoever to Christianity, Stevens asserts that Paramat protest of image worship and the large number of Paramats is due, in part, to the spread of Christianity in Burma. Stevens writes that "we have learned that [in the Paramat region] and in other places, tracts and Bibles, which have previously been distributed, are silently doing their work, 'shining as a light in a dark place,' and surely undermining the bulwarks of heathenism." This statement gives a kind of agency and power to distributed tracts and bibles, arguing that they are working to weaken Buddhism. Stevens seems very confident in the effectiveness of the missionary texts, and he also appears certain that the

Paramats see real problems with Buddhism, although he is not sure that they are becoming Christians. He concludes that these "people clearly perceived the errors of Buddhism, but are yet ignorant of the *true* way of life." In other words, Stevens agrees with their criticism of Buddhism, but he does not go so far as to say that the Paramats are Christian.[66]

This 1850 report by Stevens is the last extant missionary text on Paramats before the Second Anglo-Burmese War. This period's missionary writings on Paramats vary with regard to the amount and kinds of detail provided on the sect, but there is a consistent reluctance on the part of the missionaries to see Paramats as either potential or actual converts to Christianity. In the next section, which examines missionary writings about Paramats from the period between the Second and Third Anglo-Burmese Wars, I will show that the theory that the Paramats are nearly Christian is first maintained by Burmese Christian preachers. Then American missionaries begin to see Paramats as proof that Buddhism and its abundant material culture were losing their hold on Burma, and that there was therefore a new opening to spread Christianity throughout the land. This second period of Paramat writing also features a pair of rare texts claiming to come directly from Paramat leaders. By examining these materials along with other missionary-produced studies of the Paramats, I demonstrate what the increased attention to this sect meant for the way the missionaries imagined the future of Christianity in Burma. These sources also provide a rare window into how dissent from Buddhist orthodoxy developed at the end of the final Burmese kingdom. They are a valuable resource for the study of debates about nirvana and meditation, of criticism of the power of religious images and objects, and pervasive concerns among new religious movements.

Accounts from the End of the Anglo-War Period

The Second Anglo-Burmese War not only resulted in the British annexing lower Burma, including the valuable port city of Rangoon; it also resulted in Mindon Min taking the Burmese throne and launching a Buddhist revival that was perhaps most visible in the countless new, repaired, and regilded pagodas throughout the country, including British territories.

THE PAGODA

In 1854, the Burma-based missionary James Granger sent the American Baptist Missionary Union a letter from Rangoon to describe what Burma was like on the brink of the Buddhist revival. One section is titled "The Popular Faith Shaken—The Paramats." In the letter, the missionary credits the recent war for the current state of Buddhism in Burma in which "*the popular faith of the country has received a shock.*" Granger describes deserted pagodas, unfed monks, disrobing monks, and the British treatment of "monasteries as public property and forcibly expell[ing] their occupants, while the soldiers ... shamefully rifle[] the pagodas in searching for treasure." Granger writes that he was surprised by "what apathy all this is regarded by the people, especially when it is remembered that these sacred places have always been respected in all their civil wars." In other words, the war with the British was quite different from earlier wars in Burma between rival ethnic groups and claims to the throne; those wars did not threaten Buddhism in the way the wars with the British had. Granger argues that the Second Anglo-Burmese War had induced "a general feeling [that the] old religion had been broken down."[67]

Granger explains that, in the midst of this breaking down of Buddhism and its pagodas, larger numbers of people had started calling themselves Paramats, which he describes as "a class of freethinkers who abjure Buddhism." In this definition, Paramats come across as even more hostile to Buddhism than they had in earlier reports, even as they retain a sense of nonconformity. Granger elaborates on the teachings of the Paramats, explaining that their "leading doctrine is that *there is one self-existing and eternal law of right,* to which it is the duty of all men to conform, and in which alone resides the sum of man's religious duty. This law is a perfect rule, and is known only by the voice of conscience which proclaims it." Granger here emphasizes individual faith in the dhamma but adds the condescending remark that many of the people claiming to be Paramats have "a very imperfect knowledge of the creed they embrace." Granger explains that these new converts are simply "ranked as Paramats" because they "relinquish the worship of pagodas and images [and] cast off the rule and support of the Burman priesthood." While the Burmese people Granger is observing are expressing their distinct religious or political identity by protesting pagodas and Buddha statues, Granger is clearly more interested in their belief system. He sees a problem with these new iconoclasts not seeming to understand well enough their doctrine of devotion to the eternal law.[68]

This report raises the question of whether its missionary author is privileging belief over practice because of his own Protestant bias, which was not shared by the Paramats. Was his concern for theology over religious action more of a reflection of Baptist values? Could a prominent concern of the Paramats have been to address pagodas to express opposition to contemporary behavior by Burmese Buddhist monks and their royal supporters as well as to promote Abhidhamma doctrines on the ultimate truth?

Missionary reports like Granger's are regularly concerned with what is right and wrong about Paramat doctrine and how that doctrine and its attendant actions—especially iconoclastic ones—resembled Protestant Christianity. But I think we can learn something if we consider Paramat *practices* and their political implications. In other words, I think it might be more accurate to see Paramats as committed to *both* protesting corruption among royally empowered monks and to knowing the true dhamma. It is worth considering that they might have even been more interested in public, political action rather than in doctrinal debate—or, rather, that it is a mistake to separate the two: the political and the philosophical. I would wager that it is most productive to consider the Paramats as a kind of opposition movement against the dominant, royally sponsored monasticism that concerned itself with both the ultimate validity of religious doctrine as well as the political climate which promoted certain peoples, pagodas, and doctrines and suppressed other religious expression.

Over a decade after Granger's Paramat writings, the *Missionary Magazine* published a piece that includes a text on Paramats by the Burmese Christian preacher and self-proclaimed former Paramat Ko Kong. It is clear from this 1867 article that Ko Kong was asked to write this text to help raise support for the mission, and I suspect that it was originally written in Burmese and then translated into English. Without the original Burmese we cannot tell how literal the translation was; still, I think we can approach it as some version of what the Burmese preacher actually wrote. Seen in this way, Ko Kong's account of his journey from Buddhist to Paramat to Christian is a rare document informed by the point of view of a former Paramat. Indeed, it is the earliest text I have found said to be written by someone who explicitly identified as a Paramat. Therefore, in Ko Kong's story, we can look both for signs that it has been manipulated for American audiences, *and* signs that it speaks to a Paramat history and imagination at some remove from the influence of the Baptists.

Ko Kong writes that he was born in 1806 and moved with his family in his early years to Prome to escape robbers in his hometown. Up until the age of twelve, he earned money for his family by making bamboo flutes. Then his father died, and his mother sent him to the monastery to learn to read and write. He stayed there for two years as a lay student and two more as a monk. At sixteen, he disrobed to return home and help his mother. At nineteen, he married and had one son. It was at this point that he encountered Paramat teachers and "their views of the Buddhist religion." Ko Kong writes about "observing that they did not worship the idols of Gaudama nor the priests," and how he "examined the books on Buddhism," Then, by the age of thirty, he, "left off worshipping the idols and became a disciple of the Paramats." Ko Kong continued to identify as a Paramat for eighteen years before his conversion to Christianity at the age of forty-eight.[69]

For Ko Kong, an understanding of the sect was based on hearing their arguments against Buddhism and witnessing their refusal to participate in traditional devotional practices with Buddha images. Ko Kong went on to study Buddhist texts for himself, stop worshipping statues and monks, and become a Paramat. It is important to underscore here that he never mentioned a central philosophical or theological Paramat stance. For Ko Kong, the attraction to the sect was foremost their rejection of Buddha statues and veneration of monks. This autobiography, then, supports my hypothesis that a central concern connecting various Paramat figures and groups is an active, organized protest of mainstream Buddhist institutions and their material presence. This Buddhist materiality was powerful enough in this period to generate condemnation and practices of religious conversion examined elsewhere in this book.

Eveleth's Paramat Articles

The missionary archives have preserved two additional texts from this period between the Second and Third Anglo Burmese Wars that similarly aim to give a direct Burmese perspective on the Paramats. These texts, which claim to be transcripts of interviews with Paramat leaders, are embedded in long articles from 1881 and 1882 by Frederick Howard Eveleth, an American missionary active in the final years of the Konbaung dynasty. Eveleth writes that he included transcripts because missionaries are "so frequently charged with misrepresenting the views of the heathen."[70] These articles are not only extraordinary for their transcript format but also for the sheer amount of information they offer.

Eveleth's first article begins by explaining that "about fifty years ago a class of metaphysicians arose in Ava, called the Paramats, who respect only the Abhidama, and reject the other books that the Buddhists consider sacred, saying that they are only a compilation of fables and allegories. The founder of this sect, Ko San, with about five of his followers, was put to death by order of the king." This account resembles the Paramat histories given by Malcom, but instead of Malcom's "Kolan" we find the leader's name transcribed as "Ko San." Also, Eveleth's source specified that the Paramats only respect the Abhidhamma.[71]

Eveleth's article then goes on to detail a recent schism between the Paramats and the orthodox Buddhist Order in Toungoo. Eveleth explains that the Paramats in that region had a substantial following for "several years," but that "nothing occurred to separate them from the main body of Buddhists until the rainy season of last year." Eveleth describes the rainy season controversy in which a Paramat leader named U Alapa skillfully defended his doctrines in front of a large crowd. Despite U Alapa's persuasive defense, the monastic council tried to make him sign a contract to declare that he would stop preaching these controversial views, but the Paramat refused, and a big schism ensued that Eveleth says ended up violently separating "old friends and hitherto harmonious families."[72]

The following month, an unnamed authority issued a letter calling for the six Paramat monks, including U Alapa, to be prevented from associating with the other priests, accepting offerings from lay people, and preaching. The central Paramats in Eveleth's article, surprisingly, are monks, unlike the lay Paramats from earlier missionary reports. Eveleth explains that the prohibitions against the monks were "nearly equivalent to excommunication; and those laymen who still adhere to these priests were regarded as heretics," which, Eveleth reports, is what also happens to people in Burma who convert to Christianity. This invites his American readers to adopt a sympathetic view of the Paramat struggle as well as to reflect on the difficulties faced by local Christians.[73]

In order to reconcile, the Paramats and the mainstream Buddhists sent the case to be reviewed in Mandalay. Those court officials, according to Eveleth, "enjoined upon both parties the necessity of living peaceably together." Eveleth concludes that "it was virtually a victory for the new party." The interview transcripts then follow. The first is with U Shway Bo, who replies to Eveleth's questions about God by saying that "God is in mind," that he exists "in Nigban," and that the being that the Paramats call God is "a man who sees and knows all things." From these responses it seems that U Shway Bo was explaining an understanding of awakening that is based on Abhidhamma doctrines that hold that practitioners must investigate and ultimately know reality in its conditioned parts so that they can attain freedom from that reality, nibbana. Here the Paramat seems to referring to the example of Gotama Buddha, as the model man who saw and knew all things and attained nirvana, and suggests that all men, by understanding what Gotama understood, can also attain nirvana. U Shway Bo added that Paramats "do not worship . . . images and pagodas," but rather that "pagodas serve to remind us of him whom we worship." U Shway Bo is emphasizing that these Buddhist objects should not be seen as somehow powerful or magical or efficacious in of themselves but as symbols of the Buddha's realization of the ultimate nature of all things. Like the missionary reports on pagodas examined at the outset of this chapter, U Shway Bo's explanation of pagodas is that they are symbols of something else. The Paramats and the Baptist both claim that pagodas are reflections of more important ideas. This claim comes up against other reports we find in the missionary archives of pagoda visitors expressing a sense that the Buddha and the liberation he taught is really present in the shrine.[74] Deliberations about how Buddha images can possess the power of the Buddha and whether it is better to see them as reminders of his teachings surely occurred in Burmese culture long before Americans arrived in the country. But, with the increasing presence of Protestant Christianity and their continuous charges of idolatry, it seems that Buddhist leaders became more practiced in explaining Buddhist sensational forms as symbols of more complex and important doctrines.

There are further examples of this kind of explanation work in Eveleth's report, which includes fascinating topics not found in earlier reports. For example, when he asks the monk, "Do you hold that the gates of Nigban are closed saved when a Buddh is in the world?," U Shway Bo answers, "The mass of Buddhists so believe, but we do not." This refers to a larger debate in the kingdom about whether people's enlightenment depends on the presence of a fully enlightened Buddha in the world. The Paramat leader states that the majority of Buddhists think that full enlightenment is only possible when a Buddha is present, but that the Paramat position is that enlightenment is possible even in times like the present: the period between Gotama Buddha and the next Buddha, Maitreya (B. Metteyya). Eveleth follows up by asking how a man may "soonest attain to Nigban." Then, by way of reply, U Shway Bo "[closes] his eyes ... assum[es] a meditative attitude," and tells the American that you attain nirvana "by contemplating the body. For example, the hairs of my head; how numerous they are! But soon they will turn white, and fall off, etc. Thus on through the thirty-two parts of the body, as the nails, skin, heart, lungs, etc. By this kind of meditation a man can soonest reach Nigban, I think."[75]

This 1882 record of U Shway Bo's teaching on meditation is extraordinary. It is a rare example of a Burmese person arguing for the importance of a formal meditation practice to a foreigner in the Konbaung period. The specific meditation to which the Paramat leader refers is the meditation on the thirty-two body parts, which can be traced back to the instructions in the Pali Canon's *Satipaṭṭhāna Sutta* on body contemplation in which "a monk reviews this same body up from the soles of the feet and down from the top of the hair, bounded by skin, as full of many kinds of impurity," and then thirty-two body parts are listed. The *Sutta* continues, "In this way he dwells contemplating the body in the body internally, externally, and both internally and externally.... And he dwells independent, not clinging to anything in the world."[76] As Erik Braun has shown, the thirty-two body parts contemplation practice became popular in the late nineteenth century among revolutionary Buddhist teachers such as Hpo Hlaing, whose 1875 *Kāyānaupassanā*, or meditation on the body, builds on these canonical instructions.[77] It seems that the increased attention to this body meditation among the newly popular Vipassanā (insight meditation) teachers—the figures that Braun shows were dramatically transforming Burmese Buddhism and laying the ground work for the global popularity of Vipassanā meditation in the late twentieth and early twenty-first centuries—was also happening in Paramat communities.

Following his interview with U Shway Bo and its remarkable discussion of meditation, Eveleth includes an interview with the Paramat leader U Alapa, who says at the outset of their conversation that "we are not very far apart in our faith." Eveleth adds in parenthesis: "Would that he were as near being a Christian as he thinks!" U Alapa tells Eveleth that "God is eternal," but adds the decidedly un-Christian doctrine that God is "helpless in the matter of saving men. . . . He cannot forgive sin." This Paramat leader also says that enlightenment is possible for lay people in their very lifetimes. This claim, which U Shway Bo also made, is not in reports of the Paramats prior to Eveleth's. And it is *this* claim that U Alapa said caused him to be called to trial. In other words, the Paramats' most controversial teaching was that men can attain liberation in this very life, without being a monk, without waiting eons for another Buddha to appear. This speaks to a new wave of thought about the possibility of lay enlightenment that was beginning to gather energy in Burma at this time.[78]

Patrick Pranke has shown that "chronicles written from the perspective of the royally-backed Thudamma ecclesiastical council begin to reflect a gradual shift in opinion regarding the possibility of enlightenment in the present age."[79] Braun has argued that "the growing prominence given to the possibility of awakening in these texts signaled a change that would enable a rethinking later about the potential of meditation practice on a mass scale."[80] Braun's monograph shows how Ledi Sayadaw (1846–1923), the influential Burmese Buddhist leader of the modern Vipassanā meditation movement, advanced this rethinking and famously taught that enlightenment in this very life was even possible for lay people, something we do not find in the Konbaung chronicles. Bruan's work persuasively demonstrates that Ledi Sayadaw's movement was inspired by precolonial traditions (such as the Abhidhamma philosophical tradition) as well as by the disruption of colonial forces. The kinds of disruption Braun highlights are British political and economic control. Surely the Burmese Buddhist majority was significantly more disrupted by British colonization than they were by the presence of the American Baptist missionaries, whose efforts shifted into minority communities from remote hill and jungle regions over the course of the nineteenth century. Still the larger energy around contemplating new religious possibilities was fueled in some part by the Baptist push—in print and in person—for Christian consideration. While the Baptists argued against individually earned enlightenment, they did insist that true salvation was possible for everyone in this life as long as they truly believed in the Christian god.

The statements by U Alapa and U Shway Bo suggest that Paramats adopted the new view of the possibility of present-day enlightenment for lay people that was being advanced by teachers like Ledi Sayadaw and understood how it related to Christian doctrines on salvation. Eveleth ends his interview with U Alapa by telling his readers that this Burmese monk "has had a copy of the New Testament for the past three years, and has always listened attentively to our native preachers," and that his knowledge of the Bible was said to be "both deep and solid." The Baptist seems to imply that U Alapa's ideas about God as eternal truth and salvation as open to all people could have been influenced from missionary texts and evangelical efforts. Eveleth also notes that Paramats were persecuted as badly as the Christians, perhaps even more so, that "some of the orthodox Buddhists go so far as to declare that a man had much better be a Christian out and out than a Paramat." This point about it being politically and socially safer to identify as Christian rather than as Paramat echoes Stevens's investigation into the crucifixion of U Po described above, where Mandalay locals explained that while Christianity was tolerated, Buddhist heresy was not.[81]

I will now briefly address this chapter's last source: Eveleth's second article on the Paramats. This article focuses on the Paramat activity in Shwaygeen, which Eveleth had heard was quite different from what was going on in Toungoo. Whereas his first article reports somewhat hopeful signs that Paramats made an opening for Christian conversion among the Burmese, this second article is even more enthusiastic about what Eveleth sees as nearly Christian beliefs of the Paramats in Shwaygeen.

The Shwaygeen leader quoted by Eveleth echoed earlier Paramat statements about the supreme law: how it was unnecessary to worship images, and how he—like other Burmese—could not accept the Christian teaching that Jesus Christ died so that men can be saved by God. Following his interview with the Shwaygeen leader, Eveleth reports on what he had learned during his visit to the area about how Paramats and Christians suffer similar persecution. One Paramat who calls on Eveleth told him, "They have stoned my house, cut down my plantain trees, [cut] in pieces my jack-fruit, killed and eaten my fowls, and burned my boat. They say, 'This is Jesus Christ property, there is no hell in destroying this; these are Jesus Christ fowls, there is no sin in killing them.'" There is both religious and material violence in this attack. Clearly the attackers targeted the Paramat's shelter, food, and vehicle, threatening his life and the lives of his family. They justify their devastating assault by claiming that these materials are not, in fact, the man's, because he has converted to Christianity. As Eveleth explains, for mainstream Buddhists "any movement which appears like a departure from the old faith is construed at once as a going-over to the Christian religion."[82] This movement is a *material* movement; conversion dangerously transforms people's status and property.

These Eveleth articles not only help detail the activities and doctrinal positions of Paramats but they also point out that the persecution Paramats suffered was similar to the persecution of Christian converts. The local informants Eveleth quotes are the ones making this connection, suggesting both that the Burmese community linked Paramats and Christians, and that Paramats themselves reached out to Baptists for sympathy and support for the difficulties they faced on the fringes of Burmese society. This was not just a matter of abstract philosophical debate. This was a battle for real power.

These Paramat documents show how, over the course of the nineteenth-century American Baptist mission and the three Anglo-Burmese wars, Paramats went from being described vaguely as a group of iconoclasts to being reported on in detail as a relatively organized sect who connected their philosophies to Christian teachings and their persecution to the abuse faced by Christian converts in the country. This movement regularly pointed to pagodas and related images practices to explain their criticisms of mainstream Burmese Buddhism and its excessive materiality. This survey has also shown how American Baptist missionaries wove together visions of the country's weakening Buddhism with visions of new possibilities for Christian evangelism into their reports on Paramats. While Paramat activity seems to have peaked in the nineteenth century without creating a significant opening for Christian conversion among the Burmese majority, the story of the Paramats does point to larger trends in modernizing Burmese Buddhism that are of particular interest to scholars today, such as the growing interest in meditation, the increasingly prominent role of lay Buddhists, and the idea that enlightenment can be achieved in this very life.

* * *

This chapter's study of pagodas and Paramats offers insights into larger processes of religious transformations during Burma's final kingdom, both among the Burmese Buddhist majority as well as minority communities. By studying previously unexamined writings on the Paramats and Christian attacks on Buddhist material culture, I have detailed religious conflict and imagination in Burma. This book is working to tell more textured and inclusive stories of nineteenth-century Burma by attending to the ways various minority groups used powerful objects to challenge dominant religious-political institutions and engage with alternative religious movements. These stories complicate common narratives about Burma as a unified, tranquil Buddhist kingdom before the late nineteenth-century. By detailing histories of minority groups resisting or protesting the majority and the ways those groups were suppressed, exiled, or appeased, I hope that this book can shed light on larger patterns of religious and ethnic conflict that still plague the region to this day. In order to explore the living legacy of the nineteenth-century American Baptist mission in contemporary Myanmar, the following chapter jumps into the twenty-first century to attend to Myanmar's bicentennial celebrations of the American Baptist mission. A curious set of portraits reveals how religious objects continue to shape communal expression, transformation, and segregation in the Southeast Asian country.

FOUR

The Portrait

American Jesus in Burma

IN 2013, BAPTIST communities in Myanmar and the United States celebrated the 200-year anniversary of Ann and Adoniram Judson's arrival in Burma and the establishment of their Christian mission. Baptist churches and historical organizations had organized pilgrimages and publications on the 100-year anniversary, in 1913, and the 150-year anniversary, in 1963, and were keen to commemorate the bicentennial. At that time, I was a PhD student, just beginning research for a dissertation on nineteenth-century Burmese religious history. The previous fall, I had made a research trip to the American Baptist Historical Society archives in Atlanta, Georgia, where I learned about the historical society's plans to host the Judson200 Legacy Tour, which was planning to take about two dozen Americans to Myanmar from January 17 to 31, 2013. The tour "promise[d] to be a very special cultural and spiritual experience" and "a singular opportunity to see those places where [the Judsons] lived, studied, worked, and invested their hearts in the lives of the people they loved."[1] Additional bicentennial celebrations in Myanmar throughout the year heralded similar experiences and itineraries, inviting foreign and local Baptists to visit historic sites and worship with congregations that traced themselves back to the early American mission. With an invitation from the tour planners, the support of my dissertation advisers, and enough available credit on my American Express card, I was able to join.

THE PORTRAIT

The trip proved transformational. Although I had been to Myanmar before, I had never explored the country's Christianity. And, although I had been studying Baptist history academically, I had never spent a significant amount of time among living Baptist congregations. I had traveled to Myanmar once before for a month-long independent research trip as an undergraduate student in Antioch College's Buddhist studies program, based in Bodh Gaya, India. During that trip, which focused on Burmese Buddhist nuns, I barely noticed a Christian presence or history as I visited monasteries and meditation centers in Mandalay and Sagaing. By the time of Judson200, I had begun to learn about the Baptist mission, but my research was entirely archival. I did not personally know many Baptists. I was raised by a Catholic and an atheist, and after college I worked in the editorial department of *Tricycle: The Buddhist Review*, which involved spending a lot of time with Buddhists in New York City. On Judson200, I got my first real sense of what it was like to be among practicing Baptists. The Baptists on the tour knew I was joining as a researcher and were very accepting. Given that the American Baptist Historical Society was the organizing institution, there was an appreciation for religious history, and a few of the other participants had advanced degrees in the humanities. I joined this Christian tour planning to record oral histories from Myanmar Baptist communities and to visit historic sites and archives, but the most striking thing I learned was how deeply inspiring the story of Ann and Adoniram Judson was for the American pilgrims and the Myanmar Baptists who welcomed us.

This final chapter follows the itinerary of Judson200 Tour in order to explore the particular material practices that have shaped the Judson-centric legacy of the U.S. Baptist mission to Burma. I draw on my research during the January trip as well as on research I conducted in the summer and fall of 2013, when I returned to Myanmar independently to work in archives and collect more oral histories. That additional research allowed me to examine further how the nineteenth-century developments and objects I examine in the previous chapters have given shape to contemporary religious formations in both the United States and Myanmar. This chapter is organized according to the Judson200 Legacy Tour's itinerary in order to examine it as a constructed, communal experience. As Hillary Kaell shows in her study of American Christian participation in Holy Land pilgrimages, this kind of organized group travel is part of the understudied phenomenon of the multibillion dollar Christian leisure industry [which includes] activities such as trips to the Holy Land [that] are voluntary and are undertaken as a complement to regular church services and activities. As such, they are paradenominational or extradenominational, making them part of what is perhaps the most important trend in modern U.S. Christianity. Parachurch organizations, small prayer and study groups, pilgrimages and tours, retreats and short term missions, online chats and TV ministries, to name just a few examples, are central sites of flexible identity production and religious adherence. It is in these contexts that we see contemporary faith in action.[2]

By joining this tour and seeing it put contemporary faith in action, I was able to understand how Baptist communities in Myanmar and the U.S. continue to enliven a religious imagination of the mission as historic and holy. This tour—like other Baptist commemorative practices centered on the Judsons that I explore later in this chapter—used powerful things to imbue the mission with sacred significance. At the time of my research, the people I met in Myanmar who helped me understand the role particular objects on the tour played in constructing this experience did not ask for anonymity. But, since my travels, violence against the Rohingya accelerated, and the military launched a coup. So, for the protection of the people I quote in this chapter, I have changed their names and other details about the context of our interactions. While I foreground the sensorium that the tour's material culture produced, I also work to reproduce how the participants and our Burmese hosts spoke about the power of God and the impact of the Judson's extraordinary evangelization.

The Judson200 Legacy Tour promised a Protestant pilgrimage filled with extraordinary embodied experiences. A trek through banana fields to the now grassy spot where Adoniram Judson was imprisoned invited the group to circle around and bow heads in prayer. We spent one sunset visiting the famous Shwedagon Pagoda, where we took off our shoes to walk on the marble circumambulation path, still warm from the day's heat. The chimes of Buddhist shrine bells found their way through the curtained windows of our tour bus as we motored through cities and out to villages. Old Christian hymns at Sunday services reminded American pilgrims from rural areas of country churches back home. In between sightseeing and church visits, "Busses Welcome" restaurants prepared us mild versions of local cuisine, leaving out Chinese and Indian peppers from their fish-sauced dishes, various salads, and pickled tea leaves. All the while we practiced Burmese expressions for "hello" (*min-gala-ba*) and "thank you" (*ce-zu-tin-bah-deh*), feeling the new shapes of the words in our mouths.

Amid the sensorium of our encounters with the country's cultures, it was a visual encounter that proved the most fascinating, that provoked me to think anew about what Christian conversion has meant for the Baptists of Burma: I saw the Judsons everywhere. And Jesus, too. It was not just that people told story after story about Adoniram and Ann, and that they praised Jesus for sending them to Burma. It was *how* Jesus and the Judsons materialized that really caught my attention.

On our first Sunday, we visited the country's oldest Baptist congregation, where a huge oil-painted banner behind the center stage featured the Judsons and, above, hung a spotlit print of Warner Sallman's *Head of Christ* (see figure 4.1). The following Sunday, at the small village church in southern Burma at Ann's gravesite, I looked up to find the same Sallman painting as the only altar image and a pair of framed portraits of Adoniram and Ann hanging opposite. Many days in between and afterward included encounters with nearly identical paintings.

FIGURE 4.1 Altar at U Naw Church, Yangon. Photo by the author.

THE PORTRAIT

It is perhaps not surprising that I saw so many depictions of the Judsons. It was the bicentennial celebration of their arrival into Burma, after all, and local churches, national organizations, and American religious groups had put a lot of energy and resources into materials commemorating the event.[3] As for the many prints of Sallman's *Head of Christ*—that image is found all over the Protestant map. In fact, the 1940 painting by the Chicago artist is the most popular religious image in the world, with over five hundred million copies produced by the turn of the twenty-first century.[4]

But American Baptists tend to hang their Sallman prints in their homes or church halls, not on their altars. Why, then, do Christians in Burma give such prime church space to images of Jesus with angular facial features and golden highlights in his hair? There seemed to be something curious about the Judson images, too: instead of portraying the couple as dressed for evangelizing the Southeast Asian country, the Judson paintings consistently costumed them in the stately fashions of early nineteenth-century America. Why did these portraits not show Ann in the Burmese fashions and thin, bright local fabrics she adopted, or Adoniram in the simple cotton clothes he chose for this warm, humid climate? Why remember the founding missionaries in the heavy materials, ornate necklines, and muted colors they would wear when they sat for formal portraits in New England? What does it mean that the country's Baptist congregations gaze up at all of this exoticized religious imagery?

The answers to these questions about the relationship between this Christian portraiture and Burma's Baptists could formulate two rather different arguments: first, that the Anglo-American style of this country's church paintings reflects a lasting influence of Western imperialism; or, second, that Christians in Burma use this imagery to set themselves apart from the Burmese Buddhist majority and celebrate the powerful internationalism of their church. I want to make both arguments, simultaneously—and I want to suggest, further, that both are necessary to track the dynamic of religion in postcolonial societies like Myanmar's. The difference between these arguments hinges on the relationships of local Christians with both Westerners and Burmese Buddhists. Are Christians casualties of the cultural imperialism that attends missionary efforts? Is the Christianization among these ethnic minority groups largely a consequence of British colonialism and American cultural hegemony? Do Christians in Burma associate with Western religious and cultural forms for the promotion of other interests? Who has agency in this story, and how does that agency relate to enduring asymmetrical power structures?

This chapter argues that the Anglo-American style of Jesus and Judson imagery *does* reveal a Baptist strategy to mark themselves as distinct from Burmese Buddhists and networked with Western communities. This strategy, though, must be understood as descending from the collision and commingling of nineteenth-century empires and imagined religious worlds in Burma—British, American, and Burmese. It also comes from efforts among the country's minority communities to negotiate changing human relations and transcend them in the service of the divine. The use of Anglo-American Christian imagery in modern-day Burma, then, proceeds from the religious and political interactions narrated in the previous three chapters.[5]

By tracing the Judson200 Legacy Tour route (see figure 4.2), this chapter studies the material qualities and social contexts of religious images along the way in order to understand the relationships Burma's Baptists have

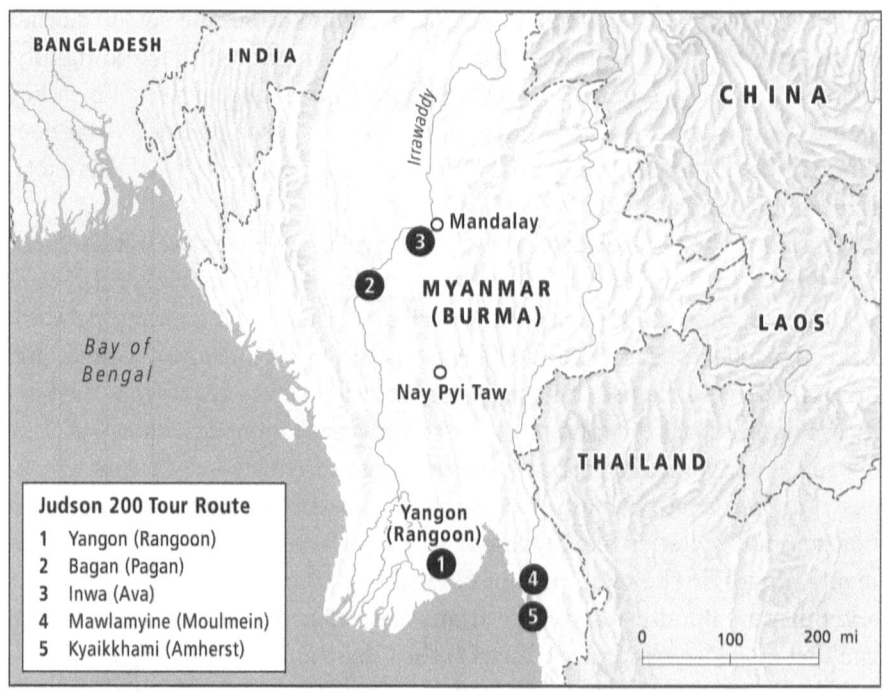

FIGURE 4.2 Judson200 tour route.

with God, the missionaries who brought his teachings to their country, and the Buddhist majority they live alongside.[6] To consider how paintings of the Judsons and Jesus work to create distinct and globally networked Christian communities in Burma, I will first turn to the tour's starting point in Yangon, where all this Baptist business began; then I will follow the Protestant pilgrimage north to Mandalay Region, where Adoniram Judson was famously imprisoned. Finally, I will wind up the tour with Judson200's final excursion into the country's southeastern region, where the Americans headquartered their mission in the mid-nineteenth century.

Yangon (Rangoon)

"After months of wandering, in July, 1813, the Judsons found their first eastern home in Rangoon," Marilla Ingalls recounted in her 1857 book on missionary life in Burma. "They found the country full of darkness, idolatry, cruelty, commotion, and superstition. The first missionaries longed to see even one Burman at the foot of the Cross." The reason the Judsons had so much difficulty converting the Burmese in Rangoon, Ingalls argued, was that Buddhism had "interwoven itself with political and civil life," and that this was made visible in the city's most holy site, Shwedagon Pagoda.[7] The Judsons, according to this nineteenth-century Baptist text, were operating their first missionary post in the monumental shadow and material excess of Burmese Buddhism, struggling to convince even one local to turn away from their beloved pagoda and toward the Christian cross. Today, Buddhist activity continues to dominate Yangon, but, in Christian corners, Baptists are surrounded by Christian imagery. Rather than at the feet of minimalist crosses, though, Baptists gather in pews below the painted faces of Jesus and the Judsons. In this most cosmopolitan of Burma's cities, Western portraiture marks a clear Christian presence alongside countless Buddhist shrines with their adorned Buddha statues, as well as among Hindu temples covered with carved devas, and mosques with their distinctive domed roofs and spiraling minarets. Buddhism, Hinduism, and Islam are old residents of this Southeast Asian port, but the exaggerated light-skinned iconography of Rangoon's Baptist churches reminds viewers that Protestant Christianity is a more recent arrival.

THE PORTRAIT

The Myanmar Baptist Convention Headquarters, Yangon

Our Judson200 Legacy Tour group got our Baptist bearings in Yangon by visiting the headquarters of the Myanmar Baptist Convention (MBC), the denomination's national oversight organization. The MBC operates out of Cushing Hall, a red-and-white brick structure built in 1908 in honor of the American Baptist missionary Josiah Nelson Cushing, who worked in Burma from 1866 to 1905.[8] There, MBC leaders shared data on their churches as well as details of their bicentennial plans. The MBC reported on 4,722 Baptist churches, which operate in 18 languages and regions and serve the 7 percent of Burma's population that identifies as Baptist. As 8 percent of the country identifies as Christian, the Baptists are the largest Christian community in Burma by far, as well as the largest religious minority group.[9] Another 80 percent of the population identifies as Buddhist, 4 percent as Muslim, and less than 2 percent as Hindu.[10]

While this visit was set up as a kind of business meeting, the visual culture at the headquarters gave it the look of a sacred space. Paintings of the Judsons and of Jesus on the walls and bicentennial materials presented Burma's Baptists as rooted in Western power and seemed to set a precedent for the visual culture at the churches our group visited throughout the country. Specific Judson and Jesus portraiture we encountered at MBC would appear again and again on our tour, as would the ways the missionaries were situated next to Christ and juxtaposed to next to national symbols.

Our tour group took our seats at conference tables arranged in a U-shape, as though we were foreign investors gathering to consider the value potential of this underfunded enterprise. We were each given a copy of the 2013 MBC datebook, the cover of which showcased a pair of black-and-white busts of Ann and Adoniram Judson, with curly-haired Ann in a puffy white ruffled neck collar and Adoniram in a formal jacket and high-collared shirt, his thinning hair brushed back (see figure 4.3). Ann and Adoniram are cast in a halo of white light within a faint bust of Sallman's *Head of Christ*. Behind Christ is an even subtler leaf design, with the top leaf outlining the shape of the country and an overlapping leaf inscribed with a white cross. This cover illustration on a mass-produced bicentennial memento pieces together the Judson legacy, Sallman's *Christ*, and a view of a Christian Burma. Out of the conglomerated Christian busts shoots a Baptist branch with Burma as its uppermost leaf. A similar visual argument about of the Western roots of

FIGURE 4.3 2013 Myanmar Baptist Convention management planner.

FIGURE 4.4 Wall mural at the Myanmar Baptist Convention headquarters, Yangon. Photo by the author.

Burma's Baptist churches is depicted in the MBC headquarters mural, although the Judsons in the wall painting are far more anglicized.

As we walked through the foyer to and from the MBC's main meeting space, we saw on the back wall a nine-foot-long, four-foot-tall painting of the Judsons arriving in Rangoon by sailboat in 1813 (see figure 4.4). In this richly colored scene, Adoniram and Ann gaze out from their ship's railing to examine Burma's Buddhist horizon. A towering Shwedagon Pagoda sits on a hill in the upper left portion of the mural, and Sule Pagoda rises on the right shore, the spires of these prominent religious landmarks nearly piercing the painting's top border. The glistening golden hues of the Buddhist shrines curiously match the hair on Ann's and Adoniram's heads, found in the mural's bottom right corner. While it is certainly exceptional to find the Judsons depicted as blondes, Ann's ruffled collar and Adoniram's formal jacket and shirt resemble the stately costumes they consistently wear in their portraits in this country's Baptist churches, confirming that these Western-dressed figures are indeed the famous founding missionaries.

The viewer looks out from behind them so that they can only see their backs and the sides of their faces, and so that they, too, are set inside their boat. This angle makes the focus of the figures not their familiar faces but the generically foreign cut of their clothes and exotic hair color. Here we find evidence that the Judsons are iconic enough among Burma's Baptists that they are recognizable by their silhouettes alone. Their old-timey American dress lines and hairstyles identify them as the country's especially famous and familiar nineteenth-century Westerners, even when they are hyperanglicized with blonde hair; their golden heads even help the viewer single them out as the first American missionaries. This rear perspective also encourages the viewer to imagine the country that the Judsons first saw in 1813: an overwhelmingly Buddhist nation about to be introduced to the teachings of the Baptist faith. And as the viewers are invited into their boat, they are incorporated into their missionary project, following them to the land where they worked to turn the people away from glistening pagodas and toward Christ.

The visual confrontation in this image between Western Christianity and Burmese Buddhism simplifies a story whose complexity lies in the diverse ethnic communities merely hinted at by the stick figures on the boats and shore between the American Baptists and the towering Theravada pagodas. The success of this evangelical mission would be decided, in large part, by the ethnic minority convert communities who energized the nineteenth-century mission and who sustained the Baptist church beyond the Anglo-Burmese war period, the colonial period, Burmese independence, the twentieth-century military dictatorship, and the bicentennial celebrations. It is mostly Karen, Kachin, and Chin communities who protect and promote this Protestantism through connections to Western organizations and negotiations with Buddhist organizations. They do not appear within the frame of MBC's wall mural or its brochure, but they are the ones doing the framing.

I returned to the MBC on my own nine months later to learn more about the ethnic relationships between present-day Baptist congregations and the country's first American evangelists. Connections I had made during the Judson200 visit to MBC in January helped me arrange interviews with the organization's leaders during my October visit to its headquarters. This second research trip overlapped with rising Buddhist-Muslim violence in Rakhine State, so I often found myself in conversations about the country's religious and ethnic conflicts, including those between Christians and Buddhists and among various Christian communities. As these conflicts began to intensify into a horrific genocide of the Rohingya people, Buddhist nationalists in government drafted the Religious Conversion Law on May 27, 2014. This law was part of a collection of proposed laws called the "Race and Religious Protection Bills." The conversion law limits the freedom of people to change religions by demanding that they go through elaborate application, interview, and education procedures. Other bills in this collection restrict interfaith marriage, ban polygamy, and establish population control measures.

I discussed Burma's religious and ethnic tensions with Reverend Tin Shwe, the MBC's director of the Evangelism and Ministry Department. He explained that one of the biggest problems for the Baptist Church in Myanmar today is the way Christians mistrust other communities, especially Buddhists, but also other ethnic Christian groups. He said that 95 to 99 percent of Christians come from minority groups, which contributes to what he called a pervasive "tribal mentality" among them. He told me a popular Christian joke to help explain this so-called tribal mentality: "Once a Karen man went to heaven and saw a Burmese man there, so he wanted to come back."[11] This joke shows how, for Reverend Tin Shwe, Baptist communities from the country's minority groups can often be more concerned with differences in ethnicity than religion and be even willing to jeopardize their own salvation to maintain distances between ethnic groups.

This joke might also help explain the ethnic markers in the Christian artwork hung in the country's Baptist churches, such as the hyperanglicized vision of the golden-haired Judsons in the MBC wall mural. By marking the Western aspects of their history, Burma's Baptist institutions brand themselves as networked to a powerful international community rather than as backed into ethnic corners of an otherwise Burmese Buddhist state. But, as I will show when I discuss the Judson200 Tour group's visit to Yangon's two most prosperous historic churches, Baptist congregations also juxtapose Jesus and Judson paintings with imagery specific to certain ethnic groups in order to privilege their church and its relationship to that ethnic group.[12]

The Judson200 Legacy Tour group had only one Sunday in Yangon to attend Sabbath services at the city's Baptist churches, so our itinerary had us attending two that morning: the 8:30 a.m. English-language service at Immanuel Baptist Church, and the 10:30 a.m. Burmese-language service a few blocks west at U Naw Church. Immanuel is the city's most prosperous and diverse Baptist church, and U Naw is the country's oldest Baptist congregation, dating back to the very first church the Judsons established. Christian artwork at both of these landmarks promote specific visions of how their congregations identify with national and international communities. Immanuel Baptist Church uses large Jesus paintings to promote a nondenominational image, whereas U Naw's emphasis on Judson imagery alongside smaller Jesus iconography emphasizes the church's specific Baptist, Burmese, and American history.

THE PORTRAIT

Immanuel Baptist Church, Yangon

You can't miss Immanuel Baptist Church. You just go downtown to the city's most important political and religious intersection and look for the big white building with the huge Jesus painting above the entrance (see figure 4.5). This larger-than-life Jesus seemingly walks out of the heavens, with clouds at his feet, light bursting around his head, and arms extended in a gesture of welcoming. His shoulder-length golden-brown locks and neatly cropped beard mark him as clearly exotic in this land of dark hair and little facial hair. Jesus's lush eyebrows frame a fair face with rosy cheeks, a small nose, and sympathetic eyes. A message across his legs quotes John 13:34 in Burmese and English: "I have loved you, that you also love another." This message of divine and brotherly love beams out across the parking lot to the golden Sule Pagoda, Yangon's second most prominent Buddhist shrine, where there are said to be relics of multiple Buddhas. This celebrated site, then, is constantly in a kind of public visual communication with Immanuel's Westernized, friendly, Christian exterior. On the northern side of this busy intersection are city hall and the building that housed the Supreme Court of Burma until 2006. And on the southern side is Maha Bandula Park, notorious for being the place where, at the height of the 1988 Uprising, the military opened fire on protesters calling for an end to the twenty-six-year, single-party military socialist rule of Ne Win. The uprising stood against the new constitution established under Ne Win that strengthened a more centralized state and revoked many protections for ethnic minorities. The political and religious history in this intersection is thick, and the iconography of Immanuel Baptist Church claims a space for a particular depiction of ecumenical Christianity within it.

Immanuel Baptist Church was founded in 1885—the year of the Third Anglo-Burmese War—but the original building was destroyed during the World War II Japanese occupation. The church was rebuilt in 1952, four years after Burmese independence and nine years before Buddhism was established as the country's official religion under Prime Minister U Nu.[13] During the 2013 Judson200 Tour, the country was experiencing relative peace after decades of military dictatorship and its attendant persecution of minorities (this period would, unfortunately prove short lived, as the Rohingya crisis escalated later that year, and the military orchestrated a putsch eight years

FIGURE 4.5 Immanuel Baptist Church, Yangon. Photo by author.

THE PORTRAIT

later). Immanuel Baptist Church openly welcomed congregants from a vast array of the country's ethnic minorities, with Sunday services held in Kayin, Telugu, Chinese, Burmese, Lisu, Shan, Mizo, as well as English and Burmese. The sounds of this diversity seem to fade away in the singular face of the Jesus image prominently posted behind the altar (see figure 4.6). It is the same image as the one on the building's exterior, this one covered in protective plastic wrap, and surrounded by lights. Above this glistening painting of Jesus is a lacquered wooden disk with a reversed *Head of Christ* at the center. As I sat with the American pilgrims looking up at the shrine, one member of our group, a historian and retired professor, commented that Sallman "really captured the likeness of our Lord." I looked up again to consider the warm glow of Jesus's face, the near halo effect of the backlighting, the golden highlights in the hair, and the radiant eyes gazing out of the painting's frame. But, rather than feel comforted by the familiarity of the image, I wondered why this particular, American painting of Jesus was being showcased in these Baptist spaces in Burma. As I began to start seeing more and more Sallman's Christs and noticing them alongside images of the Judsons, I realized that the exoticism was part of the point.

FIGURE 4.6 Immanuel Baptist Church altar, Yangon. Photo by author.

THE PORTRAIT

The prayer scripture at the Immanuel Baptist Church service came from the Book of Revelations (8:15): "Then the angel took the censer and filled it with fire from the altar and threw it on the earth; and there were peals of thunder, voices, flashes of lightening, and an earthquake." The church's senior minister, Reverend Dr. John Matthew, preached on this theme of the destructions of nations, elaborating on how many great nations have arisen and fallen, notably those of Babylonia, Persia, Greece, and Rome. He paused to suggest that the next to fall might be the United States or Russia or China. But a much greater kingdom awaited, the Kingdom of God. Reverend John Matthew delivered this message of the Kingdom above all kingdoms from a chair on the left side of the stage, rather than standing behind the pulpit. Our tour leader—a retired missionary living in Alabama and the author of a book on the Judsons—explained on the bus after the service that Reverend John Matthew had to sit because he suffered from an illness attacking his kidneys and was on dialysis. Adoniram also preached sitting down, our tour leader continued; not because he was too ill to stand, but because he understood that local people were used to hearing religious authorities speak from that position. Senior Burmese Buddhist monks today continue to preach and oversee rituals from a seated, cross-legged position on a platform or stage that is elevated above the space where the laity sits. Unlike Adoniram, Reverend John Matthew was not intentionally imitating these Buddhist postures, but his seated sermon provided the tour leader with the opportunity to recount how the first missionaries physically and visually modeled surrounding Buddhist practices. The American Protestants from two centuries ago did not go so far as to hang huge, colorful, anthropomorphic paintings in their religious spaces, but they did set a precedent for incorporating local religious practices.

There were no images of Adoniram, seated or standing, paired with Immanuel Baptist Church's Jesus paintings, but this did not strike me as odd. It was the first church I had visited in the country, and I had not yet noticed the prevalence of Judson paintings throughout the country's Baptist spaces. When I returned to Yangon seven months later, I learned more about why this particular community might emblazon a huge Westernized Jesus painting on the outside of their church, but did not advertise anywhere their connection to the nineteenth-century American mission. I visited Immanuel Baptist Church again on August 29, 2013, to attend a memorial service held for Reverend John Matthew, who had died that week. The service not only celebrated the esteemed reverend's life and work, but also the ethnic diversity and nonsectarian atmosphere of his church. Hundreds of people had come out to honor his memory, and the service was filled with performances from the church's several minority-language choirs. Many in attendance were from other denominations, including the head of Yangon's Armenian Church, Reverend Paul Than Win, who had invited me to attend the service with him. The multilingual, multidenominational Christian crowd at Reverend John Matthew's memorial service seemed to work in partnership with the church's Western Christian imagery to project an ecumenical identity.

Immanuel Baptist Church's openness to a larger Christian community also caught the eye—and nose—of the Judson200 Tour group, who all seemed interested in the incense burning at the service during our January visit. Knowing that I studied Buddhism, a couple of people asked me if this was an encroachment from the surrounding Buddhist culture. Our tour leader got wind of these grumblings and put the question directly to Reverend John Matthew, who responded that their church used incense not to appeal to the surrounding Buddhist culture, but as a way to make the space more welcoming to other Christians who had come to expect services filled with its smoky fragrance. Likewise, the colossal Jesus paintings hung on the outside of the church and behind its main altar promoted Immanuel as a place of worship for all Christians who see the son of their god with Western features but as ultimately above all ethnic and national difference, perhaps like the Kingdom of God of Reverend John Matthew's sermon.

U Naw Church, Yangon

After a visit to Immanuel, U Naw Church feels decidedly more parochial and less "high-church," as the professor on our tour from Virginia described it. (He followed his comment to me with a quick apology; he had learned the night before that I grew up going to a Catholic church and didn't mean any offence.) U Naw Church is also in downtown Yangon, but at a less prominent intersection, and the red brick building attracts less attention than Immanuel's gleaming white stucco structure. While the exterior is subtler, the richly illustrated interior of U Naw tells a much more ethnically inflected story of the Burmese congregation's specific connections to the American mission. In the place of Immanuel's universalism, we found an especially sectarian, Burmese Baptist picture of Christianity in U Naw.

U Naw Church's congregation traces itself directly back to the country's first Baptist church, established by the Judsons in 1816. The original wooden structure has been lost to the ravages of monsoon rains and the chaos of the Anglo-Burmese wars. Now the congregation named after the Burmese convert U Naw, the first person in the country to be baptized by Adoniram Judson, is housed in a mid-twentieth-century building with a prominent cross-shaped window facing Yangon's busy Anawrahta Road. It is not just its historical claim, though, that U Naw uses to promote its ties to U.S. religious history. Images of the Judsons that were hung throughout the church for the bicentennial reminded members and visitors alike that this faith came by way of two famous Americans and their god.

The Judson200 Legacy Tour group entered U Naw at the street-level community space and then climbed a stairwell to reach the large church, containing seventeen rows of pews and a spacious stage altar. Sunlight poured into the church through a large cross-shaped window. We had arrived early, and, as young men were setting up microphones onstage, we could examine

FIGURE 4.7 Altar banner at U Naw Church, Yangon. Photo by author.

the altar's centerpiece: an eight-foot tall, ten-foot-wide maroon cloth banner with a large white heart (see figure 4.7). Within the heart was the now familiar black-and-white painting of Adoniram and Ann Judson. In it Adoniram is wearing a high-collared jacket over a white shirt and a striped tie; Ann's thick, shiny hair frames her face in a kind of voluminous Edwardian updo, which is mirrored by a large, ruffled white collar. Two books are stacked in front of Adoniram's chest, with the large binding of the top volume suggesting that it contains his Burmese bible, the first translation of the Christian scriptures into the language. The book below is likely the first Burmese-English dictionary, another of Adoniram's monumental translation projects.

The banner painting of Ann and Adoniram recreates iconic imagery, specifically the Judson portraits created for the 150-year anniversary of their arrival (see figure 4.8), the biggest anniversary celebration prior to the 200-year celebration that was the occasion of our Judson200 Tour. For the 1963 celebration, the MBC (then called the Burma Baptist Convention)

FIGURE 4.8 *The Sesquicentennial Pictorial of Baptist Work in Burma, 1813–1963*. Courtesy of the American Baptist Historical Society.

distributed illustrated pamphlets printed at Rangoon University Press titled *The Sesquicentennial Pictorial of Baptist Work in Burma, 1813–1963*.[14] The *Pictorial*'s cover features a pair of portraits of Adoniram and Ann Judson nearly matching those shown on the U Naw banner, although it fills rectangular frames with buildings indicating key events in the history of the American mission: behind Adoniram is Judson Church at Judson College, now Yangon University, the country's most prestigious institute of higher education; and in front of Ann is the watchtower built by the Burmese king Bagyidaw, who imprisoned Adoniram in 1824. Traces of this tower poke out of the bottom of U Naw's heart banner, but the religious and royal landmarks are much more legible in the *Pictorial*, which therefore makes stronger visual connections between the Judsons and the institution-building work of the American mission and the obstacles Christian evangelists faced from Buddhist authorities.[15] Without prominent church towers and menacing prisons, the banner at U Naw focuses instead on a less historic and perhaps more charismatic vision of the American couple. It is a heart frame, after all, that crops the historic building out of the image and holds our gaze in the devotional pairing of these foreign founding figures, both of whom died in this country while laboring for the Baptist church. For the members of the congregation—who sit in pews below the Judsons and wear the colorful clothing with simple necklines common in this country—the banner's fixation on the Western costumes and hairstyles of the Judsons seems to emphasize that these founding figures came from a faraway place and time.

Above this huge Judson heart banner was a framed, spotlit painting of Jesus that imitates Sallman's *Head of Christ*. This *Head of Christ*, like the one in Immanuel Baptist Church, mirrors Sallman's to show Jesus facing left. But the alterations do not stop there. U Naw's Jesus wears a red robe instead of Sallman's white, and the painting's brighter, cruder illumination forms a large halo around Jesus's face, giving him a lighter, peachier complexion. Jesus's red robes nearly match the color of Burmese Buddhist monastic robes, but his beard and skin tone as well as the Judsons' clothing and hairstyles clearly communicate that this is a Christian space with Western influences.

The real twist in the iconography of U Naw Church, however, is not in how the images of the Judsons or Jesus play with earlier forms, but how a third—and explicitly Burmese—bust is added to Burma's Baptist pantheon: U Naw's. The main exhibit showcasing U Naw is found at the ground floor entrance of the church on a mural celebrating the congregation's upcoming bicentennial

THE PORTRAIT

FIGURE 4.9 Historical display at U Naw Church, Yangon. Photo by the author.

celebrations (see figure 4.9). This mural features an illustration of the *Georgiana*, the ship that brought Adoniram and Ann from India to Burma in 1813. The main sail frames paintings of the Judsons that are nearly identical to the ones displayed on the main altar and on the wall calendar, but here there are pops of color—peach in Adoniram's shirt and tie and coral in Ann's ruffled collar. On the wind-filled sail waving above the Judsons we find a painting of U Naw, wearing a traditional Burmese headband, formal jacket, and high-necked shirt. U Naw was a member of this country's majority group, and the church bearing his name serves a congregation that is nearly entirely Burmese, a rarity in a country whose Christian populations are overwhelmingly found among minority communities.

These complex identity politics play out in the anniversary mural, which places images of U Naw alongside and occasionally above the Judsons and celebrates bicentennials beyond the one marking the Judsons' arrival. The mural's uppermost sail gives the year of U Naw's conversion, 1819, and the year of the two-hundredth anniversary of that first conversion, 2019. The fore sail shows a recent picture of the exterior of U Naw Church with the founding date of Judson's first church, 1816, and its projected bicentennial, 2016. Thus, the three sails show three bicenntennials: the Judsons' arrival at the center, the founding of the first church to the left, and U Naw's conversion above. Also aboard this legendary ship is U Naw's current pastor, Rev. U Toe Toe, whose pulpit is the ship's bow. Rev. U Toe Toe's arm parallels this bow to point a dialogue bubble: "The ship Georgiana hasn't reached her destination yet, she still has to stretch out her mission to work to the end of the world." The clear message here is that this Burmese Baptist congregation is carrying on the mission established by Americans two hundred years ago, extending their work beyond the 2013 celebrations, beyond the 2016 celebrations of the church's founding, and beyond the 2019 anniversary of U Naw's baptism. Above this pastoral dialogue bubble is a cropped copy of Warner Sallman's 1950 painting *Christ Our Pilot*, with Christ's outstretched arm extending the line pointed out by the pastor. Sallman's stormy sea scene is based on an anonymous 1944 poster showing Jesus helping an American World War II sailor steer a ship out of a large wave.[16] Whereas the original audience of *Christ Our Pilot* was reminded of the obstacles facing young men in mid-twentieth-century America, here the piloting Christ and his American sailor partner with Rev. U Toe Toe to advance this historic Burmese congregation's ambitious evangelical goal. The mural's combination of Burmese- and English-language text suggests its intended audience of visitors from within the country and abroad who, like the Judson200 participants, will journey to the historic U Naw Church to celebrate the Baptist mission's bicentennial and look for signs of continued hope of the Christian conversion of the Burmese population.

The visual culture of U Naw Church—with its Judson heart banner and legacy mural of bicentennials—uses Western faces to tell a story of a groundbreaking past, an ambitious present, and an auspicious future. Paintings of Ann, Adoniram, and Jesus are paired with pictures of U Naw and Rev. U Toe Toe to place U Naw Church prominently in the picture of how Burma's Baptist church began and how it will continue on its path to "share the good news of the Salvation of Jesus Christ to the nations worldwide."[17] Whereas Immanuel Baptist Church uses welcoming Jesus paintings to project an image of a nondenominational Christianity with Western connections, U Naw's iconography focuses on distinctly American and Burmese figures. The Judson heart banner and the mural of bicentennials situate the Judsons, U Naw, and the church's present pastor as the country's leading evangelical Christians.

After our day visiting Yangon's historic churches, our Judson200 group gathered in the tony lobby of Trader's Hotel to discuss the day. The first reflections came from one of the older members of our tour, a pastor from Illinois. She spoke about the familiarity of the music and the hymns, and about how this strong connection to churches at home was powerfully combined with the recognition of how ethnically diverse the world's Baptist population is. One of the two undergraduate students from West Virginia agreed. The services that day had given the pastor a real sense of belonging to a religious community, a family. "All are children of God," she concluded, and several others nodded in agreement. These comments echoed Reverend John Matthew's Kingdom of God message as well as an observation we heard when we met the pastor of Judson Church on the Yangon University campus, who told us that seeing us Americans in the Burmese church brought joy to his heart and thoughts of the wonderful diversity we will meet in heaven.

The Yangon portion of the Judson200 Tour offered the group both a chance to experience different church communities with exotic aspects—such as incense at Immanuel or the Burmese language service at U Naw—as well as with familiar features, such as American hymns like "Jesus Paid It All," written in 1865 by Elvina M. Hall of Monument Street Methodist Church of Baltimore. This combination of American Protestant affinity and Southeast Asian variety seemed to inspire in the group a rich feeling of community, one that was not limited to a worldly, international Baptist congregation spanning the globe, but that promised to also reach heaven. Expressions of holy connection would give way to mournful reflections in Mandalay Region, where our group visited the site of Judson's imprisonment and confronted thousands of Buddhist monuments at Pagan telling not only of the country's ancient and powerful Buddhist history but also of its present Buddhist revival.

Mandalay Region (Pagan and Inwa)

After three days in Yangon, our tour group left the cosmopolitan and multireligious city to fly north to Mandalay Region to explore a couple of the country's most popular tourist attractions. Burmese rulers of the past three centuries have tended to locate their centers of power in this central part of the country. Konbaung kings from the last royal lineage built three capitals here between 1765 and their defeat in the Third Anglo-Burmese War in 1885, and the country's present capital, "Nay Pyi Taw," has been the administrative center since the government moved it to that previously remote spot in Mandalay Region in 2005. This central area is also home to two of Burma's most famous tourist destinations, Pagan and the royal city of Mandalay, founded by King Mindon in 1857. Foreign Baptist tour groups in Myanmar for the 2013 bicentennial celebrations were likely to go to these popular attractions as part of the "cultural" part of their trips, but they would have also used journeys to this central region to visit the infamous site where Adoniram Judson and other foreigners at the Ava court were imprisoned by King Bagyidaw during the first Anglo-Burmese War in 1824–1826.

This is just what the Judson200 Legacy Tour group did: we spent one day touring the Buddhist ruins at Pagan and then headed to Mandalay to visit the prison site and the nearby Baptist church. As I will show in this section, the vibrant visual cultures among Buddhists and Baptists in Mandalay Region function to distinguish the former as a national Burmese religion, and the later as an international faith with distinct American roots. Among the thousands of ancient and new pagodas in central Burma, the Christian artwork and historical displays at the Judson Baptist Church at Aungpinle, Mandalay, remind congregants and visitors of the clashing religious worlds of its past—Burmese, American, and British—as well as the negotiations and tensions that shape its present.

Pagan (Bagan)

Pagan is one of the country's most popular tourist attractions because of its vast ruins of an ancient Buddhist city, which flourished here from the ninth through the thirteenth centuries. When Adoniram visited Pagan in January 1820, he "took a survey of the splendid pagodas and extensive ruins" by climbing one of the tallest edifices one hundred feet to behold "all the country round, covered with temples and monuments of every sort and size; some in utter ruin, some fast decaying, and some exhibiting marks of recent attention and repair." This panoramic view, according to Adoniram, "conspired to suggest those elevated and mournful ideas which are attendant on a view of the decaying remains of ancient grandeur ... deeply interesting to the antiquary, and more deeply interesting to the Christian missionary." These ancient mournful ideas were, for Adoniram, teachings of Buddhism, which was "first publicly recognized and established as the religion of the empire" in Pagan a millennium ago.

Adoniram saw himself looking "back on the centuries of darkness that are past" and wondered if he stood "on the dividing line of the empires of darkness and light."[18] In today's Pagan, Adoniram's dream of emblazoning the land with God's light has clearly not been realized—Christian churches are still rare in this central region. If anything, more Buddhist monuments have been built in this area, and many historic ones have been restored.

Pagan is one key site of the current government's efforts to promote Buddhism in the country, which it sees as threatened by modernization and Westernization. In his 2013 essay collection, Hla Myint argues that the country's Buddhist promotion campaign is a response to the "impact of modernization and change ... [the] tremendous concern that traditional culture will be eroded by especially the influence of Western culture."[19] Myanmar's Department for the Promotion and Propagation of the Sāsana sees its work of building "temples and pagodas ... [and] many Buddha images of great size [and] made of different materials" as a continuation of the Theravada Buddhist activity that thrived in Pagan in the eleventh century. This department works to extend what it calls "Buddhist missionary work" into ethnic minority communities in border areas and hill regions by ensuring that "religious objects ranging from Buddha images to rosaries are distributed."[20] Signs of this ambitious Buddhist boosterism in Pagan led some on the Judson200 Legacy Tour group to express relief to leave the next morning to fly to Mandalay. By the end of our afternoon in Pagan, only a few tour members were still getting off the bus to explore historic pagodas.

Everyone, however, got off the bus the next day when we visited the Judson prison site in Inwa (Ava). The prison location has since been covered over by grass and trees, but we were able to navigate small riverboats, dirt roads, and short cuts through banana fields to find it. The following section takes a detour from the Judson200 Legacy Tour to examine closely the Judson prison story, with a focus on the visual culture it produced. I then contrast the local Burmese elements in the prison imagery with the foreign features of paintings and photographs the tour group sought out at the Baptist church we visited next to the prison site.

THE PORTRAIT

The Judson Prison Story

In May 1824, the British occupation of Rangoon escalated violence between the British and Burmese empires, and King Bagyidaw (r. 1819–1837) began incarcerating foreign residents in Ava, his royal capital.[21] As the royal examiners went through the documents of one of these residents, they found records of Henry Gouger—a young, flashy Anglo-Indian cotton merchant—having paid money to the American missionaries residing in the city, Adoniram Judson and Jonathan Price. While all three of them insisted that this was an honest transfer of funds from the American Board of Commissioners for Foreign Missions through agents in Bengal, the Burmese authorities saw it as evidence that the Americans were spying for the British and locked them up in Bagyidaw's most violent prison, Let Ma Yoon. Ann Judson, who was two months pregnant, quickly began pleading her situation to anyone with connections. She shrewdly used her stores of cotton, silver, and tobacco as bribes and, by doing so, kept Adoniram alive and fed. Eleven months later, Adoniram was marched off to a prison in nearby Aungpinle, where he expected to be executed. Instead, he was called to serve as the Burmese court's translator in negotiations with the British, a crucial role that directly led to the Treaty of Yandabo, the document that ended the war.[22] Eight months later, Ann died from a terrible fever, the last of many illnesses she had suffered during Adoniram's imprisonment. Six months after that, in another tragic development, Maria, their child born during the war, died. The two-year-old was buried next to her mother in Amherst, a port town being developed by the British in their newly acquired territory in southern Burma.

The dramatic account of Adoniram's imprisonment has become one of the most famous and most recounted episodes in history of the American mission in Burma. Even before Adoniram died in 1850, the story of his time in prison was legendary for the heroic way the pioneering missionary endured torture; for Ann's courage and selflessness in keeping Adoniram and his translation work alive; for the excellence and rarity of Adoniram's Burmese-language skills, which ultimately freed him; and, finally, for the tragic epilogue of Ann and Maria's death. For example, when Adoniram spoke on the campus of Richmond College in Virginia in 1845, the college president, Robert Ryland, introduced him by saying that although the faculty and students were meeting Adoniram for the first time, they already felt very intimately connected to his life story:

THE PORTRAIT

Your history, your character—your spirit are familiar to our minds. We heard in our childhood of your voluntary exile from your native land, we followed you over the boisterous seas—we read your earliest journals—wept over the narrative of the war and prison scenes in Burmah—stood with you in imagination at [Ann's] grave under the Hopia tree—sat with you at your work of translation—saw you kneeling to the God of Missions with the last sheet of your corrected version in your hands, and heard you dedicating it to His service and glory. We welcome you, then, not as a stranger—but as a dear friend. Your name is one of our house-hold words.[23]

Ryland's sketch of Adoniram's life story shows how celebrated the missionary already was in American Protestant society through newspaper articles, excerpts of personal letters printed in magazines, and institutional histories. This sketch further emphasizes the centrality of the scenes of Adoniram's incarceration and Ann's death to that fame, the most important events between the Judsons setting sail as the first foreign missionaries and Adoniram translating the Bible into Burmese.[24] John Corrigan highlights the large impact of the story of Adoniram's imprisonment and related accounts of the Judsons' struggles with Burmese authorities. Corrigan explains that the Judsons were two of the best known celebrities among Protestants in the U.S. antebellum period whose reports on the religious intolerance of Burmese authorities—which were not only printed regularly in Baptist periodicals but also copied in a wide range of other U.S. publications—served as a "rhetorical entwining of the fact of political struggle there with the historic Christian battle against intolerance."[25] This demonizing of intolerance in a foreign land is, Corrigan argues, an expression of the trauma of the United States' history of religious violence. The prison images I will now analyze show that this rhetorical demonizing did not just happen in words, but in illustrations as well.

In 1853, the Protestant press published its first illustration of the prison scene. This image is also likely the very first printed image showing the Judsons in Burma. American Baptist archives have preserved a detailed history of the creation of this image that reveals how the Judsons were literally drawn in the mid-nineteenth century by their inheritors through precise consciousness of iconography and concern for the way visual representations would promote certain ideas about the Baptist mission. I will show the stark contrast between this early American vision of the famous

THE PORTRAIT

FIGURE 4.10 "Mrs. Judson's Visit with Her Infant to Her Husband in Prison," *American Missionary Memorial*, 1853.

missionary couple and Burma's twenty-first century paintings. Whereas the Judson imagery examined so far in this chapter has emphasized stately American costumes, the nineteenth-century prison illustration shows Ann in an elaborate Burmese dress and hairstyle and Adoniram in simple clothing. This contrast suggests that, whereas today's Baptists in Burma celebrate their connections to America, nineteenth-century American Baptists were interested in the ways the first missionaries had integrated into Burmese culture through their knowledge of its fashion, language, and customs.

This first prison illustration was published with the heart-wrenching title "Mrs. Judson's Visit with Her Infant to Her Husband in Prison" in a volume of missionary stories that featured a piece on Ann Judson by the prominent author and editor Rev. Sewell S. Cutting (see figure 4.10). As historian Christine Heyrman explains, it was through the U.S. Protestant press that "missionary heroines found their way into their readers' imagination.... Missionary chronicles abounded in tales of drama and romance, peril and courage, unfolding in exotic settings, and like novels they beckoned readers to imagine themselves as heroines having such adventures

[192]

and inhabiting their own story." Heyrman contextualizes this within larger U.S. culture to explain that "foreign missions offered one of the few avenues to celebrity open to a respectable woman at any time during the nineteenth century."[26] Ann Judson was indeed a nineteenth-century celebrity, and the arresting illustrations that accompanied the tales of her husband's imprisonment and her lonely gravesite gave powerful visual force to her fame. I have traced the origins of the first prison image of the Judsons to a conversation between Cutting and Adoniram's third wife, Emily Chubbuck Judson, in a Boston parlor in the spring of 1852. Emily had suggested accompanying his piece with an illustration of the prison scene, and Cutting relayed this suggestion to the publisher at Harper & Brothers, who was "much pleased" with the idea.[27] Five days after Cutting wrote Emily to let her know of the publisher's interest, Emily, clearly employing her skills as a popular professional writer, replied with a description for the illustrator so vivid and so telling of how she imagined Ann and Adoniram, and how she thought the American Protestant audience should imagine them, that I quote her at length:

> The prison was very much like a New England barn—without ceiling, inner lining of any sort, and without windows or even an aperture to admit the air. There were about 100 prisoners mostly Burmans, and many of them in the stocks, and other torturing positions. The group nearest the door was composed of foreigners—two Americans, three Englishmen, one Spaniard, three Armenians, and a Portuguese priest—their clothing but little, as they were all reduced to mere shirt and trousers. They wore five pairs of fetters each on their ankles (none on their wrists) and were farther confined by a bamboo pressed between their legs and conjoined to the fetters of the two outside men; so that they could sit or lie in a row on the floor, but could not move farther, without the simultaneous movement of the whole party of them.
>
> The particular scene that I mentioned to you, was Mrs. J's first visit to the prison after the birth of little Maria, when the child was twenty days old. She had adopted for safety's sake the Burman dress (with the exception of the sandal), a correct representation of which I enclose [A note added to the end of the letter explains that Emily Judson enclosed "a picture of a Burman woman, and also a gentleman and his servant. Moung Ing would dress like a gentleman—the other would be the jailer's dress."]. This style of dress is very pretty indeed. The child was most probably wrapped in folds of plaid silk. It would be well for

the artist to know that Mrs. Judson was a particularly fine looking woman, and Mr. J. was also, as a young man, very handsome. The moment that I fixed upon for the picture was when she stood in the door (not permitted to enter) with the infant in her arms—Moung Ing, the faithful preacher close behind her, the diabolical old jailer, with great rings tattooed on his chest, and "Loo That" or "Man Killer" on his breast, laughing maliciously at her elbow and ready to order her away; and her husband, seconded by his companions in misery, making an effort to come a little nearer to the door, and extending his arms for the unconscious child. Mr. J. several times mentioned her appearance as having made a lasting impression on him, and being the best subject he had ever seen for an artist. "And what figure do you suppose *you* would cut in the picture?" I asked. "Ah, I don't know," he said, smilingly; "I suppose I should look like some poor convicted wretch bowing before a Madonna, for with all my efforts, I couldn't get above the knees."[28]

Emily's sensational, almost theatrical, prison scene takes care to explain that Ann wore very pretty Burmese clothing, that she was exceptionally good looking, and that Adoniram himself had thought about the scene as a perfect subject for a piece of art. (Of course, Emily had never met Ann, as she was only nine years old when Ann died, though Emily may have seen Ann's portrait, perhaps the miniature of her made around 1811, before she left for India [see figure 4.11].) The illustrator assigned to this *American Missionary Memorial* piece was Carl Emil Doepler (1824–1905), a German-born artist who did book illustrations for Harper & Brothers and for G. P. Putnam's Sons and who also worked as a costume designer for prominent theatrical productions, such as Richard Wagner's *Ring* at the first Bayreuth Festival in 1876.[29] Doepler did not follow Emily's description exactly, although he did go to lengths to dress Ann in an exotic, vaguely Oriental outfit of an ankle-length patterned dress, a long belted sash, and a flowing overcoat, topped with an intricate hairstyle that tames Ann's curls into a smooth side wave and elaborated bun. Adoniram, who is reduced to a shirt and trousers, as Emily prescribed, is shown on his knees looking at Ann and their infant daughter. Ann is the focal point of Doepler's image as she confidently enters through the centered doorway. Her clothes sweep back, putting her in motion and fascinating the men around her. Adoniram, the jailer, and Moung Ing, the celebrated second Burmese Baptist convert and evangelist

THE PORTRAIT

FIGURE 4.11 Miniature of Ann Judson, ca. 1811. Courtesy of the American Baptist Historical Society.

coworker of the Judsons, look at her from three sides and we viewers from the fourth. The engraver has given Ann a bright white face, and Adoniram and the baby are similarly illuminated by the absence of black ink. The couple's taut line of eye contact bisects the frame along the jailer's sword, cutting their relationship against a shadowed scene of chained, crouching bodies. Pressed against the stained darkness of the foreign prison, this engraving argues for the radiance of the late missionaries and the righteousness of their sacrifice.[30]

This first rendering of the Judsons in prison seems to have given a specific shape to Protestant concerns about the Burma mission after Adoniram's death. For missionary advocates like the prominent Baptist leader Edward Bright, the vision was gratifying. Bright, who was the secretary of the American Baptist Missionary Union at the time, wrote Emily shortly after the volume was published to say that he "was greatly pleased" with what he described as the scene's "life-like character."[31] By casting the story of the mission with these vivid, attractive, tragic white bodies, Emily's image proposed that their mortal sacrifice had a sacred, immortal purpose. And, by being placed in the prison with them, feeling their pain and power, the audience enters a thrilling shared space of religious imagination in which those who witness the Judsons' sacrifice serve God and celebrate his promise of eternal life.

Seven years later, a similar image was printed in Henry Gouger's 1860 memoir, *Personal Narrative of Two Years Imprisonment in Burmah, 1824–26* (see figure 4.12). "Interior of the Let-Ma-Yoon," as Gouger's prison scene is titled, shows Adoniram Judson as one of the three foreigners hanging from bound feet, but we do not have Burmese-costumed Ann in the scene. The vision of Judson hanging in a reverse crucifixion pose can even be seen today on wall calendars created for Burma's 2013 Baptist bicentennial.[32] The U Naw Church bicentennial calendar, for example, includes a small illustration of a dark jail holding shackled, shirtless men, including a barely identifiable Adoniram hanging from bound feet. This calendar image is taken from the 1980 film *Adoniram Judson Called to Be a Missionary*, produced by American Baptist Films; the film, too, leaves Ann out.[33]

Clearly Emily's vision of Ann and her strategic and beautiful Burmese clothes did not make a lasting imprint on Baptist cultural memory. Instead of remembering this founding missionary in the Burmese fashion she

FIGURE 4.12 "Interior of the Let-Ma-Yoon Prison," Henry Gouger's *Personal Narrative of Two Years Imprisonment in Burmah, 1824–1826*, 1860.

adopted, Burmese churches today remember her in a Western neck ruffle. In the place of forgotten visions of Ann's immersion into the local culture, we find proliferated images of a very foreign-looking lady missionary. These showcased images of a hyper–New England Ann visually emphasize the American influence on the Baptist church's beginnings and the continued effort by this Christian minority to situate itself within a powerful international religious network.

Inwa (Let Ma Yoon and Aungpinle)

The drama of Adoniram's imprisonment has not only inspired writers and artists to recreate the scene but also incited Protestant pilgrims to trek to Ava to experience the site of Let Ma Yoon prison for themselves. Foreign Baptists have been journeying here since at least the 1870s, two decades after Adoniram's death. In 1873, Marilla Ingalls wrote about her visit to the "small and very miserable looking village" where Judson's prison once stood. She "had some trouble finding the prison grounds, as the place was so overgrown with cactus and other bushes. The people told [her] that one hole was the place of a post; but [she] could not believe this to be the ground till [she] dug and found some of the brick pavement."[34] Ingalls's visit was not unlike the journey the Judson200 Legacy Tour took to the clearing where two broken pieces of carved stones lay abandoned. Weather and time had eroded the 1915 memorial inscription, but photographs at the nearby Judson Church we visited preserve photographs of the intact and inscribed memorial stone, which once marked the "unrecordable suffering" that Adoniram endured at that spot from June 1824 to May 1825.

The memorial stone photographs are part of a larger display of Judson relics in the upper right corner of the Judson Baptist Church at Aungpinle, Mandalay. When Adoniram Judson's son Edward (with Adoniram's second wife, Sarah) bought the land to build this memorial church in 1892, he chose it for its proximity to the site of the execution-grounds-turned-prison Judson was moved to after Let Ma Yoon. The church functions both as a shrine of sorts to the man who survived two Burmese prisons and as a materialization of the way the origins of Burma's Baptist church are remembered. As Pamela Klassen shows in her study of how Canada came into being through practices of believing, mediated by missionary storytelling media, material storytelling of Adoniram's imprisonment makes real the history and sanctity of the Baptist mission.[35]

The church's display contains three framed photographs of the prison memorial stone as well as a first-edition Judson Burmese bible in a glass case, a pair of formal portraits of the Judsons, and a piece of folk art known as a "jewelry painting" on account of its use of sparkling colored sand. This jewelry painting scroll, which shows a gray-haired Jesus praying in the wilderness, is one of the three Jesus images at this church, none of which are copies of Sallman's *Head of Christ* but still suggest the profile and gaze of that iconic American painting. The sparkling silver stone on which the jewelry-art Jesus prays seems to reflect the memorial stone in the trio of photographs below and perhaps reminds the viewer of the trials Jesus and Adoniram endured for the sake of their salvation. In the framed image of Adoniram, the Baptist hero is not in prison clothes, but in the costume he was wearing in Yangon: a high-collared jacket and shirt. Likewise, Ann Judson appears almost exactly as she does in the U Naw Church/1963 *Pictorial* image with her halo of thick dark hair and large white ruffled collar.[36] There are no signs here that Ann adopted local dress. In the Judson Church in Aungpinle, as in churches throughout this country, the founding missionary couple is memorialized in Western clothing. The visual reminder of the American influence on Burma's Baptist churches is coupled with a shrine of photographs of Adoniram's imprisonment during the First Anglo-Burmese War and also connected, as I will show, to a Karen flag representing the twentieth-century resistance of the Karen to persecution by the Burmese military dictatorship. This religious space memorializes the legacy of British and Burmese imperial violence.

After guiding us through the church, the pastor invited our tour group to the community room next door for fresh fruit and conversation. The space did not contain any Judson memorabilia, but it did have hanging a couple of Jesus paintings and a large Karen National Union (KNU) flag.[37] The KNU is the armed organization that has fought since 1949 for the Karen people's independence from the Burmese government. In 1976 they changed their goal from total independence to a federal system, which the government would still not allow, demanding instead that the Karen be citizens of Burma's Karen State. KNU leadership has been so overwhelmingly Christian that in 1994 a group of Buddhist soldiers broke away to establish the Democratic Karen Buddhist Army, which began working with the Burmese army to weaken the KNU. In 2012, the KNU agreed to a cease-fire and continued to participate in peace talks with the Burmese government. The red-white-and-blue KNU flag endures as a symbol of the Karen people's long struggle for justice from Burmese government, especially from the brutal military dictatorship. It also signals the crucial role religious identity plays in Burma's history of ethnic conflict and warfare.

KNU flags in Christian spaces often indicate that the building belongs to a Karen community, and this flag might very well be in Aungpinle Judson Church's community room because the pastor is Karen. But Baptist people from other ethnic groups also hang KNU flags to show their support for Karen independence efforts. The KNU flag at this church in central Mandalay Region is far from the southeastern Karen State and indicates that the pain of the Karen strife has been felt throughout the country, as has the relief of the recent peace efforts. Out of concern for the sensitive political situation, I did not ask about this political symbol, but I know that many of the tour participants knew Karen refugees in the States through their Baptist churches and were familiar with both the KNU flag and the ongoing Burmese persecution of the Karen. The following section follows the Judson200 Legacy Tour southeast from the Buddhist and Christian visual cultures of Mandalay Region toward the Karen heartland to see how visions of the country's power dynamics relate to Christian imagery in the area that was the center of the American Baptist mission after the First Anglo-Burmese War.

Southeastern Burma (Mawlamyine and Kyaikkhami)

After Ann died in Amherst in 1826, Adoniram went to Moulmein to visit Dana and Sarah Boardman, who had set up a missionary station in Moulmein after General Campbell of the British Army offered them land. Seeing how fast Moulmein was growing, Adoniram decided to move the Amherst operations to the town in the Salween River delta, where the missionary headquarters remained until the Second Anglo-Burmese War. During this period, American missionaries working from this post often commented on the particular Buddhist obstacles in the way of their evangelism. Edward Stevens, the missionary who took over work on Adoniram's English-Burmese dictionary after he died in 1850, considered the Buddhist artwork in southern Burma to pose a distinct threat to Christian conversion because it emphasized the invisibility of the Christian god. Stevens's journal from 1849 describes a seventy-foot-long Buddha statue in the reclining posture, representing Gotama achieving parinirvana. Stevens goes on to explain that "although the sacred books declare that in attaining nigban [nirvana] he utterly ceased to exist, soul and body, the people *practically* believe him in a state of existence reclining at his ease, perfectly free from all evil. Such a heaven is to them the perfection of bliss." Stevens continues that, in contrast to the country's powerful Buddhist imagery, Baptists were struggling to spread word of a god that they did not, at that time, represent in sculptures or paintings. This aniconic Protestant practice, according to Stevens, made it difficult for people in Burma to accept the "invisibility of God, while their objects of worship are before their eyes."[38] Stevens clearly saw the force religious art had in Burma, though he surely could not have imagined how, centuries later, Baptist communities would harness that force for themselves.

Mawlamyine (Moulmein)

During the quarter-century that the American Baptist mission operated out of Moulmein, many churches were established in the region. In a letter to a Mr. Anderson of Port Louis on August 5, 1849, Adoniram wrote that in Moulmein alone there were three Baptist churches—"a Burmese church, containing about one hundred and fifty members, of which I am pastor; a Karen church, containing about one hundred members, of which Mr. Binney is pastor; and an English church, containing about twenty-five members, of which Mr. Simons is pastor." In addition, Adoniram noted "two other Burmese churches in these regions, and above a dozen Karen churches."[39] While Adoniram continued to concentrate his missionary work on the Burmese population, Karen interest in Christianity drove the efforts of many other American evangelists into nearby jungles. This final section examines the iconography at the Burmese church described by Adoniram in 1848 and at Ann Judson's gravesite. These concluding images illustrate how

THE PORTRAIT

Baptist congregations in the southeast, like congregations in Yangon and Mandalay, use Christianity to establish distinct identities in this vastly Buddhist country.

On our drive to the Judson Baptist Church in Moulmein from our hotel in the capital of the Karen State, Hpa-An, one of the tour group members announced that we were not going to distribute the missionary tracts we had received from an American missionary woman in Yangon. We were in the country on tourist visas, and if we acted like missionaries we could get in trouble with the government. The group did not seem disappointed at this missed opportunity to participate in the kind of evangelical work the early American missionaries did in this region. Instead of the risky endeavor of handing out Christian texts and debating religion with locals, the Judson200 group preferred to see the historical and cultural sites within the safe spaces of guided group tours and air-conditioned buses. In twenty-first-century Burma, Americans are welcome to spend their dollars in the country on a twenty-eight-day tourist visa, but are prohibited from moving to the country to evangelize like nineteenth-century Baptists. The missionary who gave us the tracts in Yangon was illegally proselytizing, and this group was clearly not interested in taking similar risks.

Just a few blocks from the banks of the Salween River in Moulmein is the historic Judson Baptist Church. Established by Adoniram Judson in 1827, the congregation is now housed in a large, brightly painted stucco building with a multistory bell tower. This handsome mid-twentieth-century structure features a small cemetery next to the entrance containing the grave of Charles Judson, son of Adoniram and Sarah Boardman Judson, who died in 1845 at eighteen months old. Buried next to Charles is Emily Margaret Hanna, granddaughter of Adoniram and Emily, who was born in Brooklyn, New York, but died in Moulmein in 1911.

As you walk into the church, you find a white electrified cross gleaming from the center of the altar above an illuminated glass case containing an early-edition Judson bible. The rest of the large stage is filled with carved and lacquered wooden furniture. Judson Baptist Church has no images of the Judsons or Jesus on its altar. There are no figures at all depicted on its stage; to find revered portraiture, you have to look to the left side of the church where a thin shelf exhibits black-and-white portraits of six Burmese pastors and a short shelf above the left-hand side of the lineup shows a matching

THE PORTRAIT

FIGURE 4.13 Pastor portraits at Judson Baptist Church, Mawlamyine. Photo by the author.

black-and-white illustration of Adoniram (see figure 4.13). The identical framing, consistent color palette, and focus on the heads and shoulders of these leaders link them all in a single lineage. Adoniram, who is still elevated above the Burmese pastors, wears his classic Western jacket and shirt, but here his jacket is not a strong black, but rather the same light gray as his shirt, muting the foreignness of his necklines. Adoniram seems to blend in here, and, without any Jesus paintings in the church with exotic features, the markings of ethnic differences between the congregation and its founders feels softened.

After attending the Sunday service in Moulmein, the Judson Baptist Church congregation served us a lunch of carrot, cucumber, and mayonnaise sandwiches on white bread with the crusts cut off; a few French fries; Sunkist; bottled water; and trays of fruit that included red bananas, pomelos, and watermelon—a meal generously prepared with American tastes in mind. We then boarded our bus to drive an hour and a half south on National Highway 8 to the small coastal town of Kyaikkhami, called Amherst when Ann Judson was buried there.

THE PORTRAIT

Kyaikkhami (Amherst)

Ann Judson's gravesite, the southernmost point for those journeying in the footsteps of the Judsons, would be hard to find if you did not know where to look. The cemetery features only a few memorial stones and sits next to a little church built in 2011, "in loving memory of Ann Judson (Ma Ma Yuda Than) on the 185th anniversary of her death," as the dedicatory plaque explains. The altar of the church elevated a single image: a print of Sallman's *Head of Christ* (see figure 4.14). The protective plastic wrap reflected the sunlight abounding in the church, but behind this glistening layer I could still see the benevolent glow of Sallman's Jesus, the highlights in his light-brown hair, and his thick beard. Opposite this central image hung a pair of portraits featuring Adoniram and Ann Judson in their now familiar nineteenth-century New England dress (see figure 4.15). Their faces, like the face of the Jesus they look out at, are depicted in warm tones and hold soft, maybe even humble, expressions. They are distinctly Western figures that seem to suggest to the visitors to this church as well as the young Buddhist and Muslim children who come here for school that Burma's Baptists have a distinct, but friendly, international faith.

* * *

We left Amherst to travel back north on National Highway 8 to our hotel in Hpa-An. We passed through Mudon, home to the world's largest reclining Buddha, measuring over five hundred feet long and nearly one hundred feet high (see figure 4.16). Clearly, the desire for monumental parinirvana Buddhas that Edward Stevens observed in this southern region in 1849 is still around today. The grand-scale sculpture at Win Sein Taw Ya monastery in Mudon invites visitors inside through an entrance below the head that leads them to multistory, human-scale dioramas of scenes from the lives of the Buddha and especially horrific visions of Buddhist hells. In one display, a massive black demon with a hugely muscular body and frightening tusks grabs a life-sized, pale-skinned, bare-breasted woman by the crotch and prepares to butcher her with a double-edged, blood-smeared cleaver. If this giant haunted Buddha is too frightening, visitors can stay outside the structure to marvel at its size or splash down the water slides below the entrance. The Judson200 Legacy Tour only participated in the marveling

FIGURE 4.14 Interior of Judson Memorial Church, at Ann Judson's grave, Kyaikkhami. Photo by the author.

part, as the bus did not take us beyond the entrance, where we got out to snap photographs. I was not able to visit the sensational interior until I returned that fall.

Mudon's massive reclining Buddha and its interior hellscapes are certainly unique, but our encounter with them was part of a larger pattern in which the tour passed by very prominent and public Buddhist monuments on our way to see Baptist sites and their exoticized Judson and Jesus

FIGURE 4.15 Interior of Judson Memorial Church, at Ann Judson's grave, Kyaikkhami. Photo by the author.

FIGURE 4.16 Giant reclining Buddha, Mudon. Photo by the author.

portraiture. Buddhist and Christian imagery was constantly brought together on our Baptist pilgrimage. The religious landscape showed sacred images to be the modes and methods, the contours and concerns, of religious distinction, contestation, and correlation in Myanmar. Towering golden pagodas, colossal Buddha statues, and countless shrines impressed upon us the monumental power of Buddhism in the country and how, in its shadow, the nineteenth-century mission found a place for the country's Baptist church.

This chapter has asked what this Christian artwork reveals about the religious and political concerns of the country's Baptists. I have examined portraiture of Jesus and the Judsons to consider how emphasis on foreign dress, hair, and facial features connects minority Christian communities with Western powers and distinguishes them from the Burmese Buddhist majority. By following the Judson200 Tour group from Yangon, where Adoniram and Ann first looked out onto a horizon of glistening pagodas, to Mandalay Region, where Adoniram surveyed the ancient ruins of the Buddhist city of Pagan, to the southeastern coast, where Stevens beheld a seventy-foot reclining Buddha, I have spotlit Baptist shrines scattered among the public displays of the state-sponsored religion. And these Baptist spaces are not sparse meeting houses with simple crosses: they are places to hang prominent, expressive portraits of the celebrated missionaries who left their faraway New England homes to bring their religion to the people of Burma, the powerful and the oppressed. They are houses whose object of worship has been made visible in the form of Jesus Christ, who appears benevolent and Western, reminding all who gaze up at him that they are not only part of a community with affluent American leaders but also committed to a religion that promises the keys to a kingdom above all kingdoms.

In a country that has, in the last two centuries, experienced the collapse of the once powerful Burmese empire, the British occupation, and failed democratic, socialist, and military governments, ethnic minorities find great appeal in this striking visual and material culture. Through Christian art objects, Myanmar's Baptists remember celebrated pasts and claim present-day space in the Buddhist country. The limits and extent of this space continue to be shaped by the Buddhist state and Western Christian funders. But, as their paintings of Jesus and the Judsons show, Baptists are working within this contouring to define themselves.

Conclusion

AS I FINISH this book, Myanmar is embroiled in a coup that began on February 1, 2021. The military recaptured total rule over the country after a decade of sharing power with democratic bodies. The country's leading civilian party, the National League for Democracy, headed by Aung San Suu Kyi, won 83 percent of contested seats in the November 2020 election, but the military, the Tatmadaw, refused to accept the results. Declaring a state of emergency (a right granted to the military in the 2008 Constitution), the Tatmadaw seized control of the media and travel networks and swiftly began detaining civil leaders, including Aung San Suu Kyi, President U Win Myint, top ministers, writers, and activists. People in large cities began publicly calling for the return of civilian government in what were initially peaceful protests, but after forces killed unarmed protesters the civil disobedience movement quickly grew to include more disruptive actions, including a general strike and the mobilization of armed guerrilla forces. The military continues to violently suppress resistance movements throughout the country, killing, assaulting, and arresting thousands. As the coup took hold, photographs of protesters holding up three fingers in the air populated news media the world over, signaling the nightmare Myanmar is going through and the possibility of change.

This three-finger salute is from Suzanne Collins's *The Hunger Games* book and film franchise.[1] In recent years, protesters in nearby Thailand and Hong Kong have taken up the gesture in collective actions against unjust state power. In 2014, when *The Hunger Games: Mockingjay—Part 1* was playing in Thai theaters, the Thai military staged a coup, and Thai protesters began using the fictional series' salute in their real-world resistance efforts. Thai activists took up the gesture again in 2020 in opposition to King Maha Vajiralongkorn's monarchy. In uprisings in 2014 and 2019, protesters against Chinese overreach in Hong Kong adopted the salute.[2] Likewise, demonstrators against the military takeover in Myanmar raise their arms high to flash the same sign with their three middle fingers held straight up. In the spirit of the films' hero, Katniss Everdeen (played by U.S. actress Jennifer Lawrence), these protesters invoke a dramatic defiance of an oppressive regime. Their salute points to the dystopia they feel they are living through. It also points to their hope that subjugated people like them can take on a totalitarian state.

Identifying with the young tributes forced to fight to their death in *The Hunger Games*' annual tournament at Panem, Myanmar's younger generations feel betrayed by their elders. The promise of democracy, of reopening their world after decades of isolating military dictatorship, was violently taken from them. While they take lessons from the country's well-known resistance movements of 1988 and 2007, these 2021 activists have a new weapon in their arsenal: the mobile phones in their pockets. Just a decade ago, North Korea was the only country with fewer phones than Myanmar. Now, widely available smartphones connect protesters locally and to allies abroad. They exchange encrypted messages about how and where and when to protest. And the three-finger salute itself is a multimedia expression. Sometimes a spontaneous hand gesture, it is also an iterated, recorded, and disseminated image. There is the news coverage. The selfie. The graffiti. The protest sign. The Instagram photo.

Take, for instance, a colorful canvas photographed and posted to threefingers.org (see figure 5.1). The anonymous Myanmar artist centers a right hand raised with the three middle fingers held up and the pinky and thumb held together below. A golden pagoda in front of a burnt-orange setting sun establishes the scene as Burmese. The pagoda's outline is too simple to specify it as Shwedagon or any other particularly famous Myanmar landmark. Instead, its standard, iconic shape simply marks this as Myanmar, the land of the golden pagodas. A large yellow flower wraps its green leafy stem around the saluting hand's wrist and blooms brightly outward, directly at the viewer, while another opening bud stretches to the top of the canvas. The watery blue background offers a primary color contrast,

CONCLUSION

FIGURE 5.1 Three-finger salute painting from Myanmar. Courtesy of threefingers.org. Anonymous.

rendering the image striking even when small and backlit on a phone screen. That blue also surrounds an earthy jagged mass along the bottom border and a lighter terracotta mass partially seen along the top, invoking the Bay of Bengal, the Indian Ocean, perhaps even the Irrawaddy River—that central artery that carries people, materials, and power to the country's central valley region, where Konbaung kings and military dictators built their capitals.

I am tempted to read the pagoda as a Buddhist symbol and the hand as a mudra. But overt religious symbolism is conspicuously minimized in Myanmar's 2021 protest art. Yes, some protest signs have illustrations of pagodas and Buddhist monks. They are often coupled with English-language text, making me wonder if they are inspired by Western tourism's fixation on photogenic young novice monks and pagodas glistening in sunset—romantic visions of an entirely Buddhist, peaceful Burma, visions that have persisted even in the face of the ethnic cleansing of the Rohingya and the ongoing armed conflicts in border states. These themes on protest art seem to say, "If you care at all about this land you enjoy picturing as peaceful and distinct, you have to help us save it." There is not enough of a pattern, though, of protesters using religious material to change the future that the Tatmadaw has forcibly usurped. I cannot make a neat argument about particular Buddhist and Christian objects continuing to shape the course of Burmese history. This moment is not neat. It is messy.

I am not an expert in contemporary Myanmar politics, but images of the resistance are pressing me to leave the relative safety of the stories of long-dead people in the nineteenth-century and speak to connections I see affecting those living through this coup. The most glaring is one made the world over between pasts of Western imperial violence and presents of struggle for just self-rule. The British overthrow of the monarchy and colonization of the country doubtlessly depleted Burma of precious natural and cultural resources, instituted oppressive ethnoracist hierarchies, and propelled an enraged nationalism. The American Baptist mission supported this colonization by proclaiming the supremacy of Christian peoples. But this does not mean that this Southeast Asian is a monolithic land of serene Buddhists recovering from British imperial invasion. The Tatmadaw has roots in both the nationalist movements that reclaimed independence from the British and the longer history of Burmese imperialism, plotted with kings and powerful monks who crafted myths of legitimation to enlarge the power of the ruling classes.

I do not mean to naturalize Myanmar's violence. I am not arguing that the country is inherently authoritarian. The fact that there is a history behind the Tatmadaw means that it can change. The resistance movement is a belief in that change. It is a practice of making that change happen. And it finds inspiration in a Hollywood movie franchise. This brings me to the other connection to the nineteenth-century stories I have told in this book. The communities who converted to Christianity found both material and immaterial power in their participation in the American Baptist mission. I have argued that converts were not simply interested in the economic and social advantages of Protestant affiliation. They also had

CONCLUSION

more abstract interests in ultimate salvation and the nature of spirits and gods. Nineteenth-century Burma was a place of dynamic and reimagined religious worlds. These worlds materialized through religious books, schools, pagodas, and portraits.

Today the imagined world of Panem is realized in paintings like the anonymous one from threefingers.org and embodied in the three-finger salute. This is not a typical story of American culture and consumer capitalism infecting the world. This is a story of real people making meaningful connections to an invented story of suffering and salvation. They are using the global familiarity of *The Hunger Games* to advance their particular cause, and they are insisting on the truth of its promise that brave collective action can defeat totalitarianism.

As An Xiao Mina explains, "Asia seen through a Western lens [is] often misunderstood. By using a symbol that is popularly understood in the West and then globally, it's a way of encouraging people to make that connection between something they do understand, which is *The Hunger Games,* and try to start to say, 'Wait a minute, is that also what's going on in Myanmar?' " Mina adds that

> the additional power of the symbol is just how practical it is. When you are just raising your hand and raising your fingers it's almost as simple as it gets. It's something you carry with you, you can take it down with you. You can take a selfie, post drawings. It allows the images to disseminate and go viral. If the thing that this meme represents is something deeper, if it's a deeper societal issue it's very unlikely for it to go away until the society changes. And until we actually see changes on the ground, I suspect we will see this symbol not just resonate in South East Asia, but to actually start to be picked up around the world. And that's both the story of the power of fiction and the story of the power of social movements to turn fiction into reality and help us all kind of understand the story behind people's suffering and people's challenges.[3]

This book has been an attempt to understand how imagined religious worlds materialize, how communities animate objects and are animated by them. As Laura Levitt observes, "Objects facilitate human interaction.... They demand our attention.... They help us continue to tell stories and engage with one another. And in these ways they help us remember pasts even as they enable us to shape different futures."[4]

CONCLUSION

The creativity of religious communities in nineteenth-century Burma was not boundless. The strictures of Konbaung and colonial society contoured religious activity among both threatened and privileged groups. The three Anglo-Burmese wars waged during the American Baptist mission to Burma raised the stakes for this activity. The weakening Burmese kingdom defensively promoted Buddhist institutions throughout the country, as I detail with respect to the weapon-bearing spirits on Burmese manuscripts and the protests and persecutions of the sectarian movement known as the Paramats. When the First Anglo-Burmese War portioned parts of southern Burma off to the British in 1826, the American Baptist mission began to change their evangelization strategy from one that focused on the Burmese in the center of the country to one that attended to minority communities in regions being colonized by the British. In the midst of Burma's changing power structures, minority communities like the Karen found in conversion to Christianity an opportunity to redefine their identity. The lost book legend is an example of this in its told and retold versions about a Karen people that have not always been an illiterate hill tribe, as they were cast in the Burmese kingdom, but a divinely favored race with ancient ties to Christian lands and an auspicious future. Within those imperial formations, with their relentless conditions of oppression, individuals and communities found spaces for religious resistance and opportunities for religious innovation. This book tells the stories of the objects at the center of those spaces and the communities who made them meaningful. It shown how the religious book, the school house, the pagoda, and the portrait have reflected and shaped religious change in nineteenth-century Burma.

Notes

Introduction

1. The Judsons' celebrity is particularly striking considering how few women in this period achieved the level of fame that Ann Judson (and Harriet Newell, another missionary who set sail with the Judsons but died before she could evangelize abroad) did. As Christine Heyrman puts it in *Doomed Romance: Broken Hearts, Lost Souls, and Sexual Politics in Nineteenth-Century America* (New York: Knopf, 2021), "Foreign missions offered one of the few avenues to celebrity open to a respectable woman at any time during the nineteenth century," adding that "had there been a guide explaining how missionary women could leverage their status to wield power within churches, Ann Judson would have written it" (16–17). There are countless Baptist institutional histories and hagiographies honoring Judson as the sainted first American foreign missionary, with the most recent popular text being Rosalie Hall Hunt, *Bless God and Take Courage: The Judson History and Legacy* (Valley Forge, PA: Judson, 2005). Academic works on the mission movement also highlight Judson's near-celebrity status in nineteenth-century Protestant American. William Hutchison's authoritative study on American foreign missions, *Errand to the World: American Protestant Thought and Foreign Missions* (Chicago: University of Chicago Press, 1987), describes Judson as "the most celebrated of the first generation of foreign missionaries" (49).
2. I refer to the majority ethnic group as "Bamar," though many of my sources use the term "Burman," which was more common in the nineteenth century. Other scholars writing in English use "Bama" to refer to this same ethnic group.
3. Maung Shwe Wa, *Burma Baptist Chronicle* (Rangoon: Board of Publications, Burma Baptist Convention, 1963).
4. The few Catholic missionaries in the country focused on translating Buddhist scriptures and serving small local Catholic communities (such as the *bayingyi*,

INTRODUCTION

descendants from Portuguese and other traders in the port town of Syriam who were relocated to upper Burma and pressed into work as artillerymen when Burma sacked the town in 1613). British missionaries did not begin evangelizing in Burma until 1859, when the Church of England's Society for the Propagation of the Gospel established a small-scale mission whose greatest impact on Burma was through a Mandalay Christian school run by Reverend John Marks from 1869 to 1874 and supported in part by King Mindon, who sent several of his sons there to study. For more on the limited variety of Christian missionaries in Burma, see Jörg Schendel, "Christian Missionaries in Upper Burma, 1853–85," *South East Asia Research* 7, no. 1 (1999): 66–91.

5. Francis Wayland, *A Memoir of the Life and Labors of the Rev. Adoniram Judson, D.D*, 2 vols. (Boston: Phillips, Sampson, 1853), 251–52.
6. For an excellent model of a human-scale story addressing Christianity in India that also illuminates the larger processes of empire and sovereignty, see Danna Agmon, *A Colonial Affair: Commerce, Conversion, and Scandal in French India* (Ithaca, NY: Cornell University Press, 2017). Agmon's microhistory of French India at the turn of the eighteenth century avoids the binary of collaboration/resistance by closely reading legal records around the rise, imprisonment, and postmortem rise again of Nayiniyappa, a Tamil man with an important job in the French trading company governing Pondicherry. Agmon looks at the neglected area of French India to show that colonial efforts were fractured, not monolithic. I aim to similarly focus on the neglected area of American evangelism in Burma to complicate our understanding of the rise of colonialism in the region.
7. The country changed its name from "Burma" to "Myanmar" in 1989. I use "Myanmar" when referring to events after 1989.
8. D. Christian Lammerts's *Buddhist Law and Burma: A History of Dhammasattha Texts and Jurisprudence, 1250-1850* (Honolulu: University of Hawai'i Press, 2018) accounts for the central place that law played in Buddhist knowledge production from 1250 to 1850. Lammerts examines the genre of literature known as *dhammasattha* to show that its significant production and circulation speaks to larger dynamic Buddhist legal practices that extend beyond the regulatory practices of the Buddhist monastic code (*vinaya*); he points out that Burma is the only region where Buddhist law claims jurisdiction over all members of society, not just monks.
9. The term *Theravada*, which means "the doctrine of the Elders," was not widespread until the twentieth century. The nineteenth-century people I study used *Theravada* in some contexts but were much more likely to use the more general Pali term *sāsana* (B. *thathana*) to describe the teachings that the Buddha put forth in India, were preserved in Sri Lanka, and then adopted and promoted in Burma. This book uses the terms *Theravada* and *Pali* without macrons to indicate their long vowels because they are now commonly included in English-language dictionaries and written that way. For scholarship on the history and usage of *Theravada*, see Peter Skilling, "Theravāda in History," *Pacific World* 3, no. 11 (2009): 61–93. See also Peter Skilling, Jason Carbine, Claudio Cicuzza, and Santi Pakdeekham, eds., *How Theravāda Is Theravāda? Exploring Buddhist Identities* (Chiang Mai: Silkworm, 2012).

INTRODUCTION

10. Victor Lieberman's sweeping work *Strange Parallels: Southeast Asia in Global Context, c. 800-1830* (New York: Cambridge University Press, 2003) examines the Taungoo kingdom as part of his inquiry into how only three centralized Southeast Asian kingdoms emerged in 1830 when there were numerous small polities throughout the same region in 800. His complex answer views the move toward consolidation as occurring through religion, culture, demographics, agriculture, and climate change. Lieberman shows how concurrent temporal patterns in these areas led to a relatively synchronized shift toward integration throughout Southeast Asia.
11. Michael Charney's *Powerful Learning: Buddhist Literati and the Throne in Burma's Last Dynasty, 1752-1885* (Ann Arbor: Centers for South and Southeast Asian Studies, University of Michigan, 2006) draws on previously unexamined sources for Burmese political and religious history in the premodern and modern periods to argue that it was the literati in the Lower Chindwin Valley, not Burmese kings, that created myths of legitimation that Konbaung rulers used to maintain their power.
12. Alicia Turner's *Saving Buddhism: The Impermanence of Religion in Colonial Burma* (Honolulu: University of Hawai'i Press, 2014) shows how Burmese communities took over these Buddhist obligations through new technologies available in colonial Burma as well as through past techniques honed by generations of Buddhists in the county. In addition to the nuanced history it tells of late nineteenth- and early twentieth-century Burma, *Saving Buddhism* also makes strong larger claims that the category of "religion" is unstable, and that British colonial power did not omnipotently reproduce societies in its image around the globe. Importantly, Turner supports these claims by showing the particular work Buddhists in colonial Burma did to renegotiate the terms of colonialism.
13. Erik Braun's *Birth of Insight: Meditation, Modern Buddhism, and the Burmese Monk Ledi Sayadaw* (Chicago: University of Chicago Press, 2013) provides an intellectual biography of the Burmese monk Ledi Sayadaw (1846-1923), whose work teaching simplified meditation practices and incorporating study of Abhidhamma doctrine launched the insight (*vipassana*) meditation as a mass movement.
14. Chie Ikeya's *Refiguring Women, Colonialism, and Modernity in Burma* (Honolulu: University of Hawai'i Press, 2011) studies the "modern" woman who rose to prominence in the 1920s and 1930s to show that there were more options in Burma than Westernization and ethnonationalism and to offer the first book-length historical analysis of gender in the country.
15. Thomas Patton's *The Buddha's Wizards: Magic, Protection, and Healing in Burmese Buddhism* (New York: Columbia University Press, 2018) explores contemporary *weizzā* devotees and the history contextualizing their lived experiences to show that this is not some bizarre esoteric cult but rather part of a more varied Burmese Buddhism than scholars have previously recognized.
16. Following my use of the Roman alphabet for Pali and Sanskrit terms, I have transcribed all Burmese words and names in this book into Roman. There are multiple systems for transcribing Burmese into Roman. I have tried to use spellings that readers of Burmese words in English would recognize most easily. As

for place names, I use the more recent, official names (i.e., Yangon instead of Rangoon) when I am writing about recent events (as in chapter 4), but I use the names most commonly used in the nineteenth century when I am writing about that period.

17. A prime piece of evidence of the malleability of Burmese terms for people groups is the British census. Long before the introduction of British colonial bureaucracy in the nineteenth century, Burmese kingdoms kept written population and tax records that enumerated military, religious, and village activity. Those records, which date back at least to the fourteenth century, do not concern themselves with distinguishing strictly defining people groups, nor do they contain any sense of named groups being biologically determined. For more on the character of religious and social regulation in precolonial Burma, see Lieberman, *Strange Parallels*, 190. And for more on how the Burmese concept of *lumyo* was influenced by Anglo-American concepts of race and nation between the 1820s and 1870s, see Aurore Candier, "Mapping Ethnicity in Nineteenth-Century Burma: When 'Categories of People' (*Lumyo*) became 'Nations,'" *Journal of Southeast Asian Studies* 50, no. 3 (2019): 347–64. While British biopolitical projects like the census and mapping were more prolonged and instrumental in the transformation of India, the British Raj did exert a kindred impact on Burma. When the British first conducted an official colonial census of their growing Burmese territory in 1872 and started counting in Upper Burma in 1891, they fixated on *lumyo* as a kind of immutable biological category, leading it to be used and understood as a way of describing different races in Burma. See Jane M. Ferguson, "Who's Counting? Ethnicity, Belonging, and the National Census in Burma/Myanmar," *Journal of the Humanities and Social Sciences of Southeast Asia* 171, no. 1 (2015): 1–28. For an analysis of the construction of race in Burma in the early twentieth century, see Penny Edwards, "Half-Cast: Staging Race in British Burma," *Postcolonial Studies* 5, no. 3 (2002): 279–95. Edwards analyzes the role of whiteface theater from the 1910s through the 1940s, connecting this practice to European anxieties about race and control, notably their problems with the category termed "Eurasian" in the nineteenth-century Baptist missionary accounts like those I examine in the second chapter of this book. For more on the importance of bringing critical race theory into our understanding of Buddhist traditions, see Adeana McNicholl, "Buddhism and Race in the United States," *Religion Compass* (2021): 1–13.
18. Yoko Hayami, "Karen Culture of Evangelism and Early Baptist Mission in Nineteenth Century Burma," *Social Sciences and Missions* 31, nos. 3–4 (2018): 251–83.
19. The Baptists' linguistic innovations were not limited to minority languages, they also included contributions to Burmese. Adoniram Judson and his colleagues were likely the first to employ and disseminate the terms *botdabada* for "Buddhism" and *bada* for "religion." Alexy Kirichenko's study of the construction of religion in nineteenth- and early twentieth-century Myanmar shows how the creation of these terms produced a new sense of the importance of a uniform set of doctrines and allowed Burmese communities to use Western frameworks to assert the superiority of their religion. Alexy Kirichenko, "Theravada Buddhism: Constructions of Religion and Religious

Identity in Nineteenth- and Early Twentieth-Century Myanmar," in *Casting Faiths: Imperialism and the Transformation of Religion in East and Southeast Asia*, ed. Thomas David DuBois (New York: Palgrave Macmillan, 2009), 23–45.

20. As Elliot Prasse-Freeman explains in "Scapegoating in Burma," *Anthropology Today* 29, no. 4 (2013), with regard to twenty-first-century violence against the Rohingya, we see in Burmese history and politics a pattern of both community building and scapegoating. Prasse-Freeman argues that these practices are *performances* and therefore unstable, explaining that, "once one group is identified as 'not part of' Burma, or 'incompatible' with 'our traditions,' what constitutes a putatively authentic Burmese citizen or tradition is put into question, even potentially undermined" (3).

21. An especially illuminating work from these disciplines is David Chidester's *Empire of Religion: Imperialism and Comparative Religion* (Chicago: University of Chicago Press, 2014), a counterhistory of the study of religion. Chidester shows how knowledge about religion has been produced "within the power relations of imperial ambitions, colonial situations, and indigenous innovations" (xi). Chidester's material history works to "overcome lingering dualisms—imperial versus indigenous, colonizer versus colonized—by attending to the complex, multiple, and multiplying mediations in which knowledge was produced in and through the material conditions of empire" (xii). My own analysis seeks to follow Chidester's approach by paying attention to the production of knowledge about Burmese religions in and through the material conditions of empire (British, Burmese, and American).

22. Earlier work on American missionaries focused on missions as one-way processes in which missionaries abroad imposed ideas about Christ and culture on far-flung lands. For example, William Hutchison's *Errand to the World*, an influential early academic study of U.S. missions, noted that the missions of the early nineteenth century were countercyclical in their openness to the world, but it focused on the writings of missionary theorists and American-based promoters to analyze the way the foreign mission enterprise was rooted in both a Christian zeal for evangelization and a belief in America's special role to save the world. Likewise, in the academic study of Asian religions, American missionaries have long been assumed to be simply antagonistic toward Hinduism, Buddhism, and other Asian traditions. For example, Thomas Tweed's now classic *The American Encounter with Buddhism, 1844-1912: Victorian Culture and the Limits of Dissent* (Chapel Hill: University of North Carolina Press, 2000) glossed over missionary encounters because, as he claims, they were simply hostile to Buddhism. Tweed argues that "in fact, almost all of the missionaries' interpretations [of Buddhism] were hostile" before footnoting the fact that "no comprehensive study of Protestant missionary interpretations of Buddhism has yet appeared" (30, 177). This book provides a study of missionary interpretations of Buddhism in Burma while calling into question the commonly held suspicion that American missionaries were radical imperialists. *Competing Kingdoms*, a 2010 collection of essays on American Protestant missionary women, was conceived out of a recognition that the concept of cultural imperialism as unidirectional was wrong in its misunderstanding of how host cultures related to

INTRODUCTION

evangelism. This collection instead views "missions as sites of encounter and exchange where individuals met, interacted, and triggered change." Barbara Reeves-Ellington, Kathryn Kish Sklar, and Connie Anne Shemo, eds. *Competing Kingdoms: Women, Mission, Nation, and the American Protestant Empire, 1812-1960* (Durham, NC: Duke University Press, 2010), 6. Other scholars see this turn to individual encounters as denying the pervasive power of Western imperialism. For example, Emily Conroy-Krutz's 2015 *Christian Imperialism: Converting the World in the Early American Republic* (Ithaca, NY: Cornell University Press, 2015) examines American Board of Commissioners for Foreign Missions operations to show that prevalent expressions of Anglo-American superiority go as far back as the early republic. David Hollinger's 2017 *Protestants Abroad: How Missionaries Tried to Change the World but Changed America* (Princeton, NJ: Princeton University Press, 2017) swings back toward "encounter narratives" to complicate the notion that missionaries advanced U.S. power through a consistent subordination of non-Anglo-American peoples by charting cosmopolitanism and liberalism among mid-twentieth-century foreign missionaries and their children. Additional scholars focus instead on particular mission stations to tell more textured stories of how this range of U.S. missionary interests played out in specific times and places. See, for example, Adam H. Becker, *Revival and Awakening: American Evangelical Missionaries in Iran and the Origins of Assyrian Nationalism* (Chicago: University of Chicago Press, 2015); Christine Leigh Heyrman, *American Apostles: When Evangelicals Entered the World of Islam* (New York: Hill & Wang, 2015); and Melanie Trexler, *Evangelizing Lebanon: Baptists, Missions, and the Question of Cultures* (Waco, TX: Baylor University Press, 2016). Furthermore, Pamela Klassen and Heather Curtis have written two outstanding recent books on North American missionaries whose attention to both complex power dynamics and material culture inspire my study. Pamela E. Klassen, *The Story of Radio Mind: A Missionary's Journey on Indigenous Land* (Chicago: University of Chicago Press, 2018); Heather D. Curtis, *Holy Humanitarians: American Evangelicals and Global Aid* (Cambridge, MA: Harvard University Press, 2018).

23. A classic and influential study of antebellum America that asserts this claim is Mark A. Noll, *America's God: From Jonathan Edwards to Abraham Lincoln* (Oxford: Oxford University Press, 2002). A more recent example of the continuation of scholars arguing for a Protestant consensus is John Lardas Modern, *Secularism in Antebellum America: With Reference to Ghosts, Protestant Subcultures, Machines, and Their Metaphors; Featuring Discussions of Mass Media, Moby-Dick, Spirituality, Phrenology, Anthropology, Sing Sing State Penitentiary, and Sex with the New Motive Power* (Chicago: University of Chicago Press, 2011).

24. For more on American religious history scholarship on the Protestant consensus and how my work seeks to intervene, see Alexandra Kaloyanides, "America's God and the World: Questioning the Protestant Consensus," *Church History* 84, no. 3 (2015): 625–29.

25. A foundational work of scholarship examining imperialism, Christianity, and Asia is Peter van der Veer's *Imperial Encounters: Religion and Modernity in India and Britain* (Princeton, NJ: Princeton University Press, 2001), which productively complicated oppositions between modern/traditional, secular/religious,

progressive/reactionary common to earlier scholarship by showing how the national cultures in India and Britain developed through their shared colonial experiences and were greatly influenced by notions of secularity and religion. Jean and John Comaroff's history of Christianity and colonialism in Africa, *Of Revelation and Revolution: Christianity, Colonialism, and Consciousness in South Africa*, vol. 1 (Chicago: University of Chicago Press, 1991), similarly offers a nuanced analysis of evangelical Christianity and the British empire. Their study of early encounters between the Southern Tswana peoples of the South African frontier and British missionaries provides a model of scholarship that attends to both colonizer and colonized to question how particular cultural and religious forms are incorporated or rejected.

26. Felix Carey, the eldest son of the famous English Baptist missionary and translator of Indian literature William Carey, tried unsuccessfully to establish a Protestant mission in Burma in 1806.

27. Judson had been petitioning the newly formed American Board of Commissioners for Foreign Missions alongside Samuel Nott, Samuel Newell, and Gordon Hall for support to become America's first intercontinental foreign missionaries. The Board of Commissioners, not wanting these Americans to embark on this pioneering mission under the London Missionary Society (who had agreed to support them), voted at the end of 1811 to sponsor the four men in their evangelical efforts overseas. Luther Rice joined this team, and all were ordained as missionaries on February 6, 1812, at the Tabernacle in Salem, Massachusetts. Samuel and Harriett Newell set sail out of Boston with the Judsons, and Nott, Hall, and Rice left together from Philadelphia on February 18, but did not arrive in Calcutta until July 2013, the month after the Judsons. See Wayland, *Memoir*, 74–81.

28. Harriet Newell's memoirs were first published in 1815 and began a popular genre of missionary biographies celebrating women who left the comforts of American homes and families to sacrifice themselves overseas. See Candy Gunther Brown, *The Word in the World: Evangelical Writing, Publishing, and Reading in America, 1789–1880* (Chapel Hill: University of North Carolina Press, 2004), 92. See also Harriet Newell and Timothy Dwight, *Memoirs of the Life of Mrs. Harriet Newell, Wife of the Rev. Samuel Newell, Missionary to India, Who Died at the Isle of France, November 30, 1812—Aged 19 Years* (Lexington, KY: T. T. Skillman, 1815).

29. Robert G. Torbet, *Venture of Faith: The Story of the American Baptist Foreign Mission Society and the Woman's American Baptist Foreign Mission Society, 1814-1954*. (Philadelphia: Judson, 1955), vii.

30. This approach to investigating the role of visual and material culture in Asian religions follows in the footsteps of Richard Davis's celebrated *Lives of Indian Images* (Princeton, NJ: Princeton University Press, 1997), which launched an object-biographical approach in the study of South Asian religions. Like Davis's Indian images, the objects studied in this book have been animated in different ways by different communities, displaying the variegated human processes by which objects are made meaningful. Justin McDaniel's *Architects of Buddhist Leisure: Socially Disengaged Buddhism in Asia's Museums, Monuments, and Amusement Parks* (Honolulu: University of Hawai'i Press, 2016) demonstrates the continued value of studying Asian religions through a material culture lens that brings

into focus activity beyond monks and elite texts. My work hopes to do just that: to look beyond the powerful sangha to understand the religious expressions of marginalized people.

31. This material culture turn in American religious history began in larger part because of Colleen McDannell, *Material Christianity: Religion and Popular Culture in America* (New Haven: Yale University Press, 1995).

32. My approach to these sacred materials follows Birgit Meyer's call in "Religious Sensations: Why Media, Aesthetics, and Power Matter in the Study of Contemporary Religion," in *Religion: Beyond a Concept*, ed. Hent De Vries (New York: Fordham University Press, 2008) to focus the study of religion on "sensational forms," which she defines as "relatively fixed, authorized modes of invoking and organizing access to the transcendental, thereby creating and sustaining links between religious practitioners in the context of particular religious organizations" (707). Meyer's work suggests that, by studying sensational forms, the bodies that experience them, and the power structures in which they are embedded we can overcome the academic habit of reducing religious expression to symbols of something else (like God or nirvana or colonial policy). We also find this transformative approach in Christopher Pinney's book on Indian chromolithographs, *Photos of the Gods: The Printed Image and Political Struggle in India* (London: Reaktion, 2004). In this study of the politics of printed images, mass-produced Hindu lithographs are not simply reflections of some more important colonial or nationalist negotiations happening elsewhere. Instead, Pinney shows how history can be "determined in part by struggles occurring at the level of the visual" (8). Pinney's lithographs narrate a different story of modern India in which visuals are actively involved in shaping the societies around them.

33. Scholarship from Protestant missionary operations in other parts of the world helps inform my method of complicating the story of how and why communities converted to Christianity and the relationship between evangelization and colonization. As my notes show, work on Africa and India is especially informative.

34. As Tomoko Masuzawa has shown in *The Invention of World Religions, or, How European Universalism Was Preserved in the Language of Pluralism* (Chicago: University of Chicago Press, 2005), the European work of counting and mapping world religions—which overlapped with the American Baptist mission studied here—presented the West as a bastion of pluralism and a justified world power. For the case of the United States, Tracy Fessenden has demonstrated how the power of Protestant ideology has become consolidated and entrenched through displays of a kind of tolerance in which a diverse range of minorities groups are shown as harmonious through Protestant benevolence; see Tracy Fessenden, *Culture and Redemption: Religion, the Secular, and American Literature* (Princeton, NJ: Princeton University Press, 2011).

35. For more on the Buddha's unanswered questions, see Hugh Nicholson, "The Unanswered Questions and the Limits of Knowledge," *Journal of Indian Philosophy* 40, no. 5 (2012): 533–52.

36. One of the most influential Mahayana scriptures about the lifestory of the Buddha, the *Lalitavistara Sutra*, features a rather divine Buddha performing his life

as a prince who leaves the palace to find enlightenment—a theme that is highlighted in the title of the scripture, which is composed of the Sanskrit terms for "playing" (*lalita*) and "in detail" (*vistaraḥ*).
37. See the fifteenth chapter of the *Lotus Sutra*.
38. It is the commentaries on the Pali Canon that bundle these three key concepts of impermanence (*anicca*), suffering (*dukkha*), and not-self (*anattā*) as the "Three Marks of Existence" (*tilakkhaṇa*). I am grateful to Ṭhānissaro Bhikkhu for sharing his expert knowledge of the Pali Canon and the commentaries with me. Ṭhānissaro Bhikkhu describes this Buddhist teaching as "the three perceptions" and translates these key terms as "inconstancy, stress, and not-self." Ṭhānissaro Bhikkhu, "The Three Perceptions," Dhammatalks.org, May 27, 2021, https://www.dhammatalks.org/books/uncollected/ThreePerceptions.html.
39. John Strong, *Relics of the Buddha* (Princeton, NJ: Princeton University Press, 2004).
40. Pe Maung Tin, "The Shwe Dagon Pagoda," *Journal of the Burma Research Society* 24, no. 1 (1934):1–91.
41. For more on Burmese pagodas and their relationship to Pali texts, see San San Win, Aye Min, and Khin Mar Sein, "The Mahādhammarājika Pagoda, the Historical Monument in Meiktila Township," *Meiktila University Research Journal* 11, no. 1 (2020): 181–83.
42. Donald K Swearer, *Becoming the Buddha: The Ritual of Image Consecration in Thailand* (Princeton, NJ: Princeton University Press, 2004).
43. Matthew Engelke, *A Problem of Presence: Beyond Scripture in an African Church* (Berkeley: University of California Press, 2007), 12–13.
44. David Morgan, *The Thing About Religion: An Introduction to the Material Study of Religions* (Chapel Hill: University of North Carolina Press, 2021), 38.
45. Jon Butler, *Awash in a Sea of Faith: Christianizing the American People* (Cambridge, MA: Harvard University Press, 1990), 228.
46. Erik R. Seeman, *Speaking with the Dead in Early America* (Philadelphia: University of Pennsylvania Press, 2019), 189–228.
47. Bénédicte Brac de La Perrière, "An Overview of the Field of Religion in Burmese Studies," *Asian Ethnology* 68, no. 2 (2009): 185–210.
48. As I have written elsewhere, the study of Theravada Buddhism would benefit from more attention to spirits like nats and other nonhuman beings. Some scholars have already begun moving the discipline in this direction, including Thomas Patton, in his work on Myanmar's wizard-saints, and Erik Davis, who examines Cambodian Buddhists' relationships with the dead. See Alexandra Kaloyanides, "'Intercultural Mimesis,' Empire, and Spirits," *Journal of Global Buddhism* 22, no. 1 (2021): 125–31; Patton, *Buddha's Wizards*; and Erik W. Davis, *Deathpower: Buddhism's Ritual Imagination in Cambodia* (New York: Columbia University Press, 2016).
49. Howard Malcom, "Journal of Mr. Malcom," *Baptist Missionary Magazine*, May 1837, 98.
50. My treatment of the imagination throughout this book builds on Benedict Anderson's classic work on the subject, *Imagined Communities: Reflections on the Origins and Spread of Nationalism* (New York: Verso, 1983), which was, notably, produced through his study of Southeast Asia. Anderson revealed that the nation is an imagined political community, and that print culture has been

crucial to its coming into being. While Burmese nationalism is outside of the scope of this book, I do examine the role of print in creating imagined communities such as distinct ethnic minority communities and larger Protestant communities.

51. The World Religion Database counts 74.4 percent of Myanmar's population as Buddhist, 8.2 percent as Christian, 3.8 percent as Muslim, 1.7 percent as Hindu, 1.5 percent as Confucianists, and 9.5 percent as ethnoreligionists. See Todd Michael Johnson and Brian J. Grim, eds., *World Religion Database: International Religious Demographic Statistics and Sources* (Leiden: Brill, 2008). The majority of the country's Christians are Baptist, but reliable demographic studies detailing the country's various Christian denominations do not exist. The *World Factbook* published by the U.S. Central Intelligence Agency calculates a relatively low estimate for Myanmar's Christian population, 4 percent, and breaks that population down into Baptists, which it counts as 3 percent, and Roman Catholics as 1 percent. See U.S. Central Intelligence Agency, *The World Factbook: Burma*, accessed May 15, 2016, https://www.cia.gov/library/publications/the-world-factbook/geos/bm.html. For an illuminating study of evangelical Christianity in contemporary Myanmar, see Michael Edwards, "Circulating Publicness and Public Circulation," The Immanent Frame 2019, https://tif.ssrc.org/2019/06/18/circulating-publicness-and-public-circulation/ (accessed August 26, 2022). Edwards connects a close analysis of a preacher on a Yangon train to larger considerations of the mediation of publicity in Myanmar and in contemporary evangelism.

1. The Book

1. George Boardman, "Journal," *American Baptist Magazine*, January 1830, 22.
2. Boardman, "Journal."
3. Boardman.
4. Boardman.
5. Boardman.
6. Boardman goes on to note that the sorcerer "handed over his wand, saying he had no further use for it," and later reports describe him tearing his dress to pieces and throwing the pieces into a brook. This missionary account relishes these details of the destruction of material embodiments of heathen beliefs.
7. Kuthodaw Pagoda's Tipitaka is still called the "world's largest book" by travel websites and databases like Atlas Obscura, who are using a common definition of a book as a material base that humans have marked to record and communicate information. See Joshua Foer, "World's Largest Book at Kuthodaw Pagoda," Atlas Obscura, https://www.atlasobscura.com/places/world-s-largest-book-at-kuthodaw-pagoda (accessed August 26, 2022). The kinds of books this chapter focuses on largely fit this definition, in that they include printed and bound missionary publications and hand-inscribed manuscripts that record and disseminate the teachings of the Buddha. Scholars have long questioned the limitations of this definition of the book. For example, Germaine

1. THE BOOK

Warkentin demonstrates how Native peoples in Canada employ sign systems such as wampum (strings and belts of worked shell beads) and painted animal skins to show why scholars should not classify their cultures as simply "oral," given their use of material sign-making; Warkentin persuasively argues that scholars should bring sign systems like these into their understanding of writing and books. Germaine Warkentin, "In Search of 'the Word of the Other': Aboriginal Sign Systems and the History of the Book in Canada," *Book History* 2 (1999): 1–27. Similarly, D. F. McKenzie, in *Bibliography and the Sociology of Texts* (New York: Cambridge University Press, 1999), advocates for an expansive definition of the term "text" that includes "verbal, visual, oral, and numerical data, in the form of maps, prints, and music, of archives of recorded sound, of films, videos, and any computer-stored information" (13). When scholars pay attention to this range of recorded forms, they are able to show how forms effect meaning, as McKenzie's work demonstrates.

8. King Mindon [r. 1853–1878], a powerful king of the dynasty explored in the final section of this chapter, ordered this project of inscribing the Burmese Buddhist canon on huge marble slabs. King Mindon was famous for both his promotion of Buddhism and his efforts to resist the expansion of the British Raj into Burma. For more on King Mindon, see Myo Myint, *Confronting Colonialism: King Mindon's Strategy for Defending Independence (1853-1878)* (Yangon: Ministry of Religious Affairs, 2012). This chapter details the gold-painted six-volume bible missionaries Adoniram Judson and James Colman present to King Bagyidaw, elaborates on how the missionary Jonathan Wade and others formulated a written language system for a previously unlettered Karen language, and examines reports of tract-turned-earrings and worshipped devices.

9. When Adoniram and Ann Judson and Luther Rice left to evangelize in India in 1812, they were members of the Congregationalist Church, and their travels were under the auspices of the Congregationalist Board of Commissioners; however, while at sea, all three studied the issue of baptism and became convinced that the New Testament did not instruct infant baptism, instead instructing immersion for those who professed Christian faith. The Judsons and Rice formally became Baptists in India when they were baptized by a British Baptist missionary. This change of denomination led to the establishment in 1814 of the first national Baptist body in America: the General Missionary Convention of the Baptist Denomination in the United States for Foreign Missions. This leading body soon became known as the Triennial Convention on account of its practice of meeting every three years. In 1845, the Triennial Convention divided over the issue of appointing missionaries who held slaves, and the Southern Baptist Convention was formed. While this division is crucial for Baptist identity in the United States today, the shared legacy of the first foreign missionaries is celebrated by both Southern Baptists and the American Baptist Churches organization that developed out of the 1845 division. See Bill Leonard, *Baptists in America* (New York: Columbia University Press, 2005).

10. See Myint, *Confronting Colonialism*; and Michael Charney, *Powerful Learning: Buddhist Literati and the Throne in Burma's Last Dynasty, 1752-1885* (Ann Arbor: Centers for South and Southeast Asian Studies, University of Michigan, 2006).

1. THE BOOK

11. See Maung Shwe Wa, *Burma Baptist Chronicle* (Rangoon: Board of Publications, Burma Baptist Convention, 1963), 180–90. See also Hitomi Fujimura's "Disentangling the Colonial Narrative of the Karen National Association of 1881: The Motive Behind Karen Baptist Intellectual's Claim for a Nation," *Journal of Burma Studies* 24, no. 2 (2020), 275–314, on how Karen Baptist elites developed claims for a Karen nation through their engagement with the American Baptist mission and the British colonial system.
12. A Karennic word for book is *lee*, which can also include anything in written form with or without a cover, such as a letter or a note. I am grateful to Hitomi Fujimura for helping me understand this term and for sharing her translation of the Sgaw Karen entry for *lee* in the 1850 *Thesaurus of Karen Knowledge*: "When people make opinions and write their words and its meaning, or put various things that we know from talking into writing, we call it lee. [Among] many groups of people, some of them have *lee*. Those who have kings have their own *lee*. Those without their kings do not have their *lee*." As Fujimura points out, this entry makes the significant connection between practices of kingship and possession of *lee*. Sau Kau Too, *Thesaurus of Karen Knowledge: Comprising Traditions, Legends or Fables, Poetry, Customs, Superstitions, Demonology, Therapeutics, Etc. Alphabetically Arranged and Forming a Complete Native Karen Dictionary, with Definitions and Examples, Illustrating the Usages of Every Word*, vol. 4, ed. Jonathan Wade (Tavoy: Karen Mission, 1850), 259.
13. The field of religious studies has, in many ways, been built on the argument that world religions must have canons of holy texts and revered ancient histories to qualify. Tomoko Masuzawa investigates the emergence of the "world religions" system in nineteenth-century Europe, demonstrating specifically how Buddhism emerged as a world religion on the grounds that it had ancient canonical texts and a venerable history. See Tomoko Masuzawa, *The Invention of World Religions, or, How European Universalism Was Preserved in the Language of Pluralism* (Chicago: University of Chicago Press, 2005), 121–46.
14. For more on how new methods within the comparative study of languages in the eighteenth and nineteenth centuries gave rise to particular fantasies of an Indo-European past, see Maurice Olender, *The Languages of Paradise* (Cambridge, MA: Harvard University Press, 1992). For more on how developments in print technology contributed to American evangelicalism, see Candy Gunther Brown, *The Word in the World: Evangelical Writing, Publishing, and Reading in America, 1789-1880* (Chapel Hill: University of North Carolina Press, 2004). For more on how developments in nautical science shaped those traveling to Burma in this period, see Sunil S. Amrith, *Crossing the Bay of Bengal: The Furies of Nature and the Fortunes of Migrants* (Cambridge, MA: Harvard University Press, 2013).
15. The most comprehensive account of the Baptist church in Burma, the institutional history published in 1963 on account of the 150th anniversary of the Judson's arrival, the *Burma Baptist Chronicle*, records the story of the Karen lost book that had been standardized by the mid-twentieth century. See Shwe Wa, *Burma Baptist Chronicle*, 69, 305.
16. Anthropologist Theodore Stern's study of millenarian expectations among nineteenth-century Karen offers a similar argument to the one I put forth here

1. THE BOOK

in that he argues that millenarian movements among the Karen developed out of contact with American Baptist religious ideas and elements of Theravada Buddhism. Stern focuses on how Karen chiliasm arose out of this period of cultural confrontation and desire for aspects of Western civilization. The Karen legend of the lost book is examined in Stern's essay, but analyzed for the way it emphasized millenarian expectations, not for how evolving versions point to concern with religious book practices shared among Theravada Buddhism and American Protestantism in Burma. Theodore Stern, "Ariya and the Golden Book: A Millenarian Buddhist Sect Among the Karen," *Journal of Asian Studies* 27, no. 2 (1968): 297–328.

17. Scholarship throughout the academy, especially in the field of anthropology, has long been interested in the oral traditions of unlettered cultures. Lawrence Sullivan encourages scholars of religious studies to similarly pay attention to the inventive productions of people that fall outside of our limited definition of texts worthy of study, productions such as folklore. Sullivan argues, "The long-standing creativity of unlettered peoples—the existence of their shrewd reflections and exfoliating aesthetic life—challenges the choice of 'text' as the most exemplary vehicle of intelligibility." Lawrence E. Sullivan, "Seeking an End to the Primary Text," in *Beyond the Classics? Essays in Religious Studies and Liberal Education*, ed. Frank E. Reynolds and Sheryl L. Burkhalter (Atlanta: Scholars Press, 1990), 41. This book works to heed Sullivan's advice and include nontextual data in its analysis, and the final chapter examines oral histories among Burma's minority groups; however, with regard to the Karen book legend, the earliest extant versions are the ones that were rendered in text by the missionaries in the nineteenth century.

18. The Karen did not write down their own histories until the late 1920s and 1930s, the end of the British colonial period. The *Kayin Chronicle* by U Pyinnya, a Buddhist history of the Karen, was published in 1929; U Saw's *Kuyin Great Chronicle*, a second Buddhist Karen history, was published in 1931; and a Christian Karen history, *A History of the Pgakanyaw*, was published by Saw Aung Hla in 1939. As Kazuto Ikeda has shown, the two Buddhist Karen histories work to establish the Karen as a legitimate people comparable to the Burmese and Mon on account of their having had ancient dynasties and practices of supporting Buddhist communities. The histories also emphasize the dominant impact of Buddhism among the Karen, complicating the popular image of Karen as monolithically Christian, pro-Western, anti-Burmese, and separatist. Kazuto Ikeda, "Two Versions of Buddhist Karen History of the Late British Colonial Period in Burma: Kayin Chronicle (1929) and Kuyin Great Chronicle (1931)," *Southeast Asian Studies* 1, no. 3 (2012): 431–60.

19. Fujimura, "Disentangling the Colonial Narrative."

20. Ananda Rajah, "A 'Nation of Intent' in Burma: Karen Ethno-Nationalism, Nationalism, and Narrations of Nation," *Pacific Review* 15, no. 4 (2002): 533.

21. This approach of considering Karen historical understandings of the lost book alongside American Baptist presentations of it follows the work of other scholars of Christian missionary history who employ this approach to show the

limitations of seeing adoption of foreign forms as symptoms of Western colonialism. For example, Nicholas May's work on the oral histories of Nisga'a Church Armies shows that this late nineteenth-century Christian movement in Canada was driven by a Nisga'a priority to secure the continuity of exuberant forms of worship that were crucial to their collective cultural survival. This resonates with Karen stories of the lost book that ensure a continuity between their past their Christian present. May's work shows that paying attention to this kind of indigenous historical practice gives us a "deeper grasp of a phenomenon such as the adoption and appropriation of what was initially a foreign religious form." Nicholas May, "Marching to the Beat of a Newer Drum: Cultural Continuity and Revival in Nisga'a Church Armies, 1894–1970," *Ethnohistory* 62, no. 4 (2015): 784.
22. Saw Quala's letter to the English governor-general, published in Francis Mason, *The Karen Apostle* (n.p., 1843), 14–28. In Mason's reprinting, Saw Quala's name, which includes the Karen honorific "Saw" and means "hope," is transliterated as "Sau Qua-la," but I have written his name here as "Saw Quala" to follow the standard English spelling used today.
23. Mason, *Karen Apostle*, 14–28.
24. Mason, 23.
25. Mason, 24.
26. Mrs. Mason, *Civilizing Mountain Men: Sketches of Mission Work Among the Karens* (London: James Nisbet, 1862), 103.
27. Mason, *Civilizing Mountain Men*, 103.
28. Mason, 103.
29. Religious Tract Society, *The White Foreigners from Over the Water: The Story of the American Mission to the Burmese and the Karens* (London: Religious Tract Society, 1868), 106. This same translated song appears in the afterward to Ellen Mason's *Civilizing Mountain Men*. Mason's editor, Ellen Ranyard, notes that "this rendering is slightly different from that given [by Ellen Mason earlier in the book], but is accounted for by the variations in oral tradition." Ranyard does not, however, say from where she obtained this rendering. Mason, 366–67.
30. Religious Tract Society, *White Foreigners*, 107.
31. Religious Tract Society, 139–40.
32. An institutional history published in 1981 by the Karen new religious movement the Lekhai tells a version of this lost book story that also includes the dogs devouring the sacred text. The Lekhai account explains that the Karen ancestor forgets about the book, leaving it on a tree stump for the entire rainy season, and it is "only at the end of the rainy season that he remembered the message left on the tree stump. When he went to look for it, all that was left of the parchment, were bits of leather chewed by dogs, that lay scattered on the ground scratched by fowls." Saw Kya Shin, Kyaw Paung-Yei, Kyau Taing Lone Gay, Mahn Gyi Sein, and Hlaingbwe, "A Brief Outline of the Traditional Background of the Lekhai (Ariya) Religious Sect [and] Its Leit-Hsan Wait," *Karen Heritage* 1, no. 1 (2004): 11.
33. Donald Mackenzie Smeaton, *The Loyal Karens of Burma* (London: Kegan Paul, Trench, 1887), 68.

1. THE BOOK

34. Smeaton, *Loyal Karens of Burma*, 75.
35. Smeaton, 1.
36. Matthew Engelke, *A Problem of Presence: Beyond Scripture in an African Church* (Berkeley: University of California Press, 2007), 5–6.
37. May, "Marching to the Beat," 784.
38. Linford D. Fisher, *The Indian Great Awakening: Religion and the Shaping of Native Cultures in Early America* (New York: Oxford University Press, 2012), 5–12.
39. Sylvester A. Johnson, *African American Religions, 1500-2000: Colonialism, Democracy, and Freedom* (New York: Cambridge University Press, 2015), 138.
40. Johnson, *African American Religions*, 144–45.
41. Kathryn Gin Lum shows how Euro-American attitudes toward the Hawaiians and Chinese in the nineteenth century reveal the way they conceived of history in opposition to their perception of others' lack of history. Kathryn Gin Lum, "The Historyless Heathen and the Stagnating Pagan: History as Non-Native Category?," *Religion and American Culture: A Journal of Interpretation* 28, no. 1 (2018): 59–91. Burmese and British elite employed similar techniques as representing minority groups in the Southeast Asian country as either not having histories or having wrong histories in contrast to the noble and true histories of the Burmese or British.
42. Performance studies scholar Joseph Roach's theorization of how culture recreates itself provides an alternative to strict utilitarian readings of the advent of origin myths. Roach uses the term "surrogation" to mean a process in which "actual or perceived vacancies occur in the network of relations that constitute the social fabric" and "into these cavities . . . survivors attempt to fit satisfactory alternates." The Karen lost book legend might be seen as a kind of surrogate that was intended to substitute lost communal memories of Karen history. As Roach suggests, "Improvised narratives of authenticity and priority may congeal into full-blown myths of legitimacy and origin." For the Karen, the lost book legends seem to have begun as extemporized accounts of authenticity, but then evolved into a fully developed origin story. Roach's work suggests that this progression comes out of "loss through death or other forms of departure." While we do not have the data to explore this question sufficiently, it is worth noting that this kind of loss or departure for the Karen could be their subjugation by the Burmese. See Joseph R. Roach, *Cities of the Dead: Circum-Atlantic Performance* (New York: Columbia University Press, 1996), 2–3.
43. Francis Mason, "Journal of Mr. Mason," *American Baptist Magazine*, September 1835, 366–72.
44. Mason, "Journal of Mr. Mason."
45. Homi Bhabha writes about the very similar "scene in the cultural writings of English colonialism which repeats so insistently after the early nineteenth century. . . . the sudden, fortuitous discovery of the English book." Bhabha analyzes scenarios in which the English book is "an insignia of colonial authority and a signifier of colonial desire" in colonial India, Africa, and the Caribbean. Bhabha explains that his scholarship repeats the scenario of the English book—a genre in which the English books found among the Karen mostly fit despite the fact that the discoverers are Americans and not British colonists—because it

seeks to represent a colonial difference, to show "the effect of uncertainty that afflicts the discourse of power, an uncertainty that estranges the familiar symbol of English 'national' authority and emerges from its colonial appropriation as the sign of its difference." Bhabha names this displacement of value "hybridity" to articulate the "ambivalent 'turn' of the discriminated subject into the terrifying, exorbitant object of paranoid classification." Furthermore, Bhabha analyses the technology of the printed world in rural, nineteenth-century India as possessing a penetrative power that is both psychic and social. Homi K. Bhabha, *The Location of Culture* (New York: Routledge, 1994), 102, 13, 16–17. Bhabha's work helps to explain the particular power Protestant printed tracts wielded in Burma and indicates that what is happening in these Karen scenes is being repeated throughout the British empire.

46. Thomas Simons, "Journal of Mr. Simons," *Baptist Missionary Magazine*, May 1837, 109–13.

47. Simons, "Journal." For an illuminating analysis of another Protestant missionary account of local people cutting up printed Christian pages and inserting them into holes in earlobes, see McKenzie's analysis of nineteenth-century reports on the Maori of New Zealand. McKenzie examines this practice as part of a larger phenomenon of people in oral societies who treat books as ritual objects when first encountering them McKenzie, *Bibliography and the Sociology of Texts*, 107.

48. The issue of the Buddhist cult of the book has been perhaps most famously explored by Gregory Schopen, who has argued in "The Phrase '*Sa Pthivīpradeśaś Caityabhūto Bhavet*' in the *Vajracchedikā*: Notes on the Cult of the Book in Mahāyāna," *Indo-Iranian Journal* 17, no. 3 (1975) that the earliest formation of Mahayana Buddhism was a "loose federation of a number of distinct though related cults, all of the same pattern, but each associated with a its specific text" (181). Schopen suggests that the shift to the cult of the book from the cult of *stūpa*/relic allowed early Mahāyāna communities to center cultic activity such as flower-*pūjā* and dancing at the site where books containing the words of the Buddha were stored, instead at fixed geographical locations recognized as associated with the life and relics of the Buddha. While the data Schopen examines dates to centuries before the Buddhist book material analyzed in this chapter and also comes from Indian and Tibetan materials, rather than Southeast Asian ones, I will show that the Burmese Buddhist book the Kammavāca, like the books Schopen studies, allows its communities to relocate centers of power.

For a study of sacred, magical objects among modern Theravada communities in Southeast Asia, see Stanley Jeyaraja Tambiah, *The Buddhist Saints of the Forest and the Cult of Amulets: A Study in Charisma, Hagiography, Sectarianism, and Millennial Buddhism* (New York: Cambridge University Press, 1984). While Tambiah does not study book cults, his examination of amulet practices in Thailand explores the power of portable religious objects. Tambiah argues that the "traditional preoccupation [with amulets is] now reaching the pitch of fetishistic obsession" (3) and is connected to the charisma of saints in present-day Thailand, lay fascination with meditation, and the power amulets are understood to possess.

49. Despite Protestant theologies of privileging inner, private, direct, immaterial connections with God over material and mediated practices, scholars have long

1. THE BOOK

demonstrated that Protestants in practice have long and complex histories with religious things like books. Colleen McDannell's exploration of the Bible in the Victorian home, for example, offers a case study that is contemporaneous with the Karen book legend explored in this chapter. In *Material Christianity: Religion and Popular Culture in America* (New Haven: Yale University Press, 1995), 67–102, McDannell show how American bibles were sacred objects that communicated a message of family stability and a sense of style alongside a commitment to God and domestic space.

50. Mark 16:15–16.
51. Claudius Buchanan, *The Star in the East: A Sermon* (Boston: Munroe & Francis, [1809] 1811).
52. Edward Judson, *The Life of Adoniram Judson* (New York: A. D. F. Randolph, 1883), 3.
53. Francis Wayland, *A Memoir of the Life and Labors of the Rev. Adoniram Judson, D.D.* (Boston: Phillips, Sampson, 1853), 1:37.
54. Wayland, *Memoir*, 1:37.
55. Wayland, 1:38. Judson's "high-wrought enthusiasm," "engrossing," and full-hearted missionary views suggest the ecstatic states that Ann Taves explores in *Fits, Trances, and Visions: Experiencing Religion and Explaining Experience from Wesley to James* (Princeton, NJ: Princeton University Press, 1999), a study of how believers and detractors in this period of Protestant revivalism drew on popular psychology to interpret complex experiences, such as those named in her title.

Janet Lindman considers similar phenomena in her study of the corporeal nature of Baptist practice in eighteenth-century America, *Bodies of Belief: Baptist Community in Early America* (Philadelphia: University of Pennsylvania Press, 2008). Lindman argues that, for these Baptists, the body became a channel of belief and behavior that was penetrable by both holy and earthly forces; faith, then, was achieved by these Baptists through prolonged and trying religious turmoil in this penetrable body. Reading this Burmese missionary data with Taves and Lindman in mind suggests that the impassioned responses to Buchanan's sermon explored here come out of specifically American Baptist traditions and were connected to larger frameworks built in nineteenth-century Protestant revivalism.

Additionally, Jonathan Edwards—the American theologian whose 1749 biography of David Brainerd, an early missionary to the Native Americans, inspired missionaries in the second half of the eighteenth century and throughout the nineteenth century—articulated an emphasis on religious feelings and affections similar to what I find in the writings of Adoniram Judson and his contemporary American Baptists. As Harry S. Stout shows in his study of colonial New England, *The New England Soul: Preaching and Religious Culture in Colonial New England* (New York: Oxford University Press, 1986), Edwards's treaties on the affections insisted that "ethical and religious ideas were never emotionally neutral but laden with a range of feelings and sentiments"; as Stout explains, Edwards "reclothed the old Calvinist teachings of sin and grace in a new rhetoric of sentiment" (206, 207).

In addition to the influence of Edwards's theological treatises on sentiment, there is also an imprint of Edward's linkage of mission and millennial drama in nineteenth-century American Baptist missionary writings an imprint of Edwards's linkage of mission and millennial drama. As William R. Hutchison shows in *Errand to the World: American Protestant Thought and Foreign Missions* (Chicago: University of Chicago Press, 1987), Edwards and Cotton Mather were key proponents of the notion that the New World was God's staging area in which native Americans must and would be converted before Christ's return by American Protestant missionary acting as God's instrument. Mather especially, according to Hutchison, "gave some credence to the possibility that the Native Americans were Jews—descendants, that is, of the Lost Tribes of Israel" (38). This notion that those in the mission field once knew God, but subsequently lost their way, became important for American missionaries in Burma who argued, as I have shown in the case of the Karen, that the communities targeted for mission work were once peoples of God.

Robert Caldwell's study of Adoniram Judson's missionary theology, New England's New Divinity and the Age of Judson's Preparation," in *Adoniram Judson: A Bicentennial Appreciation of the Pioneer American Missionary*, ed. Jason G. Duesing (Nashville, TN: B&H, 2012), 31–54, elaborates on connections between Jonathan Edwards and Adoniram Judson. Caldwell argues that Judson was shaped by the New Divinity or Edwardsean movement that saw itself as a branch of the Calvinist tradition rooted in both Edwards's distinction between "a sinner's natural ability and moral inability to choose Christ . . . [as well as Edwards's promotion of] radical self-denial among America's early missionaries" (31).

56. Crane to Judson, December 6, 1851, in *The Life and Letters of Emily Chubbuck Judson (Fanny Forester)*, ed. George H. Tooze (Macon, GA: Mercer University Press, 2009), 5:77–78.
57. Marilla Baker Ingalls, *Ocean Sketches of Life in Burmah* (Philadelphia: American Baptist Publication Society, 1857), 76.
58. Wayland's biography of Judson reprints excerpts from a handful of letters that further attest to the powerful impact of the "Star in the East" sermon on American Protestants in the early years of the nineteenth century. Two of these letters, quoted below, resemble Judson's own reflections on the sermon in noting its incredibly rousing force, a force they praise for cutting the audience's attachment to home as well as recognize as being based on incorrect assertions. The first of these letters is from Reverend Chapin, president of Columbian College, Washington, who writes that his first missionary impressions were occasioned by reading "The Star in the East" in 1809 at Andover Theological Seminary, which "produced a very powerful effect on my mind. For some days I was unable to attend to the studies of my class, and spent my time in wondering at my past stupidity, depicting the most romantic scenes in missionary life, and roving about the college rooms, declaiming on the subjects of missions. My views were very incorrect, and my feelings extravagant; but yet I have always felt thankful to God for bringing me into that state of excitement, which was perhaps necessary, in the first instance, to enable me to break the strong attachment I felt to home and country" (Wayland, *Memoir*, 1:51–52). Here Chapin is processing his passionate response to Buchanan's sermon in very much the same way that Judson did: characterizing his excitement as

1. THE BOOK

overzealous and based on views that he would come to learn were incorrect, but also as strong enough to cut his ties to home.

Wayland further quotes an undated letter to Adoniram Judson from a Reverend Staughton that similarly explains that the author's views of missionary work are "different from what they were, when [he] was first set on fire by Buchanan's 'Star in the East.' " This interpretation matches Judson's: the missionary supporter recalls his fiery and excited response to Buchanan and notes that he has come to see the sermon's arguments as problematic in substance, but effective in their work of cutting the readers' attachments to home in order to commit to the cause of foreign missions. This pattern suggests that as this generation of American supporters of the missionary cause grew older, they were in conversation about how to rectify Buchanan's erroneous assertions about the history of Christianity in India with his celebrated effect of launching the American missionary era. See Wayland, 1:178.

59. Buchanan, "Star in the East."
60. See Pandurang Vaman Kane, *History of Dharmasastra: Ancient and Medieval Religious and Civil Law*, 5 vols. (Poona: Bhandarkar Oriental Research Institute, 1930).
61. Buchanan does not name this Sanskrit text, but cites a "learned Orientalist" who "has deposited the originals among the archives of the Asiatiac Society." From these, and from other documents, he has compiled a work entitled "The History of the Introduction of the Christian Religion into India: Its Progress and Decline," at the conclusion of which he writes: "I have written this account of Christianity with the impartiality of an Historian; fully persuaded that our holy Religion cannot receive any additional lustre from it." This Orientalist is named "Mr. Wilford." Buchanan, "Star in the East," 7. Buchanan must have read a version of the essay that Francis Wilford eventually published as "Origin and Decline of the Christian Religion in India," the fifth essay in his series "And on the Sacred Isles in the West, with Other Essays, Connected with That Work," which Wilford began publishing in *Asiatic Researches* in 1808. Francis Wilford, "Origin and Decline of the Christian Religion in India," *Asiatic Researches* 10 (1811): 27–126.
62. This approach of freely quoting bits and pieces of Sanskrit literature that the scholar, his British colleague, or his Indian translator and language teacher has found to resemble Western stories or philosophies was becoming popular in this early period of Western interest in Indian texts. Nigel Leask argues in "Francis Wilford and the Colonial Construction of Hindu Geography, 1799–1822," in *Romantic Geographies: Discourses of Travel, 1775–1844*, ed. Amanda Gilroy (New York: St. Martin's, 2000), 204–22, that Wilford was "simply following the methodology of Sir William Jones and other eighteenth-century orientalists in syncretising Sanskrit with classical and biblical narratives, establishing transcultural correspondences by means of often crude conjectural etymologies" (205). While Leask is certainly correct that Wilford was not alone in his approach to Sanskrit materials, it is important to see how his methodologies were not only problematic in that they led to erroneous readings of Indian texts, but also in the way they promoted appropriative techniques in philology, colonial practices, and missionary approaches.

63. The name Śālivāhana is given to princes in Brahmanical, Jain, and Buddhist texts. The Monier-Williams Sanskrit dictionary lists "Siṃhāsana-Dvātriṃśikā or Vikramāditya-Caritra, Jaina recension, Subhāṣitāvali, Buddhist literature" as literary sources and identifies Śālivāhana as the "name of a celebrated sovereign of India (said to be so called either from having ridden on a yakṣa—called śāli -, or from śali—for śāla -, the Sal tree, śāli—vāhana—being represented as borne on a cross made of that or other wood; he was the enemy of Vikramāditya—and institutor of the era now called śaka—q.v; his capital was pratiṣṭhāna—on the godāvarī—)." Monier Monier-Williams, *A Dictionary, English and Sanskrit* (London: W. H. Allen, 1851), 1002. I have not been able to find a source of this statement that Śālivāhana is represented on a cross, a suggestive image that Wilford employs.

    With regard to references to this king in Jain literature, Phyllis Granoff has shown that a King Śālivāhana appears in the second episode of the popular Śvetāmbara Jain story *Kālakācārya kathā* [The story of the teacher Kālaka], in which the monk Kālaka agrees to change the date of a Jain festival (*paryuṣaṇā*) because it overlaps with an important Hindu festival. Granoff explains that this story accounts for why manuscripts of the *Kalpa sūtra*, which is recited at *paryuṣaṇā,* often included versions of the story of Kālakācārya. Futhermore, there is a biography of Śālivāhana in the *Prabandhakosa* in which Śālivāhana is the child of a Brahmin woman and the nagaraja Śeṣa. Phyllis Granoff, "Kālakācārya Kathā the Story of the Teacher Kālaka," (unpublished manuscript, last modified October 31, 2013).
64. Francis Wilford, "An Essay on the Sacred Isles in the West, with Other Essays Connected with That Work," *Asiatic Researches* 10 (1811): 40.
65. Wilford, "Essay," 46.
66. For a classic analysis of British philology and colonialism, see Edward Said, *Orientalism* (New York: Pantheon, 1978).
67. Wilford, "Essay," 47.
68. Wilford, 47.
69. Questions regarding the dating of the Śaka era and the equation of Śaka and Śālivāhana were debated by Western scholars throughout the nineteenth century, starting with Wilford's essay and in the research of the colleague he cites throughout the essay as a source of much of his data, Colin Mackenzie, a British officer in Madras. A century after these debates began, J. F. Fleet revisited this issue in an article, "Salivahana and the Saka Era," published in the very same journal in which Wilford published, known in Fleet's time as the *Journal of the Royal Asiatic Society of Great Britain and Ireland*. Fleet used epigraphic records to demonstrate that there was no real king named Śālivāhana reigning in 78 AD, and that this argument came out of cloudy associations between Śālivāhana and King Vikrama and terminology for a lineage of kings coming out of the Dekkan who had nothing to do with the establishment of an era for dating. Fleet traces the equation of Śaka and Śālivāhana to the work of paṇḍits in the court of the kings of Vijayanagara in the fourteenth century. See J. F. Fleet, "Salivahana and the Saka Era," *Journal of the Royal Asiatic Society of Great Britian and Ireland* (1916): 809–20.

1. THE BOOK

70. See Wilford's "Essay," in which he describes working with his pundit on the Sanskrit texts and then learning that this language teacher/domestic servant had deceived him by forging Sanskrit manuscripts so that they echoed biblical stories. For example, one such text they read together that the pundit, according to Wilford, claimed was from the *Padma Purāna*, told of Noah and his three sons; Wilford later realized that this was a fake manuscript and explained the whole embarrassing fiasco in "Origin and Decline of the Christian Religion in India." *Asiatic Researches* 10 (1811): 352–60.
71. Buchanan, "Star in the East," 5–6.
72. Buchanan, 6.
73. William Jones, "On the Hindus: The Third Discourse," *Asiatic Researches* 1 (1799): 422–23.
74. The first chair in Sanskrit language and literature was founded for Antoine Léonard de Chézy at the Collège de France in 1814, the year after Judson's arrival in Burma, and in 1816 Franz Bopp started work on his *Comparative Grammar*—the landmark book that created a system for the study of Indo-European languages out of the haphazard conjecture of prior scholarship. See Franz Bopp, *A Comparative Grammar of the Sanscrit, Zend, Greek, Latin, Lithuanian, Gothic, German, and Sclavonic Languages* [Vergleichende Grammatik des Sanskrit, Zend, Griechischen, Lateinischen, Litthauischen, Gothischen und Deutschen] (London: Madden & Malcolm, 1845–1850).
75. Max F. Müller, *Lectures on the Science of Language Delivered at the Royal Institution of Great Britain in February, March, April, and May, 1863* (New York: C. Scribner, 1865), 136–37.
76. Olender, *Languages of Paradise*, 8.
77. Friedrich Schlegel, *The Aesthetic and Miscellaneous Works of Frederick Von Schlegel*, trans. E. J. Millington (London: Henry G. Bohn, 1849), 427–28.
78. James Darmesteter, "Rapport Annuel," *Journal Asiatique*, July–August 1890, 25.
79. The Burmese dynastic chronicles of the country's last lineage of kings, a key body of source material for this book, claims to account for the history of the Buddha's religion from its earliest period in ancient India, through its phases of decline and reinstatement in India, Sri Lanka, and Burma, up to the contemporary circumstances of the Konbaung kingdom. There are four major chronicles of the Konbaung dynasty: Mehti Sayadaw's 1799 *Vaṃsadīpanī*; the 1812 Pali *Sāsanasuddhidīpaka* by Nandamāla; the 1831 Burmese language *Thathanalinkara Sadan* by Mahadamma Thingyan; and the 1861 *Sāsanavaṃsa* by Paññasāmi, the tutor to the Burmese king Mindon.
80. For more on the religious reformations of King Bodawpaya, see Jacques P. Leider, "Text, Lineage, and Tradition in Burma: The Struggle for Norms and Religious Legitimacy Under King Bodawphaya (1782–1819)," *Journal of Burma Studies* 9 (2004), 82–129. See also Patrick Pranke, " 'Treatise on the Lineage of Elders' (*Vaṃsadīpanī*): Monastic Reform and the Writing of Buddhist History in Eighteenth-Century Burma" (PhD diss., University of Michigan, 2004), 1–33. See also Charney, *Powerful Learning*, 89–108. For more on the military campaigns along Burma's western frontier in the first period of Konbaung rule, especially during the reign of King Bodawpaya, see William J. Koenig, *The Burmese Polity, 1752-1819: A Study of Kon Baung*

1. THE BOOK

Politics, Administration, and Social Organization (Ann Arbor: Center for South and Southeast Asian Studies, University of Michigan, 1990), 22–30.
81. Wayland, *Memoir*, 1:250.
82. Wayland, 1:254.
83. Wayland, 1:254–55.
84. Wayland, 1:255.
85. Wayland, 1:256.
86. Burmese prohibitions of Christian evangelism kept American Baptist missionaries from overtly proselytizing until the British Raj began to occupy Burma during the Anglo-Burmese War period, and even then they limited their proselytizing to British-controlled territories.
87. Buddhist activity in Burma dates to at least the fifth century, when the Pyu people began to establish the country's first urban centers near modern-day Prome. These people were in contact with peoples in southeastern India and built stupas featuring Pali and Sanskrit inscriptions. The height of medieval Buddhist culture in Burma was during the Pagan period, which peaked in the eleventh and twelfth centuries. During this time, there were Buddhist communities practicing what are now called Mahayana and Theravada traditions, but, by the end of this period, royal support went exclusively to Theravada communities. Following the Pagan period, a lineage of kings ruled out of Pegu and included Dhammaceti (r. 1472–92), a famous reformer of Theravada Buddhism. The kings at Pegu were subjugated by kings based out of Taungoo, who then moved their courts to Pegu and then Ava. This second major lineage of Burmese kings—most famous for the foreign campaigns of Tabinshweti and Bayinnaung—was overthrown by Mon rebels, who were then deposed by the first king of the Konbaung dynasty, Alaungpaya. For a concise political-religious history of Burma, especially as it relates to the artistic practices discussed in this chapter, see Ralph Isaacs and T. Richard Blurton, eds., *Visions from the Golden Land: Burma and the Art of Lacquer* (Chicago: Art Media Resources, 2000).
88. Many of these ethnic groups, including the Shan, Lao, Mon, Arakanese, and Tai, practiced forms of Theravada Buddhism as well as ancestor worship, making Buddhist activity key for political control. See Juliane Schober, *Modern Buddhist Conjunctures in Myanmar: Cultural Narratives, Colonial Legacies, and Civil Society* (Honolulu: University of Hawai'i Press, 2011), 16.
89. The Pali Canon (P. *Tipiṭaka*), a product of the Theravada school of Buddhism, has been a strategic work legitimizing the Mahāvihāra lineage in Sri Lanka (formerly Ceylon). Collins demonstrates that it is not the specific texts in the Pali Canon that have been important, but the idea of such a collection—that one lineage has a definitive list of the teachings of the Buddha. See Steven Collins, "On the Very Idea of the Pali Canon," *Journal of the Pali Text Society* 15 (1990): 89–126. As it did in Ceylon, the Pali Canon served to legitimize the dominant Buddhist lineage in Burma that traced itself, through its possession of the Pali Canon, back to the Mahāvihāra lineage.

A second text collection that served to legitimate Theravada schools in Ceylon and then in Burma is a genre of juridical and historical writing known as *sāsana-katikāvata* that claims to account for the history of the Buddha's religion

1. THE BOOK

from its earliest period in ancient India, through its phases of decline and reinstatement in Theravada countries. This literary tradition traces back to the Theravada Buddhist reforms in Sri Lanka in the twelfth and thirteenth centuries and developed in Burma Konbaung chronicle tradition. See Pranke, "Treatise on the Lineage of Elders."

90. The first of these unique Konbaung chronicles, the *Treatise on the Lineage of Elders* (P. *Vaṃsadīpanī*), was written at the end of the eighteenth century, just over a decade before the Judsons arrived in Rangoon, and was explicitly designed as an instrument of the royal Buddhist reformation, known as the Sudhammā Reformation, executed by King Bagyidaw's predecessor, Bodawpaya. See Pranke, "Treatise on the Lineage of Elders."
91. See Charney, *Powerful Learning*.
92. Patrick Pranke, "'Bodawpaya's Madness': Monastic Accounts of King Bodawpaya's Conflict with the Burmese Sangha," *Journal of Burma Studies* 12 (2008): 1–28.
93. Pranke, "Treatise on the Lineage of Elders," 278–79.
94. For more on Burmese Buddhist legal systems, see Christian Dietrich Lammerts, *Buddhist Law in Burma: A History of Dhammasattha Texts and Jurisprudence, 1250–1850* (Honolulu: University of Hawai'i Press, 2018).
95. While the Pali-language *Sāsanavaṃsa* was sponsored by King Mindon, Victor Lieberman has shown that this text is a revised translation of the Burmese-language work *Tha-thana-wun-tha sa-dan thathana-lin-ga-ya kyan* [History of the religion which is an adornment of the religion], which was completed in 1831 during the reign of King Bagyidaw. While Lieberman notes that there are original sections in the *Sāsanavaṃsa*, he shows that the majority of the Pali chronicle's material is found in the earlier Burmese text. Lieberman's revelation demands that scholars studying the *Sāsanavaṃsa* for information on nineteenth-century Burmese Buddhism recognize that it was King Bagyidaw, not the later King Mindon, who sponsored the chronicle. Scholars must therefore also acknowledge that the chronicle, then, is a response to the threat posed to Buddhism on account of the First Anglo-Burmese War, not the Second. See Victor Lieberman, "A New Look at *Sāsanavaṃsa*," *Bulletin of the School of Oriental and African Studies* 39 (1976), 137–49.
96. "Imañca dhammikarājānaṃ nissāya marammaraṭṭhe sammāsambuddhassa sāsanaṃ ativiya joteti. Vuḍḍhiṃ virūḷiṃ vepullaṃ āpajjati." *Chaṭṭha Saṅgāyana Pāli Tipiṭaka* (including Paññasāmi's *Sāsanavaṃsa*), http://www.tipitaka.org (accessed August 26, 2022).
97. "Idañhi suṇantehi sādhujjanehi anumoditabbaṃ, asukasmiṃ kira kāle asukasmiṃ raṭṭhe asuko nāma rājā sāsanaṃ pagganhitvā vuḍḍhiṃ virūḷiṃ vepullamāpajji, seyyathāpi nāma rukkho bhūmodakānaṃ nissāya vuḍḍhiṃ virūḷiṃ vepullamāpajjīti." *Chaṭṭha Saṅgāyana Pāli Tipiṭaka*.
98. There are illustrated astrological manuscripts in Burma, but this tradition of illustrated manuscripts does not use precious substances such as gold, silver, copper, or jewels. Portions of this chapter's analysis of the Kammavāca have been adapted with permission from Alexandra Kaloyanides, "The Flower, Then the Sword: The Militarization of Burma's Most Beautiful Book," *Journal of Southeast Asian Studies* 54, no. 1 (2023).

99. Kammavāca in other Theravada settings with simple, incised palm-leaf folios will occasionally feature illustrated cover boards. There are some rare examples of illustrated manuscripts from other Theravada countries—namely, Thailand, where we find painted Kammavāca from the nineteenth century. These Thai manuscripts have expertly illustrated margins, but they do not use lacquered cloth pages or the special script that distinguishes the Burmese Kammavāca.

While the geographic extent and premodern history of Kammavāca texts are outside of the scope of this article, I will note here that we also know of early Sanskrit versions, Karmavācanā, and versions in other languages found throughout Asia, with fragments found in places as far flung as Maral-Bashi in Xinjiang, China. For a study of a fascinating Maral-Bashi manuscript written in the Iranian dialect Tumshuq, see H. W. Bailey, "The Tumshuq Karmavācanā," *Bulletin of the School of Oriental and African Studies* 13, no. 3 (1950): 649–70.

100. I would like to thank Ṭhānissaro Bhikkhu for his help understanding these rituals. For more of his studies and translations of monastic ceremonies, see Ṭhānissaro Bhikkhu, *The Buddhist Monastic Code* (self-published, 2007). Theravada rituals in Burma place great importance on the ritual use of the canonical language of Pali, although they regularly employ Burmese language pieces as well. As Jason Carbine has shown, in *Sons of the Buddha: Continuities and Ruptures in a Burmese Monastic Tradition* (New York: Walter de Gruyter, 2011), higher ordination rituals among the Shwegyin, the second largest monastic order in Burma, are mostly conducted in Burmese, but key portions are always in Pali, because, as Carbine writes, those texts are "considered to be the very words of the Buddha himself ... so they must be recited with precision in Pali. Ritual continuity with the teachings and practices of the Buddha is thus predicated upon certain types of linguistic fidelity to him. The ritual process allows for deviation from direct usage of the Pali, but only up to a point" (118).

101. In addition to these conservative language practices, Buddhist communities in Burma and throughout Southeast Asia have a rich history of inventing liturgical texts. As Trent Walker has shown, the fact that there is not a standard set of Theravada Buddhist chants has led to cultures creating new liturgies or borrowing them from neighbors. Trent Walker, "A Chant Has Nine Lives: The Circulation of Theravada Liturgies in Thailand, Cambodia, and Vietnam," *Journal of Vietnamese Studies* 15, no. 3 (2020): 38. Walker has also demonstrated the sophisticated ways that mainland Southeast Asian communities have rendered Pali into local vernaculars, including Burmese. For more on how Southeast Asian vernaculars were developed through Pali-vernacular bitexts, see Trent Walker, "Indic-Vernacular Bitexts from Thailand: Bilingual Modes of Philology, Exegetics, Homiletics, and Poetry, 1450–1850," *Journal of the American Oriental Society* 140, no. 3 (2020): 675–99. I am using the term "Theravada" here because the Thai, Sri Lankan, and Burmese communities that use Kammavāca texts today use it to name their form of Buddhism; however, it was not widespread until the twentieth century. The nineteenth-century Buddhists who commissioned, crafted, employed, and circulated Kammavāca likely did not use this term. For scholarship on its history and usage, see Peter Skilling, "Theravāda in History," *Pacific World* 3, no. 11 (2009): 61–93.

1. THE BOOK

102. For example, in the beginning of Clough's translation, when he is translating the first part of the higher ordination (*upasampadā*) section of the Kammavāca—which prescribes the assembly of the sangha; the appointment of a head monk to lead the ritual; and the opening dialogue, when the head monk asks the candidate if he has his requisite begging bowl and robes—Clough adds lengthy footnotes explaining what the Sangha is, why Buddhist monks beg for their food, and how monastic robes are comprised of three garments. Rev. Benjamin Clough, "The Ritual of the Budd'hist Priesthood, Translated from the Original Pali Work, Entitled *Karmawakya*," *Miscellaneous Translations from Oriental Languages Published for the Oriental Translation Fund of Great Britain and Ireland* 2 (1834): 1–30.
103. J. F. Dickson, "The Upasampadā-Kammavācā: Being the Buddhist Manual of the Form and Manner of Ordering of Priests and Deacons," *Journal of the Royal Asiatic Society of Great Britain and Ireland* 7, no. 1 (1875): 149–59. For more on how these translations fit into the large history of Buddhist studies, see J. W. deJong, "A Brief History of Buddhist Studies in Europe and America," *Eastern Buddhist* 7, no. 1 (1974): 55–106.
104. Charles Hallisey, "Roads Taken and Not Taken in the Study of Theravada Buddhism," *Curators of the Buddha* (1995): 46.
105. An outstanding exception is Sinéad Ward, who has done extensive research into Burmese Kammavāca in Asian and Western collections. See Sinéad Ward, "Stories Steeped in Gold: Narrative Scenes of the Decorative Kammavaca Manuscripts of Burma," in *From Mulberry Leaves to Silk Scrolls: New Approaches to the Study of Asian Manuscript Traditions*, ed. Justin McDaniel and Lynn Ransom (Philadelphia: University of Pennsylvania Press, 2015), 70–106. Another scholarly work that has given sustained attention to Burmese Kammavācas since Hallisey's article is Dietrich Christian Lammerts's "Buddhism and Written Law: Dhammasattha Manuscripts and Texts in Premodern Burma" (PhD diss., Cornell University, 2010). Lammerts's overview of the Burmese Kammavāca tradition is part of his larger survey of styles of ornamentation in Burmese Buddhist manuscripts. The book Lammerts published that is based in part on this dissertation is *Buddhist Law in Burma: A History of Dhammasattha Texts and Jurisprudence, 1250–1850* (Honolulu: University of Hawai'i Press, 2018).
106. By making a popular craft practice the focus of this study, this section takes its cue from the fields of material culture studies and art history, whose work in the last few decades has demonstrated the fruits of turning to nontextual data. As Buddhist historian Gregory Schopen has articulated so persuasively, it is decidedly peculiar that Western scholarship has focused on Buddhist scripture rather than the other materials Buddhist communities produced, especially considering how few monks and lay people actually engaged these texts. See Gregory Schopen, "Archaeology and Protestant Presuppositions in the Study of Indian Buddhism," *History of Religions* 31, no. 1 (1991): 1–23. Furthermore, by focusing on traditional crafts, such as the making of the Kammavācas, we include the creative work of peoples outside the educated elite. Classic scholarship paving the way for this approach to nontextual materials includes Donald McCallum, *Zenkōji and Its Icon: A Study in Medieval Japanese Religious Art* (Princeton, NJ: Princeton University Press, 1994). See also Davis, *Lives of Indian Images*

1. THE BOOK

(Princeton, NJ: Princeton University Press, 1997); and Henry Glassie, *Material Culture* (Bloomington: Indiana University Press, 1999).
107. Richard Fox, *More than Words: Transforming Script, Agency, and Collective Life in Bali* (Ithaca, NY: Cornell University Press, 2018), 1, 46, 47. See also Matthew Engelke's exploration of the Friday Masowe apostolics of Zimbabwe dynamically engaging the fundamental Christian question of how God becomes present, which demonstrates how "the significance of material culture is not always subordinate to that of language" (*Problem of Presence*, 10).
108. The longer history and speculation about the origins of this manuscript tradition are not only beyond the scope of this section but also quite impossible to uncover, given the lack of evidence from before the eighteenth century. I have found just one reference to this manuscript tradition in a Konbaung Buddhist chronicle (B. *thathanawin*); it appears in final chronicle of this textual tradition, the *Sāsanavaṃsa*, composed by Paññasāmi in 1861, which briefly notes the unique Burmese practice of preparing polished books adorned with red and gold paint. Paññasāmi dates this practice to the reign of King Siripavaramahārājā, who, he writes, ruled from years 1035 to 1060 of the Kali age. Paññasāmi writes:

Kaliyuge pana aṭṭhatiṃsādhike vassasahasse sampatte vesākhamāsassa kāḷapakkhaaṭṭhamito paṭṭhāya lokasaṅketavasena uppajjamānaṃ bhayaṃ nivāretuṃ navaguhāyaṃ tena devacakkobhāsattherena kathitaniyāmena paṭhamaṃ marammikabhikkhū paṭṭhānappakaraṇaṃ vācāpesi. Tato pacchā jeṭṭhamāsassa juṇhapakkhapāṭipadadivasato rāmaññaraṭṭhavāsike bhikkhū paṭṭhānappakaraṇaṃ vācāpesi. Mahāchaṇañca kārāpesi. Raṭṭhavāsinopi bahupūjāsakkāraṃ kārāpesi. Tassa kira rañño kāle potthakaṃ aṭṭhibhallika-rukkhaniyyāsehi parimaṭṭhaṃ katvā manosilāya likhitvā suvaṇṇena limpetvā piṭakaṃ patiṭṭhāpesi. Tato paṭṭhāya yāvajjatanā idaṃ potthakakammaṃ marammaraṭṭhe akaṃsūti "Pāḷi Tipiṭaka," Paññasāmi, "Sāsanavaṃsappadīpikā," Mandalay 1861, *Chaṭṭha Saṅgāyana Pāli Tipiṭaka* (including Paññasāmi's *Sāsanavaṃsa*), http://www.tipitaka.org (accessed August 26, 2022).

Here is B. C. Law's translation of this passage:

"In the year of one thousand and thirty-eight of the Kali age, in order to remove a fear that arose through common disturbance, the monks of the Maramma country first recited, according to the manner spoken by that Elder Devacakkobhāsa, the Paṭṭhānapakaraṇa in the Nava cave beginning from the eighth day of the dark half of the month of Vesākha. Thereafter the monks of the Rāmañña country recited the Paṭṭhānapakaraṇa beginning from the first day of the bright half of the month Jeṭṭha. He caused a great festival to be held. He also caused the inhabitants of the country to be much honored and respected. At the time of that king, they say, when he had polished a book with bones and the juice of the Bhallika tree and had written on it with red arsenic and smeared it with gold, he established the Piṭaka. From that time up to the present day, they adopted this method for the preparation of books in the Maramma country." Bimala Churn Law, *The History of Buddha's Religion (Sāsanavaṃsa)* (Calcutta: Sri Satguru, 1952), 123.

Law's translation of *aṭṭhi* as "bones" here is exciting, because this could refer to the use of cremation ashes in the manuscript preparation, a practice known

1. THE BOOK

to happen in the creation of twentieth-century Kammavācas; however, that term could also be referring to the nuts of the Bhallika tree, leading to the revised translated phrase "the juice from the nut-Bhallika tree."

109. I also cautiously draw from Noel F. Singer, "Kammavaca Texts: Their Covers and Binding Ribbons," *Arts of Asia*, May–June 1993, 97–106. This is not a carefully sourced academic article, but it does assemble a large collection of Kammavācas.
110. Material culture has played an important role in marking distinct groups and forging political alliances in related Southeast Asian contexts. For example, in "Power Dressing: Female Court Dress and Marital Alliances in Lan Na, the Shan States and Siam," *Orientations* 32, no. 4 (April 2001): 42–49, Susan Conway shows how female court dress displayed the identities of a princess's homeland and signaled the extensive influence of the prince she was married to. Conway considers marital alliances in Lan Na, the Shan States, and Siam by focusing on the textiles princesses wore in intermarriages among royalty in valley and hill regions. This example reminds us how displays of diversity as well as performances of unity fabricated images of royal power in Southeast Asia.
111. Michael Charney's study of religion, politics, and literature in the Konbaung dynasty demonstrates how "control over texts—who wrote them, how they were written, and how they were circulated—became a central concern of the Burmese throne" from the late eighteenth century into the nineteenth. I add to Charney's argument that control over how texts were illustrated was also crucial for the Konbaung kingdom's mobilization of religious texts to secure power throughout the country. See Charney, *Powerful Learning*, 9.
112. For more on Konbaung practices of enslaving artists, alongside other specialists and elite captives, see Bryce Beemer, "The Creole City in Mainland Southeast Asia: Slave Gathering Warfare and Cultural Exchange in Burma, Thailand, and Manipur, Eighteenth to Nineteenth Century" (PhD diss., University of Hawai'i at Manoa, 2013).
113. Ivory Ka Ma Wa, eighteenth century, Manuscripts, Yangon University Library, Yangon.
114. Singer has suggested that Burma's oldest dated ornamented manuscript, a *Pañcanipāt aṅguttuir aṭṭhakathā* from 1683, features a title page adorned in Kammavāca style ("Kammavaca Texts," 99). As Lammerts persuasively writes, "We should be cautious about attributing a Kammavāca 'style' to the 17th century, as few (if any other) securely-dated decorated manuscripts from this era survive, and thus it is impossible to know whether Kammavāca comprised a model for manuscripts ornamented in this way" ("Buddhism and Written Law," 215).
115. Ivory Kammavāca, eighteenth century, Oriental Manuscripts, 12010h, F. 1r, British Library, London.
116. Isaacs and Blurton, *Visions from the Golden Land*, 138.
117. Singer, "Kammavaca Texts." For more on Burmese warfare and Thai artisans, see Isaacs and Blurton, *Visions from the Golden Land*, 15. See also Beemer, "Creole City."
118. Kammavācā with sazigyo, 1792, Manuscripts, Royal Asiatic Society, London. The folio with the Buddha illustrations was previously published in Singer, "Kammavāca Texts," 100.

1. THE BOOK

119. For a well-preserved example of an earlier *chinthe*, see the 1628 bronze Buddha sculpture protected by 4 *chinthes* published in Sylvia Fraser-Lu and Donald Martin Stadtner, *Buddhist Art of Myanmar* (New Haven: Yale University Press, 2015), 156.
120. This folio was published in Isaacs and Blurton, *Visions from the Golden Land*, 140.
121. The Asian Art Museum in San Francisco holds another Kammavāca that features images of the Buddha, but this piece does not show the enlightened Buddha; rather, it features a scene of Prince Siddhartha renouncing his life in the palace to become an ascetic. Forrest McGill provides an excellent analysis of the illustrations on this rare manuscript, which is dated to the first half of the nineteenth century. See Forrest McGill, Chirapravati Pattaratorn, Peter Skilling, Kazuhiro Tsuruta, and Asian Art Museum of San Francisco, *Emerald Cities: Arts of Siam and Burma, 1775-1950* (San Francisco: Asian Art Museum, Chong-Moon Lee Center for Asian Art and Culture, 2009), 79–80. A similar scene is painted on the first and last leaves of the Kammavāca, nineteenth century, Oriental Manuscripts, Or. 13896, British Library, London. Most relevant for the analysis of this paper is the royal dress and sword donned by Prince Siddhartha, which resemble the costuming and weaponry on the guardian figures on the late Konbaung-era manuscripts. The sword in this Siddhartha Kammavāca is carried by the prince as part of his royal apparel and becomes important when he cuts off his hair, the gesture most symbolic of his and his disciples' monastic renunciation of worldly life. This scene would obviously resonate for the community performing ordination rituals in nineteenth-century Burma, reminding them that the men shaving their heads and taking vows were following in the footsteps of the Buddha.

    This manuscript, then, suggests an alternative meaning to swords found in other manuscripts: those held by the guardian figures might have been meant for the tonsure of those being ordained in the Kammavāca rituals. In other words, perhaps I should see them as tools rather than weapons, as ritual devices rather than displays of courtly power. But I think that to make this distinction between religion and politics—to put Kammavāca manuscripts into a sacred sphere separate from the messy, mundane matters of the court—is to miss the opportunity Kammavāca offer us to glimpse how the religious and the royal were so entwined in this period.
122. See Myo Myint, *Confronting Colonialism: King Mindon's Strategy for Defending Independence, 1853-1878* (Yangon: Ministry of Religious Affairs, 2012), 190–241. François Tainturier has also demonstrated that King Mindon used Buddhism to transform the kingdom's landscape in a direct response to the British takeover of Lower Burma. Tainturier's detailed study of the construction of Mandalay shows how King Mindon built the land around this new royal city to be a "Buddha-land" (Buddha-*desa*) fortified against non-Buddhist foreigners (*meissa deithi kala*). François Tainturier, *Mandalay and the Art of Building Cities in Burma* (Singapore: NUS Press, 2021), 5.
123. Alicia Marie Turner, *Saving Buddhism: The Impermanence of Religion in Colonial Burma* (Honolulu: University of Hawai'i Press, 2014); Braun, *The Birth of Insight: Meditation, Modern Buddhism, and the Burmese Monk Ledi Sayadaw* (Chicago: University of Chicago Press, 2013).

1. THE BOOK

124. Abbreviations of the Sacred Books of Gautama, n.d., Burmese palm-leaf books and Kammavacas, American Baptist Historical Society, Atlanta, Georgia. For more on the looting of Thibaw's palace, see Terence R. Blackburn, *The British Humiliation of Burma* (Bangkok: Orchid, 2000).
125. Ingalls is also the author of an early English-language description of Burma's book practices, including the maintenance of Kammavācas. In a vignette titled "A Morning Visit to a Monastery, or Kyoung," Ingalls writes that "the sacred books were written in a Pali (sometimes written Bali) character; the letters square and angular. The books were composed of the Palmyra leaf covered with gold and black varnished letters, or painted black and lettered with gold. These were kept together by a string and then placed between two boards richly covered with figures in gold." This description begins a longer section detailing a range of the book types and practices she encountered at this monastery, including common palm-leaf manuscripts with Burmese script, parabeik account books, and practice slates. Ingalls listens to a star student read loudly for her and then tells the novices and monks that, in America the schoolrooms are, by contrast, very quiet. Before leaving, Ingalls distributed Protestant tracts to a few of the students and one of the old priests. Marilla Baker Ingalls, *Ocean Sketches of Life in Burmah* (Philadelphia: American Baptist Publication Society, 1857), 149.
126. Kammavāca, nineteenth century, Works on Paper–Manuscripts, 2007.145.15, Yale University Art Gallery, New Haven, Connecticut.
127. Kammavāca, nineteenth century, Works on Paper–Manuscripts, 2010.93.1, Yale University Art Gallery, New Haven, Connecticut.
128. Kammavāca, nineteenth century, Oriental Manuscripts, Or. 4949, British Library, London.
129. Konbaung Kammawa, n.d., Manuscripts, National Library of Myanmar, Yangon.
130. Than Htun, *Lacquerware Journeys: The Untold Story of Burmese Lacquer* (Bangkok: River, 2013), 136.
131. Bénédicte Brac de la Perrière, "The Burmese Nats: Between Sovereignty and Autochthony," *Diogenes* 44, no. 174 (1996): 45–60.
132. Brac de la Perrière, "Burmese Nats," 49.
133. Furthermore, scholarship on Burma should take care to consider the role nats have played in Burmese history and lived religion rather than give excessive attention to the place of Theravada Buddhism in the country. As Bénédicte Brac de la Perrière cautions in "An Overview of the Field of Religion in Burmese Studies," *Asian Ethnology* (2009): 186, ignoring the nats in order to focus again and again on Buddhism promotes a false view of Burma as essentially Buddhist.
134. Juliane Schober, *Modern Buddhist Conjunctures in Myanmar: Cultural Narratives, Colonial Legacies, and Civil Society* (Honolulu: University of Hawai'i Press, 2011), 16.
135. Contemporary non-Buddhist imagery allows us to further work out the symbolic value of the late Konbaung-era Kammavāca characters. An 1852 drawing from the *Illustrated London News* depicts a soldier from the Second Anglo-Burmese War. His turban, bayonet, and belted uniform suggestively resemble the headpiece, weapon, and costume lines from the turbaned guardians figures we have seen,

such as those found on the cover board of the first Yale Kammavāca. A hand-colored engraving from the London periodical the *Graphic* of Thibaw and Queen Suphayarlat in 1886, standing next to an empty throne after their defeat by the British raj, shows that the visual choices for costuming and accessorizing late Konbaung-era Kammavāca were clearly influenced by royal dress. Blackburn, *The British Humiliation of Burma* (Bangkok: Orchid, 2000), 65, 132.

136. Braun, *Birth of Insight*, 83.
137. Wayland, *Memoir*, 1:176.
138. This chapter has not considered parallel book cults in other Southeast Asian and North American communities. The most relevant non-Burmese example is the legend of lost literacy among the Hmong (Miao) people, who assert that their knowledge and practice of literacy was lost in China hundreds of years ago on account of Chinese oppression. Anthropologist Nicholas Tapp writes about the variety of Hmong explanations for their lost literacy, from losing written texts when escaping from Chinese attacks to legends of a pair of brothers—Chinese and Hmong—who in ancient times received a book each from the Jade emperor, but then fell asleep on a bridge. They awoke to discover that the Hmong brother's book was entirely eaten by animals, whereas the Chinese brother's book was only half eaten; the Hmong say that this is why the Chinese were able to maintain their literacy while the Hmong lost it. Tapp explains that this legend is part of a larger effort among Hmong to emphasize the "affinity and original unity of the Hmong with the Chinese," whereas other stories about losing literacy while fleeing the Chinese tell a different history of "fighting and opposition to the Chinese." See Nicholas Tapp, *The Hmong of China: Context, Agency, and the Imaginary* (Boston: Brill, 2001), 445. As with the Karen lost book legend, the Hmong lost literacy stories explore the relationship between an illiterate minority group and the literate majority, with the Chinese and the Burmese cast as obstacles to Hmong and Karen literacy, respectively. Both stories use the relationship of brothers, but the Karen version sees the Anglo-American missionary as the long-lost brother, whereas the Hmong were once brothers with the Chinese.

The most obvious example of a North American book cult in this period is centered on the Book of Mormon, which was published by Joseph Smith in 1830, seventeen years into the Baptist mission in Burma, and thirteen years before the first recorded version of the Karen lost book legend. For an excellent study of Mormon history and material culture, see David Walker, *Railroading Religion: Mormons, Tourists, and the Corporate Spirit of the West* (Chapel Hill: University of North Carolina Press, 2019).

2. The School

1. Jonathan Price, "Burman Mission," *American Baptist Magazine*, November 1826, 332.
2. Jonathan Price, "Dr. Price's Journal," *American Baptist Magazine*, February 1828, 49.

2. THE SCHOOL

3. Jonathan Price, "Burman Mission," *American Baptist Magazine*, June 1828, 186.
4. Eugenio Kincaid, "Interesting News from Burmah," *Baptist Missionary Magazine*, July 1834, 277.
5. Simons, "Journal of Mr. Simons," *Baptist Missionary Magazine*, May 1837, 111.
6. Simons, "Journal of Mr. Simons," 111.
7. Manuscript journal of Edgar Jacob (1844–1920), India Office Records and Private Papers, Mss Eur F559, British Library, London.
8. Alexandra Green, *Buddhist Visual Cultures, Rhetoric, and Narrative in Late Burmese Wall Paintings* (Hong Kong: Hong Kong University Press, 2018), 116.
9. Turner, *Saving Buddhism: The Impermanence of Religion in Colonial Burma* (Honolulu: University of Hawai'i Press, 2014), 47.
10. For more on ordination rituals and the roles that monasteries and monastics play in Theravada societies, see Kate Crosby, *Theravada Buddhism: Continuity, Diversity, and Identity* (Malden, MA: Wiley Blackwell, 2014), 197–217.
11. Juliane Schober, "Colonial Knowledge and Buddhist Education in Burma," in *Buddhism, Power, and Political Order*, ed. Ian Harris (Routledge, 2007), 57. For more on the subject of law as it fit into Burmese Buddhist education, see Lammerts, *Buddhist Law in Burma: A History of Dhammasattha Texts and Jurisprudence, 1250–1850* (Honolulu: University of Hawai'i Press, 2018).
12. Turner, *Saving Buddhism*, 54.
13. Schober, "Colonial Knowledge and Buddhist Education in Burma," in *Buddhism, Power, and Political Order*, ed. Ian Harris (New York: Routledge, 2007), 61.
14. For more on how British colonialism undertook a project of cultural control in India through the subjects of language, law, art, and clothing, see Bernard S. Cohn, *Colonialism and Its Forms of Knowledge: The British in India* (Princeton, NJ: Princeton University Press, 1996).
15. Thongchai Winichakul examines a parallel phenomenon in Thailand in *Siam Mapped: A History of the Geo-Body of a Nation* (Honolulu: University of Hawai'i Press, 1994). Winichakul explores "how a map created the geo-body of a nation" (18) by focusing on moments when premodern and modern kinds of knowledge collided. *Siam Mapped* emphasizes the relationship between mapping and military force to show that they are mutual operations of power that execute the truth of geography. The indigenous concepts of space that Winichakul shows were displaced by modern geographic and mapping knowledge practices features Traiphum (Three Worlds) cosmography, a prominent Theravada doctrinal system influential in Burma as well and determined by the merit system discussed above. Winichakul insightfully points out, though, that this Buddhist cosmology was not the only premodern indigenous special conception; imaginations of space were also shaped by Hinduism and Islamic traditions as well as more local practices. This surely was true to some extent in Burma.
16. I am drawing here on the chapter "Christian Schools and Publications: 1833–1845" in Maung Shwe Wa, *Burma Baptist Chronicle* (Rangoon: Board of Publications, Burma Baptist Convention, 1963), 115–26.
17. Deborah Wade, "State of the Schools," *Baptist Missionary Magazine*, July 1841, 223.
18. Editorial Board, "The Tenasserim Provinces," *Calcutta Review* 8, no. 16 (1847): 140–45.

2. THE SCHOOL

19. As Barbara Reeves-Ellington, Kathryn Kish Sklar, and Connie A. Shemo explain in their introductory essay in *Competing Kingdoms: Women, Mission, Nation, and the American Protestant Empire, 1812–1960* (Durham, NC: Duke University Press, 2010), foreign evangelism created dramatically new opportunities beyond marriage and domestic life for Protestant American women. They write that "the opportunity to carry the good news abroad offered [women] extra benefits that addressed their gendered location in American society, namely, an alternative to marriage, meaningful work, and emancipation from at least some of the gendered constraints of their culture" (3–4).
20. Editorial Board, "The Death of Mrs. Lydia L. Simons," *Baptist Missionary Magazine*, March 1899, 90.
21. For example, Joan Brumberg's *Mission for Life: The Story of the Family of Adoniram Judson, the Dramatic Events of the First American Mission, and the Course of Evangelical Religion in the Nineteenth Century* (New York: Free Press, 1980)—one of the few academic studies of the American Baptist mission and the only book-length work devoted to the Judson family and their relationship to nineteenth-century American evangelical religious culture—does not mention Lillybridge's close friendship and working relationship with Emily Chubbuck. The social history it gives of the Judson family is primarily interested in its significant influence on American Protestant print culture and pays little attention to foreign dimensions of this history. Even the book's passing references to Baptist encounters with Asian religions simply dismisses them as part of some simple Protestant struggle with "heathenism."
22. Emily Chubbuck Judson's letter collections speak to her many deep and enduring friendships and to larger practices of female relations in this period that were not only based in the northeastern United States but also had global connections, such as when women became missionaries. As Carroll Smith-Rosenberg explains in her study of close emotional relations between American women in the late eighteenth century through the mid-nineteenth century, female worlds were both highly structured and varied, and that they complemented heterosocial worlds; see "The Female World of Love and Ritual: Relations Between Women in Nineteenth-Century America," *Signs* 1, no. 1 (1975): 1–29.
23. Lillybridge to Peck, August 21, 1850, in *The Life and Letters of Emily Chubbuck Judson (Fanny Forester)*, ed. George H. Tooze (Macon, GA: Mercer University Press, 2009–2013), 4:388–89.
24. Lillybridge to Judson, April 27, 1851, in Tooze, ed., *Life and Letters*, 4:528.
25. Hillary Kaell's study of child sponsorship in the United States explores the way that missionaries portrayed heathen children as both innocent and damned, an ambivalence that Lillybridge seems to be struggling with in her correspondences. She is invested in their potential to be educated and converted to Christianity but she also recognizes the pervasive power of Buddhism in the country. Hillary Kaell, *Christian Globalism at Home: Child Sponsorship in the United States* (Princeton, NJ: Princeton University Press, 2020), 28.
26. Lillybridge to Peck, August 21, 1850, in Tooze, ed., 4:388–90.
27. Solomon Peck, "For What Departments of Labor Are Missionaries at the Present Time Most Needed? Or, The Due Gradation of Missionary Labor,"

2. THE SCHOOL

Baptist Missionary Magazine, July 1849, 206–10. Notably, Peck did not include medical work as part of important missionary labor. Although, early on, the American Baptist mission had featured missionaries practicing medicine (such as Jonathan Price, who is discussed at the outset of this chapter), they did not begin more formal medical missionary work until 1855, when J. Dawson started vaccinating Karen children against smallpox. For more on the larger role American Baptist missionaries played in the smallpox vaccination campaign in colonial Burma, see Atsuko Naono, *State of Vaccination: The Fight Against Smallpox in Colonial Burma* (Hyderabad: Orient Blackswan, 2009).

28. Many women also assisted in translation work. As Peck acknowledges in his 1849 report, the Missionary Union was indebted to female assistant missionaries for creating "idiomatic tracts and books," and it is clear that all missionaries, male and female, were in the business of handing out tracts and books and bibles. Peck, "For What Departments?"
29. Peck.
30. Judson to Newell, March 25, 1817, Postal History, Western Manuscripts, RP 4428, British Library, London.
31. This prized 1817 Judson letter highlights the fact that the developments in the international postal system not only enabled the work of the American Baptist mission in Burma (in sending crucial U.S. resources and information to Burma and vice versa) but also enabled my scholarship, in that this book relies so heavily on correspondence that passed through the mail and was then collected into archives. In *The Potlatch Papers: A Colonial Case History* (Chicago: University of Chicago Press, 1997), a study of the impact of the postal system on the First Nations of British Columbia from the 1860s through the 1930s, Christopher Bracken argues that correspondence related to potlatches and the Parliament of Canada's 1884 law banning their performance largely "aimed to define, regulate, and ultimately destroy the social systems of the British Columbia First Nations" (1). Further research would be needed to see to what extent the Burmese postal system contributed to systematic violence by Westerners and powerful Burmese peoples against marginalized people in Southeast Asia.
32. For more on the rise of modern evangelical notions of conversion, especially through the work of the famous eighteenth-century Anglo-American revivalist George Whitefield, see Harry S. Stout, *The Divine Dramatist: George Whitefield and the Rise of Modern Evangelicalism* (Grand Rapids, MI: Wm. B. Eerdmans, 1991).
33. Lincoln A. Mullen, *The Chance of Salvation* (Cambridge, MA: Harvard University Press, 2017).
34. I am building here on William Womack's excellent study of Mason and the politics of her work for female and local authority, "Contesting Indigenous and Female Authority in the Burma Baptist Mission: The Case of Ellen Mason," *Women's History Review* 17, no. 4 (2008): 543–59.
35. For more on Charles Canning's role in the 1857 rebellion and the influence of the event on the relationship between Great Britain and India, see Thomas R

2. THE SCHOOL

Metcalf, *Aftermath of Revolt: India, 1857-1970* (Princeton, NJ: Princeton University Press, 2015).

36. Lesley Shapland, "Charlotte Canning's Burning Tent," Untold Lives, British Library, April 26, 2018, https://blogs.bl.uk/untoldlives/2018/04/charlotte-cannings-burning-tent.html.
37. This was also the period in which the Cannings led the British Raj in their response to the Indian Rebellion of 1857, the implementation of the Hindu Widow's Remarriage Act of 1856, and the establishment of the first three "modern" Indian universities: the University of Calcutta, the University of Madras, and the University of Bombay.
38. Mason to Canning, February 7, 1857, Papers Relating to Schools, Nursing, and Charity, India Office Records and Private Papers, Mss Eur F699/2/5/30, British Library, London.
39. Mason to Canning, October 10, 1857, Papers Relating to Schools, Nursing & Charity, October 10, 1857, India Office Records and Private Papers, Mss Eur F699/2/5/30, British Library, London.
40. Wade to Brother Lester, July 11, 1853, Deborah B. Lapham Correspondence, Missionaries, RG-1135, American Baptist Historical Society, Atlanta, Georgia.
41. For more on how the British worked to cultivate the Karen as allies, see Harry Ignatius Marshall, *The Karen People of Burma: A Study in Anthropology and Ethnology* (Columbus: University at Columbus, 1922).
42. Mason to Viscountess Canning, October 10, 1857.
43. Mason.
44. Mason.
45. T. L. Seccombe, ed., *Education*, vol. 42, *Accounts and Papers of the House of Commons: East India (Progress and Condition)* (London: 1863), 730.
46. Colonel Lawrie, "Dispatch from Colonel Lawrie," *Journal of the Society of the Arts*, February 28, 1873, 267.
47. This section has been adapted with permission from Alexandra Kaloyanides, "'Show Us Your God': Marilla Baker Ingalls and the Power of Religious Objects in Nineteenth-Century Burma," *Religions* 7, no. 81 (2016): 1–19.
48. Sir Dietrich Brandis, "Mrs. Marilla B. Ingalls," *Standard*, June 6, 1903, 8.
49. Brandis, "Mrs. Marilla B. Ingalls."
50. Brandis.
51. Marilla Baker Ingalls, "My Dumb Teacher," *Baptist Missionary Magazine*, May 1896, 137–39.
52. Ingalls, "My Dumb Teacher," 139.
53. Ingalls, 138.
54. Kate Crosby's overview of Buddhist consecration practices in Theravada cultures in *Theravada Buddhism* summarizes the practice of consecrating a Buddha statue as one in which the statue "is empowered not through the Buddha himself being immanent in the statue, but through a process of empowerment, in which the Buddha's powers are transmitted into the statue" (53).
55. Swearer, *Becoming the Buddha: The Ritual of Image Consecration in Thailand*, (Princeton, NJ: Princeton University Press, 2004)184.

2. THE SCHOOL

56. One of the most famous nat stories in Burma is about Min Mahagiri, a renowned blacksmith in the Pyu kingdom. In this story, the Pyu king marries Min Mahagiri's sister, Taunggyi Shin, so that he can lure the famous blacksmith to enter his city and then have him executed by fire. Taunggyi Shin is so upset when this happens that she throws herself onto the flames engulfing her brother's murdered body. Their angry spirits then live in a tree, so the king orders that tree cut down and thrown in the Irrawaddy River. The tree trunk washes up in the kingdom of Pagan, and the Burmese king there—inspired by a dream—carves their images onto the trunk and establishes the trunk on the sacred Mount Popa so that the nats can be appeased there. For more on this particular nat story and the Burmese nat tradition at large, see Bénédicte Brac de La Perrière, "Sibling Relationships in the *Nat* Stories of the Burmese Cult to the 'Thirty-Seven,'" *Moussons*, no. 5 (2002): 31–48.
57. For more on moral conduct and merit-making in Theravada Buddhism, see Kate Crosby's chapter "The Good Buddhist" in *Theravada Buddhism*.
58. Ingalls, "My Dumb Teacher," 139.
59. Ingalls, "Our Great Sign Tree," 602.
60. Ingalls, 602.
61. Ingalls, 602.
62. Ingalls, 603.
63. Ingalls, 603.
64. Ingalls, 604.
65. "Perry Davis' Vegetable Pain Killer," *Baptist Missionary Magazine*, August 1883, 1.
66. Marilla Baker Ingalls, "A Morning at Thongzai," *Baptist Missionary Magazine*, June 1877, 140.
67. Ward Keeler's 2018 *The Traffic in Hierarchy: Masculinity and Its Others in Buddhist Burma* (Honolulu: University of Hawai'i Press, 2017) argues that while scholarship by Chie Ikeya and Tharaphi Than convincingly demonstrates that women in Burma have been made to endure "long-standing prejudices concerning women's capacities, their proper roles, and their appropriate relations with masculine authority," scholars must appreciate that in Burmese society women's limited autonomy is context specific and makes sense "to so many men and even a fair number of women" (235). Keeler is writing about contemporary Burmese society, and my research here into an 1861 text about women cannot contribute to this debate about how much equality or autonomy Burmese women really have in today's society. My analysis shows that female characters are used as devices in a male-authored and -circulated story about the power of male monastic and royal authorities in Konbaung Burma. This analytical attention to patriarchies' rhetorical use of female status is therefore more in line with Ikeya's and Tharaphi Than's findings about how authorities in Burma and India worked to idealize women's conditions rather than honestly acknowledge the many ways they were subordinated. Ikeya, *Refiguring Women, Colonialism, and Modernity in Burma* (Honolulu: University of Hawai'i Press, 2011); Tharaphi Than, *Women in Modern Burma* (New York: Routledge, 2014). See also Turner, *Saving Buddhism*.

2. THE SCHOOL

68. Portions of this section have been adapted with permission from Alexandra Kaloyanides, "The Women Who Mastered Pali," in *From Jetavana to Jerusalem: Sacred Biography in Asian Perspectives and Beyond, Essays in Honour of Professor Phyllis Granoff*, ed. Jinhua Chen (Singapore: World Scholastic, 2022), 458–73.
69. Mabel Haynes Bode, *Sāsanavaṃsa* (London: Pali Text Society, 1897).
70. Michael Charney, "Review of Michael Aung-Thwin *Mists of Ramanna: The Legend That Was Lower Burma*," H-net Asia Book Reviews, February 2006 (no longer available).
71. Lieberman calculates the number of sections using chapter divisions and section headings in the 1897 edition of the *Tha-thana-wun-tha sa-dan thathana-lin-ga-ya kyan* published in Rangoon and the 1952 translation of the *Sāsanavaṃsa* by B. C. Law. In these versions, the *Sāsanavaṃsa* is divided into ten chapters. The *Tha-thana-wun-tha sa-dan the-thank-lin-ga-ya* does not have chapter divisions but has over one hundred small section headings. "A New Look at *Sāsanavaṃsa*," *Bulletin of the School of Oriental and African Studies* 39 (1976): 137–49.
72. Lieberman, 142–43.
73. Kitsiri Malalgoda, *Buddhism in Sinhalese Society, 1750-1900: A Study of Religious Revival and Change* (Berkeley: University of California Press, 1976), 161–65.
74. Chaṭṭha Saṅgāyana Pāli Tipiṭaka (including Paññasāmi's *Sāsanavaṃsa*), http://www.tipitaka.org (accessed August 26, 2022).
75. Anne M. Blackburn, "Buddhist Connections in the Indian Ocean: Changes in Monastic Mobility, 1000-1500," *Journal of the Economic and Social History of the Orient* 58, no. 3 (2015): 238.
76. Hema Goonatilake, "Sri Lanka-Myanmar Historical Relations in Religion, Culture, and Polity," *Journal of the Royal Asiatic Society of Sri Lanka* 55 (2009): 78.
77. This particular scene of King Satabahana's wives making fun of his poor Sanskrit grammar from the *Kathāsaritsāgara* was featured in King Akbar's illustrated translation of the *Kathāsaritsāgara* into Persian. Heike Franke shows how this imperial *Kathāsaritsāgara* features an illustration of this scene; see "Akbar's *Kathāsaritsāgara*: The Translator and Illustrations of an Imperial Manuscript," *Muqarnas* 27 (2010): 338. I am grateful to Phyllis Granoff for pointing out this connection to the *Kathāsaritsāgara*.
78. As Erik Braun has shown in *The Birth of Insight: Meditation, Modern Buddhism, and the Burmese Monk Ledi Sayadaw* (Chicago: University of Chicago Press, 2013), the Burmese have long considered themselves distinctive in their understanding of and appreciation for the Abhidhamma. Braun writes about a Burmese folk tale that narrates how a ship carrying the Tipiṭaka sank and the basket carrying the suttas went to Sri Lanka, the Vinaya to Thailand, and the Abhidhamma to Burma (62–63).
79. I published an earlier version of this second vignette in "Female Pali Masters in the Burmese Kingdom of Pagan," *Sakyadhita* 30 (Winter 2022): 16–17.
80. The version of the *Sāsanavaṃsa* I am translating from is Paññasāmi, "Sāsanavaṃsa."

3. The Pagoda

1. Shwe Wa, *Burma Baptist Chronicle* (Rangoon: Board of Publications, Burma Baptist Convention, 1963), 132, 273.
2. The Burmese term for pagoda, *zedi*, comes from the Pali term *cetiya*, which refers to mounds in which the remains of the Buddha or other prominent figures are interred. The Burmese term *phaya* is used to refer to pagodas, but it is a more general term that can also be used for Buddhas, kings, monks, and images of the Buddha. The now English-language *pagoda* comes from a sixteenth-century Portuguese word, *pagode*, which derives either from the Persian *but nada* (habitation for idols) or from an Indic terms with roots in the Sanskrit *bhagavat* (divine).
3. Donald Stadtner, "Ancient Pagan," from *Buddhist Art of Myanmar*, ed. Sylvia Fraser-Lu and Donald M. Stadtner (New Haven, CT: Yale University Press, 2015), 58.
4. George Boardman, "Mr. Boardman's Journal," *American Baptist Magazine*, July 1829, 245.
5. Charles Hallisey, "Roads Taken and Not Taken in the Study of Theravada Buddhism," in *Curators of the Buddha: The Study of Buddhism Under Colonialism*, ed. Donald S. Lopez (Chicago: University of Chicago Press, 1995), 33.
6. For my extended reflection on the influence of Charles Hallisey's notion of "intercultural mimesis" on the study of Theravada Buddhism, see Kaloyanides, "'Intercultural Mimesis,' Empire, and Spirits," *Journal of Global Buddhism* 22, no. 1 (2021): 125–31. This article is part of a special section that I edited with Trent Walker in which we survey the impact of Hallisey's 1995 essay "Roads Taken and Not Taken" and call for new directions in the field, including more attention to materiality and power dynamics.
7. The *Sāsanavaṃsa* is a Burmese Buddhist history composed in 1861 by Paññasāmi, the tutor to the Burmese king Mindon. The *Sāsanavaṃsa* is the last of four Buddhist chronicles composed during the Konbaung kingdom.
8. Pranke, "'Treatise on the Lineage of Elders' (*Vaṃsadīpanī*): Monastic Reform and the Writing of Buddhist History in Eighteenth-Century Burma," (PhD diss., University of Michigan, 2004), 110.
9. Pranke, "Treatise on the Lineage of Elders," 99–100.
10. Patrick Pranke, "Buddhism and Its Practice in Myanmar," from *Buddhist Art of Myanmar*, ed. Sylvia Fraser-Lu and Donald M. Stadtner (New Haven, CT: Yale University Press, 2015), 31.
11. In this context, conversion means the process of taking refuge. Traditionally Buddhists take refuge in the Buddha, the dharma, and the sangha. But these first converts only took refuge in the Buddha and the dharma, as there was not yet a community of monks, or a *sangha*. While historians have not found evidence of a shrine in the region—or any Buddhist material, for that matter—from the time of the historical Buddha, there is some evidence that an ancient stupa could have existed on this hilltop since the first millennium of the common era. The earliest dated evidence of Shwedagon comes from

3. THE PAGODA

fifteenth-century inscriptions. For more on the history of Shwedagon and on Burmese Buddhist foundation myths, see Pranke, "Buddhism and Its Practice."

12. Donald M. Stadtner, *Sacred Sites of Burma: Myth and Folklore in an Evolving Spiritual Realm* (Bangkok: River, 2010), 72.
13. Robert A. Orsi, *History and Presence* (Cambridge, MA: Harvard University Press, 2016), 8.
14. Ingalls, *Ocean Sketches*, 77–78.
15. King Mindon also helped the Society for the Propagation of the Gospel build a lavish church in 1873 featuring a marble font from Queen Victoria and space for three hundred, but, as it only ever seemed to attract a dozen or two congregants, it was derided by both Burmese court officials and British officials. Schendel contrasts the late arrival and limited presence of Anglican missionaries in upper Burma with the longer presence of Roman Catholic missionaries, who date back to the sixteenth century. Schendel explains that "the few thousand Catholic residents in Upper Burma, known as *bayingyi*, were descended from Portuguese and other foreigners, who had been trading in Burma, most of them in the costal town of Syriam. Burma sacked the city in 1613 and took the foreigners captive, settled them in several villages in Upper Burma, and made them liable for services as riflemen and artillerymen. The *bayingyi* intermarried with Burmese and assumed local customs, habits, and appearance." As for Catholic evangelism, Schendel explains that "for long periods, only a few Catholic missionaries came to Burma, and even they did little evangelizing. The Barnabites and their successors were not allowed to visit non-Catholic villages in the interior, and the government continued to restrain missionary work until the annexation. Consequently, the Catholics converted few Burmese, and those converts did not overtly display their new faith." Schendel, "Christian Missionaries in Upper Burma, 1853–85," (*South East Asia Research* 7, no. 1 (1999): 68–69.
16. Boardman, "Mr. Boardman's Journal."
17. Cohn, *Colonialism and Its Forms of Knowledge: The British in India* (Princeton, NJ: Princeton University Press, 1996), 7–8.
18. Boardman, "Mr. Boardman's Journal."
19. Edwin Bullard, "Maulmain Mission: Extracts from a Letter of Mr. Bullard," *Baptist Missionary Magazine*, December 1845, 311–15. For more on consecration practices of Buddha statues in Southeast Asia, see Donald K. Swearer, *Becoming the Buddha: The Ritual of Image Consecration in Thailand* (Princeton, NJ: Princeton University Press, 2004).
20. Bullard, "Maulmain Mission."
21. Bullard.
22. Francis Mason, "Mr. Mason's Description of His Arrival Among the Burmans," *American Baptist Magazine*, November 1831, 341–43.
23. Ingalls, *Ocean Sketches*, 77–78.
24. Edward Stevens, "Shway Dagong, at Rangoon: Description," *Baptist Missionary Magazine*, February 1876, 34–36.
25. Stevens, "Shway Dagong."

3. THE PAGODA

26. Talal Asad, "The Construction of Religion as an Anthropological Category" (Baltimore, MD: Johns Hopkins University Press, [1982] 1993), abridged and reprinted in Michael Lambek, ed., *A Reader in the Anthropology of Religion* (Hoboken, NJ: Blackwell, 2002), 122.
27. Charney, *Powerful Learning: Buddhist Literati and the Throne in Burma's Last Dynasty, 1752-1885* (Ann Arbor: Centers for South and Southeast Asian Studies, University of Michigan, 2006), 207.
28. Maung Htin Aung, *A History of Burma* (New York: Columbia University Press, 1967), 189.
29. E. Michael Mendelson, *Sangha and State in Burma: A Study of Monastic Sectarianism and Leadership* (Ithaca, NY: Cornell University Press, 1975), 73.
30. Erik Braun, *The Birth of Insight: Meditation, Modern Buddhism and the Burmese Monk Ledi Sayadaw,* (Chicago: University of Chicago Press, 2013), 46-47.
31. Charney, *Powerful Learning*, 207.
32. John Ferguson, "The Symbolic Dimensions of the Burmese Sangha" (PhD diss., Cornell University, 1975), 205.
33. Mendelson, *Sangha and State in Burma*, 73, 77.
34. Father Sangermano, *The Burmese Empire a Hundred Years Ago, with an Introduction and Notes by John Jardine* (London: Archibald Constable, 1983), 111-12.
35. Sir Henry Yule, *A Narrative of the Mission Sent by the Governor-General of India to the Court of Ava in 1855: With Notices of the Country, Government, and People* (London: Smith, Elder, 1858), 241-42.
36. For more on the impact of Brian Hodgson's manuscript collecting on the emergence of Buddhist studies, see the introduction by Katia Buffetrille and Donald S. Lopez Jr. to Eugène Burnouf, *Introduction to the History of Indian Buddhism* (Chicago: University of Chicago Press, 2010).
37. Shway Yoe (a.k.a. Sir James Scott), *The Burman: His Life and Notions* (New York: MacMillan, [1910] 1882), 147.
38. Mendelson, *Sangha and State in Burma*, 77.
39. Maung Htin Aung, *History of Burma*, 189.
40. Charney, *Powerful Learning*, 208.
41. Lammerts, *Buddhist Law in Burma: A History of Dhammasattha Texts and Jurisprudence, 1250-1850* (Honolulu: University of Hawai'i Press, 2018), 21-22.
42. Alexey Kirichenko, "The Making of the Culprit: Atula Hsayadaw Shin Yasa and the Politics of Monastic Reform in Eighteenth-Century Burma," *Journal of Burma Studies* 15, no. 2 (2011): 189-229.
43. Chris Wingfield, "'Scarcely More than a Christian Trophy Case?' The Global Collections of the London Missionary Society Museum (1814-1910)," *Journal of the History of Collections* 29, no. 1 (2017): 114.
44. In addition to Shahzad Bashir's work on religious imagination considered in this chapter, another example of related insightful scholarship is David Morgan's work on imagination and visual culture, *The Embodied Eye: Religious Visual Culture and the Social Life of Feeling* (Berkeley: University of California Press, 2012). Morgan attends to imagination in his very definition of the key term "religions," which he gives as "communities of feeling or sentiment that

are held together by shared forms of intuition, imagination, and body practices" (6).
45. Shahzad Bashir, "Shah Ismaʿil and the Qizilbash: Cannibalism in the Religious History of Early Safavid Iran," *History of Religions* 45, no. 3 (2006): 234–56.
46. Edward Stevens, "Tour to Mandelay," *Missionary Magazine*, June 1870, 161–66.
47. I am using "U," the common English spelling of the Burmese honorific used today. Missionary sources, including this report by Stevens, tend to spell it "Oo." The Royal Administration of Burma uses "U," so I have used "U" for the sake of consistency. This same honorific is used in other names later in the chapter, but since those names are only cited in missionary sources that spell them as "Oo," I have also used "Oo."
48. Stevens, "Tour to Mandelay."
49. Stevens. For more on King Mindon's promotion of Buddhism, see Myo Myint, *Confronting Colonialism: King Mindon's Strategy for Defending Independence (1853-1878)* (Yangon: Ministry of Religious Affairs, 2012).
50. King Mindon supported the church and school run by John Ebenezer Marks, a Society for the Preservation of the Gospel missionary from England. Marks's memoir recounts how King Mindon, in response to his request for permission to work as a Christian missionary in the capital and build a church and school said that Marks had the king's "full sanction to preach my religion in his dominions, and that no one should be molested for listening or even for becoming Christian." See John Ebenezer Marks, *Forty Years in Burma* (London: Hutchinson, 1917).

    Myo Myint details how King Mindon lavishly supported Marks's Christian school—even sending nine of his sons there—in order to influence public opinion abroad. British newspapers reported on the money King Mindon spent to build the school (30,000 kyat), and on how the English design was executed by Burmese carpenters. Queen Victoria got the message and gifted a font of multicolored marble to show her gratitude to King Mindon. See Myint, *Confronting Colonialism*, 237.
51. James George Scott, *Burma: A Handbook of Practical Information* (London: Alexander Moring, 1906), 378.
52. Scott, *Burma*, 379.
53. Scott, 209.
54. U Tin also served under Mindon's successor, King Thibaw, the last king of Burma, and went on to work in government service for the British colonial administration.
55. U Tin, *The Royal Administration of Burma*, trans. Euan Bagshawe (Bangkok: Ava, 2001), 359–60.
56. Turner, *Saving Buddhism: The Impermanence of Religion in Colonial Burma* Honolulu: University of Hawai'i Press, 2014); Braun, *Birth of Insight*.
57. Shwe Wa, *Burma Baptist Chronicle*, 125.
58. Isabel Hofmeyr, *Gandhi's Printing Press* (Cambridge, MA: Harvard University Press, 2013), 13.
59. Thomas Simons, "Extracts from the Journal of Mr. Simons," *Baptist Missionary Magazine*, November 1837, 265–68.

3. THE PAGODA

60. Eugenio Kincaid served in Burma for nearly thirty years, beginning in 1830. Kincaid published many accounts of his evangelization among British soldiers, his experiences at the Burmese royal court, and his adventures on itinerant preaching tours in Burma's remote areas. Kincaid also made history for carrying a royal letter of friendship from King Mindon to U.S. president James Buchanan. The letter was enclosed in red velvet and set in an ivory case. Buchanan sent a kind reply back with Kincaid along with a gift package of U.S. publications.
61. Simons, "Extracts."
62. Howard Malcom, *Travels in South-Eastern Asia: Embracing Hindustan, Malaya, Siam, and China / with a Full Account of the Burman Empire; with Dissertations, Tables, Etc.* (Boston: Gould, Kendall & Lincoln, 1838), 211; casing in original.
63. Francis Mason, "Maulmain Burman Mission: Journal of Mr. Mason," *Missionary Magazine*, February 1850, 47.
64. This Burmese Buddhist view of world religions presents an interesting parallel to the concurrent development of European world religions system, which worked to privilege Christianity even while it added more religions, including Buddhism, to the European pantheon of world religions. For more on the contemporary European practice of tracking world religions, see Tomoko Masuzawa, *The Invention of World Religions* (Chicago: University of Chicago Press, 2005).
65. This example of a Burmese history of world religions that works to privilege Buddhism offers an interesting parallel to the ways European authorities defined world religions, which Masuzawa has shown worked to promote European Christianity above all; see *Invention of World Religions*.
66. Edward Stevens, "Letter of Mr. Stevens," *Missionary Magazine*, January 1850, 14.
67. James Granger, "Letters from Mr. Granger," *Missionary Magazine*, March 1854, 65–78; italics in original.
68. Granger, "Letters from Mr. Granger."
69. Ko Kong, "Ko Kong's Narrative," *Missionary Magazine*, February 1867, 42–43.
70. Frederick Howard Eveleth, "The Paramats," *Baptist Missionary Magazine*, January 1882, 4–8.
71. Eveleth, "Paramats."
72. Eveleth.
73. Eveleth.
74. Eveleth.
75. Eveleth.
76. *Majjhima Nikāya* 10, in *In the Buddha's Words: An Anthology of Discourses from the Pāli Canon*, ed. Bhikkhu Bodhi (Boston: Wisdom, 2005), 283.
77. Braun, *Birth of Insight*, 31–32.
78. Eveleth, "Paramats."
79. Patrick Pranke, "On Saints and Wizards," *Journal of the International Association of Buddhist Studies* 33, nos. 1–2 (2010): 458.
80. Braun, *Birth of Insight*, 29.
81. Eveleth, "Paramats."
82. "The Paramats.—II," *Baptist Missionary Magazine*, September 1882, 331–33.

4. The Portrait

1. Deborah Van Broekhoven, Jan Ballard, and Rosalie Hunt, letter attached to email message to author, September 6, 2012; Rosalie Hunt, letter attached to email message to author, November 5, 2012.
2. Hillary Kaell, *Walking Where Jesus Walked: American Christians and Holy Land Pilgrimage* (New York: New York University Press, 2014), 199.
3. For example, the Myanmar Baptist Convention funded bicentennial celebrations through contributions from the country's churches. The Sgaw Karen churches were asked to pay $1,400,000, whereas the Pwo Karen churches, fewer in number and congregation size, paid $200,000. These funds went to feeding and housing pilgrims who came to Yangon to celebrate as well as to the production of anniversary materials. Reverend Ko Ko Lay (president of Pwo Kayin Theological Seminary), interview with the author, August 6, 2013.
4. Stephen R. Prothero, *American Jesus: How the Son of God Became a National Icon* (New York: Farrar, Straus and Giroux, 2003), 116. For more on the place of Warner Sallman's religious art in mainstream American culture and thought, see David Morgan, *Icons of American Protestantism: The Art of Warner Sallman* (New Haven: Yale University Press, 1996).
5. This argument that Baptist artwork in Burma is both a reaction and a response to nineteenth-century imperialism builds on the work of Michael Taussig and his use of the term "mimetic faculty," which he defines in *Mimesis and Alterity: A Particular History of the Senses* (New York: Routledge, 1993) as "the faculty to copy, imitate, make models, explore difference, yield into and become Other" (xiii). Taussig argues that in postcolonial societies the emergence of dissolved borders and new interactions between the West and the rest, between those understood as selves and others, created a "mimetic excess," which Taussig defines as "mimetic self-awareness, mimesis turned on itself, on its colonial endowment, such that now, in our time, mimesis as a natural faculty and mimesis as a historical product turn in on each other as never before" (252). Taussig concludes that the products of this postcolonial mimetic excess "provides a welcome opportunity to live subjunctively as neither subject nor object of history but as both, at one and the same time" (55). If we see paintings of Jesus and the Judsons as forms of postimperial mimetic excess, we can begin to understand that when Burma's Baptist minority continuously copies and alters earlier versions of these American images, they are both subjects and objects of the history of their encounters with Western religion and power.
6. This approach to religious artwork follows the scholarship of Richard Davis, whose study *Lives of Indian Images* (Princeton, NJ: Princeton University Press, 1997) understands them "as fundamentally social beings whose identities are not fixed once and for all at the moment of fabrication, but are repeatedly made and remade through interactions with humans" (7–8). Like Davis's Indian artwork, Burma's paintings of Jesus and the Judsons can be considered social in that they communicate ideas about this worldly and otherworldly communities. When congregations place them in prominent positions in their churches

4. THE PORTRAIT

and homes, these Anglo-American images remind Baptists of the American influence on their religious lives and the Western-rooted, global institution to which their church belongs.

The scholarship of Sally Promey and David Morgan on the visual cultures of American religions in *The Visual Culture of American Religions* (Berkeley: University of California Press, 2001) extends this line of reasoning by encouraging us to recognize images as cultural devices that "participate significantly in religious practice" (2). Promey and Morgan highlight two key operations in which images participate that are especially relevant for the analysis in this chapter: the operations of communion and commemoration. Communion, as defined by Promey and Morgan, is the device by which "images identify individuals as members of kinship networks, communities, or nation as well as religious denominations, traditions, or institutions. This kind of image helps establish a *communitas*, incorporating a set of horizontal relations among individuals as well as vertical communion with a reality greater than the self" (6). For Burma's Baptists, paintings of Jesus and the Judsons identify the communities as a part of an international network of Baptist churches with special ties to the United States. This horizontal network intersects with a vertical vision of the heaven to which the congregants aspire: a Kingdom of God occupied by Jesus, the Judsons, other American missionaries to Burma, the country's first converts, later generations of Burma's Baptists, and a vast array of Christians from all over the world. In addition to forming a *communitas*, this Protestant portraiture also works to shape communal memory and empower acts of commemoration. Promey and Morgan argue that religious imagery has "long been used as a way of seeding the memory with information vital to maintaining a religious group's identity," such as "ritually observing sacred events and commemorating heroes" (10). Judson paintings in Burma help congregations ritually remember the nineteenth-century American origins of the Baptist faith in the country and preserve the denomination's distinct identity within a vastly Buddhist land.

7. Marilla Ingalls, *Ocean Sketches of Life in Burmah* (Philadelphia: American Baptist Publication Society, 1857), 76–78.
8. Cushing's career in Burma was extraordinary, distinguished not only by his publications on the Shan language but also by his leadership work at the Baptist College in Rangoon, now University of Yangon, the most distinguished university in Burma. After his death in 1905, Cushing's manuscript comparing Buddhism and Christianity was published through the efforts of Henry Melville King, Pastor Emeritus of the First Baptist Church in Providence, Rhode Island. See Josiah Nelson Cushing, *Christ and Buddha* (Philadelphia: American Baptist Publication Society, 1907). My investigations into Cushing's manuscript collection at the American Baptist Historical society suggest that the views of Buddhism he expresses in his book were formed in larger part from his time in Sri Lanka, rather than his experience working in Burma.
9. To compare to U.S. figures, 15 percent of Americans identify as Baptist or Southern Baptist making them nearly one third of the Protestants in the country. A

4. THE PORTRAIT

2014 ABC News/Beliefnet poll tallied 83 percent of Americans Christian, with 53 percent of Americans identifying as Protestant. This poll reports that Baptist account for 15 percent of the American population with "no other Protestant denomination coming close in size." Gary Langer, "Poll: Most Americans Say They're Christian," ABC News, July 18, 2014, abcnews.go.com/US/story?id=90356.
10. Pew Research Center, "The Future of World Religions: Population Growth Projections, 2010–2050," April 2, 2015, http://www.pewforum.org/2015/04/02/religious-projections-2010-2050/
11. Thawng Khan Siing (director of the Evangelism and Mission Department, Myanamr Baptist Convention), interview with the author, October 1, 2013.
12. Another Yangon resident who used humor to explain to me ethnic and religious issues for Burma's Christians is V. Kam, an amateur historian of the Chin people. When I met with V. Kam in September, he shared illuminating information about why minority Christians prominently displayed Jesus imagery. V. Kam invited me to his home to talk about his unpublished book manuscript, a history of the Chin people from nearly time immemorial with connections to China, India, the Near East, even Africa and Europe. This work is, V. Kam told me, "very tender, sensitive." V. Kam explained that part of the difficulty for the Chin is that the "Burmese people blame Christianity as a foreign religion," so V. Kam's research reaches way back in time, well before the colonial period to explore early possible connections between the Chin and the tribes of Israel. To the left of V. Kam's front door is a framed Sallman *Head of Christ* with two lines of overlay text, the one along the right frame reading "Tedim Baptist Church," the name of Rangoon's largest Chin church, and the bottom line reading a quote from Isaiah 41:10 in Chin: "Do not fear, for I am with you." I asked V. Kam's family about the image, and he and his daughters explained that "every church member has to have this painting in their house and a cross on the outside. But," they added with a smile, "it's not free! You have to pay!" V. Kam told me that when they got the images in 2005 he had to pay 2000 kyat for the *Head of Christ* (a little over $2) and 3300 kyat (approximately $3.5) for the jewelry-scroll painting of the church. Perhaps this church simply wants the images to help remind their congregants of the message of Isaiah: that they should not fear, for God is with them. It seems that the required paintings and cross outside also remind them and their neighbors that they belong not to the Buddhist majority, but to a distinct Christian minority with Western ties. V. Kam, interview with the author, September 29, 2013.
13. Non-Buddhist minority communities protested the passage of the State Religion Act in 1961, and General Ne Win used this pushback to justify the military coup of 1962. Once in power, Ne Win undid many of the features of this act, and Buddhism has not officially been established as a national religion since, although the 2008 constitution gave it "special status."
14. *The Sesquicentennial Pictorial of Baptist Work in Burma, 1813–1963*, created by the Burma Baptist Convention in 1963 and published for the Burma Baptist Convention Board of Publications by U Maung U, printed at the Rangoon University

4. THE PORTRAIT

Press, Rangoon, Burma, held at the American Baptist Historical Society, Atlanta, Georgia.

15. The 150-year celebration materials seem to have taken many visual cues from the first wide-scale anniversary celebration in 1913. The 100-year commemoration produced multiple leaflets for the occasion, including *Arrival of Judson in Burma*, featuring a portrait of Judson on the cover, as well as *Mrs. Judson's Story of Her Arrival in Burma*, which also featured a portrait of Ann. There was even a centennial medal: a bronze watch fob, featuring the bust of Adoniram Judson. Unlike the materials made for the 1963 anniversary, the 1913 event distributed leaflets and other memorabilia created in the United States and overseen by the American Baptist Foreign Mission Society in Boston. The images in the American-made 1913 materials more closely match the official nineteenth-century portraits of the Judsons, including the miniatures painted before their first departure from America and portraits they sat for after achieving celebratory status. These portraits were reprinted in the many biographies and memoirs published after their deaths.
16. David Morgan, *Icons of American Protestantism: The Art of Warner Sallman* (New Haven: Yale University Press, 1996), 47.
17. Matthew 28:19, as quoted on the U Naw bicentennial mural; casing theirs.
18. Francis Wayland, *A Memoir of the Life and Labors of the Rev. Adoniram Judson, D.D,* (Boston: Phillips, Sampson, 1853), 1:251–52.
19. Hla Myint, *The State's Role in Purifying and Perpetuating Buddha Sāsana Through History: Myanmar's Experience and Selected Conference Papers* (Yangon: International Theravada Buddhist Missionary University, 2013), 32.
20. Hla Myint, *State's Role,* 3–32. Here Hla Myint is referring to stringed Buddhist prayer beads, often called malas, when he uses the term "rosaries."
21. With permission from *Material Religion,* I have extracted and adapted much of this section from Alexandra Kaloyanides, "Peering into Prisons, Gazing upon Graves: Early U.S. Missionary Media from Burma," *Material Religion* 17, no. 2 (2021): 117–201.
22. In her critical translation and study of the Treaty of Yandabo, *The End of the First Anglo-Burmese War: The Burmese Chronicle Account of How the 1826 Treaty of Yandabo Was Negotiated* (Bangkok: Chulalongkorn University Press, 1994), Anna Allott writes that, without Adoniram's work, "it is doubtful if the British and the Burmese would have been able to conduct any negotiations at all, let alone conclude a treaty" (ii).
23. Ryland to Judson, December 8, 1851, in *The Life and Letters of Emily Chubbuck Judson (Fanny Forester),* ed. George H. Tooze (Macon, GA: Mercer University Press, 2009–2013), 5:83–84.
24. For more of my analysis of the history of images of Ann Judson's gravesite and its crucial place in an imagined world of redemptive missionary sacrifice in Burma, see Kaloyanides, "Peering into Prisons."
25. John Corrigan, *Religious Intolerance, America, and the World: A History of Forgetting and Remembering* (Chicago: University of Chicago Press, 2020), 73.
26. Christine Leigh Heyrman, *Doomed Romance: Broken Hearts, Lost Souls, and Sexual Politics in Nineteenth-Century America* (New York: Knopf, 2021), 16.

4. THE PORTRAIT

27. Cutting to Chubbuck Judson, June 22, 1852 Framingham, Massachusetts, AJ 15, no. 613, vol. 5, 419–20, American Baptist Historical Society, Atlanta, Georgia; Tooze, ed., *Life and Letters*, 5:419–20.
28. Tooze, ed., 5:422–23.
29. J. Rigbie Turner, "Richard Strauss to Cäcilie Wenzel: Twelve Unpublished Letters," *Nineteenth-Century Music* 9, no. 3 (1986): 165.
30. Hamilton W. Pierson, *American Missionary Memorial, Including Biographical and Historical Sketches* (New York: Harper, 1853), 121.
31. Tooze, ed., *Life and Letters*, 6:117.
32. Kent Brintnall, *Ecce Homo: The Male-Body-In-Pain as a Redemptive Figure* (Chicago: University of Chicago Press, 2011) explores representations of the suffering male body and the way they enlist viewers in the "fantastic work of valorizing triumphant heroism as the meaning of masculine subjectivity and the criterion of human dignity." Brintnall argues that the brutal spectacle of crucifixion keeps Christianity from becoming profane, suggesting that the sustained interest in depicting Adoniram in a tortured, reverse-crucifixion position worked within a larger network of representations of male suffering to make the Burma mission a sacred enterprise. *Ecce Homo* also shows how "eroticism, like religion, is a search for lost continuity" and that, "like sacrifice and eroticism, art is a form of transgressive expenditure," pressing us to see how artistic representations of Adoniram's sacrifice in a Burmese prison worked to loosen the bounds of the individual viewer place them in intersubjective relation (20, 12, 13).
33. Ronald E. Schlosser, writer, *Adoniram Judson Called to Be a Missionary* (Valley Forge, PA: American Baptist Films, 1980).
34. Marilla Baker Ingalls, "Visit to Mandelay," *Baptist Missionary Magazine*, August 1873, 311–16.
35. Pamela Klassen, *The Story of Radio Mind: A Missionary's Journey on Indigenous Land* (Chicago: University of Chicago Press, 2018).
36. Ann's portrait looks rather new and shows no signs of weather damage. Adoniram's portrait, by contrast, shows water stains and sun fading, marking it as clearly older than Ann's. Furthermore, this depiction of Adoniram is far more subtly rendered and could be a late nineteenth-century print installed shortly after this church was built in 1905. This shows more details than the later reproductions of this or similar images. For example, we see in this portrait that between Judson's shirt and jacket is a buttoned vest, and the shading around his face and the texture in the cloth backdrop suggests a more formal-style portrait.
37. The Jesus paintings in the community room included another depiction of Jesus praying in the wilderness. The community room's wilderness oil painting shows Christ with peach-colored skin and brown hair. The second Jesus painting in the room features the familiar Sallman-style Christ head, but zooms out to show Jesus standing at a lacquered cross-carved pulpit in the style found throughout this country. It seems odd to show Christ preaching in front of a bible, and I found myself wondering if the artist had in mind Judson's first Burmese-language translation. With all the attention that the church gives to its first-edition Judson bible, this painting of Christ at a Burmese-style

lacquered pulpit in front of a bible seemed to almost conflate Adoniram and Jesus, but maybe I had just gone a bit cross-eyed at this point in the tour.
38. Edward Stevens, "Maulmain—Journal of Rev. Mr. Stevens," *Baptist Missionary Magazine*, December 1849, 409–13.
39. Francis Wayland, *A Memoir of the Life and Labors of the Rev. Adoniram Judson. D.D.* (Boston: Phillips, Sampson, 1853), 1:325.

Conclusion

1. Suzanne Collins's trilogy of young adult novels are titled *The Hunger Games* (2008), *Catching Fire* (2009), and *Mockingjay* (2010). Scholastic Corporation, headquartered in New York City, published them in 2008, 2009, and 2010, respectively. The American-Canadian entertainment company Lionsgate, headquartered in Santa Monica, California, has distributed three major motion pictures based on these novels: *The Hunger Games* (2012), *The Hunger Games: Catching Fire* (2013); *The Hunger Games: Mockingjay—Part 1* (2014); and *The Hunger Games: Mockingjay—Part 2* (2015).
2. In analyzing the global popularity of *The Hunger Games* with a focus on Thailand, Malisa Kurtz argues that the film's generic narrative of oppression and precarity "encourages ambiguity and adaptability," and that this "ambiguity also increases its appeal to audiences precisely because this ambiguity itself expresses a shared sense of uncertainty, a collective failure to understand our current historical condition, and an inability to fully capture the traumas of globalization. See Malisa Kurtz, " 'The Dark Side of Hope': Genre and Globalization in *the Hunger Games*," *Extrapolation* 58, nos. 2–3 (2017): 255–72.
3. Tessa Wong, "Hunger Games Salute: The Symbol of Protest Against Asia's Military Regimes," BBC, March 7, 2021, https://www.bbc.com/news/av/world-asia-56289575.
4. Laura Levitt, *The Objects That Remain* (University Park: Penn State University Press, 2020), 15.

Works Cited

Abbreviations of the Sacred Books of Gautama, n.d. Burmese palm-leaf books and Kammavacas. American Baptist Historical Society, Atlanta, Georgia.
Agmon, Danna. *A Colonial Affair: Commerce, Conversion, and Scandal in French India.* Ithaca, NY: Cornell University Press, 2017.
Allott, Anna. *The End of the First Anglo-Burmese War: The Burmese Chronicle Account of How the 1826 Treaty of Yandabo Was Negotiated.* Bangkok: Chulalongkorn University Press, 1994.
Amrith, Sunil S. *Crossing the Bay of Bengal: The Furies of Nature and the Fortunes of Migrants.* Cambridge, MA: Harvard University Press, 2013.
Anderson, Benedict. *Imagined Communities: Reflections on the Origins and Spread of Nationalism.* New York: Verso, 1983.
Asad, Talal. "The Construction of Religion as an Anthropological Category." Baltimore, MD: Johns Hopkins University Press, [1982] 1993. Abridged and reprinted in *A Reader in the Anthropology of Religion*, edited by Michael Lambek. Hoboken, NJ: Blackwell, 2002.
Aung Htin. *A History of Burma.* New York: Columbia University Press, 1967.
Bailey, H. W. "The Tumshuq Karmavācanā." *Bulletin of the School of Oriental and African Studies* 13, no. 3 (1950): 649–70.
Bashir, Shahzad. "Shah Ismaʿil and the Qizilbash: Cannibalism in the Religious History of Early Safavid Iran." *History of Religions* 45, no. 3 (2006): 234–56.
Becker, Adam H. *Revival and Awakening: American Evangelical Missionaries in Iran and the Origins of Assyrian Nationalism.* Chicago: University of Chicago Press, 2015.
Beemer, Bryce. "The Creole City in Mainland Southeast Asia: Slave Gathering Warfare and Cultural Exchange in Burma, Thailand, and Manipur, Eighteenth to Nineteenth Century." PhD diss., University of Hawai'i, 2013.
Bhabha, Homi K. *The Location of Culture.* New York: Routledge, 1994.

WORKS CITED

Bhikkhu, Ṭhānissaro. "The Three Perceptions." Dhammatalks, May 27, 2021. https://www.dhammatalks.org/books/uncollected/ThreePerceptions.html.
——. *The Buddhist Monastic Code*. 2 vols. Valley Center, CA: self-published, 2007.
Blackburn, Anne M. "Buddhist Connections in the Indian Ocean: Changes in Monastic Mobility, 1000–1500." *Journal of the Economic and Social History of the Orient* 58, no. 3 (2015): 237–66.
Blackburn, Terence R. *The British Humiliation of Burma*. Bangkok: Orchid, 2000.
Blurton, Ralph Isaacs, and T. Richard, ed. *Visions from the Golden Land: Burma and the Art of Lacquer*. Chicago: Art Media Resources, 2000.
Boardman, George. "Journal." *American Baptist Magazine*, January 1830, 22–23.
——. "Mr. Boardman's Journal." *American Baptist Magazine*, July 1829, 242–46.
Bode, Mabel Haynes. *Sāsanavaṃsa*. London: Pali Text Society, 1897.
Bodhi, Bhikkhu, ed. *In the Buddha's Words: An Anthology of Discourses from the Pāli Canon*. Boston: Wisdom, 2005.
Bopp, Franz. *A Comparative Grammar of the Sanscrit, Zend, Greek, Latin, Lithuanian, Gothic, German, and Sclavonic Languages* [Vergleichende Grammatik des Sanskrit, Zend, Griechischen, Lateinischen, Litthauischen, Gothischen und Deutschen]. London: Madden & Malcolm, 1845–1850.
Brac de La Perrière, Bénédicte. "An Overview of the Field of Religion in Burmese Studies." *Asian Ethnology* 68, no. 2 (2009): 185–210.
——. "Sibling Relationships in the *Nat* Stories of the Burmese Cult to the 'Thirty-Seven.'" *Moussons*, no. 5 (2002): 31–48.
——. "The Burmese Nats: Between Sovereignty and Autochthony." *Diogenes* 44, no. 174 (1996): 45–60.
Bracken, Christopher. *The Potlatch Papers: A Colonial Case History*. Chicago: University of Chicago Press, 1997.
Brandis, Sir Dietrich. "Mrs. Marilla B. Ingalls." *Standard*, June 6, 1903, 8.
Braun, Erik. *The Birth of Insight: Meditation, Modern Buddhism, and the Burmese Monk Ledi Sayadaw*. Chicago: University of Chicago Press, 2013.
Brintnall, Kent. *Ecce Homo: The Male-Body-in-Pain as Redemptive Figure*. Chicago: University of Chicago Press, 2011.
Brown, Candy Gunther. *The Word in the World: Evangelical Writing, Publishing, and Reading in America, 1789–1880*. Chapel Hill: University of North Carolina Press, 2004.
Brumberg, Joan Jacobs. *Mission for Life: The Story of the Family of Adoniram Judson, the Dramatic Events of the First American Mission, and the Course of Evangelical Religion in the Nineteenth Century*. New York: Free Press, 1980.
Buchanan, Claudius. *The Star in the East: A Sermon*. Boston: Munroe & Francis, [1809] 1811.
Bullard, Edwin. "Maulmain Mission: Extracts from a Letter of Mr. Bullard." *Baptist Missionary Magazine*, December 1845, 311–15.
Burnouf, Eugène. *Introduction to the History of Indian Buddhism*. Chicago: University of Chicago Press, 2010.
Butler, Jon. *Awash in a Sea of Faith: Christianizing the American People*. Cambridge, MA: Harvard University Press, 1990.

WORKS CITED

Caldwell, Robert. "New England's New Divinity and the Age of Judson's Preparation." In *Adoniram Judson: A Bicentennial Appreciation of the Pioneer American Missionary*, edited by Jason G. Duesing, 31–54. Nashville, TN: B&H, 2012.

Candier, Aurore. "Mapping Ethnicity in Nineteenth-Century Burma: When 'Categories of People' (*Lumyo*) became 'Nations.'" *Journal of Southeast Asian Studies* 50, no. 3 (2019): 347–64.

Carbine, Jason A. *Sons of the Buddha: Continuities and Ruptures in a Burmese Monastic Tradition*. New York: Walter de Gruyter, 2011.

Chancey, Karen. "The Star in the East: The Controversy over Christian Missions to India, 1805–1813." *Historian* 60, no. 3 (1998): 507–22.

Charney, Michael. "Review of Michael Aung-Thwin *Mists of Ramanna: The Legend That Was Lower Burma*." H-Net Asia Book Reviews, February 2006 (no longer available).

———. *Powerful Learning: Buddhist Literati and the Throne in Burma's Last Dynasty, 1752–1885*. Ann Arbor: Centers for South and Southeast Asian Studies, University of Michigan, 2006.

Chaṭṭha Saṅgāyana Pāli Tipiṭaka (including Paññasāmi's *Sāsanavaṃsa*). Accessed August 26, 2022. http://www.tipitaka.org.

Chidester, David. *Empire of Religion: Imperialism and Comparative Religion*. Chicago: University of Chicago Press, 2014.

Clough, Rev. Benjamin. "The Ritual of the Budd'hist Priesthood, Translated from the Original Pali Work, Entitled *Karmawakya*." *Miscellaneous Translations from Oriental Languages Published for the Oriental Translation Fund of Great Britain and Ireland* 2 (1834): 1–30.

Cohn, Bernard S. *Colonialism and Its Forms of Knowledge: The British in India*. Princeton, NJ: Princeton University Press, 1996.

Collins, Steven. "On the Very Idea of the Pali Canon." *Journal of the Pali Text Society* 15 (1990): 89–126.

Comaroff, Jean, and John L. Comaroff. *Of Revelation and Revolution: Christianity, Colonialism, and Consciousness in South Africa*. Vol. 1. Chicago: University of Chicago Press, 1991.

Conroy-Krutz, Emily. *Christian Imperialism: Converting the World in the Early American Republic*. Ithaca, NY: Cornell University Press, 2015.

Conway, Susan. "Power Dressing: Female Court Dress and Marital Alliances in Lan Na, the Shan States, and Siam." *Orientations* 32, no. 4 (April 2001): 42–49.

Corrigan, John. *Religious Intolerance, America, and the World: A History of Forgetting and Remembering*. Chicago: University of Chicago Press, 2020.

Crosby, Kate. *Theravada Buddhism: Continuity, Diversity and Identity*. Malden, MA: Wiley Blackwell, 2014.

Curtis, Heather D. *Holy Humanitarians: American Evangelicals and Global Aid*. Cambridge, MA: Harvard University Press, 2018.

Cushing, Josiah Nelson. *Christ and Buddha*. Philadelphia: American Baptist Publication Society, 1907.

Darmesteter, James. "Rapport Annuel." *Journal Asiatique*, July–August 1890, 19–180.

Davis, Erik W. *Deathpower: Buddhism's Ritual Imagination in Cambodia*. New York: Columbia University Press, 2016.

Davis, Richard. *Lives of Indian Images*. Princeton, NJ: Princeton University Press, 1997.

Deborah B. Lapham Correspondence. Missionaries. American Baptist Historical Society, Atlanta, Georgia.

de la Perrière, Bénédicte Brac. "An Overview of the Field of Religion in Burmese Studies." *Asian Ethnology* (2009): 185–210.

deJong, J. W. "A Brief History of Buddhist Studies in Europe and America." *Eastern Buddhist* 7, no. 1 (1974): 55–106.

Dickson, J. F. "The Upasampadā-Kammavācā: Being the Buddhist Manual of the Form and Manner of Ordering of Priests and Deacons." *Journal of the Royal Asiatic Society of Great Britain and Ireland* 7, no. 1 (1875): 149–59.

Editorial Board. "The Death of Mrs. Lydia L. Simons." *Baptist Missionary Magazine*, March 1899, 90.

——. "The Tenasserim Provinces." *Calcutta Review* 8, no. 16 (1847): 140–45.

Edwards, Michael. "Circulating Publicness and Public Circulation." The Immanent Frame, June 19, 2019. https://tif.ssrc.org/2019/06/18/circulating-publicness-and-public-circulation/.

Edwards, Penny. "Half-Cast: Staging Race in British Burma." *Postcolonial Studies* 5, no. 3 (2002): 279–95.

Engelke, Matthew. *A Problem of Presence: Beyond Scripture in an African Church*. Berkeley: University of California Press, 2007.

Eveleth, Frederick Howard. "The Paramats." *Baptist Missionary Magazine*, January 1882, 4–8.

——. "The Paramats.—II." *Baptist Missionary Magazine*, September 1882, 331–33.

Ferguson, Jane M. "Who's Counting?: Ethnicity, Belonging, and the National Census in Burma/Myanmar." *Journal of the Humanities and Social Sciences of Southeast Asia* 171, no. 1 (2015): 1–28.

Ferguson, John. "The Symbolic Dimensions of the Burmese Sangha." PhD diss., Cornell University, 1975.

Fessenden, Tracy. *Culture and Redemption: Religion, the Secular, and American Literature*. Princeton, NJ: Princeton University Press, 2011.

Fisher, Linford D. *The Indian Great Awakening: Religion and the Shaping of Native Cultures in Early America*. New York: Oxford University Press, 2012.

Fleet, J. F. "Salivahana and the Saka Era." *Journal of the Royal Asiatic Society of Great Britian and Ireland* (October 1916): 809–20.

Foer, Joshua. "World's Largest Book at Kuthodaw Pagoda." Atlas Obscura. Accessed August 26, 2022. https://www.atlasobscura.com/places/world-s-largest-book-at-kuthodaw-pagoda.

Fox, Richard. *More than Words: Transforming Script, Agency, and Collective Life in Bali*. Ithaca, NY: Cornell University Press, 2018.

Franke, Heike. "Akbar's *Kathāsaritsāgara*: The Translator and Illustrations of an Imperial Manuscript." *Muqarnas* 27 (2010): 313–56.

Fraser-Lu, Sylvia, and Donald M. Stadtner, eds. *Buddhist Art of Myanmar*. New Haven: Yale University Press, 2015.

Fujimura, Hitomi. "Disentangling the Colonial Narrative of the Karen National Association of 1881: The Motive Behind Karen Baptist Intellectual's Claim for a Nation." *Journal of Burma Studies* 24, no. 2 (2020): 275–314.

Glassie, Henry. *Material Culture*. Bloomington: Indiana University Press, 1999.

Goonatilake, Hema. "Sri Lanka-Myanmar Historical Relations in Religion, Culture, and Polity." *Journal of the Royal Asiatic Society of Sri Lanka* 55 (2009): 77–114.

Granger, James. "Letters from Mr. Granger." *Missionary Magazine*, March 1854, 65–78.

Granoff, Phyllis. "Kālakācārya Kathā the Story of the Teacher Kālaka." Unpublished manuscript. Last modified October 31, 2013.

Green, Alexandra. *Buddhist Visual Cultures, Rhetoric, and Narrative in Late Burmese Wall Paintings.* Hong Kong: Hong Kong University Press, 2018.

Hallisey, Charles. "Roads Taken and Not Taken in the Study of Theravada Buddhism." *Curators of the Buddha* (1995): 31–61.

Hayami, Yoko. "Karen Culture of Evangelism and Early Baptist Mission in Nineteenth-Century Burma." *Social Sciences and Missions* 31, nos. 3–4 (2018): 251–83.

Heyrman, Christine Leigh. *American Apostles: When Evangelicals Entered the World of Islam.* New York: Hill & Wang, 2015.

———. *Doomed Romance: Broken Hearts, Lost Souls, and Sexual Politics in Nineteenth-Century America.* New York: Knopf, 2021.

Hla Myint. *The State's Role in Purifying and Perpetuating Buddha Sāsana Through History: Myanmar's Experience and Selected Conference Papers.* Yangon: International Theravada Buddhist Missionary University, 2013.

Hofmeyr, Isabel. *Gandhi's Printing Press.* Cambridge, MA: Harvard University Press, 2013.

Hollinger, David A. *Protestants Abroad: How Missionaries Tried to Change the World but Changed America.* Princeton, NJ: Princeton University Press, 2017.

Hunt, Rosalie Hall. *Bless God and Take Courage: The Judson History and Legacy.* Valley Forge, PA: Judson, 2005.

Hutchison, William R. *Errand to the World: American Protestant Thought and Foreign Missions.* Chicago: University of Chicago Press, 1987.

Ikeda, Kazuto. "Two Versions of Buddhist Karen History of the Late British Colonial Period in Burma: Kayin Chronicle (1929) and Kuyin Great Chronicle (1931)." *Southeast Asian Studies* 1, no. 3 (2012): 431–60.

Ikeya, Chie. *Refiguring Women, Colonialism, and Modernity in Burma.* Honolulu: University of Hawai'i Press, 2011.

India Office Records and Private Papers. British Library, London.

Ingalls, Marilla Baker. "A Morning at Thongzai." *Baptist Missionary Magazine*, June 1877, 139–40.

———. "My Dumb Teacher." *Baptist Missionary Magazine*, May 1896, 137–39.

———. *Ocean Sketches of Life in Burmah.* Philadelphia: American Baptist Publication Society, 1857.

———. "Our Great Sign Tree." *Baptist Missionary Magazine*, November 1897, 602–4.

———. "Visit to Mandelay." *Baptist Missionary Magazine*, August 1873, 311–16.

Isaacs, Ralph, and T. Richard Blurton. *Visions from the Golden Land: Burma and the Art of Lacquer.* London: British Museum, 2000.

Johnson, Sylvester A. *African American Religions, 1500–2000: Colonialism, Democracy, and Freedom.* New York: Cambridge University Press, 2015.

Johnson, Todd Michael, and Brian J. Grim, eds. *World Religion Database: International Religious and Demographic Statistics and Sources.* Leiden: Brill, 2008.

Jones, William. "On the Hindus: The Third Discourse." *Asiatic Researches* 1 (1788): 415–31.

Judson, Adoniram. Letter to Mr. Samuel Newell in Bombay from Rangoon, March 25, 1817. Postal History. Western Manuscripts. British Library, London.

Judson, Edward. *The Life of Adoniram Judson*. New York: A. D. F. Randolph, 1883.

Ivory Ka Ma Wa, eighteenth century. Manuscripts, Yangon University Library, Yangon.

Kaell, Hillary. *Walking Where Jesus Walked: American Christians and Holy Land Pilgrimage*. New York: New York University Press, 2014.

———. *Christian Globalism at Home: Child Sponsorship in the United States*. Princeton, NJ: Princeton University Press, 2020.

Kaloyanides, Alexandra. "America's God and the World: Questioning the Protestant Consensus." *Church History* 84, no. 3 (2015): 625–29.

———. "Female Pali Masters in the Burmese Kingdom of Pagan." *Sakyadhita* 30 (Winter 2022): 16–17.

———. "'Intercultural Mimesis,' Empire, and Spirits." *Journal of Global Buddhism* 22, no. 1 (2021): 125–31.

———. "Peering into Prisons, Gazing upon Graves: Early U.S. Missionary Media from Burma." *Material Religion* 17, no. 2 (2021): 117–201.

———. "'Show Us Your God:' Marilla Baker Ingalls and the Power of Religious Objects in Nineteenth-Century Burma." *Religions* 7, no. 81 (2016): 1–19.

———. "The Flower, then the Sword: The Militarization of Burma's Most Beautiful Book." *Journal of Southeast Asian Studies* 54, no. 1 (2023).

———. "The Women Who Mastered Pali." In *From Jetavana to Jerusalem: Sacred Biography in Asian Perspectives and Beyond, Essays in Honour of Professor Phyllis Granoff*, edited by Jinhua Chen, 458–73. Singapore: World Scholastic Publishers, 2022.

Kammavācā with sazigyo, 1792. Manuscripts, Royal Asiatic Society, London.

Kane, Pandurang Vaman. *History of Dharmasastra: Ancient and Mediæval Religious and Civil Law*. 5 vols. Poona: Bhandarkar Oriental Research Institute, 1930.

Keeler, Ward. *The Traffic in Hierarchy: Masculinity and Its Others in Buddhist Burma*. Honolulu: University of Hawai'i Press, 2017.

Kincaid, Eugenio. "Interesting News from Burmah." *Baptist Missionary Magazine*, July 1834, 277–85.

Kirichenko, Alexey. "The Making of the Culprit: Atula Hsayadaw Shin Yasa and the Politics of Monastic Reform in Eighteenth-Century Burma." *Journal of Burma Studies* 15, no. 2 (2011): 189–229.

———. "Theravada Buddhism: Constructions of Religion and Religious Identity in Nineteenth- and Early Twentieth-Century Myanmar." In *Casting Faiths: Imperialism and the Transformation of Religion in East and Southeast Asia*, edited by Thomas David DuBois, 23–45. New York: Palgrave Macmillan, 2009.

Klassen, Pamela E. *The Story of Radio Mind: A Missionary's Journey on Indigenous Land*. Chicago: University of Chicago Press, 2018.

Ko Kong. "Ko Kong's Narrative." *Missionary Magazine*, February 1867, 42–43.

Koenig, William J. *The Burmese Polity, 1752–1819: A Study of Kon Baung Politics, Administration, and Social Organization*. Ann Arbor: Center for South and Southeast Asian Studies, University of Michigan, 1990.

Konbaung Kammawa, n.d. Manuscripts, National Library of Myanmar, Yangon.

Kurtz, Malisa. "'The Dark Side of Hope': Genre and Globalization in *The Hunger Games*." *Extrapolation* 58, nos. 2–3 (2017): 255–72.

Lambek, Michael, ed. *A Reader in the Anthropology of Religion*. Hoboken, NJ: Blackwell, 2002.

Lammerts, Dietrich Christian. "Buddhism and Written Law: Dhammasattha Manuscripts and Texts in Premodern Burma." PhD diss., Cornell University, 2010.

———. *Buddhist Law in Burma: A History of Dhammasattha Texts and Jurisprudence, 1250-1850*. Honolulu: University of Hawai'i Press, 2018.

Langer, Gary. "Poll: Most Americans Say They're Christian." ABC News, July 18, 2014. https://abcnews.go.com/US/story?id=90356.

Law, Bimala Churn. *The History of Buddha's Religion (Sāsanavaṃsa)*. Calcutta: Sri Satguru, 1952.

Lawrie, Colonel. "Dispatch from Colonel Lawrie." *Journal of the Society of the Arts* (February 28, 1873): 267.

Leask, Nigel. "Francis Wilford and the Colonial Construction of Hindu Geography, 1799–1822." In *Romantic Geographies: Discourses of Travel, 1775-1844*, edited by Amanda Gilroy, 204–22. New York: St. Martin's, 2000.

Leider, Jacques P. "Text, Lineage, and Tradition in Burma: The Struggle for Norms and Religious Legitimacy Under King Bodawphaya (1782–1819)." *Journal of Burma Studies* 9 (2004): 82–129.

Leonard, Bill. *Baptists in America*. New York: Columbia University Press, 2005.

Levitt, Laura. *The Objects That Remain*. University Park: Penn State University Press, 2020.

Lieberman, Victor. "A New Look at *Sāsanavaṃsa*." *Bulletin of the School of Oriental and African Studies* 39 (1976): 137–49.

———. *Strange Parallels: Southeast Asia in Global Context, c. 800-1830*. New York: Cambridge University Press, 2003.

Lindman, Janet Moore. *Bodies of Belief: Baptist Community in Early America*. Philadelphia: University of Pennsylvania Press, 2008.

Lopez, Donald S., ed. *Curators of the Buddha: The Study of Buddhism Under Colonialism*. Chicago: University of Chicago Press, 1995.

Lum, Kathryn Gin. "The Historyless Heathen and the Stagnating Pagan: History as Non-Native Category?" *Religion and American Culture: A Journal of Interpretation* 28, no. 1 (2018): 52–91.

Malalgoda, Kitsiri. *Buddhism in Sinhalese Society, 1750-1900: A Study of Religious Revival and Change*. Berkeley: University of California Press, 1976.

Malcom, Howard. "Journal of Mr. Malcom." *Baptist Missionary Magazine*, May 1837, 4–8.

———. *Travels in South-Eastern Asia: Embracing Hindustan, Malaya, Siam, and China / with a Full Account of the Burman Empire; with Dissertations, Tables, Etc.*. Boston: Gould, Kendall & Lincoln, 1838.

Marks, John Ebenezer. *Forty Years in Burma*. London: Hutchinson, 1917.

Marshall, Harry Ignatius. *The Karen People of Burma: A Study in Anthropology and Ethnology*. Columbus, OH: University at Columbus, 1922.

Mason, Francis. "Journal of Mr. Mason." *American Baptist Magazine*, September 1835, 366–72.

———. *The Karen Apostle. Or, Memoir of Ko Thah-Byu, the First Karen Convert, with Notices Concerning his Nation*. Boston: Gould, Kendall & Lincoln, 1843.

———. "Maulmain Burman Mission: Journal of Mr. Mason." *Missionary Magazine*, February 1850, 44–48.

———. "Mr. Mason's Description of His Arrival Among the Burmans." *American Baptist Magazine*, November 1831, 341–43.

Mason, Ellen B. *Civilizing Mountain Men: Sketches of Mission Work Among the Karens*. London: James Nisbet, 1862.

Masuzawa, Tomoko. *The Invention of World Religions, or, How European Universalism Was Preserved in the Language of Pluralism*. Chicago: University of Chicago Press, 2005.

Maung Htin Aung. *A History of Burma*. New York: Columbia University Press, 1967.

Maung Shwe Wa. *Burma Baptist Chronicle*. Rangoon: Board of Publications, Burma Baptist Convention, 1963.

May, Nicholas. "Marching to the Beat of a Newer Drum: Cultural Continuity and Revival in Nisga'a Church Armies, 1894–1970." *Ethnohistory* 62, no. 4 (2015): 781–801.

McCallum, Donald. *Zenkōji and Its Icon: A Study in Medieval Japanese Religious Art*. Princeton, NJ: Princeton University Press, 1994.

McDaniel, Justin Thomas. *Architects of Buddhist Leisure: Socially Disengaged Buddhism in Asia's Museums, Monuments, and Amusement Parks*. Honolulu: University of Hawai'i Press, 2016.

McDannell, Colleen. *Material Christianity: Religion and Popular Culture in America*. New Haven: Yale University Press, 1995.

McGill, Forrest, Chirapravati Pattaratorn, Peter Skilling, Kazuhiro Tsuruta, and the Asian Art Museum of San Francisco. *Emerald Cities: Arts of Siam and Burma, 1775–1950*. San Francisco: Asian Art Museum, Chong-Moon Lee Center for Asian Art and Culture, 2009.

McKenzie, D. F. *Bibliography and the Sociology of Texts*. New York: Cambridge University Press, 1999.

McNicholl, Adeana. "Buddhism and Race in the United States." *Religion Compass* 15, no. 8 (2021): 1–13.

Mendelson, E. Michael. *Sangha and State in Burma: A Study of Monastic Sectarianism and Leadership*. Ithaca, NY: Cornell University Press, 1975.

Metcalf, Thomas R. *Aftermath of Revolt: India, 1857–1970*. Princeton, NJ: Princeton University Press, 2015.

Meyer, Birgit. "Religious Sensations: Why Media, Aesthetics, and Power Matter in the Study of Contemporary Religion." In *Religion: Beyond a Concept*, edited by Hent De Vries, 704–23. New York: Fordham University Press, 2008.

Modern, John Lardas. *Secularism in Antebellum America: With Reference to Ghosts, Protestant Subcultures, Machines, and Their Metaphors; Featuring Discussions of Mass Media, Moby-Dick, Spirituality, Phrenology, Anthropology, Sing Sing State Penitentiary, and Sex with the New Motive Power*. Chicago: University of Chicago Press, 2011.

Monier-Williams, Monier. *A Dictionary, English and Sanskrit*. London: W. H. Allen, 1851.

Morgan, David. *The Embodied Eye: Religious Visual Culture and the Social Life of Feeling*. Berkeley: University of California Press, 2012.

———. *Icons of American Protestantism: The Art of Warner Sallman*. New Haven: Yale University Press, 1996.

———. *The Thing About Religion: An Introduction to the Material Study of Religions.* Chapel Hill: University of North Carolina Press, 2021.
Morgan, David, and Sally M. Promey. *The Visual Culture of American Religions.* Berkeley: University of California Press, 2001.
Mullen, Lincoln A. *The Chance of Salvation.* Cambridge, MA: Harvard University Press, 2017.
Müller, Max F. *Lectures on the Science of Language Delivered at the Royal Institution of Great Britain in February, March, April, and May, 1863.* New York: C. Scribner, 1865.
Myo Myint. *Confronting Colonialism: King Mindon's Strategy for Defending Independence (1853-1878).* Yangon: Ministry of Religious Affairs, 2012.
Naono, Atsuko. *State of Vaccination: The Fight Against Smallpox in Colonial Burma.* Hyderabad: Orient Blackswan, 2009.
Newell, Harriet, and Timothy Dwight. *Memoirs of the Life of Mrs. Harriet Newell, Wife of the Rev. Samuel Newell, Missionary to India, Who Died at the Isle of France, November 30, 1812—Aged 19 Years.* Lexington, KY: T. T. Skillman, 1815.
Nicholson, Hugh. "The Unanswered Questions and the Limits of Knowledge." *Journal of Indian Philosophy* 40, no. 5 (2012): 533–52.
Noll, Mark A. *America's God: From Jonathan Edwards to Abraham Lincoln.* Oxford: Oxford University Press, 2002.
Olender, Maurice. *The Languages of Paradise.* Cambridge, MA: Harvard University Press, 1992.
Oriental Manuscripts. British Library, London.
Orsi, Robert A. *History and Presence.* Cambridge, MA: Harvard University Press, 2016.
"Pāḷi Tipiṭaka." Vipassana Research Institute.
Paññasāmi. "Sāsanavaṃsa." Vipassana Research Institute, 1861.
———. "Sāsanavaṃsappadīpikā." Mandalay, 1861.
Patton, Thomas Nathan. *The Buddha's Wizards: Magic, Protection, and Healing in Burmese Buddhism.* New York: Columbia University Press, 2018.
Pe Maung Tin. "The Shwe Dagon Pagoda." *Journal of the Burma Research Society* 24, no. 1 (1934): 1–91.
Peck, Solomon. "For What Departments of Labor Are Missionaries at the Present Time Most Needed? Or, The Due Gradation of Missionary Labor." *Baptist Missionary Magazine*, July 1849, 206–10.
"Perry Davis' Vegetable Pain Killer." *Baptist Missionary Magazine*, August 1883, 1.
Pierson, Hamilton W. *American Missionary Memorial: Including Biographical and Historical Sketches.* New York: Harper, 1853.
Pinney, Christopher. *"Photos of the Gods": The Printed Image and Political Struggle in India.* London: Reaktion, 2004.
Pranke, Patrick. " 'Bodawpaya's Madness': Monastic Accounts of King Bodawpaya's Conflict with the Burmese Sangha." *Journal of Burma Studies* 12 (2008): 1–28.
———. "Buddhism and Its Practice in Myanmar." In *Buddhist Art of Myanmar*, edited by Sylvia Fraser-Lu and Donald M. Stadtner, 27–34. New Haven: Yale University Press, 2015.
———. "On Saints and Wizards." *Journal of the International Association of Buddhist Studies* 33, nos. 1–2 (2010: 453–88.

———. " 'Treatise on the Lineage of Elders' (Vaṃsadīpanī): Monastic Reform and the Writing of Buddhist History in Eighteenth-Century Burma." PhD diss., University of Michigan, 2004.
Prasse-Freeman, Elliott. "Scapegoating in Burma." *Anthropology Today* 29, no. 4 (2013): 2–3.
Price, Jonathan. "Burman Mission." *American Baptist Magazine*, June 1828, 182–86.
———. "Burman Mission." *American Baptist Magazine*, November 1826, 332–39.
———. "Dr. Price's Journal." *American Baptist Magazine*, February 1828, 42–49.
Prothero, Stephen R. *American Jesus: How the Son of God Became a National Icon*. New York: Farrar, Straus and Giroux, 2003.
Rajah, Ananda. "A 'Nation of Intent' in Burma: Karen Ethno-Nationalism, Nationalism, and Narrations of Nation." *Pacific Review* 15, no. 4 (January 2002): 517–37.
Reeves-Ellington, Barbara, Kathryn Kish Sklar, and Connie Anne Shemo, eds. *Competing Kingdoms: Women, Mission, Nation, and the American Protestant Empire, 1812-1960*. Durham, NC: Duke University Press, 2010.
Religious Tract Society. *The White Foreigners from Over the Water: The Story of the American Mission to the Burmese and the Karens*. London: Religious Tract Society, 1868.
Roach, Joseph R. *Cities of the Dead: Circum-Atlantic Performance*. New York: Columbia University Press, 1996.
Said, Edward. *Orientalism*. New York: Pantheon, 1978.
San San Win, Aye Min, and Khin Mar Sein. "The Mahādhammarājika Pagoda, the Historical Monument in Meiktila Township." *Meiktila University Research Journal* 11, no. 1 (2020): 181–83.
Sangermano, Vincenzo, Padre. *The Burmese Empire a Hundred Years Ago, with an Introduction and Notes by John Jardine*. London: Archibald Constable, 1983.
Sau Kau Too. *Thesaurus of Karen Knowledge: Comprising Traditions, Legends, or Fables, Poetry, Customs, Superstitions, Demonology, Therapeutics, Etc. Alphabetically Arranged and Forming a Complete Native Karen Dictionary, with Definitions and Examples, Illustrating the Usages of Every Word*. Vol. 4. Edited by Jonathan Wade. Tavoy: Karen Mission, 1850.
Saw Kya Shin, Kyaw Paung-Yei, Kyau Taing Lone Gay, Mahn Gyi Sein, and Hlaingbwe. "A Brief Outline of the Traditional Background of the Lekhai (Ariya) Religious Sect [and] its Leit-Hsan Wait." *Karen Heritage* 1, no. 1 (2004): 10–25.
Schendel, Jörg. "Christian Missionaries in Upper Burma, 1853–85." *South East Asia Research* 7, no. 1 (1999): 66–91.
Schlegel, Friedrich von. *The Aesthetic and Miscellaneous Works of Frederick Von Schlegel*. Translated by E. J. Millington. London: Henry G. Bohn, 1849.
Schlosser, Ronald E, writer. *Adoniram Judson Called to Be a Missionary*. Valley Forge, PA: American Baptist Films, 1980.
Schober, Juliane. "Colonial Knowledge and Buddhist Education in Burma." In *Buddhism, Power, and Political Order*, edited by Ian Harris, 68–86. New York: Routledge, 2007.
———. *Modern Buddhist Conjunctures in Myanmar: Cultural Narratives, Colonial Legacies, and Civil Society*. Honolulu: University of Hawai'i Press, 2011.
Schopen, Gregory. "Archaeology and Protestant Presuppositions in the Study of Indian Buddhism." *History of Religions* 31, no. 1 (1991): 1–23.

———. "The Phrase '*Sa Pthivīpradeśaś Caityabhūto Bhavet*' in the *Vajracchedikā*: Notes on the Cult of the Book in Mahāyāna." *Indo-Iranian Journal* 17, no. 3 (1975): 147–81.
Scott, James George. *Burma: A Handbook of Practical Information*. London: Alexander Moring, 1906.
Seccombe, T.L., ed. *Education: Vol. 42, Accounts and Papers of the House of Commons, East India (Progress and Condition)*. London: House of Commons, 1863.
Seeman, Erik R. *Speaking with the Dead in Early America*. Philadelphia: University of Pennsylvania Press, 2019.
Shapland, Lesley. "Charlotte Canning's Burning Tent." Untold Lives, British Library, April 26, 2018. https://blogs.bl.uk/untoldlives/2018/04/charlotte-cannings-burning-tent.html.
Shway Yoe [a.k.a. Sir James Scott]. *The Burman: His Life and Notions*. New York: Macmillan, [1910] 1882.
Simons, Thomas. "Extracts from the Journal of Mr. Simons." *Baptist Missionary Magazine*, November 1837, 265–68.
———. "Journal of Mr. Simons." *Baptist Missionary Magazine*, May 1837, 109–13.
Singer, Noel F. "Kammavaca Texts: Their Covers and Binding Ribbons." *Arts of Asia* 23, no. 3 (1993): 97–106.
Skilling, Peter. "Theravāda in History." *Pacific World* 3, no. 11 (2009): 61–93.
Skilling, Peter, Jason Carbine, Claudio Cicuzza, and Santi Pakdeekham, eds. *How Theravāda Is Theravāda? Exploring Buddhist Identities*. Chiang Mai: Silkworm, 2012.
Smeaton, Donald Mackenzie. *The Loyal Karens of Burma*. London: Kegan Paul, Trench, 1887.
Smith-Rosenberg, Carroll. "The Female World of Love and Ritual: Relations Between Women in Nineteenth-Century America." *Signs* 1, no. 1 (1975): 1–29.
Stadtner, Donald M. *Sacred Sites of Burma: Myth and Folklore in an Evolving Spiritual Realm*. Bangkok: River, 2010.
Stern, Theodore. "Ariya and the Golden Book: A Millenarian Buddhist Sect Among the Karen." *Journal of Asian Studies* 27, no. 2 (February 1968): 297–328.
Stevens, Edward. "Letter of Mr. Stevens." *Missionary Magazine*, January 1850, 13–15.
———. "Maulmain—Journal of Rev. Mr. Stevens." *Baptist Missionary Magazine*, December 1849, 409–13.
———. "Shway Dagong, at Rangoon: Description." *Baptist Missionary Magazine*, February 1876, 34–36.
———. "Tour to Mandelay." *Missionary Magazine*, June 1870, 161–66.
Stout, Harry S. *The Divine Dramatist: George Whitefield and the Rise of Modern Evangelicalism*. Grand Rapids, MI: Wm. B. Eerdmans, 1991.
———. *The New England Soul: Preaching and Religious Culture in Colonial New England*. New York: Oxford University Press, 1986.
Strong, John. *Relics of the Buddha*. Princeton, NJ: Princeton University Press, 2004.
Sullivan, Lawrence E. "Seeking an End to the Primary Text." In *Beyond the Classics? Essays in Religious Studies and Liberal Education*, edited by Frank E. Reynolds and Sheryl L. Burkhalter, 41–59. Atlanta, GA: Scholars Press, 1990.
Swearer, Donald K. *Becoming the Buddha: The Ritual of Image Consecration in Thailand*. Princeton, NJ: Princeton University Press, 2004.

Tainturier, François. *Mandalay and the Art of Building Cities in Burma*. Singapore: NUS Press, 2021.

Tambiah, Stanley Jeyaraja. *The Buddhist Saints of the Forest and the Cult of Amulets: A Study in Charisma, Hagiography, Sectarianism, and Millennial Buddhism*. New York: Cambridge University Press, 1984.

Tapp, Nicholas. *The Hmong of China: Context, Agency, and the Imaginary*. Boston: Brill, 2001.

Taussig, Michael T. *Mimesis and Alterity: A Particular History of the Senses*. New York: Routledge, 1993.

Taves, Ann. *Fits, Trances, and Visions: Experiencing Religion and Explaining Experience from Wesley to James*. Princeton, NJ: Princeton University Press, 1999.

Than Htun. *Lacquerware Journeys: The Untold Story of Burmese Lacquer*. Bangkok: River, 2013.

Tharaphi Than. *Women in Modern Burma*. New York: Routledge, 2014.

Thongchai, Winichakul. *Siam Mapped: A History of the Geo-Body of a Nation*. Honolulu: University of Hawai'i Press, 1994.

Tooze, George H., ed. *The Life and Letters of Emily Chubbuck Judson (Fanny Forester)*. 7 vols. Macon, GA: Mercer University Press, 2009–2013.

Torbet, Robert G. *Venture of Faith: The Story of the American Baptist Foreign Mission Society and the Woman's American Baptist Foreign Mission Society, 1814–1954*. Philadelphia: Judson, 1955.

Trexler, Melanie. *Evangelizing Lebanon: Baptists, Missions, and the Question of Cultures*. Waco, TX: Baylor University Press, 2016.

Turner, Alicia. *Saving Buddhism: The Impermanence of Religion in Colonial Burma*. Honolulu: University of Hawai'i Press, 2014.

Turner, J. Rigbie. "Richard Strauss to Cäcilie Wenzel: Twelve Unpublished Letters." *Nineteenth-Century Music* 9, no. 3 (1986): 163–75.

Tweed, Thomas A. *The American Encounter with Buddhism, 1844–1912: Victorian Culture and the Limits of Dissent*. Chapel Hill: University of North Carolina Press, 2000.

U.S. Central Intelligence Agency. *The World Factbook: Burma*. Accessed May 25, 2016. https://www.cia.gov/library/publications/the-world-factbook/geos/bm.html.

U Tin. *The Royal Administration of Burma*. Translated by Euan Bagshawe. Bangkok: Ava, 2001.

Veer, Peter van der. *Imperial Encounters: Religion and Modernity in India and Britain*. Princeton, NJ: Princeton University Press, 2001.

Wade, Deborah. "State of the Schools." *Baptist Missionary Magazine*, July 1841, 223–24.

Walker, David. *Railroading Religion: Mormons, Tourists, and the Corporate Spirit of the West*. Chapel Hill: University of North Carolina Press, 2019.

Walker, Trent. "A Chant Has Nine Lives: The Circulation of Theravada Liturgies in Thailand, Cambodia, and Vietnam." *Journal of Vietnamese Studies* 15, no. 3 (2020): 36–78.

———. "Indic-Vernacular Bitexts from Thailand: Bilingual Modes of Philology, Exegetics, Homiletics, and Poetry, 1450–1850." *Journal of the American Oriental Society* 140, no. 3 (2020): 675–699.

Ward, Sinéad. "Stories Steeped in Gold: Narrative Scenes of the Decorative Kammavaca Manuscripts of Burma." In *From Mulberry Leaves to Silk Scrolls: New Approaches* to the Study of Asian Manuscript Traditions, edited by Justin McDaniel and Lynn Ransom, 70–106. Philadelphia: University of Pennsylvania Press, 2015.

Warkentin, Germaine. "In Search of 'the Word of the Other': Aboriginal Sign Systems and the History of the Book in Canada." *Book History* 2 (1999): 1–27.

Wayland, Francis. *A Memoir of the Life and Labors of the Rev. Adoniram Judson, D. D.* 2 vols. Boston: Phillips, Sampson, 1853.

Wilford, Francis. "An Essay on the Sacred Isles in the West, with Other Essays Connected with That Work." *Asiatic Researches* 10 (1811): 27–126.

——. "Origin and Decline of the Christian Religion in India." *Asiatic Researches* 10 (1811): 27–126.

Wingfield, Chris. " 'Scarcely More than a Christian Trophy Case?' The Global Collections of the London Missionary Society Museum (1814–1910)." *Journal of the History of Collections* 29, no. 1 (2017): 109–28.

Womack, William. "Contesting Indigenous and Female Authority in the Burma Baptist Mission: The Case of Ellen Mason." *Women's History Review* 17, no. 4 (2008): 543–59.

Wong, Tessa. "Hunger Games Salute: The Symbol of Protest against Asia's Military Regimes." BBC, March 7, 2021. https://www.bbc.com/news/av/world-asia-56289575.

Works on Paper–Manuscripts. Yale University Art Gallery, New Haven, Connecticut.

Yule, Sir Henry. *A Narrative of the Mission Sent by the Governor-General of India to the Court of Ava in 1855: With Notices of the Country, Government, and People.* London: Smith, Elder, 1858.

Index

Abhidhamma tradition: Burmese understanding and appreciation for, 135–36, 248n78; Kusalattika ("The Triad of the Wholesome") text of, 112–13; and the modern Vipassanā meditation movement, 161–62, 215n13; Paramat respect for, 120, 136, 137, 152, 156, 158, 159; *paramattha* as a key notion for, 135–36; understanding of awakening, 159

absence and presence: of the Buddha in Buddha statues, 98, 246n54; Burmese pagoda building tradition, 123–24, 128–30; Christian paradox of God's simultaneous presence and absence, 16, 200; of God among the Friday Mosawe apostalics of Zimbabwe, 238n107; objects used as tools for remembering Buddha's teachings and example, 14–15

Africa, Friday Masowe apostolics of Zimbabwe, 32, 238n107

Agmon, Danna, 214n6

Alaungpaya. *See* Konbaung dynasty-Alaungpaya

Allott, Anna, 257n22

American Baptist Missionary Union: Baptist Triennial Convention as its former name, 8, 223n9. *See also* Peck, Solomon

American Baptist mission to Burma: Burmese prohibitions on Christian evangelism, 234n86; fixation on Burmese pagodas, 117, 119–20; geographical materials used in their evangelical work, 20, 66–67, 69–70, 76–77; male leadership of, 68, 84; as a story of conversion—both failed and sweeping, 2–3. *See also* Cushing, Josiah Nelson; Granger, James; Ingalls, Marilla Baker; Judsons; Kincaid, Eugenio; Lillybridge, Lydia; Mason, Ellen Bullard; Simons, Thomas; Wade, Jonathan

American Baptist mission to Burma—schools: the labor of female missionaries assigned to, 83–84, 89–90. *See also* Lillybridge, Lydia; Mason, Ellen Bullard

American Baptist tradition: corporeal nature of Baptist practice, 229n55; development of Sunday schools in the nineteenth century, 85, 130;

[275]

INDEX

American Baptist tradition (*continued*)
  percent of Americans identifying as Baptist or Southern Baptist, 255n9
American Board of Commissioners for Foreign Missions: financing of the first American mission to "the East," 7; transfer of funds flagged by Burmese authorities, 190
Anderson, Benedict, 221–22n50
Anglo-Burmese War period: Burma occupied by the British Raj during, 2, 234n86; convert communities sustaining the Baptist church, 175; God understood as part of the British war effort, 131–32; pagodas as a key site for expression of religious difference during, 135; political and religious significance of criticism of Burmese Buddhist objects during, 142; political anxiety between the First and Second Anglo-Burmese Wars, 149–50
Anglo-Burmese Wars—First Anglo-Burmese War (1824–1826), 5; evangelization strategy of the American Baptist mission shifted to the Karen following, 212; Karen alliances with the British during, 28; Treaty of Yandabo, 190, 257n22
Anglo-Burmese Wars—Second Anglo-Burmese War (1852–1826), 5, 48; British annexation of lower Burma, 154–55; depiction of a soldier from, 241n135
Anglo-Burmese Wars—Third Anglo-Burmese War (1885): British colonization of Burma, 97; dethronement of the last Burmese king, 2, 5
Asad, Talal, 133–34
Asiatic Society of Bengal, Wilford's articles on Christian and European equivalencies published by, 38, 231n62
Atlas Obscura, 222n7

Bagyidaw. *See* Konbaung dynasty—Bagyidaw (r. 1819–1837)
Bamar people: "Bamar" as a term, 213n2; education of males at Buddhist monasteries, 90; incursions into Karen communities, 27–28; influence during the British colonial period of, 5; pagodas and temples built by, 121; resistance to Christian conversion efforts, 2, 164; wizard-saints of, 5, 215n15, 221n48
Baptist tradition. *See* American Baptist Missionary Union; American Baptist tradition; Cushing, Josiah Nelson; Immanuel Baptist Church; Mason, Ellen; Mason, Francis; Myanmar Baptist Convention (MBC); U Naw Church
Baptist Trienniel Convention. *See* American Baptist Missionary Union
Bashir, Shahzad, 143
Bhabha, Homi K., 227–28n45
Bible: American Baptist missionaries' employment of, 35, 41, 64–65; American bibles as sacred objects, 229n49; Burmese translation by Adoniram Judson (1834), 2, 64, 183, 198; gilded bibles offered to Burmese kings in their pleas for permission to proselytize, 23, 44–45, 64; the Karen's lost book of God identified with, 26–32, 64
Bible—quotes: Isaiah 28:10–13 quoted by Lillybridge, 83; Isaiah 41:10 quoted on images posted by Chin Christians, 256n12; John 3:16, 101; John 13:34 in the painting on exterior of the Immanuel Baptist Church, 177; Mark 16:15 ("Go ye into all the world"), 35, 133; Matthew 28:19 on the U Naw bicentennial mural, 257n17; Revelations 8:15, 180; Romans 5:7–8 recited by Ingalls, 193
bicentennial celebrations: cultural attractions for Baptist tour groups, 188; depictions of the Judsons

featured, 169, 172, *173*f4.3, 182, 186; funding of, 254n3; 2013 celebration, 4, 20–21, 165; at U Naw church, 184–86, 196
Blackburn, Anne M., 110
Boardman, George: books introduced to the Karen, 22–23, 222n6; focus on pagodas and the eradication of idolatry, 126–28
Boardman, Sarah. *See* Judsons-Sarah Judson
Bodawpaya. *See* Konbaung dynasty—Bodawpaya (r. 1782–1819)
Bode, Mabel Haynes, 107
book cult. *See* cult of the book
Brac de la Perrière, Bénédict, on the foundation myth of Burma's pantheon of thirty-seven nats, 61–62, 241n133, 247n56
Bracken, Christopher, 245n31
Brandis, Sir Dietrich, 95
Braun, Erik: on a Burmese folktale about a ship carrying the Tipiṭaka, 248n78; on Burmese anxiety about the decline of the *sāsana*, 55, 149; on Burmese monk Ledi Sayadaw, 63, 161, 215n13; on the notion of *paramattha* in the Abhidhamma system, 135; on thirty-two body parts contemplation practice, 160
Brintnall, Kent, 258n32
British Library: Ivory Kammavāca folio, *51*f1.2, 52, 58, *59*f1.9; Adoniram Judson's 1817 letter preserved in, 84–85, 245n31; Kammavāca Or. 13896, 240n121; Mount Meru featured in a Burmese Buddhist cosmology manuscript, 73, *73*f2.2
British Museum, Mount Meru featured in a Burmese *parabaik*, 71, *72*f2.1, 73
Brumberg, Joan Jacobs, 244n21
Buchanan, Claudius—"Star in the East" sermon: criticisms of, 230–31n58; fascination with Sanskrit writings, 38, 40–41, 231n61; impassioned responses to, 35–38, 229n55, 230–31n58; Ingalls on the martyrdom it inspired, 37
Buddhism: American missionaries presumed to be antagonistic toward, 217n22; early Buddhist culture in Burma, 234n87; emergence as a world religion, 153, 224n13, 253nn64–65; imaginations of space, 243n15; monumental parinirvana Buddha in Mudon, 203–4, *205*f4.16; nats and Burmese Buddhism, 61–62, 99, 241n133, 247n56; work of Burmese communities to renegotiate the terms of colonialism, 215n12, 216–17n19. *See also* pagodas; *sāsana*
Buddhism—Mahayana Buddhism: on Buddha's lifestory, 13–14, 220–21n36; cult of the book, 228n48; theory of a Mahayana-Paramat connection, 137–40
Buddhism—Theravada Buddhism: on Buddha's life on earth and his achievement of parinirvana, 13; Buddhist connections in the Indian Ocean region, 110; Buddhist monastic orders in Sri Lanka, 109–10; consecration practices of, 98, 246n54; establishment in Burma by King Bagyidaw, 45; Konbaung Buddhist chronicles (B. *thathanawin*) commissioned by Theravada Buddhist rulers, 43, 45–47, 233n79; magical objects among modern Theravada communities, 228n48; notion of *paramattha*, 135–36; practices of ethnic groups in Burma, 234n88; rituals in Burma conducted in Pali and Burmese, 236n100; *sāsana-katikāvata* literary tradition associated with, 214n9, 234–35n89; *Theravada* ("the doctrine of Elders") as a term, 214n9; Traiphum (Three Worlds) cosmography, 243n15; wizard saints and nat practices of, 5, 17–18, 61–62, 99, 215n15, 221n48,

[277]

INDEX

Buddhism—Theravada Buddhism (*continued*) 241n133, 247n56; *zedi* (P. *cetiya*) monuments with the Buddha's power (P. *ānubhāva*), 16, 121, 249n2. *See also* Abhidhamma tradition; Buddhist canon—Pali Canon; Kammavāca (B. *Kammawa*)

Buddhist canon—Pali Canon: Abhidhamma tradition, 112–13, 135–36, 137, 152, 156, 215n13, 248n78; Burmese folktale about a ship carrying the Tipiṭaka, 248n78; emergence of Buddhism as a world religion based on, 224n13; Kuthodaw Pagoda Tipitaka, 23, 222n7; legitimization of the Theravada school in Lanka and Burma, 234–35n89; marble inscription ordered by King Mindon, 223n8; "Three Marks of Existence" (*tilakkhaṇa*), 14, 220n38. *See also* Abhidhamma tradition; Kammavāca (B. *Kammawa*)

Buddhist cosmology: indigenous concepts of space, 71, 73, 243n15; Mount Meru featured at Pakokku built in 1813, 73; Mount Meru featured in Burmese manuscripts, 71, 72f2.1, 73, 73f2.2; Traiphum (Three Worlds) cosmography of Theravada Buddhism, 243n15

Buddhist monastic schools: refusal to introduce Western subjects into their curriculum, 75–76; teaching of worldly knowledge (*lokāyata*) in, 75

Bullard, Edwin, 128–29

Burma Baptist Convention. *See* Myanmar Baptist Convention (MBC)

Burmese education: literacy of Burma reflected in British census taken in 1872, 74. *See also* Buddhist monastic schools

Caldwell, Robert, 230n55
Calvinism: Congregationalist background of the Judsons associated with, 8, 17, 223n9, 230n55; influence of Jonathan Edwards's treatises on sentiment on, 229–30n55
Canning, Charles, 88, 245–46n35
Canning, Charlotte, 88–93
Carbine, Jason A., 236n100
Catholicism: *bayingyi*, 126, 213–14n4; Buddhist scriptures translated by, 126; Catholic schools in Burma, 89; evangelism in Burma, 2, 7, 126, 213–14n4, 250n15; Father Vincenzo Sangermano on the Zodi, 138–39; Roman Catholic population of Myanmar's Christian population, 222n51
Charney, Michael: on the etymology of "Paramat," 136; on the Mans being founded by U Po, 147; on the *Sāsanavaṃsa*, 107; study of the Buddhist literati in the Konbaung dynasty, 141, 215n11, 239n111
Chidester, David, 217n21
Chin people: conversion to Christianity, 3, 176; Jesus imagery displayed by, 256n12
Clough, Rev. Benjamin, 49, 237n102
Cohn, Bernard S., 127
Collins, Steven, 234n89
Collins, Susan—*The Hunger Games*: global popularity of, 259nn1–2; three-finger salute from, 207–8
Conroy-Krutz, Emily, 218n22
Conway, Susan, 239n110
Corrigan, John, 191
Crane, William, 37
Crosby, Kate, 98, 246n54
cult of the book: Book of Mormon, 242n138; books treated as ritual objects by the Maori of New Zealand, 228n47; definition of a book, 24, 222–23n7; legend of lost literacy among the Hmong (Miao) people, 242n138; Mahayana Buddhism associated with, 228n48; practices of kingship and possession of *lee* (Karennic word for book),

[278]

224n12; printed tracts molded into amulets, 9, 23–24; Protestant text worship and book cults, 35, 41–43, 228–29n49; role of print in creating imagined communities, 22–25, 221–22n50; sacred books as integral to interactions between Christian missionaries and the Karen, 22–25, 34–35, 64–65, 227–28n45. *See also* Bible; Kammavāca (B. *Kammawa*); Karen—lost book of God; Konbaung Buddhist chronicles (B. *thathanawin*)

Curtis, Heather D., 218n22

Cushing, Josiah Nelson: career of, 172, 255n8; Cushing Hall built in honor of, 172; initial transcription of Jingphaw, 6

Darmesteter, James, 42–43
Davis, Erik, 221n48
Davis, Richard, 219–20n30, 254n6
Dickson, J. F., 49

Edwards, Jonathan, 229–30n55
Edwards, Michael, 222n51
Edwards, Penny, 216n17
Engelke, Matthew, 32, 238n107
Eveleth, Frederick Howard, 158–60, 162–63

Ferguson, John, 137
Fisher, Linford D., 50–51
Fleet, J. F., 232n69
Fox, Richard, 50
Franke, Heike, 248n77
Fujimura, Hitomi, 26–27, 224n12

Geertz, Clifford, 134
Goonatilake, Hema, 110–11
Granger, James: Buddhist revival following the Second Anglo-Burmese War described by, 154; Paramats described as iconoclasts by, 155–56
Granoff, Phyllis, 232n63
Green, Alexandra, 73

Hall, Gordon, 219n27
Hallisey, Charles: on academic attention paid to the Kammavāca, 49–50; "intercultural mimesis" identified by, 122, 249n6
Heyrman, Christine Leigh, 192–93, 213n1
Hinduism: American missionaries presumed to be antagonistic toward, 217n22; Hindoo images criticized by Boardman, 127; Hindu population of Myanmar, 221n51; Hindu Widow's Remarriage Act of 1856, 246n37; mass-produced Hindu lithographs, 220n32. *See also* Sanskrit studies
History of the Buddha's Religion, The (P. *Sāsanavaṃsa*). *See* Konbaung Buddhist chronicles (B. *thathanawin*)—*Sāsanavaṃsa* (*The History of the Buddha's Religion*)
Hla Myint, 189, 257n20
Hollinger, David A., 218n22
Hutchison, William R., 213n1, 217n22, 229–30n55

idolatry: Baptist evangelism focused on ridding Burma of idolatry, 3, 13, 89–90, 117, 119, 124, 126–27; multimedia education authorized by women viewed as idolatry by Baptist evangelists, 68, 87–88; pagodas as idols in the Baptist imagination, 121–25; Protestantism's historic concern with images, 16–17
Ikeda, Kazuto, 225n18
Ikeya, Chie, 215n14, 247n67
image-centric religious practices: agency of visuals in shaping the societies around them, 8–10, 201–6, 220n32; Burmese displays of Sallman prints, 169; Christian condemnation of Buddha statues and spirit shrines, 124–25, 142, 144; iconoclasm of the Paramat movement, 143–44; imagination incorporated into the

[279]

INDEX

image-centric religious practices (*continued*)
definition of "religions," 251–52n44; objects used as tools for remembering the Buddha's teachings and example, 14–15; stories of the Buddha's life, 123–24; *zedi* (P. *cetiya*) monuments with the Buddha's power (P. *ānubhāva*), 16, 121, 249n2. *See also* absence and presence; Kammavāca (B. *Kammawa*)—illuminated versions of; pagodas

Immanuel Baptist Church: nondenominational image promoted by Jesus paintings at, 176, 186; painting of Jesus on its exterior of its entrance, 177

Ingalls, Marilla Baker: on Buchanan's "Star in the East" sermon, 37; on Burma's book practices, 241n125; enshrined dog statue of, 95–99, 96f2.3, 105–6; independence of her work, 68–69; Kammavāca obtained from King Thibaw's court minister, 56–57, 56f1.5, 57f1.6; medicinal advertisements showcased on her banyan tree, 101, 102f2.4, 103–5; *Sayama* ("female teacher") as what she was called, 95; on Shwedagon Pagoda, 131–32; train car reading rooms, 95

Ingalls, Marilla Baker—*Ocean Sketches*: bent idolatry giving way to upright Christianity pictured in, 117, 119, 128; paired illustrations "BURMAH AS IT WAS" and "BURMAH AS IT IS," 117, 118f3.1, 119, 119f3.2; poverty in Burma portrayed in, 125–26

Islam. *See* Muslims and Islam

Johnson, Sylvester A., 33
Jones, William, 41, 231n62
Judson200 Legacy Tour: Baptist churches in Yangon visited, 176, 181–82, 186–87; embodied experiences of, 167–68; monumental parinirvana Buddha in Mudon visited, 203–4, 205f4.16; site of Adoniram Judson's imprisonment visited, 167; tour route, 170–71, 170f4.2; visit to Pagan, 188–89

Judson Baptist Church at Aungpinle: Jesus paintings in the community room of, 198, 258–59n37; KNU flag in the community room of, 198–99; location near the site of Adoniram's imprisonment, 197; memorial stone photographs at, 197, 197–98

Judson Baptist Church at Mawlamyine (Moulmein), 201–2, 202f4.13

Judsons: Joan Jacobs Brumberg's social history of, 244n21; Calvinist Congregationalist background of, 8, 17, 223n9, 230n55; celebrity among Protestants in the U.S. antebellum period, 190–92; denunciation of infant baptism, 12, 223n9; as the first foreign missionaries, 223n9; 100-year anniversary (1913), 165, 257n15; 150-year anniversary (1963), 165, 183–84, 183f4.8, 224n15, 256–57n14, 257n15; U Naw Church founded by, 176. *See also* bicentennial celebrations

Judsons—Adoniram Judson: as the Burmese court's translator during the First Anglo-Burmese War, 1, 190, 257n22; Burmese-English dictionary, 183, 200; Burmese translation of the Bible (1834), 2, 183, 198; death in 1850, 81; direct oral preaching addressed in his 1817 letter to Newell, 84–85, 245n31; first meeting with King Bagyidaw, 43–45; gilded Bible offered to King Bagyidaw, 44–45, 64; impact of Buchanan's "Star in the East" sermon on, 35, 230–31n58; imprisonment of, 1, 188, 190–98, 192f4.10, 196f4.12, 258n32; Pagan's Buddhist monuments viewed as idolatrous by, 3, 188–89; Ryland's sketch of his life story, 190–91

[280]

INDEX

Judsons—Ann Judson: celebrity of, 193, 213n1; death of, 1, 190; image of her visit to Adoniram in prison, 192–94, 192f4.10; images of her gravesite, 203, 204f4.14, 257n24; pictured in Burma, 195f4.11, 196–97

Judsons—Edward Judson, on Adoniram's fascination with Buchanan's claims, 36

Judsons—Emily Chubbuck Judson: on Adoniram's missionary zeal, 37; as Adoniram's third wife, 37, 81; death in 1854, 81; evidence of emotional relations between nineteenth-century American women in her letters, 244n22; hair relics of, 17; letters exchanged with Lillybridge, 81–82

Judsons—paintings and portraits of Jesus and the Judsons: of Adoniram's sacrifice in a Burmese prison, 195–96, 196f4.12, 258n32; Ann Judson pictured in Burma, 195f4.11, 196–97; at Ann Judson's gravesite, 203, 204f4.14, 205f4.15; Ann's visit to Adoniram in prison, 192–94, 192f4.10; *communitas* established by, 255n6; as forms of postimperial mimetic excess, 254n5; Jesus and Judson iconography employed by churches in Yangon, 176; memorial stone photographs at Judson Baptist Church at Aungpinle, 197–98, 258n36. *See also* Sallman, Warner—Christ head; U Naw Church–heart banner

Judsons—Sarah Judson (Sarah Hall Boardman): as Adoniram Judson's second wife, 77, 81; school building with Karen women, 77; son Charles Judson, 201; son Edward Judson, 197

Kachin: conversion to Christianity, 3, 175; Jingphaw studied by American missionaries, 6, 64

Kaell, Hillary, 100, 166–67, 244n25

Kali Yuga: dates for Śālivāhana's lifetime related to, 39–40, 232n69; polished books produced during the reign of King Siripavaramahārājā (1035 to 1060), 238n108

Kammavāca (B. *Kammawa*): academic attention paid to, 49–50, 237n105; craft practices associated with the making of Kammavācās, 237n106; extracts from the Tipiṭaka's set of ritual formulas, 48–49; Maral-Bashi manuscript written in Tumshuq, 236n99; nonilluminated manuscripts of, 48; royal and religious relations in Burma empowered by, 49–51, 63–64; the Theravada community's claim to authority supported by, 49, 236n101; translation into Western languages, 49, 237n102

Kammavāca (B. *Kammawa*)—illuminated versions of: American Baptist Historical Society Kammavāca obtained by Ingalls, 56–57, 56f1.5, 57f1.6; in the Asian Art Museum in San Francisco, 240n121; British Library's ivory Kammavāca, 51f1.2, 52, 58, 59f1.9; British Library's Kammavāca Or. 13896, 240n121; Chester Betty Library folio, 52, 53f1.3; content of, 47–48; impact of non-Buddhist imagery on, 241–42n135; in the Kayin State Cultural Museum, 58; manuscript featuring images of the Buddha acquired by Captain Frederic Marryat dated before 1826, 54; in the Mon State National Museum and Library, 50–51, 58, 60f1.10; in the National Library of Myanmar, 50, 58, 60, 61f1.11; ritual spaces purified by ornamented and illustrated manuscripts of, 63; in Theravada settings other than Burma, 236n99; weapon-bearing spirits on, 9, 48, 54–58, 56f1.5, 57f1.6, 59f1.9, 60–63,

INDEX

Kammavāca (B. *Kammawa*) (*continued*) 212, 240n121; Yale University Art Gallery versions of, 57f1.7, 58, 58f1.8

Karen: American Baptist mission in Tavoy, 22–23; Bamar incursions into Karen communities, 27–28; Christianity as a strategic way of surviving British Burma, 24, 33, 212, 224n11; Dawson's vaccination of Karen children, 245n27; education of Karen women fostered by Ellen Mason, 87, 91–94; exclusion from Burma's monastic school system, 90; female Karen Christian missionaries, 84, 91; folk traditions of, 31–32; histories of, 225n18; KNU flag in Christian spaces, 198–99; *lee* as the Karennic word for book, 224n12; sacred books as integral to interactions between Christian missionaries and the Karen, 22–25, 34–35, 64–65, 227–28n45. *See also* Saw Quala

Karen—lost book of God, 227n42; Karen historical understandings of, 25–27, 31, 64, 170, 225–26n21, 227n42; Lekhai version of, 226n32; Ellen Mason's version, 29–30, 226n29; millenarian expectations, 225n16; Religious Tract Society version of, 29–31, 226n29; Donald Mackenzie Smeaton on Karen folk legends, 31–32

Karen—Pwo Karen: Asho script devised by the Pwo Karen missionary to the Chin Myat Goung, 6; contributions to funding bicentennial celebrations, 254n3; pagoda practices of, 128–29

Karen—Sgaw Karen: contributions to funding bicentennial celebrations, 254n3; script devised by Jonathan Wade, 6

Keeler, Ward, 247n67

Kincaid, Eugenio, 70, 151, 253n60

Kirichenko, Alexey, 216–17n19

Klassen, Pamela E., 197–98, 218n22

Ko Kong, 156–57

Konbaung Buddhist chronicles (B. *thathanawin*): list of four, 233n79; Theravada Buddhist rulers' commissioning of, 43, 45–47, 233n79

Konbaung Buddhist chronicles (B. *thathanawin*)—*Sāsanavaṃsa* (*The History of the Buddha's Religion*): Burma depicted as a model Buddhist realm in, 47, 110–11, 114–15; on the Burmese practice of preparing polished books adorned with red and gold paint, 238n108; Lieberman's analysis of, 107–8, 235n95, 248n71; on the pagoda building tradition, 123; Paññāsami's composition of (1861), 47, 108–10, 233n79, 238n108, 249n7; section on women, 67, 69, 106–8, 110–15; the *Tha-thana-wun-ta sa-dan tha-thana-lin-ga-ya kyan* [History of the religion which is an adornment of the religion] as its base, 235n95; translation by B. C. Law (1952), 247n69

Konbaung Buddhist chronicles (B. *thathanawin*)—*Vaṃsadīpanī* (*Treatise on the Lineage of Elders*): completion in 1799 by Mehti Sayadaw, 46–47, 233n79; as an instrument of Buddhist reformation, 46, 235n90; on the pagoda building tradition, 122–23

Konbaung dynasty: mobilization of religious texts, 141, 215n11, 239n111; practice of enslaving artists, 239n112

Konbaung dynasty—Alaungpaya, as the first Konbaung king, 5, 234n87

Konbaung dynasty—Bagyidaw (r. 1819–1837): Adoniram Judson imprisoned by (1824), 1, 188, 190–91, 196–98; gilded Bible offered by Adoniram Judson to, 43–45, 64; interest in telescopes and geographical materials, 70; sponsorship of the *Sāsanavaṃsa*, 235n95; Theravada

Buddhism installed in Burma by, 45; watchtower in Yangon built by, 184

Konbaung dynasty—Bodawpaya (r. 1782–1819), 233n80; and the history of the Paramats, 141; Kammavāca from the reign of, 53–54; Sudhammā Reformation executed by, 46, 235n90

Konbaung dynasty—Mindon Min (r. 1853–1878): Anglican church for the Society for the Propagation of the Gospel supported by, 149, 250n15; Buddhist revival, 55, 154–55; lacquered Kammavācas favored by, 60–61; literacy of Burma reflected in British census taken in 1872, 74; Mandalay Christian school supported by, 126, 147, 214n4, 252n50; Mandalay's lacquer industry sponsored by, 60; marble inscription of the Buddhist canon ordered by, 223n8; monastic order challenged by the Paramats during, 141; royal letter of friendship sent to President Buchanan, 253n60; *Sāsanavaṃsa* (*The History of the Buddha's Religion*) sponsored by, 47, 235n95; speaking against mainstream Buddhism not tolerated by, 147

Konbaung dynasty—Thibaw Min (r. 1878–1885): circulation of Buddhist objects into Western communities by, 56–57; dethronement of, 5; looting of his palace, 56, 241n124; pictured with Queen Suphayarlat in the *Graphic,* 242n135; U Tin's service to, 252n54

Kurtz, Malisa, 259n2

Kuthodaw Pagoda Tipitaka, 23, 222n7

Lammerts, Dietrich Christian: on Buddhist law in Burma, 214n8; on the Kammavāca, 237n105, 239n1143

Law, B. C., translation of the *Sāsanavaṃsa*, 238n108, 248n71

Lawrie, Colonel, 93–94

Leask, Nigel, 231n62

Levitt, Laura, 211

Lieberman, Victor: on the emergence of centralized Southeast Asian kingdoms in 1830, 215n10; the *Sāsanavaṃsa* analyzed by, 107–8, 235n95, 248n71

Lillybridge, Lydia: criticism of Baptist education in Burma, 79–83; dismantling of Buddhist education targeted by, 85–86; educational approach of, 81–83; Isaiah 28:10–13 quoted to support her educational approach, 83; limited scholarship on, 80–81, 244n21; marriage to Thomas Simons, 80

Lindman, Janet More, 229n55

London Missionary Society: global collections of, 143; Judson's attempt to secure connections and funds from, 7, 219n27

Lum, Kathryn Gin, 227n41

Mahayana Buddhism. *See* Buddhism—Mahayana Buddhism

Malcom, Howard: Kolan identified as the leader of the Paramats, 151–52, 158; Paramats described by (1838), 151–52, 153; on Shwedagon Pagoda, 18

mapmaking and geography: Burmese maps of the universe, 71; depictions of Buddhist cosmology, 71, 73, 243n15; globes, maps, and other world-conjuring devices as tools of the American Baptist mission in Burma, 76–77, 84, 92; illustrated astrological manuscripts, 235n98; mapmaking used to strengthen British hold over Burma, 76; sign systems in oral cultures, 222–23n7. *See also* Buddhist cosmology

Marks, John Ebenezer, 126, 214n4, 252n50

Mason, Ellen Bullard: on Burmese women, 89–90; death in 1894, 94; education of Karen women fostered

INDEX

Mason, Ellen Bullard (*continued*) by, 87, 91–94; fundraising for the American Baptist Mission, 93–94; her Baptist activity in Burma viewed as idolatry by the American Baptist Missionary Union, 87–88; Karen traditional folk song on the lost book in *The White Foreigners from Over the Water,* 29–30, 226n29; letters exchanged with Charlotte Canning, 88–93; lost book of the Karen discussed in *Civilizing Mountain Men,* 28–29; Society for the Propagation of the Gospel joined by, 88

Mason, Francis: on Burmese reverence for pagodas, 129–30; on the Paramats, 152–53; peacock-feathered prophet story, 33–34

Masuzawa, Tomoko, 220n34, 224n13, 253n65

material culture: geographical materials used in American Baptist evangelical work, 20, 66–67, 69–71, 76–77, 126; nontextual data as the focus of scholarship, 219–20n30, 237n106, 255n6; religious change in nineteenth-century Burma reflected and shaped by, 3–5, 8–12, 21, 71, 73, 210–12. *See also* cult of the book; image-centric religious practices; Judsons–paintings and portraits of Jesus and the Judsons; pagodas; religious imagination

Mather, Cotton, 229–30n55

Maung Htin Aung, 140–43

May, Nicholas, 32, 225–26n21

McDaniel, Justin Thomas, 219–20n30

McDannell, Colleen, 220n30, 229n49

McGill, Forrest, 240n121

McKenzie, D. F., 223n7, 228n47

medicine and medical work: American Baptist medical missionary work, 244–45n27; medicinal advertisements showcased on Ingall's sign tree, 101, 103–5

Mendelson, E. Michael: etymology of "Paramat," 135, 147; theory of a Mahayana-Paramat connection, 137–40

Meyer, Birgit, 220n32

Mina, An Xiao, 211

Mindon Min. *See* Konbaung dynasty— Mindon Min (r. 1853–1878)

missionaries: accounts of the Paramats, 20, 143–44; American missionaries presumed to be antagonistic toward Asian religious traditions, 217n22; contribution of female Baptist missionaries summarized, 68–69, 90–91, 105–7; new opportunities for women provided by foreign evangelism, 244n19; Protestant mission in Burma led by Felix Carey in 1806, 219n26. *See also* American Baptist Missionary Union; American Baptist mission to Burma; American Board of Commissioners for Foreign Missions; Catholicism; Ingalls, Marilla Baker; Judsons; Lillybridge, Lydia; London Missionary Society; Malcom, Howard; Mason, Ellen Bullard; Myanmar Baptist Convention (MBC); Price, Jonathan

Modern, John Lardas, 218n23

Morgan, David, 251–52n44

Morgan, David, and Sally M. Promey, 255n6

Moulmein (Mawlamyine): Baptist missionary station in, 199, 200; Baptist schools run by Simons and Lillybridge in, 80; Judson Baptist Church, 201–2, 202f4.13; Karen Christian schools in, 89; Karen Christian women from, 77

Mullen, Lincoln, 85

Müller, Max F., 41–42

Muslims and Islam: Buddhist-Muslim violence in Rakhine State, 175; Christian tracts used in Burma for earrings by, 34; Muslim population of Myanmar, 221n51; violence

[284]

against Rohingya Muslims, 6, 175, 177, 210, 217n20
Myanmar Baptist Convention (MBC): Burma Baptist Convention as the former name of, 183; Cushing Hall headquarters of, 172; impact of religious and ethnic tensions on the Baptist Church in Myanmar, 176; Judson and Jesus portraiture, 172, 173f4.3; *The Sesquicentennial Pictorial of Baptist Work in Burma, 1813-1963*, 183–84, 183f4.8, 257–58n14; wall mural featuring the Judsons's arrival in Burma, 174–75, 174f4.4, 176. *See also* Immanuel Baptist Church; U Naw Church
Myanmar today: as a Bamar nation, 5, 215n15, 221n48; "Burma" changed to "Myanmar," 214n7; Department for the Promotion and Propagation of the Sāsana, 289; religious demographics, 119, 222n51; twentieth-century dictatorship, 4, 207, 210; violence against Rohingya Muslims, 6, 175, 177, 210, 217n20; women in Burmese society, 247n67. *See also* Judson200 Legacy Tour
Myo Myint, 252n50

National Library of Myanmar, Kammavāca manuscripts in the collection of, 50, 58, 60, 61f1.11
Newell, Harriet: death of, 8; memoirs of, 219n28
Newell, Samuel, as one of America's first intercontinental foreign missionaries, 7–8, 219n27
Noll, Mark A., 218n23
Nott, Samuel, 219n27

Olender, Maurice, 42
oral histories: creativity of unlettered cultures, 225n17; of the Karen book legend, 10, 26–27, 31, 170, 225–26n21; of Nisga'a Church armies in Canada, 32, 226n21; nonpragmatic religious concerns associated with, 32; Joseph Roach's theorization on improvised narratives, 227n42
Orsi, Robert A., 124

Pagan (previously Bagan): Adoniram's visit to, 3, 188–89; Buddhism promoted by the current government in, 189; height of medieval Buddhist culture in Burma, 234n87; Judson200 Legacy Tour visit to, 188–89; King Anawratha (r. 1044–1077), 61; stone inscription from 1249 CE debating the propriety of monastic possessions, 142; Theravada Buddhism traced to the eleventh century, 189
pagodas: impact on Baptist evangelists, 18, 121–25; Mahazedi pagoda, 122–23; Pwo Karen practices attacked by Edwin Bullard, 128–29; Stevens on the tenets of Buddhism propelling pagoda practices, 133–34; as symbols of Buddha's teachings, 159; *zedi* (P. *cetiya*) monuments with the Buddha's power (P. *ānubhāva*), 16, 121, 249n2. *See also* Shwedagon Pagoda; Sule Pagoda
Pali Canon. *See* Buddhist canon—Pali Canon
Paramat movement: attainment of enlightenment for lay people explained by U Alapa, 161, 162; Baptist missionaries' fascination with, 20, 143–44, 149–54; and Buddhism during the Konbaung dynasty, 138, 141; Burmese Buddha imagery criticized by, 115–16, 120–21, 163; Christian beliefs of the Paramats in Shwaygyeen, 162–63; crucifixion of U Po, 145–49, 153, 162; groundwork of Vipassanā meditation laid by, 160, 161; Ko Kong's story, 156–57; Kolan identified as their leader by Malcom, 151–52, 158; Ko San identified as their leader by

Paramat movement (*continued*)
Eveleth, 158; opposition to the dominant, royally sponsored monasticism, 155–56; Sangermano's account of the Zodi sect identified with, 138–39; schism with the orthodox Buddhist Order in Toungoo, 158; strategic connection to Christianity of, 144–45, 163; theory of a Mahayana-Paramat connection, 137–40

Patton, Thomas Nathan, 215n15, 221n48

Peck, Solomon: correspondence with Lydia Lillybridge, 81–83; education prioritized in the order of operations of missionary labor outlined by, 83–84, 244–45n27; female assistant missionaries acknowledged by, 84, 245n28

Pinney, Christopher, 220n32

Pranke, Patrick: of the royally backed Konbaung Buddhist chronicles, 161; study of monastic accounts of the Sudhammā Reformation, 46, 123

Prasse-Freeman, Elliott, 216n20

Price, Jonathan, 66–67, 69–70, 126, 190, 245n27

Protestantism: American missionaries presumed to be antagonistic toward Asian religious traditions, 217n22; aniconic practice of, 96, 142–43, 200; cosmopolitan, modern identity associated with conversion to, 86, 218n22; Judson family influence on American Protestant print culture, 244n21; material and mediated practices of, 228–29n49; power of Protestant printed tracts in Burma, 227–28n45; Protestant consensus during the antebellum period, 7, 218nn23–24; text worship and book cults of, 35, 41–43, 228–29n49; transformation into a kind of Southeast Asian religion, 3, 8, 12, 26, 212. *See also* American Baptist tradition; Calvinism; Society for the Propagation of the Gospel

Pyu people: early Buddhist culture in Burma traced to, 234n87; story about Min Mahagiri, 247n56

race and racial identity: "Bamar" as the term used for the majority ethnic group, 213n2; Burmese terms for people groups in the British census, 6, 216n17; *lumyo* ("type of person"), 6, 216n17; Race and Religious Protection Bills (2014), 175; religious origins of Indo-Europeans, 42–43; the term *tainghyinta* ("indigenous races"), 6; women as agents for Christianizing races in Burma, 89–91. *See also* Bamar people; Chin people; Kachin; Pyu people; Shan people

Rajah, Ananda, 27

Rangoon. *See* Yangon (Rangoon)

Raynard, Ellen, 226n29

Reeves-Ellington, Barbara, Kathryn Kish Sklar, and Connie Anne Shem, 218n22, 244n19

religious imagination: cannibalism as an act of symbolic meaning, 143; impact of globes, maps, and other world-conjuring devices as tools of the American Baptist mission in Burma, 4, 10, 76–77, 84, 92; role of the sacred book, the school, the pagoda, and the portrait in shaping religious change in Burma, 3–4, 9–12, 19, 204, 206, 212. *See also* absence and presence; image-centric religious practices; material culture; pagodas

resistance and images of resistance: Bamar people's resistance to Christian conversion efforts, 2, 164; of female Baptist missionaries, 68–69, 90–91, 105–6; images of the Judsons and the Sallman Christ head at U Naw Church, 164, 168–69,

INDEX

185–86; the Karen flag used as, 198–99. *See also* Paramat movement; three-finger salute

Rice, Luther, 219n27, 223n9

Roach, Joseph R., 227n42

Royal Asiatic Society: Fleet's article on Śaka and Śālivāhana published by, 232n69; folios of the Kammavāca held by, 52, 53, 53f1.4

Śālivāhana: Christ's life related to, 38–40, 232n63; dating of his lifetime, 39–40, 232n69

Sallman, Warner, *Christ Our Pilot* painting, 186

Sallman, Warner–Christ head: in a Chin church in Rangoon, 256n12; at Ann Judson's grave at Judson Memorial Church, 203, 204f4.14; Burmese displays contrasted with American displays of, 169; on the cover of the 2013 MBC planner, 172, 173f4.3; global popularity of, 169; its profile and gaze suggested in Jesus images at Judson Baptist Church at Aungpinle, 198, 258–59n37; in U Naw Church, 168, 184–85

Sangermano, Vincenzo, Padre, account of the Zodi sect, 138–39

Sanskrit studies: Buchanan's focus on Sanskrit writings on the coming of Christ, 35–38, 40–41; establishment at the Collège de France (1814), 233n74; linguistic kinship between Sanskrit, Greek, and Latin identified, 36, 41–42, 231n62; philological work employed as a form of religious evangelicalism, 38–43, 231n62. *See also* Royal Asiatic Society

sāsana: Burmese fear of its decline, 55–56, 144, 149; Burmese responsibility for the upholding of, 74–75, 107–11, 142, 144, 149; militarized beings on Burmese Kammavācas associated with the protection of, 48, 56–58, 56f1.5, 57f1.6, 59f1.9, 60–63;

sāsana-katikāvata literary tradition associated with Theravada Buddhism, 214n9, 234–35n89; Sudhammā Reformation of King Bodawpaya design to uphold it, 46–47, 235n90. *See also* Konbaung Buddhist chronicles (B. *thathanawin*)—*Sāsanavaṃsa* (*The History of the Buddha's Religion*)

Saw Kya Shin, Kyaw Paung-Yei, Kyau Taing Lone Gay, Mahn Gyi Sein, and Hlaingbwe, 226n32

Saw Quala: on the brutality of Bamar toward the Karen, 27–28; spelling of his name, 226n22

Sayadaw, Ledi: on the richly ornamented and illustrated Kammavācas, 63; Vipassanā meditation movement led by, 161, 215n12

Sayadaw, Mehti: history of the Sudhammā Reformation, 46; *Vaṃsadīpanī* chronicle of the Konbaung dynasty, 46–47, 233n79

Schendel, Jörg, 250n15

Schlegel, Friedrich von, 42

Schober, Juliane, 62, 76

Schopen, Gregory, 228n48, 237n106

Scott, James George ("Shwe Yoe"): *The Burman*, 140; on U Po, 147

Shan people: American missionaries' interest in, 64; female court dress of, 239n110; in regions of southwest China, 5; school established by Ellen Mason for, 92; Shan language studied by Cushing, 255n8; Theravada Buddhism and ancestor worship of, 234n88

Shway Yoe. *See* Scott, James George ("Shwe Yoe")

Shwedagon Pagoda: described by American Baptist Howard Malcom, 18; earliest dated evidence of, 249–50n11; Ingalls on its power and magnitude, 131–32; on the Judson200 Legacy Tour, 167; location in

INDEX

Shwedagon Pagoda (*continued*) Rangoon (Yangon), 1, *133*f3.3, 171; relics of the Buddha's hairs enshrined at, 15, 123–24; Stevens's report on, 132; in the wall mural at the MBC, 174, *174*f4.4

Simons, Thomas, 34; death of, 80; encounters with Paramats recorded by, 150–51; marriage to Lydia Lillybridge, 80; two- and three-dimensional depictions of the world displayed by, 70–71

Singer, Noel F., on Kammavāca texts, 52, 239n114

Smeaton, Donald Mackenzie, 31–32

Smith-Rosenberg, Carroll, 244n22

Society for the Propagation of the Gospel: Anglican church built with the support of King Mindon, 147, 250n15; British evangelists sent to Burma, 2–3, 7; Ellen Mason's association with, 88; Mandalay Christian school run by Rev. John Marks, 126, 147, 214n4

Sri Lanka: Buddhist monastic order, 109–10; Cushing's time in, 255n8

Stadtner, Donald M., 123–24

Stern, Theodore, 224–25n16

Stevens, Edward: crucifixion of U Po investigated by, 146–47, 149, 153, 162; monumental parinirvana Buddha in Pagan beheld by, 200, 206; Shwedagon Pagoda described by, 132; on the tenets of Buddhism propelling pagoda practices, 133–34

Stout, Harry S., 229n55

Sudhammā Reformation, King Bodawpaya's execution of, 46, 235n90

Sule Pagoda: location opposite the Immanuel Baptist Church, 177; in the wall mural at the MBC, 174, *174*f4.4

Sullivan, Lawrence E., 225n17

Swearer, Donald K., 98, 246n54

Tambiah, Stanley Jeyaraja, 228n48

Tapp, Nicholas, 242n138

Taungoo dynasty, 5, 215n10, 234n87

Taussig, Michael T., 254n5

Taves, Ann, 229n55

Than Htun, 60

Ṭhānissaro, Bhikkhu, 220n38

Tharaphi Than, 247n67

Theravada Buddhism. *See* Buddhism—Theravada Buddhism

Thibaw Min. *See* Konbaung dynasty—Thibaw Min (r. 1878–1885)

Thongchai, Winichakul, 243n15

three-finger salute: during the 2020 protests in Thailand, 208; during the 2021 coup in Myanmar, 207; on Myanmar's 2021 protest art, 209–10; *The Hunger Games* as its source, 207–8, 211; from threefingers.org, 208–9, *209*f5.1

Turner, Alicia, 55, 74, 215n12

Tweed, Thomas A., 217n22

U Alapa: attainment of enlightenment for lay people explained to Eveleth, 161, 162; on the schism between the Paramats and the orthodox Buddhist Order in Toungoo, 158

U Naw Church: Baptist, Burmese, and American history emphasized in Jesus and Judson paintings at, 176; mural featuring the *Georgiana*, 185–86, *185*f4.9; as Myanmar's oldest Baptist congregation, 168, 176; Sallman Christ head featured at, 168, 184

U Naw Church—heart banner: books stacked in front of Adoniram's chest, 183; iconic imagery of the Judsons recreated on, 183–84, *183*f4.8; Judsons pictured on, *168*f4.1, *182*f4.7, 183

U Po: "anti-clerical" group "Mans" founded by, 147; crucifixion of, 146–49, 153, 162

U Shway Bo: on pagodas as symbols of Buddha's realization of the ultimate nature of all things, 159; teaching on meditation, 159–61

[288]

INDEX

U Tin: career of, 252n54; on U Po in his *The Royal Administration of Burma*, 148

Veer, Peter van der, 218–19n25

Wade, Deborah: on the exclusion of the Karen from Burma's monastic school system, 90; on Karen schools in Tavoy, 78
Wade, Jonathan, Sgaw Karen script devised by, 6
Walker, Trent, 236n101, 249n6
Ward, Sinéad, 237n105
Warkentin, Germaine, 222–23n7
Wayland, Francis, 230–31n58
Western imperialism: agency of Burmese minority communities in their use of Anglo-American Christian imagery, 3, 10–11, 26–27, 170, 225–26n21; Baptist artwork in Burma as both a reaction and response to, 254n5; British surveying of the British's Bengal territories, 127; Christian conversion in colonial contexts, 32–33, 225–26n21; contribution of American Christian missions to, 6–7, 11; the English book as "an insignia of colonial authority," 227n45; impact of the Burmese postal system on, 245n31; Karen Christianity as a strategic way of surviving British Burma, 33, 224n11; mapmaking used to strengthen British hold over Burma, 76; the present struggle for just self-rule in Myanmar connected with, 210–11; work of Burmese communities to renegotiate the terms of colonialism, 215n12, 216–17n19
Wilford, Francis: fascination with Sanskrit literature, 40–41, 231nn61–62, 233n70; on Śālivāhna, 38–40, 232n63, 232n69
Wingfield, Chris, 143

Yangon (Rangoon): British annexation after the Second Anglo-Burmese War, 154; Kammavāca manuscripts at the National Library of Myanmar, 50, 58, 60, 61f1.11; Tedim Baptist Church, 256n12. *See also* Immanuel Baptist Church; Shwedagon Pagoda; Sule Pagoda; U Naw Church
Yangon University: Ivory Kammavāca folio, 51f1.1, 52; Judson Church at, 187, 198; pictured as Judson College on the U Naw heart banner, 184
Yule, Sir Henry, theory of a Mahayana-Paramat connection, 139–40

[289]

RELIGION, CULTURE, AND PUBLIC LIFE
Series editor: Matthew Engelke

After Pluralism: Reimagining Religious Engagement, edited by Courtney Bender and Pamela E. Klassen
Religion and International Relations Theory, edited by Jack Snyder
Religion in America: A Political History, Denis Lacorne
Democracy, Islam, and Secularism in Turkey, edited by Ahmet T. Kuru and Alfred Stepan
Refiguring the Spiritual: Beuys, Barney, Turrell, Goldsworthy, Mark C. Taylor
Tolerance, Democracy, and Sufis in Senegal, edited by Mamadou Diouf
Rewiring the Real: In Conversation with William Gaddis, Richard Powers, Mark Danielewski, and Don DeLillo, Mark C. Taylor
Democracy and Islam in Indonesia, edited by Mirjam Künkler and Alfred Stepan
Religion, the Secular, and the Politics of Sexual Difference, edited by Linell E. Cady and Tracy Fessenden
Boundaries of Toleration, edited by Alfred Stepan and Charles Taylor
Recovering Place: Reflections on Stone Hill, Mark C. Taylor
Blood: A Critique of Christianity, Gil Anidjar
Choreographies of Shared Sacred Sites: Religion, Politics, and Conflict Resolution, edited by Elazar Barkan and Karen Barkey
Beyond Individualism: The Challenge of Inclusive Communities, George Rupp
Love and Forgiveness for a More Just World, edited by Hent de Vries and Nils F. Schott
Relativism and Religion: Why Democratic Societies Do Not Need Moral Absolutes, Carlo Invernizzi Accetti
The Making of Salafism: Islamic Reform in the Twentieth Century, Henri Lauzière
Mormonism and American Politics, edited by Randall Balmer and Jana Riess
Religion, Secularism, and Constitutional Democracy, edited by Jean L. Cohen and Cécile Laborde
Race and Secularism in America, edited by Jonathon S. Kahn and Vincent W. Lloyd
Beyond the Secular West, edited by Akeel Bilgrami
Pakistan at the Crossroads: Domestic Dynamics and External Pressures, edited by Christophe Jaffrelot
Faithful to Secularism: The Religious Politics of Democracy in Ireland, Senegal, and the Philippines, David T. Buckley
Holy Wars and Holy Alliance: The Return of Religion to the Global Political Stage, Manlio Graziano

The Politics of Secularism: Religion, Diversity, and Institutional Change in France and Turkey, Murat Akan
Democratic Transition in the Muslim World: A Global Perspective, edited by Alfred Stepan
The Holocaust and the Nabka, edited by Bashir Bashir and Amos Goldberg
The Limits of Tolerance: Enlightenment Values and Religious Fanaticism, Denis Lacorne
German, Jew, Muslim, Gay: The Life and Times of Hugo Marcus, Marc David Baer
Modern Sufis and the State: The Politics of Islam in South Asia and Beyond, edited by Katherine Pratt Ewing and Rosemary R. Corbett
The Arab and Jewish Questions: Geographies of Engagement in Palestine and Beyond, edited by Bashir Bashir and Leila Farskah
At Home and Abroad: The Politics of American Religion, edited by Elizabeth Shakman Hurd and Winnifred Fallers Sullivan

GPSR Authorized Representative: Easy Access System Europe, Mustamäe tee
50, 10621 Tallinn, Estonia, gpsr.requests@easproject.com

www.ingramcontent.com/pod-product-compliance
Lightning Source LLC
Chambersburg PA
CBHW022036290426
44109CB00014B/882